Sexual Reckonings

Sexual Reckonings

Southern Girls in a Troubling Age

Susan K. Cahn

Harvard University Press
Cambridge, Massachusetts
London, England

In Chapter 9, lyrics from the song "My Boy Elvis," written by
Aaron Schroeder, a/k/a Doc Rockingham, and Claude DeMetruis,
a/k/a Virginia Fitting, published by Rachel's Own Music,
administered by A. Schroeder International LLC, are
used by permission, International Copyright Secured.

"My Boy Elvis," by Doc Rockingham and Virginia Fitting,
© 1956 (Renewed) Unichappell Music Inc. and Rachel's Own Music.
Lyrics Reprinted by Permission of Alfred Publishing Co., Inc.

"Single Girl, Married Girl" by A.P. Carter
© 1927 by Peer International Corporation. Copyright Renewed.
International Copyright Secured. Used by Permission. All Rights Reserved.

Designed by Gwen Nefsky Frankfeldt

First Harvard University Press paperback edtion, 2012

Library of Congress Cataloging-in-Publication Data
Cahn, Susan K.
Sexual reckonings : southern girls in a troubling age / Susan K. Cahn.
p. cm.
Includes bibliographical references and index.
ISBN 978-0-674-02452-6 (cloth : alk. paper)
ISBN 978-0-674-06393-8 (pbk.)
1. Teenage girls, White—Southern States—Social conditions.
2. Teenage girls, White—Southern States—Sexual behavior.
3. African American teenage girls—Southern States—Social conditions.
4. African American teenage girls—Southern States—Sexual behavior.
5. African Americans—Segregation—Southern States.
6. Dating (Social customs)—Southern States.
7. Interracial dating—Southern States.
8. School integration—Southern States.
9. Southern States—Social life and customs.
10. Southern States—Race relations.   I. Title.
HQ798.C24   2007
306.70835'209750904—dc22
2006102565

To Emily,
whose insights made completing this book possible, and

To Tandy,
who makes all things possible

Contents

introduction

Scarlett Redux

On December 15, 1939, the Atlanta School Board ordered all schools to close at one o'clock and the city government encouraged area businesses to do the same, so that Atlanta residents of all ages might participate in festivities surrounding the opening of the movie *Gone with the Wind*. Many would line the streets and cheer as the parade of celebrities passed by in the grand march to the *Gone with the Wind* ball. If lucky, some would be among the two thousand people who packed into Loew's Grand Theater for the show's opening night while a throng of thousands jammed their way toward the theater to catch a glimpse of Vivien Leigh, Clark Gable, other cast members, director David O. Selznick, and the many political officials, Hollywood figures, and members of Atlanta "society" invited to the film's debut.[1] Or possibly, some formed part of the "volunteer corps of 200 negro *[sic]* servants" costumed in period dress, marshaled by the city to clear the stage after the hour-long program and prepare the area for the dance that followed.[2] The appearance of "voluntary" servants—slaves, in their historical role—revisited the myth of racial harmony between "good" blacks and whites in the years surrounding the Civil War, an image that Atlanta officials surely intended to project for present-day Atlanta as well. Mayor William Hartsfield had wrested the rights to the film's opening night from New York City, flexing all his political muscle to ensure that his city would host the movie of Margaret

Mitchell's famous Civil War novel set in Atlanta and its north Georgia environs. With the national spotlight shining on the city, Atlanta itself was making its debut, showing itself as the model city of the New South.

Since the book's beloved protagonist Scarlett O'Hara symbolized the classic southern belle, events surrounding the premiere featured Atlanta's own current crop of "belles." The Junior League held its annual ball in conjunction with the movie's opening, featuring debutantes in period costume to make the "Old South Come to Life," according to the *Atlanta Constitution*. The young Junior Leaguers competed to see whose figure conformed most closely to Vivien Leigh's, with the winner to lead the grand march wearing one of Scarlett's costumes from the film. Young white women from a local college played similar, if somewhat less prestigious, roles as the escorts of celebrities involved in the week's festivities. To be chosen, these modern-day Scarlett O'Haras had to provide firm evidence of family ties to the old Confederacy.[3]

Yet city leaders did not invite all adolescent girls with ties to the Confederacy to compete for these positions. They ignored African American teens, excluding as well the many middling and poor whites whose ancestors had not owned slaves or their own land. Although in all likelihood these girls were descended from enslaved southerners or conscripted Confederate soldiers, neither group fit the image of the "authentic" past that the movie and Atlanta's boosters chose to project; neither the girls nor their ancestors resembled the wealthy young "southern belles" whose charm and beauty brought elite white suitors flocking to their doors. With personal histories that fit uneasily into the memory of the South celebrated by the movie, these adolescent girls could not be pressed into service as representatives of the mythic South of the defeated yet honorable "Lost Cause."

The Confederacy itself seemed to be not so much a lost cause as a found one, undergoing its own revival. Events surrounding the film's premiere celebrated the Old South's glory and transformed the humiliating defeat of past generations into the victorious rising of a new Confederacy, at once distinct from and at one with the larger nation. On stage, the lucky "debs" joined six "southern [white] ladies" who had survived the war and now sat draped in Confederate flags, six very elderly Civil War veterans, and the current governors of the eleven former Confederate states. The program featured the raising of the Confederate flag by movie stars Gable and Leigh, who thus joined the tribute to a resurrected Confederacy. A joyful Margaret Mitchell exulted: "It was a great thing for Georgia to see the Confederates come back."[4]

The movie premiere honored the antebellum period as a time when whites ruled with ease and grace; the Old South represented an era of chivalry, civility, wealth, and honor shared by white patriarchs and revered wives and mothers who had, in their teenage years as southern belles, cast a mesmerizing charm over the region's young men. Their dazzling allure lay behind the marital unions that reproduced the society from one generation to the next. Although Mitchell's novel reinvigorated this version of the past, she also created a soft critique of that society that, in turn, supported an image of Atlanta rising from the ashes of defeat, a harbinger of the "New South." She showed individuals—epitomized in the character of Scarlett—recovering from financial and heartbreaking personal loss through hard work, shrewd bargains, manifest aggression, and business acumen. The most memorable characters in Mitchell's novel suffer devastating losses but still find the courage to endure and to change without sacrificing loyalty to the past.

Although Clark Gable captured his share of glory as the charismatic rogue Rhett Butler, Vivien Leigh, her character Scarlett O'Hara, and the many "Scarlettesque" white debutantes of Atlanta captured the limelight during the premiere.[5] For it was Scarlett who accomplished what southern politicians and business leaders had been attempting to do for decades. Through her protagonist, Mitchell represented the South as imbued with "modern" or industrial values: rapid change, industry, competition, risk taking, and a shrewdness that shaded into occasional chicanery masked by charm, manners, and fashionable beauty. Scarlett O'Hara was a "modern" girl who merged values long pushed by promoters of the "New South" with an ardent loyalty to the "Old South," symbolized in Scarlett's undying love for the serenity and goodness of Tara, the family plantation.

This powerful narrative, though heralded for its authenticity, not only distorted the past; it also created a deceptive view of the present. The canonical status of *Gone with the Wind* in popular culture engendered a lasting image of the southern belle, updated through time as the fashionable debutante. This mythic picture overpowered other representations of southern girlhood. For example, in the film Scarlett's shadow image is her personal servant, Prissy, who hovers nearby as more of an annoyance than a helping hand. Whereas Scarlett is beautiful, full-breasted, and wasp-waisted, the young Prissy appears at twelve "with skinny legs like a bird and a myriad of pigtails carefully wrapped with twine sticking stiffly out from her head." Although Mitchell credits her as having "sharp knowing eyes that missed nothing," in the movie Prissy is simple-minded and lacking in sexual knowledge—less an adolescent than a sexless, overgrown "pickaninny" who is loyal but helpless as a child and worthless as a servant.[6] Images of black adolescent girls, even as stereotyped as Prissy, were rare in national consumer culture, for upon puberty the African American girl moved instantly from child status to an image of a sexually promiscuous, enticing woman or the older, rotund, asexual "Mammy."

The mismatched pair of Scarlett and Prissy nevertheless captured some of the key qualities of modern adolescence as understood by the public: childlike yet knowing; innocent yet cunning; physically mature and alluring, yet emotionally immature and impetuous. An imperfect hero, Scarlett as drawn by Mitchell hints at the discomfiting contradictions of girlhood in the New South. She reveals the flaws of pride and vanity—preening over her seventeen-inch waist, the smallest in the county. She is brash and calculating, a girl who "found the road to ladyhood hard," since "most of her natural impulses were unladylike" and poorly concealed behind the "helpless, clinging, doe-eyed" masquerade she enacted for boys, a necessity of elite courtship.[7] Her "true self," according to Mitchell, is mercurial and willful. Mitchell describes her as a "hoyden who was not above a few kisses," animated by "frighteningly vital" desires as big as her waist was small.[8] In this sense Scarlett, who made frequent impulsive decisions without thinking through the consequences, epitomized female adolescence with her famous iteration, "I'll think about it tomorrow."

This tension between rebellion and conformity resonated with a new generation of "frighteningly vital" teenage girls, in the South and across the nation, who dreamed of being as strong-willed, impetuous, and aggressive as Scarlett but, like their heroine, ultimately loyal to—and protected by—her race and class. *Gone with the Wind* provided a fantasy in which teenage girls could imagine themselves as both the classic southern belle, emblematic of goodness and beauty, and a modern girl who might pursue her impassioned desires without being expunged from the roster of respectable girls and marriageable women.

While readers of *Gone with the Wind* may have bypassed the tensions surrounding modern girlhood, outside the novel and the fantasy world it opened neither adults nor teens found such problems easy to traverse. The disquieting changes of World War I and the 1920s generated a protean discourse about the dangers posed by sexually assertive teenage girls, regionally and nationally. Adults responded with apprehension, especially to the public presence of older girls in the workforces, shops, and streets of rapidly growing towns and cities. Yet the blossoming bodies and volatile emotions that alarmed adults also attracted them to the figure of the unpredictable adolescent girl. This nexus of apprehension and attraction toward adolescent girlhood characterized much of the twentieth century and is, arguably, still with us today. But the idea of the "girl problem" also has a history, nationally and regionally. In the South this story, while not always different from the national one, is particularly consequential and illuminates the region's history in unexpected ways.

By the 1920s the penetration of commercial culture and urban migration made proudly "modern" adolescent girls highly visible to a nervous public concerned about the direction of regional change. Social critics, professionals, parents, and young people themselves struggled to understand and regulate the assertiveness, sexual interest, and seemingly rash actions of girls who ranged in background from the most impoverished to the most privileged. From the brazen middle-class flapper to the diseased wartime white prostitute and reputedly immoral black servant girl, these adolescents forced older generations to confront the influence of sexual modernism on a society still steeped in antebellum and late Victorian traditions of racial and sexual hierarchy. When adolescent girls from diverse class and racial backgrounds used work and recreation to explore a new sexual morality, they threatened white southerners' commonsense beliefs about racial and sexual difference.

The defense that the South needed segregation and that lynchings were necessary to protect the "purity" of southern white womanhood—both her sexual virtue and purity of "bloodlines"—depended on a notion of passive, sexually innocent and vulnerable white women opposed by a contrasting notion of black women as sinful and assailable. The publication and movie release of *Gone with the Wind* in the late 1930s stands as the midpoint in a period of several decades during which the potential or actual sexual behavior of adolescent girls threw this equation into doubt. Self-assertive teenage girls did not fit smoothly into prevailing social codes that supported a systemic form of white male supremacy. In bold profile, they served as a flashpoint for many of the most controversial issues in southern society.

Southern adolescent girls wrestled with problems not unlike those of Scarlett, but less easily resolved. Negotiating work, courtship, and marriage generated uncertainty as well as opportunity. Similarly, making decisions about sexual restraint and expression proved difficult, requiring an accurate assessment of the benefits of short-term gratification versus the long-term respectability earned through moral conformity. Published in 1937 just one year after the book *Gone with the Wind,* Zora Neale Hurston's *Their Eyes Were Watching God* explored these dilemmas from the perspective of a black southern teenager also living in rural Georgia at the opening of the tale.

At sixteen, Janie Crawford's "conscious life" begins after spending days lying under a pear tree discovering the mystery of sexuality by watching bees pollinate the tree's blossoms. Her observations of nature stir feelings that had "buried themselves in her flesh" and now "caressed her in her sleep" and "quested about her consciousness." Janie feels like "the rose of the world was breathing out smell," hinting at an elusive yet yearned-for vibrancy missing in her young life.[9] This impulse leads to a chance meeting at the nearby gate post with Johnny Taylor, who initiates her into the pleasures of kissing.

Janie's fiercely protective grandmother observes the scene and angrily summons Janie back to the house, where she is berated for her forward behavior. Her grandmother, a former slave once raped and impregnated by her white owner, has resolutely determined to create a different life for Janie by securing marriage to a respectable man with an adequate income and good reputation. Under great pressure,

Janie marries an older widower, Logan Killins, whose ownership of a sixty-acre farm, a house, and the only organ in the black community promises to protect her from the plight of most black women, that is, becoming what her grandmother calls "de mule uh de world." Logan offers Janie respectability at the price of a joyless marriage in which she cannot find love, sexual pleasure, or personal power. In this exchange, Hurston tells us, "Janie's first dream was dead, so she became a woman," seemingly a status without dreams.[10]

Published within a year of each other, *Their Eyes Were Watching God* and *Gone with the Wind* take as their subject adolescents' very real struggles with sexuality, coming of age, and the conventions of society. Yet Hurston's novel, now considered a literary masterpiece, quickly fell into obscurity. Hurston was a black woman writing about an African American southern girl's coming-of-age and adult experiences as a sexually active woman in a contemporary setting. Her novel did not restore a mythic past or play on already popular images of southern belles and Confederate glory. Instead, the novel explored a taboo subject: the sexual subjectivity of black girlhood and womanhood. It rejected stereotypes of wanton black women to examine the feelings, decisions, and dilemmas faced by ordinary African American women in the South. As a story of sexual coming of age set in the present, Hurston's novel came closer to Mitchell's in capturing the real-life dilemmas faced by a generation of southern girls who found that pursuing sexual self-determination often drew harsh responses from adult authorities.

In a racially divided region, embarrassed by its deplorable conditions yet defensive of its history and culture, white southerners worried about the consequences of shifting sexual attitudes and behaviors. If girls of all races claimed a sexuality derived from a desire—in Janie's words—to bring her buried jewel of self and love to the surface and "gleam it around," would men suffer a loss of sexual privilege? Some feared a loss of basic social order, wondering what would limit the aggressive sexual desires of men if not controlled by the virtue of respectable women. Even more threatening, the sexual polarities underlining the imagined difference between black and white womanhood might cease to exist.[11]

The perceived instability of adolescence—and, in particular, adolescent female sexuality—came to stand for larger instabilities of the

region. Southerners living between 1920 and 1960 saw their world undergo tremendous changes, of which some were interpreted as progress, but others were seen as signs of social and moral breakdown. In
the interwar period, mass-marketed consumer culture reached the
South through department stores, mail-order catalogs, radios, records,
and automobiles. The family also underwent profound change. Economic and cultural transformations eroded the patriarchal family,
while intellectuals encouraged in its stead a new "democratic" family
model in which hierarchies softened and every family member had a
voice. A democratic ideal also took root in public education, as southern states agreed on the need to spend state and local funds to educate the children of their region, however unequally. A corollary to
educational liberalism was racial liberalism, articulated by intellectuals in the concept of cultural pluralism. In this view cultural differences were simply dissimilarities among equally valid cultures; they
did not indicate degrees of civilization or the relative superiority and
inferiority of races. Embraced by some southern intellectuals, racial
liberalism made little headway among ordinary whites but nevertheless hovered like a thundercloud over the Jim Crow system of segregation and subordination. Eventually, in the post–World War I years,
racial liberalism became more of a direct threat due to a coinciding increase of federal intervention in southern state governments, a persistent if small group of civil rights activists, and an embryonic youth
culture that blurred formerly rigid lines of class and race. This convergence culminated with the political firestorm over segregated
schools in the 1950s, in which the possibility of open interracial sexuality stood at the heart of white panic.

Adolescent girls played a significant role in many of the controversies that wracked the South in these decades. Although adult responses dominate official records, the behaviors and values of southern girls themselves prompted their alarm. The history of adolescence,
in the South or anywhere, is first and foremost a story of how teenagers act in a particular historical context, and how we come to understand those actions in relation to adolescent economies, family relations, social opportunities, personal desires, and "commonsense" beliefs
about sexual development and morality. Collectively, their actions
came to symbolize an eroding social order and a new morality, providing a terrain on which southerners negotiated conflicts over moder-

nity, class relations, sexual mores, and racial inequality between 1920 and 1960.

It is important, therefore, to understand adolescents not simply as an age group with a history but as an age-based social grouping that influences any historical age or time period. The history of adolescence has until recently focused primarily on boys, examining issues of crime, delinquency, schooling, and the transition from dependent child to independent adult.[12] The experience of teenage girls has most often been depicted as a dim reflection of male adolescence. In women's history much has been written about the change from a sexually reticent Victorian culture to a new era of sexual liberalism that acknowledged female sexual desire as central to modern marriage and femininity. Yet few have asked how this expectation of active female desire shaped the process of coming of age; instead teenage experiences are usually folded into generalized histories of women's work, education, and culture.

Historians have not ignored adolescent sexuality but rather chosen not to distinguish adolescent girls from the larger category of "young women," in large part because reformers, the law, and other authorities did not make this distinction.[13] Yet even as public rhetoric often merged teenagers with other "unruly" women, laws and social policies tended to apply more frequently or harshly toward teenage girls, even when not explicitly stated. Incarceration and sterilization, for example, fell disproportionately on adolescents primarily because the state had more access to minors than to adult women. Moreover, even though the public eye tended to merge teenagers with other young women, in the decades before World War II, critics, sympathizers, and reformers had begun to develop a social scientific discourse that specifically named adolescent girls as a social problem.

This book, then, builds on the insights of historians who have looked more generally at "unruly women." It examines adolescent girls as a separate group to discuss how regulatory policies applied to female minors and to trace the early twentieth-century emergence of a new sexual category—the adolescent girl—that gained greater prominence by midcentury. We can ask, for instance, how adolescents felt, understood, and acted on the desires we define as "sexual." In turn, how have adults interpreted and regulated the sexuality of adolescent girls? The South's relatively compressed transition from farm to factory and its intensely politicized racial and class divides magnify and complicate issues of adolescent sexuality in compelling ways.

Youth culture does not exist in a vacuum but rather develops in reciprocity with broader political and cultural trends or conflicts. For the first two-thirds of the twentieth century, assertive sexual behavior among African American and white teenage girls formed a lightning rod for anxieties about a perceived threat to a "southern way of life." When white girls expressed their own sexual interests, they rejected an ideal of the alluring but chaste southern belle, a class-specific image that elites nevertheless employed as representative of an idyllic South. African American girls were equally important social actors. Their own communities vested in them the power of racial uplift through chaste respectability, a responsibility some accepted and others rejected.

The sexual self-determination of adolescent girls threatened the South's foundational association between chastity and whiteness.[14] Challenging the racial imperative of white sexual purity, adolescent girls behaving in similarly "modern" ways across class and racial divides helped unhinge the established coupling of race and sex that fortified the power of white elites and a growing middle class. By putting adolescents and sexuality at the center of southern history, we can better understand a region usually studied from political, racial, and economic vantage points—not because sexuality is more important, but because sexuality is integral to all these dimensions of history.

Studying the history of adolescent girlhood raises a number of conceptual and methodological challenges. One is determining the meaning of adolescence itself. Current definitions of adolescence incorporate several separate but related aspects. Some define it chronologically as a time span consistent with the teenage years. Age-based conceptualizations often emphasize physiological developments, pointing to a set of predictable changes from the onset of puberty to the mature body of a young adult. Others point to adolescence as a period of emotional volatility signaled by rebelliousness, moodiness, precocious adult behavior, and conversely, the rejection of adult values. Such instability forms a necessary step in the process of emotional maturation, which marks the endpoint of adolescence. In another popular conception that combines the physiological and emotional, sexual changes form the core of this life stage. Adolescents experience an erotic awakening expressed in fantasy, in new signs of sexual interest, and in sexual encounters, some of them incorporated into teenage rituals of dating, romance, and physical intimacy. These same rituals capture a more psychosocial theory of adolescence in which, employing traditional gender conventions, girl and boy children grow toward mature femininity or masculinity in preparation for adult intimacy and marriage.

Since the mid-twentieth century, experts have viewed psychological development as the overarching theme of adolescence, informed by physical, social, sexual, and emotional changes. In particular, adolescence stands for a period of changing identity. As children enter their teens they adopt a stronger peer orientation, initiating a separation from parental control and from primary identification with the natal family. The adolescent gains a more individuated sense of self as a person with meaningful identifications beyond primary family bonds. Psychologists and sexologists have also viewed identity formation as less a process of separation from adults than a progression toward adult sexual identity. A more conservative view holds that over the years of adolescence a primary sense of self coheres around culturally condoned sexual and gender identities (as a heterosexual feminine/ woman or masculine/man). Any other outcome, such as homosexuality, constitutes an "arrested development" in which sexual growth ceases prematurely. More liberal interpretations note a similar process, but find other sexual (and sometimes gender) identities such as homosexuality or bisexuality acceptable.

Notably, if adolescence ends with a secure sense of self and sexual identity, the adolescent herself is always in the process of becoming, lacking a fully formed subjectivity. If the outcome is a well-adjusted self, then the adolescent is a person who is less than fully adjusted, by definition. In this view, early childhood and mature adulthood signal relative stasis, in which individuals undergo predictable physical and mental changes that do not significantly alter one's interior sense of self. With childhood and adulthood as stable bookends, adolescence stands for instability and unpredictability, a phase of life that is necessary but also in need of containment.[15]

These varied conceptualizations make clear that adolescence is an idea, not a fact. Yet it is a lived idea. The adolescent years entail a set of changes (and rarely mentioned consistencies) in which the idea of adolescence mediates experience, forming the lens through which we understand those changes. For this reason I have adopted a somewhat loose definition that recognizes the truth of the many physical, emotional, social, psychological, and sexual changes that accompany the teenage years without defining any particular set of developments or outcomes as "the truth." As a time in which self-awareness sharpens and persons come to recognize themselves as individuals who belong—or don't belong—to various collective identifications (for example, middle-class, heterosexual, white southern womanhood), adolescence is a meaningful and often poignant life stage worth separating out for historical analysis. While identity formation stresses the psychosocial dimensions of adolescent development, the psychological is inseparable from the material; unconscious desires are underwritten by consciousness of goods, means, opportunities, and limitations. The experience of coming of age, then, involves physical, emotional, sexual, and psychological changes shaped by the idea of adolescence itself, by processes of identity formation and change, and by the material world that forms the context for cultural belief and emotional subjectivity.

Given this framework, an imposing methodological difficulty is how to gain culturally sensitive and accurate insights into the subjective experience of adolescents. Especially difficult is the search for evidence of sexual experience, which is typically considered private. Since sexuality and the self come together as much in fantasy, hopes, and fears as in behavior, by looking at sexual subjectivity—an adolescent's sense of personhood and conscious awareness in relation to her sexuality—we enter a much more nebulous history of desire in which sexual and other kinds of longings are inseparable.

Margaret Mitchell and Zora Neale Hurston understood this connection. At nineteen Scarlett O'Hara feels her first wave of sexual desire as a "treacherous warm tide of feeling that made her want to . . . [feel Rhett's] lips upon her mouth." These feelings do indeed seem treacherous when Rhett spurns marriage, instead offering to make Scarlett his mistress. She refuses but is later so desperate for money to save Tara that she reconsiders. Preparing to visit Rhett and accept his terms in exchange for a loan, Scarlett dons a dress made by Mammy out of draperies, one of the few remnants of beauty that survived Yankee depredation. With a glance at the mirror, delight momentarily replaces desperation: "It was so nice to know that she looked pretty and provocative, and she impulsively bent forward and kissed her reflection in the mirror."[16] Scarlett saw in her new dress a reflection of the person she believed herself "truly" to be; this time the kiss of desire was for her old self, and for the money she hoped to lure from Rhett so she could salvage a life in which that self could exist.

Similarly, in *Their Eyes Were Watching God,* Janie's desire for sexual intimacy gets tangled between her sense of self and the value of material goods. When she meets disappointment in her second marriage to a businessman named Jody Starks, she hangs on to the belief that while he feels like "nothin'," he is at least "something in my mouth. He's got tuh be else Ah ain't got nothin' tuh live for." Unless she lies to herself about Jody's worth as a person, "life won't be nothin' but uh store and uh house."[17] Sexual longings form part of a much bigger landscape of desires, none understandable apart from the others. These desires, in part, form the mirror that adolescents gaze into searching for a recognizable "self," a person with power to call her own life into being. Identity and sexual desire never stray far from emotional and material need, which in turn operate in the context of the South's caste-like racial order.

The term "girl" itself has a racialized history. White southerners typically reserved the term for white female children and adolescents, using upon adulthood "woman" or "lady," depending usually on class. But they almost always addressed black women as girls even into late adulthood, at which point they might have switched to "auntie" or some other presumptively familiar terminology. To see the word "girl" used to refer to black adolescents as old as twenty may unsettle readers, given the tradition of racism behind this usage for black women.[18] And indeed some argue that black teens, because of the economic responsibility that rested on their shoulders, their lack of extended education, and their vulnerability to sexual assault by white men, never had an adolescence in any meaningful sense. Similarly many historians of working-class women have treated teenage workers as part of an undifferentiated group of "women workers." Yet by saying that black or white working-class teens did not have an adolescence or by always placing them as members of a larger group of adult women, historians define them out of the history of girlhood and adolescence. Economic responsibility, stunted education, and sexual vulnerability characterized the teenage years of many girls in the South, and thus those experiences must become part of the history of girlhood. To explore the personal and political meanings of female adolescence, I call teenagers from all class and racial backgrounds "girls" in an effort to focus on a distinct life stage and to pay close attention to the transitions girls underwent as they came of age as "women," a term that is equally appropriate for late adolescents who under other circumstances might reasonably be included within the category of adult women.

That the racial order of the South could determine which females were "girls," "women," and "ladies" illustrates the powerful analytical place of race in southern history. Race forms a central, and at times the central, category of analysis in southern history. Yet it should not preclude studying commonalities across racial lines. Experiences shared across race may encompass delimiting attributes such as relative poverty or wealth, rural or urban location, religiosity, or similarities in sexual desire. Nevertheless, one's identification as "black" or "white" in the South crucially informed the meaning of those experiences, even when similar or shared, and the ways they influenced any given life. The history of sexual reckonings is always and at once a story about race relations, class relations, and gender relations, as well as about how all of these connections permeate the formal politics and everyday social practices of the past. To "reckon" with teenage sexuality in the South of the 1920s through the 1950s was indeed to come face to face with the fundamental fault lines of race, class, and gender on which southern society rested.

To reflect a history that is at once personal, cultural, and political, the narrative of this book weaves between two main themes: the public controversies and policies regarding the "girl problem" in its various guises during these decades and, alternately, the lives of ordinary southern girls—"girls' problems" one might say—as they encountered the world around them, including its sexual possibilities and dangers. The movement back and forth between public policy and personal lives occurs within an overarching chronological narrative set roughly between 1920 and 1960. The forty-year period begins with early controversies over the "girl problem" prompted by the migration, urbanization, and self-conscious modernization of southern teenage girls. It ends just before the onset of the 1960s student-led civil rights movement in which high school and college students politicized their own lives and for a time became the lead actors in a dramatic social movement. This moment marks the beginning of a new period in the history of teenagers, sexuality, race relations, and politics in the South that has yet to be told as a single story.

From 1920 to 1960, however, whether as the subject of controversy or as "ordinary" teens going about the business of living their lives, southern girls symbolized—and participated in—the remaking of their society. The many "sexual reckonings" that make up this narrative can teach us about southern history as well as about girlhood and sexuality, historically and in the present. Adolescents bring into relief some of the most disturbing issues with which any society must grapple— crime, education, sexual pleasure and power, and the well-being of individuals and communities—issues that are never isolated to adolescents, even if attributing them to "troubled teens" appeals to adults by displacing societal problems onto a younger generation. As southern adolescent girls came of age, their sexuality provided a terrain on which Americans publicly negotiated and profoundly altered relations of race, class, and region—some of the defining issues of the past century and of our own time.

chapter one

"Holding Excitement in Their Hands"

The Southern "Girl Problem"

F. Scott Fitzgerald's fiction captured the mood of the immediate post–World War I decade. Novels like *The Great Gatsby* and *This Side of Paradise* glamorized a generation of young people no longer interested in politics, social reform, or war but rather in immediate pleasures. Southerners, like other Americans, indulged in drinking alcohol, frequent parties, and sexually provocative and shocking dance steps, reveling in the new music that defined the decade as the Jazz Age. During the 1920s a confluence of modernism, youthful rebellion, and sexual revolution led to a new consciousness among youth of all regions and a new sense of generational divide between adults and their adolescent children. The most sensational and representative figure of this period is the "flapper," whose public dancing, drinking, smoking, and bold sexuality caused a nationwide stir that crystallized at least two decades of adult unease over the changing attitudes and behaviors of women and youth.

Though in retrospect we may think of the flapper as a woman in her twenties, frequenting the scandalous speakeasies of urban nightlife, her contemporaries often described her as a young girl in her teens. In a 1922 article on the "Flapper Americana Novissima," renowned psychologist G. Stanley Hall argued that not since the dawn of civilization had the young teenage girl "seemed so self-sufficient and sure of herself, or made such a break with the rigid traditions of propriety and convention which have hedged her in."[1] A later essay titled "The Flapper" begins with a quote from a young man of twenty-two explaining, with seasoned wisdom, "It's not the sixteen-year-olds who're wild, it's the fourteen." The author goes on to describe early adolescent flappers who donned the latest fashions, danced with abandon, and talked easily of sexual matters from kissing to syphilis, embarrassing their male escorts while raising not even a blush in their own rouged cheeks.[2]

If Fitzgerald's novels captured this era for American literary audiences, it was Zelda Fitzgerald whose life became the model of the prototypical flapper, both in her husband's fiction and in her self-creation as a glamorous female rebel. Born Zelda Sayre in 1900, she grew up in Montgomery, Alabama, in a staid, upper-middle-class family who counted themselves among the South's "best people." Zelda appeared to be proceeding along the path of a budding debutante, receiving notice in the local society pages for her impressive beauty and popularity among the country-club set. Yet she quickly distinguished herself from her peers, acquiring a reputation for smoking and drinking, as well as for a dauntless spirit that flouted respectability in favor of drama and excitement. Like other teenage rebels of the 1910s, she bobbed her hair, wore mascara and rouge, and cultivated a fearlessness that shocked her elders. An indifferent student, she lived instead for the nightly round of parties and dances she attended with high school boys, college men, and young military officers-in-training stationed in Alabama during the war years. She also flaunted convention through irreverent acts like swimming in a flesh-colored bathing suit that gave the impression of nakedness. Although scandalizing her parents and others in their elite set, Zelda belonged to a class in which indiscretions were often overlooked and reputations survived minor disgraces. At age nineteen Zelda Sayre married F. Scott Fitzgerald, and they moved north just as he emerged on the national literary scene. As Zelda Fitzgerald she lived her twenties as the model of the 1920s flapper, while Scott used his wife's teenage experience and letters to create a type of fictional heroine he made famous: the romanticized adolescent femme fatale.[3]

Zelda Fitzgerald symbolized a national phenomenon that in retrospect we do not associate with the South. But her exploits as an Alabama teenager had been exceptional only in degree. With the growth of southern towns and cities in the early twentieth century, new commercial products and entertainments permeated the region—cars, movies, theaters, roadhouses, department stores. Young people seized on these goods and venues to develop both an individual and generational sense of being "modern." By the early 1920s, southern girls' fascination with ragtime and jazz music, "joyriding" in automobiles, and the latest dance styles and fashions had elicited panicky reproach from an older generation of moralists. Since participation in commercial culture usually required access to cash, youth from wealthier backgrounds joined easily in those activities signaling a "New Morality." But even poorer teenagers in towns and cities, who typically worked for wages in factories, shops, or private homes, participated in the quest for novel and modern forms of entertainment. One black journalist complained in 1915 that Atlanta's dance halls were frequented by the "lower classes of people . . . [who] dance all kinds of vulgar motions and expressions."[4] At the same time astonished white critics noted that "girls from the best families" joined in activities like joyriding, "the principal features of which are petting, using the contents of hip flasks and patronizing road houses."[5] They spoke to a common concern about new forms of amusement and sexual boldness that crossed racial and class lines.

Driven to pleasure, southern adolescents from diverse class backgrounds joined in a national transformation of youth culture that coincided with a redefinition of adolescence and a clear sense of generational divide. Yet while the rest of the nation vigorously debated the merits and morals of the teenage "flapper," the South's discussion of female adolescence took a distinct turn due to the particular economic and racial pressures of the region. The public significance of teenage sexuality was not new, having been a topic of southern concern for at least two decades.[6] Yet the issues came to a head when the agricultural crisis of the 1920s, triggered by the boll weevil and falling cotton prices, caused a flood of rural teenage women to enter the city in search of work. Social workers, politicians, and urban residents portrayed them as helpless, vulnerable victims of a harsh economic system, yet also as dangerous and disorderly interlopers who fell easily under the tempting sway of urban vice. A perceived moral decline joined with a steep economic decline to produce panic among south-

Mill workers like these adolescent girls from Spartanburg, South Carolina, flooded southern cities in search of work in the 1910s and 1920s. Reformers portrayed them as victims of economic and sexual exploitation or, alternatively, as wholesome but naive country girls tempted by modern urban amusements. Lewis Hine, Library of Congress, LC-H5–2985A.

erners, whose confident vision of a promising New South receded before a sense of regional failure and impending class crisis.[7]

While economic recession generated a discussion of class differences, the clash over modernity simultaneously communicated the instability of race relations and racial categories. Despite the implementation of legal segregation and the political disfranchisement of black southerners, the line dividing black from white remained unstable by definition, since this reputedly "natural" separation required formal law and extralegal terror to maintain it. In this era of frustrated political ambitions, many African Americans enacted their resistance to white supremacy in cultural venues. Lacking avenues for overt political challenges, they used popular culture—fashion, street life, dance, music—to display both their sense of pride and their refusal to break under an oppressive racial regime. Young black women responded to mistreatment and constant disrespect by signifying their individual and collective worth through the pursuit of cultural self-expression and displays of style.[8]

Defenders of the South's white supremacist patriarchal traditions responded with hostility to "flappers" of any race or class. Viewing modern adolescence, womanhood, and sexuality as a direct challenge to their established authority, antimodern elites turned "problem girls" into conspicuous subjects of social policy and regional imagination. Teenage girls, in turn, made their own public statements through consumption, sexual expression, and other "modern" behaviors—prompting reforms that ranged from the vigilante justice of Klansmen defending the authority of white fathers to campaigns for female reformatories, strict conduct codes imposed on female students by African American educators, or the eugenic sterilization policies passed by Virginia and North Carolina.

The range and depth of responses suggests that the sexuality of teenage girls struck an important political nerve, one connected to a larger regional crisis of identity. Rocked by a perceived moral decline and genuine economic collapse, anxious critics questioned the desirability of the vaunted New South and turned against beliefs and values labeled modern. The bold presence and assertive sexuality of teenagers represented not only change, but also challenge. The adolescent girl, on the verge of becoming something new and permanently different, became a trope for the South's modernity—whether viewed as the region's salvation or its damnation.

By the 1920s, both experts and the general public had begun to understand adolescence in new ways. Americans of an earlier time defined adolescence in social and economic terms as a period of "semidependency" occurring at some point between the ages of ten and twenty-one when the young person—often living away from home in an apprenticeship or at school—no longer occupied a fully dependent status in the family but did not yet have the financial resources to live independently of parents and other family members. Since with the exception of early factory workers teenage girls learned household labor in their own home or that of a neighbor and typically moved from parental dependence to economic dependence on a husband, the concept of adolescence prevalent before the twentieth century applied primarily to males.[9]

By the late nineteenth century, changes in the Victorian family and the rise of professional psychology and medicine occasioned a revised concept of adolescence. As middle-class family life gradually became more intimate and child-centered, parents reared children in an atmosphere designed to promote physical and mental health, moral rectitude, and the qualities of character that would allow a child to succeed in the world. Younger children received greater individualized attention from parents, nursemaids, and teachers, while the older child's period of economic dependence extended into the late teens and early twenties, altering the meaning of adolescence. In contrast to working-class parents, who received the most economic return from children employed during their teen years, middle-class parents, because of the extended time and education it took to acquire the social and financial resources necessary for a "good" marriage or career, now put more money than ever into the support of nonworking adolescent children. These years of preparation formed a nervous time for well-to-do parents; their children's fates seemed to ride on an extended period of training and transition, much of it spent away from home in day schools, boarding schools, and colleges.[10]

Consequently, Victorians began to understand adolescence as a time of vulnerability and peril. Literature from the newly professionalized fields of medicine and psychology explicated this view.[11] Late-nineteenth-century scientists defined adolescence as a psychological and physiological life stage in which biological maturation awakened a complex set of impulses toward sexuality, love, idealism, religious fervor, and intense experience. Believing that the adolescent's body had surged ahead of the mind's capacity for reason and emotional control, experts defined adolescence as a time of "storm and stress" in which the maturation process itself created a dangerous period of precocious activity.[12]

The leading proponent of this approach was G. Stanley Hall, who in 1904 published a landmark two-volume study, *Adolescence*. Hall, like his contemporary Sigmund Freud, viewed childhood as a series of stages that could be generalized for all of Western society. He argued that the stages of childhood development recapitulated the stages of societal development from primitive to advanced civilization. Based on this presumed correspondence, Hall viewed adolescence as a crucial time in which the individual acquired the necessary skills and values for mature adulthood and, by extension, guaranteed the future of advanced "civilized" society.[13] But this very process spawned conflicts, rebellions, and distress. Pulled between strong emotion and a gradually maturing mind, adolescents experienced, according to Hall, a "stormy period . . . when there is peculiar proneness to be either very good or very bad."[14]

It was, of course, the "very bad" adolescent who excited the most concern among turn-of-the-century parents, medical experts, and social reformers. In every city, thousands of young workers in their teens and early twenties gravitated toward dance halls, amusement parks, movie theaters, and the lively culture of the street, finding opportunities as well as hardships in the conditions of urban life. Young women, figured either as the heroically energetic or tragically downtrodden "working-girl," were the most conspicuous proponents of the new youth culture. Typically entering wage work in their early to mid-teens, they utilized inexpensive fashions, popular film and fiction narratives, modern dance styles, and a work-based peer culture to construct themselves as "modern" working-class American women.[15] By the 1910s this behavior had prompted wide-ranging criticism and diverse reform efforts. The common impression of youth in rebellion, spread by books like Jane Addams's *The Spirit of Youth and the City Streets,* created a popular knowledge consistent with new scientific theories that considered emotional tumult and social rebellion to be natural characteristics of adolescence.[16]

This understanding developed deeper roots in the 1920s when changes first noted among working-class youth became prominent among the lives of middle-class teenagers.[17] The perceived problem lay in the manners and morals of a "jazz" generation that seemed interested in little more than frivolity and sensuality. In the so-called Era of Good Times, a youthful middle-class clientele flocked to lavish "movie palaces," cabarets, and dance venues. Neither the expansion of commercial leisure nor the hedonism of the prosperous 1920s were limited to young people. But all combined to form a recognizable youth culture in which young factory workers were joined by middle-class high school and college students in creating a set of practices and values distinct from those of adults.

More than any other factor, youth culture was distinguished by its embrace of sexual values that challenged the mores of earlier generations. Adolescents abandoned an older custom of "calling" in which the male suitor called on a young woman at home and visited under the supervision of nearby adults. Their new system, "dating," entailed an adolescent male asking his female love-interest to go "out" on a romantic date, perhaps to a movie, restaurant, or a park. The public nature of the "date" paradoxically permitted a new level of intimacy, since the young couple could use either the car or a relatively secluded public area to explore physical and emotional intimacy away from home and the supervision of adults. The hallmark of the new dating system was the practice of "petting"—kissing, hugging, and other sexual touch that typically stopped short of sexual intercourse.[18] Although premarital sexual activity was not a new phenomenon, the new morality's boldness, visibility, and widespread acceptance among the young of all social classes drew shocked notice from adults. For wealthier parents, the "girl problem" ceased to be about pitiable urban factory girls and became one that involved their own daughters' sexual behavior and reputations.

To nonsoutherners, the South had come to represent the "primitive" within the United States, the last place where modernity or youthful libertinism would blaze a trail. National audiences saw the region through the eyes of journalists like H. L. Mencken, who mocked the South as a backward land populated by "the very sort of dull, shaky, fearful anthropoid who is now the chief obstacle to all true progress in the South, and a shame to all humanity."[19] The Scopes trial of 1925, in which the State of Tennessee defended its ban on teaching the theory of evolution, only confirmed popular impressions of southerners' intellectual and cultural backwardness.

The resulting image of the "benighted South" found little favor among white southerners. They preferred a sense of regional distinctiveness rooted in the claim to a glorious past and a separate, distinctly superior culture.[20] African American southerners rejected this romanticized view. They did, however, perceive the South as unique for its overt racism and de jure segregation, conditions they were only too willing to flee when the employment opportunities of World War I initiated a great northward migration among southern blacks. Consequently when the South, like the rest of the nation, endured during the 1920s battles between "modernity" and "tradition," the problem of rebellious youth assumed particular meanings. Trends in education and labor force participation, a sharp tension between religious moralism and modern leisure, and the constant pressure to maintain lines of racial separation and difference shaped approaches to adolescent girlhood in the South.

Until approximately 1930 most American teenagers between the ages of fourteen and seventeen still did not attend or complete high school, while a far smaller percentage went to college. In 1920–1921 only 35 percent of the nation's fourteen- to seventeen-year-olds attended high school, with only 16.8 percent matriculating. A decade later 55 percent of high-school-age students attended secondary school, with the percentage of graduates almost doubling, to 32 percent. Yet by the end of the 1930s, fewer than 7 percent of white students and only 2 percent of black students had completed a four-year college education.[21]

National averages obscure a far more dismal picture in the South. In 1930 ten southern states ranked as the worst in the country for education. Mississippi, at the very bottom, enrolled just under 22 percent of its high-school-age students.[22] Across the South fewer than 18 percent of black teenagers attended either public or private high schools into the early 1930s. The availability of black education, not its desirability, determined enrollment. In the 1925–1926 school year, Georgia had only twelve accredited high schools for African Americans, only three of them public, compared to 309 accredited white high schools.[23] The gap was greatest in rural areas. The South's purported leader in education, North Carolina, provided seven rural white high schools to every one for black students, though African Americans made up 30 percent of the state's population. Mississippi, with a 50 percent black population, had only fifteen accredited black secondary schools compared to 290 for white youth.[24]

Though education varied greatly by race, the typical black or white southern teenager left school after seventh grade and worked full-time in farming or in one of the growing number of factories spawned by the New South's industrial development. In an agricultural economy, children had always worked doing chores or full-time farm labor. When industries sprouted throughout the South in the late nineteenth century, the practice of hiring children as young as six to ten years old to work in the mills and mines remained largely unquestioned. The low wages that employers paid to female and child labor enabled southern mills to attract business away from an older northern textile industry. This pattern came under attack in the 1910s and 1920s when a national campaign against child labor focused much of its energy on southern employment practices, imprinting on the national consciousness the image of the undernourished, poorly clad southern child. By the late 1920s compulsory education laws and the pressure of child labor reform ensured that nearly all young children attended school for at least several years.[25] But although more of the region's teenagers entered high school than ever before, most left school at some point to seek employment. Work, not school, remained the normative experience.

Adolescents joined the flow of rural southerners who, since the late nineteenth century, had steadily made their way to urban areas searching for a better living or easier life. As individuals or members of family groups, young women abandoned the dreariness of farm life for jobs in textile mills, cigarette factories, five and dime stores, or private homes. Although since at least the 1880s politicians and reformers had been issuing jeremiads about dangerous young women set loose in the city, during the 1920s the agricultural crisis and general weakness of the region's economy accelerated the pace of migration and thus the sense of urgency. One national study reported that of the children between ten and twenty years of age living on farms in 1920, approximately 40 percent had moved to towns and cities by 1930, a trend even more notable in the South because of its predominantly rural population.[26]

Southern reformers were acutely aware of this phenomenon, especially among girls. In 1930 the reform-oriented Southern Woman's Educational Alliance published *Rural Girls in the City for Work,* a study warning readers that a "surge of dissatisfaction with country life" more common to girls than boys had yielded "an increasing army of very young, untrained and uninformed girls" flocking to southern cities in search of both work and opportunities to meet new people and experience new pleasures.[27] The author, O. Latham Hatcher, argued that the move to the city was both sensible and justifiable given the lack of opportunities in rural areas, a conclusion supported by her interview subjects, 255 young migrants to Durham or Richmond who reported overall satisfactory experiences in the city.[28] Yet the tone of the study is ominous rather than affirming. Reformers like Hatcher feared that "pent-up desires for things which money can buy" combined with the "intensity of youth at its keenest" too often led the rural migrant into situations that could "degrade her standards for all the future."[29] *Rural Girls in the City for Work,* although probably read by a limited audience of social workers and educators, echoed a set of concerns shared by a broad sector of southerners.

During and after World War I, innovations like movies, jazz, and the automobile provoked a clash over the moral underpinnings of southern society. By the 1920s evangelical moralists had declared war on modernity and mass culture.[30] Fundamentalist preachers condemned the city as a centripetal force pulling young people into a "spiritually anemic" culture of "worldliness," where "the endless pull of petty things that promise amusement" produced a "consuming desire for life's luxuries."[31] Secular critics of modernity voiced similar dismay. In *The Changing South,* William J. Robertson noted sadly that southern girls and young women now "walk about the streets as freely and readily as men." One of the most painful sights for an old southerner "is to see young girls loafing at cigar and drug store corners day or night in the same fashion that young men loafed at such places twenty-five or thirty years ago."[32]

Social critics from across the political spectrum spoke out on the matter of youthful immorality. In cities like Atlanta and Nashville, black educators, ministers, and social workers collectively deplored urban amusements that tempted African American girls during their after-work hours.[33] Older African Americans found young people's behavior scandalous because it violated a longstanding ethos of self-denial aimed at saving every penny for the purchase of land, and with it independence from the poverty and social humiliations of sharecropping. But as adolescents increasingly left agriculture for wage labor, they appeared to have exchanged one American Dream of economic independence for a new one of immediate consumption of goods and entertainment.[34]

At the opposite end of the political spectrum, the Ku Klux Klan (KKK) also engaged in moral "clean-up" campaigns aimed at defending traditions of parental authority and Christian morality. When Klansmen like E. F. Stanton complained that "girls have lost their timidity and are now more brazen than boys," he implied that lurking behind

KKK efforts to restore male chivalry and bolster white power lay a condemnation of women and children's increased sexual and social autonomy.[35] The Klan joined with the Woman's Christian Temperance Union and other women's clubs to advocate for special curfews and public crackdowns on youthful immorality. They found support not only among ministers who called for a return to "traditional" religious values, but also from "progressive" reformers who believed that legal regulation and state intervention held the answer to stabilizing the social order. Reformers who took a variety of positions on matters of race, religion, and activist government agreed that the younger generation—especially bold daughters—posed a threat to the moral fabric of southern society.

The South's moral panic about adolescent sexuality grew, in part, from an unstable foundation of interracial dependency and proximity, despite Jim Crow laws and customs of racial separation. African American leaders used this instability to their advantage by pressing, carefully, for access to social services and schools. Ingeniously entering politics through the administrative state rather than the electoral realm, they asked the government for assistance in controlling disease and delinquency—which knew no racial boundaries—through funding of black health care, education, and recreation. Hairline fractures in the system deepened when during World War I African Americans began a decades-long process of mass out-migration. Denied the ballot, black southerners voted with their feet, abandoning the region or, alternately, moving from farm to city within the region. One-half of the 2.1 million African Americans who moved to urban areas between 1900 and 1925 relocated in southern cities, at least initially.[36] Migration remapped the region, as thousands upon thousands of African Americans sought jobs, schooling, and pleasure in new urban locations. As strangers who literally and figuratively no longer knew their "place," newcomers left white elites less certain of their own place atop the social order.

Reverend William McGlothlin of South Carolina framed the issue of youthful immorality in racial terms, calling on white citizens to observe "the solemn duty of the home, of the parents, to conserve the morals of the [white] race."[37] Similarly, in Athens, Georgia, a 1922 grand jury report advised that curtailing sexual immorality among

youth involved nothing short of "the preservation of the social structure and racial purity."[38] That popular entertainment often took place
in areas of town where the two races came into contact and sometimes intentionally mingled made the dangers of racial "mixing" all
the more real and threatening.

Decatur Street in Atlanta had a reputation as a rough, unsafe
African American thoroughfare populated by less-than-respectable
black businesses, houses of prostitution, and generally "lower-life
elements."[39] Working around segregation laws, popular nightclubs
opened their doors to whites on designated nights.[40] Even if they did
not mix with blacks in the actual seating areas, whites who entered
this racial "interzone" encountered a certain sector of the black community working as musicians or club employees, or simply gathering
on the streets. The search for bootleg alcohol also led white Atlantans
into black neighborhoods, where many ordinary homes doubled as so-
called liquor houses, selling liquor by the glass to white and black
customers alike.[41] To outraged whites, allowing the races to intermin-
gle in a sexualized space threatened to further erode the presumption
of "natural" racial difference on which white supremacy rested.

Concerns about interracial leisure receded when the economic skid
of the 1920s brought renewed attention to either the "plight" or "menace" of the white tenant farmer, low-paid mill worker, and "rural girl
in the city for work." Within these groups, the troublesome adolescent
girl stood at the borders of the very social distinctions that white
southerners held most dear. Was she an innocent child or an immod-
est woman? Was she of sound Anglo-American "stock" or was she
white "trash" who resembled the black race in her weakness of body,
mind, and morals? Did her youthful energy and active pleasure signal
a successful transition to modernity or a trend toward sinful de-
cadence—modernity gone awry?

These questions shifted attention away from the compellingly modern flapper toward the dangerously autonomous working-class girl.
Child guidance counselor Edith Farrell highlighted the dangerous
conditions for mill children in Columbus, Georgia. Noting that some
young people of the town enjoyed "the usual high school dances, play
and athletic sports," the "country club and the Muscogee Club," she
complained that "commercialized recreation still held sway" for the
great group of underprivileged out-of-school young people who

flocked to gambling machines, drank quantities of Coca Cola and possibly alcohol, and listened to "popular airs" on the Victrola. Regrettably, such "cheap" entertainment held the greatest attraction for "those who had the price," especially unmarried adolescent workers experiencing "a heady new freedom from parental control."[42]

Popular music from the period made reference to this "heady new freedom" and its all too short duration. In "Single Girl, Married Girl," recorded by the Carter Family in the late 1920s, each verse compares the relative freedom of single life to marriage for young women. One stanza contrasts the single girl who is "going dressed so fine" with the married girl who "wears just any kind." In the next verse, the single girl "goes to the store and buys" while the married girl "rocks the cradle and cries." Finally, the single girl is "going where she please," while the married girl has only "a baby on her knees."[43] The song depicts—and laments, from the married woman's point of view—the physical and financial independence of adolescent girls in the new commercial economy. Ironically, their very freedom to buy nice dresses and exert autonomy facilitated the courtship process and transition to married life, with its baleful return to the economic dependency, poverty, and family responsibility that working girls had briefly escaped.

Southern welfare workers portrayed factory work itself as dangerous. Middle-class southerners saw the "shiftingness" of factory girls, who changed jobs often, as a sign of immorality and poor work ethic. The very dullness of work could create "an abnormal taste for change and excitement," encouraging the inexperienced worker to pursue "the strongest of many urges"—the desire for male company and eventually an advantageous marriage. In her search for excitement, the working girl became an easy mark for the menacing "married man seeking the young girl as his prey."[44]

The danger originated only partially from men and equally in girls' own pent-up desires. O. Latham Hatcher reported that far from passive "prey," migrant girls craved crowds, action, romance, and excitement. Moreover, "there seemed no preventing or frightening many girls from being 'picked up' by strange men in automobiles."[45] A social worker from Winston-Salem, North Carolina, described as typical the case of fifteen-year-old Tilly Hill, an unclean, poorly dressed, "slow-witted" but typically "good natured 'country girl'" with a "friendly and yielding nature." Living at the edge of the city in a semirural neighborhood, Tilly and her sister began joyriding with older, rougher companions and eventually met boys for sexual relations at prearranged spots on the road or at home, "where only the 'honk' of the horn was necessary to bring them out." Although Tilly turned her life around after a stint in reform school, her story illustrates the liminal status of the teenage migrant, situated at the border between country and city, between stable home life and the excitement of the road, and between violation and volition.[46]

Such pessimism, however, was not universally shared. In a 1927 *New Republic* essay on progress "Away Down South," Bruce Bliven described a thrilling newness in southern life, including "new roads, new automobiles, new hot dog stands, tea shops, movie palaces, radio stores, real estate subdivisions, tourist campgrounds."[47] Bliven unintentionally mapped the new geography of adolescent sexuality, noting the roads and automobiles that gave teenagers mobility and privacy as well as the commercial gathering points and pleasures that allowed youth to forge a new morality. The same travel, consumption, and entertainment opportunities that to Bliven stood for "big tomorrows" unnerved evangelical moralists and social workers.

As the proportion of southerners living in urban areas jumped in the 1920s from one-quarter to nearly one-third of the region's population, shifting geographies became a trope for shifting power relations.[48] Social reformers and other urban elites exhibited a deep suspicion of both rural and city life. Often romanticizing the countryside as wholesome, innocent, and stable, they also depicted rural life as dull, hopeless, and lonely, populated by lethargic, slow-witted rubes. The rural girl's image as lovely and pure in her primitive state presented an antithesis to the sexual, sleazy working-class mill girl or waitress. Yet a contrary set of images reversed the value placed on urban and rural. The southern "New Woman" or college girl—educated, active in civic and social life, but not too assertive and always modest in dress and demeanor—embodied the best future of the South, the future that stupid, uncultured rural girls threatened to destroy.

Contrasts between urban and country girls provided handy dichotomies for framing the battle over modernity. As adolescents, working-class girls were by definition in an unstable, highly emotional, and sexually charged state. Although teenage migrants often garnered attention for their vulnerability, most observers could not ignore the social and sexual independence of young working-class women. A divided portrait of sexually active white adolescents as alternately troubled but pitiable young girls or defiant miscreants permeated the South's ongoing discourse about "modernity."

African American activists pointed to similar problems among teenage girls of their own communities. In particular, middle-class parents worried that their daughters might be enticed by the dancing and drinking common in "rough" working-class districts like Atlanta's Decatur Street. In his 1927 sociological study _Recreation and Amusement among Negroes in Washington, D.C._, William Jones called attention to "vulgar, sexually suggestive modern dances" that threatened to escape the "lower anti-social groups in which they originated" and "spread upwards into and engross the so-called higher classes."[49] Black activists worked on multiple fronts to prevent this kind of upward mobility. Their community-based rescue and prevention efforts attempted to deal head-on with the problematic sexuality of the most active or troubled adolescent girls. And their strong commitment to education functioned to "uplift" more industrious working-class teens while insulating middle-class girls from threats to their chastity and reputation, whether they came from assaultive white men, disreputable black street life, or their own erotic desires.

At the level of family and community, a largely middle-class group of African Americans tried to protect their daughters and advance the race by adhering to strict notions of personal modesty, formality in manners, and sexual propriety. Activists believed that a conservative, near-Victorian code of sexual respectability would gradually earn the respect of white elites who, upon acknowledging that the best people of every race shared a common set of morals and manners, would be more willing to extend social and political privileges. This goal went hand in hand with a strong desire to protect youth from the psychological damage of racism and the physical danger of white violence and sexual assault.[50]

Middle-class clubwomen, who in the Jim Crow era took a leading role in black political life, placed their greatest faith not in white acceptance but in their own powers of moral tutelage. The National Association of Colored Women (NACW), which had state and local chapters throughout the southern states, included among its numerous goals establishing homes for working girls and solving "the problem of the Adolescent period."[51] Many NACW members worked locally to establish community centers, clubs, and YWCA branches, with programs aimed at teaching girls the principles and practices of domesticity, morality, and chastity. Clubwomen believed that, left unchecked, the assertive sexuality of teenagers put them in danger of sexual abuse and placed a stain on the image of all black women by confirming the stereotype of black female promiscuity.

Baptist women's organizations joined clubwomen in their focus on unchaste young African American women who threatened the race from within. They shared with white Southern Baptists a critique of jazz music, dancing, modern fashion, and urban street life. The National Training School for Women and Girls, a secondary institution founded by black Baptist women under the leadership of Nannie Helen Burroughs, spoke plainly to the relative merits of domesticity over modern sexuality. Accompanying its motto of "Bible, bath and broom," a 1926 school brochure appealed to parents with the statement, "There are no flappers in Nannie Burroughs's school."[52]

Burroughs may have expressed more of a wish than a reality. Much to the frustration of reformers, many working-class adolescents rejected this moral code for a more vibrant, sexually permissive working-class culture expressed most compellingly in the "blues" music of the period. Even in middle-class institutions like Atlanta's Spelman College for women, students gave classmates appellations such as "the eternal flapper," "modern to the minute," and with "a skin you love to touch."[53] Indeed, refinement and spirituality may not have been the top priority of students at Spelman or coed black institutions like North Carolina's Livingstone College where men described female classmates as "bee-ooot-iful," chic, having the "It" personality, and "good 'timey.'" Women, in turn, used slang terms of their time to designate particular men as plenty hot!, sharp, slick, head over heels in love and broke, a ladies' man, a vagabond lover, a good lover, suave, smooth, and devilish.[54] College administrators' depictions of their schools as training grounds of respectability, refinement, and spiritual leadership did not spare them from experiencing a generation gap common to the 1920s.

A tremendous effort by African American communities in the 1920s produced private schools like the Delmount School of Lafayette County, Mississippi. Although such schools promoted sexual protection and respectability, students like these 1927 graduates rejected a strict Victorian ethos for modern "flapper" styles, evident in short dresses and bobbed hair. Special Collections, University of Mississippi Libraries.

While by the late 1920s the public discourse of southern whites had become almost exclusively focused on white working-class adolescents, African American reformers continued to work simultaneously on two related fronts—"uplifting" the masses and addressing the needs of the smaller, better-off group of middle-class youth. A tremendous effort to improve black education, both private and public, reached toward both constituencies at once. By enrolling poorer children in primary and secondary schools, educators and reformers hoped to inculcate a set of values that included middle-class standards of sexual propriety. At the same time, the tremendous growth of black colleges in the 1920s, many of which offered preparatory secondary schooling as well, created privately controlled African American spaces to prepare middle-class youth for adulthood.

Nationally, the number of black college students more than quadrupled in the 1920s, with the overwhelming majority attending schools located in southern states.[55] Black colleges provided a level of protection for all black youth and, for girls, a kind of sexual insulation. Given that black girls often encountered their first harassment from white employers or men on the street during their middle and late teens, high schools and colleges offered both physical separation and social supervision to vulnerable adolescents. Employing strict rules and vigilant supervision, educators taught the kind of self-controlled "ladylike" behavior that would ensure a girl's reputation in the community, establish her as a respectable representative of her race in the broader society, and shield her from sexual danger in the form of white assault or her own desires.[56]

Except for a small number of white religious and clubwomen involved in early interracial cooperation, public discussions of black adolescent sexuality remained confined entirely within black communities during the 1920s. One aspect of sexuality that black and white women might have had a common interest in addressing was the accessibility of black girls and young women to older white men. The sense of violation experienced by black women forced into nonconsensual sexual relations with white men resonated with the violation and shame of white women who stood by silently as their husbands, fathers, and sons pursued relationships with black women outside of marriage, sometimes fathering biracial children who served as visible reminders of male infidelity.

While black leaders analyzed most interracial sex, especially with young black girls, as simple assault or coercion at the hands of physically and socially empowered men, white women's loyalty and racial training led them to see the situation as one of male weakness in the face of young black women's seductive allure. Except for rare cases like the antilynching campaign organized by the Association of Southern Women for the Prevention of Lynching, white women remained unwilling to admit that the men they loved, licensed by patriarchy and white supremacy, could willingly violate not only young black women but also their own vows of fidelity and racial solidarity.[57] Instead they found common cause with the vast majority of white men in the South who believed that interracial sex and assault were best left unexamined, with a crucial exemption for black men's alleged rape of white women.

One important exception to the general white silence on African American teenage sexuality is a novel by white southerner Dubose Heyward. *Mamba's Daughters,* the seventh-best-selling novel in the nation in 1929, illustrates the very assumptions that usually remained unstated.[58] Heyward's novel tells the story of three generations of black women, starting with the poor, elderly, but cunning matriarch, Mamba, who schemes her way into a servant position with "good white folks" of Charleston, South Carolina, in order to obtain protection for her daughter, Hagar, and granddaughter, Lissa. As the novel develops, Hagar and Lissa come to represent the opposing rough and respectable elements of Charleston black society. Hagar accidentally kills a man over a two-dollar debt and is banished from the city to the rural phosphate mines where, blessed with the strength and physique of a man, she earns enough to pay for music lessons for her daughter, Lissa, who remains under the care of her grandmother. Mamba raises Lissa with every advantage in the hope that she will be accepted into the upper-crust black society of Charleston. Lissa assimilates into the city's color-conscious mulatto elite through her "pale lustred bronze" skin and remarkable singing voice.[59]

Yet as much as she embraces her grandmother's dreams of class mobility, Lissa cannot break free from the essential emotionalism and sexuality that, for Heyward, defines the Negro. The novel culminates in the immediate post–World War I years, when Lissa comes to maturity and faces a choice between her grandmother's dreams of high society and her own inarticulate longings for something both distantly African and insistently youthful, a hunger for "music—dancing—throbbing young bodies."[60] A friend introduces Lissa to a life of parties and dancing as well as to Prince, a conniving hustler. Prince woos and charms her until, on a fateful night, he spirits Lissa away from the relative safety of the dance hall to a crude cabin in the swamps, where he intends to rape her. Mamba, sensing that something is amiss, drives to the country to find Hagar who, following her "natural" instincts, reaches the cabin just as Prince is about to violate Lissa. In her rage to protect her daughter, Hagar kills Prince. The three genera-tions of women then face the age-old dilemma of black Americans in the South—how to escape the wrath of white law.

Lissa escapes to New York City where, supported by Mamba's sav-ings, she trains as a singer and begins to enjoy life and approach suc-cess. But her success is predicated on tragedy. Fearful that if the real story came to light Lissa would be hunted down and prosecuted, Hagar confesses to Prince's murder, claiming that he scorned her as a lover. She then drowns herself to end all investigation into the case, sacrificing her life for her daughter's. When Lissa learns of her mother's fate, she wants to return to the South to right the record and atone for her selfishness, but she realizes that this will only undo her mother's wishes. Instead she repays her debt with her own success, consummating Mamba's dreams of color, caste, and class mobility by pioneering a musical form that is "savage, tender, reckless. Something saved whole from a race's beginnings and raised to the nth degree by Twentieth Century magic—a blues gone grand opera."[61] Lissa subli-mates her racial passions in high art, thus at once preserving the past and breaking free toward a new beginning.

Mamba's Daughters is both a lurid tale of black sexuality and a story of racial striving and success. Intended as a sympathetic narrative, Heyward's assumptions about black female sexuality tell another story. The three white adolescent girls in the story, all minor charac-ters, move smoothly from girlhood into womanhood, entering mar-riages that provide the social rank and security they desire. Lissa also succeeds, but she does so outside of marriage and only after a great struggle with her baser desires and at the cost of her mother's life. Heyward offers no explanation for either Hagar's or Lissa's birth, but implies that neither mother had ever married and that Lissa's father may have been white. He allows Mamba's and Hagar's sexuality to stand alone, evident in a motherhood lacking any signs of paternity, marriage, or respectability.

Lissa, by contrast, is raised for respectability yet her sexuality breaks free of restraint, driven by a primal desire for the vitality of her "true" heritage. To Heyward, the sexuality of the black adolescent girl cannot be contained; it exists and must not be repressed or de-nied. He eventually reconciles this image of unquenchable sexuality with his belief in black progress through Lissa's migration, growing maturity, and sublimation of passion into music. But the crisis in the story is produced by the animal passions of a girl bred to repress them. Lissa's failure to control her natural eroticism leaves a trail of death in her forsaken South.

The novel resurrects a set of assumptions prevalent in the dominant white culture, providing clues to the far more typical silence about black adolescent girls in the 1920s public discourse on sexuality. Their invisibility represents not a genuine absence, but an unstated necessary presence. It formed the essential and unchanging backdrop against which white adolescent sexuality was defined and measured. Black southerners, given their weak political position and vulnerability to retaliation, chose to challenge this view mostly from within their own communities. Some simply accepted teenage sexuality as a legitimate expression of feeling, acknowledging the activity but rejecting its negative evaluation. Less tolerant African Americans attempted to reform and regulate adolescent girls' public behavior through education and uplift activities. White southerners focused their energies on correcting and controlling the behavior of poor white girls whose sexuality muddied the ground between artificially drawn lines of black vice and white purity.

The sexuality of middle-class white girls also received comparatively little public notice. Earlier, regional observers and moral reformers had commented on the middle-class flapper's fondness for dance, cars, fashion, and assorted other recreational activities that repudiated the modesty and propriety expected of southern belles. But by the end of the 1920s migration, economic strain and the increasingly long reach of social reform and government intervention had shifted the focus toward controlling working-class female sexuality so as to protect both race and class stability.

Privately, parents remained anxious about rearing middle-class daughters. Both the family's reputation and the daughter's future security depended on living up to the moral standards of southern white womanhood. But they dealt with the issue without public fanfare by providing the academic and social training necessary for their daughters' success, that is, for a "good" marriage within or above one's social station. Several factors gave elite parents confidence in their own powers. In the 1920s, high schools, and certainly colleges, were predominantly attended by middle-class students. Thus school social life guaranteed that adolescents mixed with members of their own class, providing a certain amount of insulation from less respectable mill workers, African Americans, and rural dwellers. The strict rules and close scrutiny governing student life also ensured conformity, at least externally, to established customs of dress and deportment. Private country clubs, summer camps, and social clubs provided further insulation, creating social opportunities in which courtship could occur within narrow class circles and under the scrutiny of adults.

Daughters provided with high school and college educations, swimming pools and social clubs, fine clothing, and the other social privileges of their race and class had little reason to reject forthrightly the world of their parents. Surely some girls, following in the path of the rebellious Zelda Fitzgerald, veered from traditionally prescribed behaviors or mores. But in the relative protection of the middle-class high school and college, students found a degree of autonomy that permitted them to express their "modern" morality without posing a serious threat to the values of their parents' generation. Thus, while the most vocal white southerners publicly denounced the "immorality" of working-class adolescent girls, the majority of well-to-do parents turned to private clubs, colleges, and cotillions to keep their daughters fixed along the path to southern white womanhood.

Middle-class confidence did not eliminate all doubt, however. Lingering anxieties about the new morality offered fertile ground for an enterprising author, William Faulkner, who in 1929 set out to write a novel exploiting these themes. A controversial, sensational best seller when released in 1931, *Sanctuary* tells the story of Temple Drake, a middle-class college girl whose weekend jaunt with a college-educated man turns into a nightmare of rape, murder, abduction, and lynching.[62]

Faulkner introduces Temple Drake as a seventeen-year-old University of Mississippi student with a reputation for being "fast." He paints the long-legged, stylishly rouged and powdered redhead as sexually appealing but not quite containable, so that when the novel opens she is confined to campus for curfew violations and must sneak away to attend an out-of-town football game with her date, Gavin Stevens. The drama begins when Gavin insists on stopping at a country moonshine operation. A car accident strands them there, and

Gavin soon drinks himself into oblivion, leaving Temple to fend for herself among the several predatory men who operate the illegal business. Her only protection comes from a slightly older woman, Ruby Goodwin, who has previously "jazzed"—or sold herself sexually—in order to pay the lawyer fees to free her husband Lee from prison.

After Ruby shepherds Temple through a terrifying night of threatened assault, the frightened Temple escapes to the barn only to be raped there, with a corn cob, by Popeye, the novel's heartless, impotent antagonist. He then kills Tommy, a naive underling who witnessed the rape, and whisks Temple away to a Memphis whorehouse where she languishes in her shame, violation, and growing dependence on liquor. Popeye visits her regularly, accompanied by Red who, by prior arrangement, has sex with Temple while Popeye watches for his own pleasure. When sex with Red awakens Temple's erotic desire, Popeye kills his rival, leaving Temple no way out of the hell to which her adventurous but naive sexual interest has led.

Temple's unanticipated reprieve comes when the lawyer representing Lee Goodwin, arrested for the murder of Tommy, locates Temple in Memphis and begs her to come home to attest to Goodwin's innocence at his trial. She agrees to testify, returning to the care of her father, a respected judge. But whether from fear or love of Popeye, she falsely implicates Goodwin in both her rape and Tommy's murder. Outraged townsmen lynch Goodwin while Popeye temporarily escapes justice, only to be arrested and wrongfully hung for another man's murder. With chaos and destruction trailing in her wake, Temple escapes, much like Lissa did in *Mamba's Daughters,* by traveling to a distant city. In Paris, accompanied by her father, her economic privilege can compensate for the reputation she has squandered.

Sanctuary seems ironically titled, since none of the characters find either protection or solace from the chain of horrors initiated by a young, middle-class couple's intrusion into the rural demimonde of bootlegging and hard-edged, sometimes violent, sex. Faulkner implies that when removed from the enclave of middle-class youth culture, the provocative sexuality of adolescent white women becomes a chaotic force, triggering evil and mayhem. In the end, almost everyone who comes into contact with the sexualized, no-longer-sacralized "Temple" suffers irreparable harm. Tommy, Popeye, Red, and Lee are murdered. Temple's would-be protector, Ruby, becomes a pitiful indigent whose sickly infant lies on the brink of death. Temple Drake herself comes to a more ambiguous end, eventually restored to the protective arms of white male patriarchy. Yet Faulkner concludes the novel with an image of Temple in Paris gazing first at her own image in a compact mirror, then shifting the mirror's angle to catch a view of the sky "lying prone and vanquished in the embrace of the season of rain and death."[63] Does Temple see an image of herself in the sky's reflection? In a rare moment of self-contemplation, Temple conveys a nebulous unhappiness, leaving the reader to wonder at its source: Does it emanate from the experience of violation itself, her damaged reputation, or quite the opposite—unfulfilled sexual longings?

White, middle-class womanhood traditionally represented the "temple" or sacred body of southern worship, and thus the "sanctuary" or place of safety and protection for all that the white South valued. In Faulkner's novel, though, the Temple is violated—by rough men of a working-class underworld, by the symbolically rural corn cob, in an urban Memphis whorehouse, and most of all as a result of Gavin's and her own hedonistic pursuit of pleasure. When the safe haven offered by middle-class status inexplicably gives way, Temple ruefully recalls the safety of life as she recently knew it, summoning visions of campus couples slowly "strolling toward the sound of the supper bell, and of her father sitting on the porch at home, his feet on the rail, watching a negro mow the lawn." To ward off her impending violation, she reimagines the social order: first, a beatific college campus, bells chiming, with nothing wilder than hand-holding couples strolling toward dinner; and second, a pleasant scene of home, where her father sits in the power of repose—his feet propped upon the symbolic "top rail"—while a servile black man performs manual labor beneath him. This image fails to calm, and the terrified adolescent frantically attempts to pray for her safety. Unable to think "of a single designation for the heavenly father" she instead invokes her biological father, chanting over and over the mantra-like prayer, "My father's a judge; my father's a judge" in the desperate hope that she can marshal the powers of the patriarch to protect her sexual innocence, which she mistakenly valued too little, too late.[64]

The literary figure of Temple Drake demonstrates a lingering uncertainty and fascination with the sexuality of modern, liberated girlhood among the privileged classes. Although Faulkner's own moral stance remains largely concealed, he successfully engaged the popular regional concern about modern female sexuality in the context of deteriorating class and racial boundaries and potential social chaos. Like many movies of the era (the novel itself was turned into a movie in 1933), the story offers a titillating spectacle of sexual and social conventions torn asunder, while the conclusion reaffirms existing social hierarchies. The threatening working-class men have died, Ruby's already difficult life gets even harder, and the three middle-class main characters return "home" after long estrangements. In *Sanctuary,* the rich survive and the immoral poor die, the racial and class order remains unshaken, and white women return to the sheltering wing of white patriarchs. But the sensational plot also suggests a literary echo to the social discourse of sexual danger and disorder more often personified in the late 1920s by the working-class adolescent girl.

The changes of the 1920s stand as both a culmination and preface. The penetration of commercial culture and the migration from country to city announced the arrival of the New South, spawning a more visible, sensual youth culture that struck many southerners as a sign of declension, not progress. As girls from diverse class and racial backgrounds sought out a new independence in the 1920s, they used work and recreation to explore sexuality and a variety of other new experiences. By the end of the decade, working-class white girls sparked the most determined response, but they were not alone in their independent, sexually "modern" ways; just more visible and controversial.

Recognition of the modern adolescent girl's sexuality did not usually translate directly into articulated ideologies or government policies. Representations of female sexuality emanated from many parts of southern society, reflecting varied material interests, political agendas, and cultural expressions. But popular culture and public debate did provide important sites of contestation over political and moral values, figuring into frameworks of knowledge that helped policy makers comprehend and take action in any given political moment.

The prominence of teenage girls in southern cultural politics marks the 1920s as distinctive, yet we can also see the decade as a precursor to developments that made adolescent sexuality a salient theme in southern politics and social imagination for decades to come. In every case, the cultural uneasiness and controversy surrounding female sexuality occurred in the context of tensions within an economically and racially stratified region. As they came of age, modern teenage girls, seeking both immediate pleasures and longed-for futures, excited concerns that were integrally linked to volatile social relations in a region that often argued questions of racial and class power through the politics of sexuality.[65]

$\mathcal{S}$pirited $\mathcal{Y}$outh or $\mathcal{F}$iends $\mathcal{I}$ncarnate?

On March 12, 1931, two residential cottages at Samarcand Manor, the North Carolina state training school for delinquent girls, went up in flames. Four days later, sixteen Samarcand inmates, aged thirteen to nineteen, were charged with arson, a capital crime in North Carolina. The accused would stand trial for their lives. The citizens of North Carolina, who were suffering through one of the worst periods of the Depression, were diverted and enthralled by the fire, trial, and surrounding events, which over a period of three months included a state investigation into Samarcand's management, two jail uprisings staged by some of the teenage defendants awaiting trial, and the intervention of one of the state's most famous women, journalist and socialite Nell Battle Lewis, who in her first courtroom appearance stepped in as defense attorney. After much sensation, two suspects were released for lack of evidence, two received suspended sentences, and the remaining twelve were convicted and sentenced to eighteen months to five years in state prison on a plea bargain that reduced the charge to a noncapital offense.[1] Although these events could hardly seem further removed from typical teenage life, a public debate developed around the question of exceptionalism: Were these adolescent firebugs to be understood as uncommonly dangerous and corrupted youth ("fiends incarnate" in the words of one correspondent), or were they ordinary, passionate adolescents who had been led astray by the unfortunate circumstances of their impoverished and unstable lives?[2]

The Samarcand investigations and trial served as a focal point for a public controversy over juvenile delinquency in white girls.[3] The question of delinquency, in turn, formed part of an effort to come to terms with the sexuality and self-assertiveness attributed to "normal" girls. Efforts to define and regulate female adolescent sexuality occurred across the nation during the Progressive and interwar periods, as Progressive reformers returned again and again to the endangered young working-class woman who figured first as the "woman adrift" and later as the teenage "sex delinquent."[4] The Samarcand incident brought these issues to a head in the South, where by the late 1920s the social dangers raised by assertive, sexually active, young working girls held particular resonance. White southerners had long exalted and defended the purity of "southern womanhood" as the linchpin of social order. But what did it mean to become a southern woman in modern times, when expressions of female sexual agency challenged the pristine virtue of the idealized "southern lady"?[5] What behaviors were appropriate for female adolescents in a fast-changing region that was nevertheless still rooted in traditions of patriarchy and white supremacy? In a society that justified its racial caste system on the grounds that segregation protected the sexual and racial purity of white womanhood, recognition that sexual desire was common to all teenage girls might hasten the collapse of racialized distinctions between white virtue and black vice, not to mention the racial order that such ideas buttressed.

The 1931 Samarcand arson trial offers an unusually visible example of the process by which public officials and the public at large grappled with changing female adolescent behaviors in the context of regional, racial, and class concerns. Although ostensibly about arson, the trial and surrounding public controversy returned repeatedly to the issue of sexuality—the sexual "delinquency" in these girls' pasts and the sexual energy thought to infuse and explain their riotous behavior. The disruptive actions of troubled and defiant working-class girls forced a moment of reckoning in which the public and the courts had to draw a line between adolescents' punishable deviance and understandable misbehavior, in the process articulating the modern social parameters for female adolescent sexuality.

The fervor and ambivalence that characterized public discussion of the Samarcand incident suggest that these issues were pressing but not easily resolved. State officials and middle-class citizens wavered between a faith in the state's redemptive power to restore the essential goodness of white teenage girls damaged by poverty and personal misfortune and a strong apprehension that female sex delinquents bred social chaos and degenerate offspring, thereby diluting the quality of the white body politic. In the end, while many sympathetic citizens attempted to incorporate modern definitions of adolescent sexuality into a charitable embrace of white delinquent girls, the State of North Carolina opted for a far harsher approach that treated female delinquents as sexually immoral, physically degenerate criminals subject to severely punitive measures.

Since at least the 1880s, reformers around the nation had dedicated themselves to finding answers to what became known as the "girl problem." This phrase conveniently merged three separate problems: the problems of economic and sexual exploitation that girls or young women often encountered in urban industrial settings; the generational tensions occasioned by young women's bold styles and actions, especially their sexual and reproductive behavior; and the conceptual problem of defining the passage from girlhood to womanhood in legal practice and social theory. Efforts to solve the "girl problem" sometimes focused proactively on providing decent jobs, housing, and education to young women in the city. But equal or greater energy went into more punitive legal and penal reforms designed to protect adolescent women from the perceived hazards of modern city life and their own youthful inclinations.[6]

Late-nineteenth-century campaigns used statutory rape laws to raise the age at which a girl could legally consent to sexual intercourse. This legal reform attempted to contain adolescent sexuality within a protective framework of childhood innocence. Subsequent reform efforts, however, demonstrated less faith in the innocence of sexually experienced girls. Early-twentieth-century activists increasingly viewed female offenders as deliberate actors who participated willingly in dangerous or "immoral" activities that, if not criminal by adult standards, were serious enough to warrant incarceration and rehabilitative training.[7] Thus newly built female reformatories, which originated in private efforts, gradually secured state support. By 1924, there were fifty-seven publicly funded institutions for delinquent girls, with only two states failing to provide at least one reformatory. These "training schools," and a number of private institutions established for the same purpose, served a population of girls and young women who might be as old as twenty-one but typically fell between the ages of thirteen and eighteen.[8]

Southern institutions followed the national pattern but developed some regional distinctions as well. Juvenile reformatories in the South were often founded later and granted far fewer funds by penurious legislatures. Like the others, they were divided by gender, but in the South inmates were separated by race as well. States typically established reformatories for white boys, black boys, and white girls, with training schools for black girls left to the private efforts of African American communities.[9] Attempts in North Carolina to obtain state funding for a "Training School for Negro Girls" met continued opposition from whites who, according to the *Charlotte Observer*, believed that this type of institution would quickly be overrun with black girls who fit the criteria for sex delinquency.[10] By implication, sexual misbehavior among black girls was so common it did not constitute delinquent behavior, while among white girls it was an exceptional and correctable condition.

A final wrinkle in the picture of southern reformatories was the practice of sending delinquent girls who tested low in intelligence to state schools for feebleminded children. Although the practice was not unheard of in the North, by the 1930s it occurred more extensively in the South, where institutions for the feebleminded served as a kind of wastebasket for cases of a mental, physical, or moral nature. Female reformatory superintendents nevertheless complained frequently that the state institutions for the feebleminded accepted far too few transfers, saddling them with girls mentally incapable of successful rehabilitation and, as a result, lowering their success rates.

Although apparent before World War I, southern concern about female "sex delinquents" crystallized during the war. North Carolina, for example, established Samarcand Manor in 1917 and opened its doors one year later supported by federal funds earmarked for the reduction of venereal disease in wartime.[11] These concerns did not recede in the war's aftermath, but rather garnered greater attention due to the crisis in southern agriculture. In the 1920s, as farms failed and rural incomes dropped, individuals and families fled rural areas for the cities, lured by anticipated employment and the attractions of urban entertainment and sociability. Migrants experienced both satisfactions and disappointments, but middle-class urbanites and reformers focused only on the many problems that accompanied the transition. Chronic unemployment, crime, substandard housing, high rates of venereal disease and other diseases, and the sight of naive and "loose" young women roaming city streets led reformers to propose supervised recreation and vocational education—"constructive" reforms designed to safeguard the adolescent in her transition from girlhood to marriage and motherhood.[12]

In actuality, such programs rarely materialized and most teenage girls did not benefit from vocational or recreational guidance. The most troublesome cases, however, came to the attention of local police and welfare officials and could result in incarceration at state institutions such as Samarcand. The North Carolina reformatory annually housed between 160 and 260 girls in the late 1920s and early 1930s, averaging 215 for the decade 1926–1935.[13] Most of the girls were charged with vagrancy or immoral conduct as a result of encounters with the police, county welfare workers, community members who lodged complaints, or family members who opted to place disobedient daughters in the hands of the law. Inmates typically spent between one and three years at Samarcand, receiving treatment for venereal disease if necessary, minimal academic training, and many hours of "vocational training"—obtained while performing the domestic and agricultural tasks necessary to run the institution.

Frequent escape attempts suggest that many inmates actively disliked and resisted their treatment. Delinquent girls incarcerated at Samarcand and similar institutions perceived their reformatory term not as an educational opportunity but as an unfairly harsh and undeserved punishment. "This is a prison, not a school to teach girls a trade," wrote one angry Alabama inmate. Another girl appealed to the governor to "please for gods sakes do some thin for us girls" suffering under the horrible "conditions at this place that is called a school." In the letter, signed from "an inmate," the author sarcastically rejected the term "industrial school" as a misnomer employed to hide from the public the institution's prisonlike conditions.[14]

The desire to escape scheduled punishments and intolerable conditions prompted Samarcand inmates to set fire to two dormitories, one of them a "disciplinary cottage" where staff meted out punishments. Although most denied setting the fire, upon their arrest and removal from Samarcand to a local county jail the defendants all but indicted themselves when seven of them set fire to mattresses in their jail cells. Several weeks later, still awaiting trial and having been removed to another county jail, five of the inmates once again rioted, reportedly keeping up "a continual stream of verbal vulgarity, curses and imprecations" as they "set fire to their cell bunks, smashed every window pane they could reach . . . and finally attacked members of the local fire department who came to their rescue, with pocket knives."[15] Although the fires were quickly doused, many wondered whether the flames that burned inside such rebellious female spirits could be so easily contained.

The months of publicity surrounding the Samarcand arson case sparked statewide interest. North Carolinians pondered whether these were innocent little girls, behaving like any other teenagers but for the particularly harsh circumstances in which they found themselves. Or were they—as one newspaper headline wondered—modern-day "vixens" who had merely gotten an early start on the road to adult vice and dissolution?[16] Although phrased as an issue of age-appropriate behavior, much more was at stake in this controversy. The question of whether the Samarcand inmates were misguided yet salvageable teenagers or fiendishly carnal women was freighted with political and social implications.

The South of the 1920s and 1930s lurched unsteadily and painfully toward a modern economy as coal, furniture, textiles, steel, and retail industries drew rural sharecroppers, tenants, and small landholders toward the cities and into the wage economy. Champions of the New South held up modern industries and fast-growing cities as examples of regional prosperity, but they also worried about the instability of the new order. Massive displacement of rural whites and blacks raised social, economic, and political uncertainties soon heightened by the Depression. Moreover, despite the strength of legally implemented racial segregation and black disfranchisement, southern race relations always depended on extralegal terrorism to maintain a hierarchy that was never accepted by the region's African American citizens. Hopes for stability rested on continued economic development and the creation of a dependable, well-adjusted, and cohesive white population that supported the existing political and social order.[17]

To many, the unruliness, illicit sexuality, and high rates of out-of-wedlock pregnancy and venereal disease common to female delinquents became emblematic of the instability of the New South. The defiant wills and the sexually precocious, frequently diseased bodies of sex delinquents raised a disturbing specter of social disorder and racial degeneracy within the state's white population. But others responded more hopefully, seeing in delinquent girls a raw spirit that if harnessed represented the vigor and spark of modernity. These contrasting views were entertained but ultimately not resolved by the media, concerned citizens, state officials, and trained social workers as they responded to the disturbances at Samarcand.

The initial response to the fire took place in the press, where articles, editorials, and letters featured competing interpretations of the accused girls' conduct and character. The majority opinion commented that these were foolish, restless girls whose boundless energy and "school spirit" had merely taken a destructive turn due to unfortunate childhoods and the harsh conditions at Samarcand. "These girls are just like girls everywhere," stated one editorialist, while a Raleigh reporter concluded that the girls who took part in the latest jailhouse ruckus might just as easily "walk into a high school class room and not be different from the average."[18] These authors implied that whether in high school or reform school, the typical adolescent girl was high-spirited, sexually interested, and drawn toward a reckless search for fun and freedom. While the enthusiasms of adolescence might get any girl into a modicum of trouble, in the case of Samarcand inmates, poverty and misfortune had led to more serious harm.

In contrast, a vocal minority viewed these girls as a precocious version of sexually immoral, "low-class" women who menaced society, perceiving "a certain corrosion which strikes much deeper than the 'mistake' or 'false step' with which they are credited."[19] Anger and an absence of control were the most noted features of this debased condition. After quoting one girl's explanation that "I just feel mean," an account of the second jailhouse mutiny described faces distorted with rage, eyes gleaming, and hair and clothes disheveled such that

Several of the Samarcand arson defendants mounting the stairs to the courthouse on the day they were convicted and sentenced to state prison, May 21, 1931. Their short dresses, bobbed hair, and, on the left, cigarette smoking suggest their modern sexuality, which became a central issue in their trial. *Raleigh News and Observer.* Courtesy of the North Carolina Office of Archives and History, Raleigh, North Carolina.

"they seemed to be angered to the point of temporary insanity."[20] What in "normal" girls might be an urge for excitement had become in these girls a wanton search for thrills expressed in irrational, uncontrollable fury.

Proponents of both views emphasized two connected themes: the inmates' sexuality and their modernity.[21] In a trial that on the surface had nothing to do with sex, the papers often noted that the girls had been raised in "immoral" environments and had been incarcerated for sexual offenses. Their lawyer, Nell Battle Lewis, compiled a casebook in which she noted the sexual history of each defendant and her age at first intercourse.[22] Beyond these direct references, sexuality often appeared as a subtext in press descriptions of the defendants' rebellious modernity. The girls were described as wearing "attractive silk and cotton prints," rolling their stockings down under their knees, and begging visitors for magazines, cigarettes, and, of course, matches. Their incessant thrill-seeking seemed to come from an irrepressible sexual energy linked to modern pleasures. Their juvenile records were sprinkled with references to cafes, automobiles, and "running around" in towns and cities. And they reportedly explained that their final jail-house fire had been set as a calculated attempt to win release from their cells to a recreation room where they could listen to the Victrola and dance.[23]

The adventuresome sexualized adolescent represented a dangerous current in female modernity, a view accentuated by the contrasting presence of a more palatable New Woman, the refined yet dynamic figure of defense counsel Nell Battle Lewis. Although she ended her life as a reactionary defender of southern conservatism, in the 1920s and early 1930s Lewis stood out among southern women as a leading exemplar of New Womanhood. Born to a prominent North Carolina family and educated at St. Mary's College in Raleigh, she lived briefly in the North and then returned to the South to become a columnist for the *Raleigh News and Observer.* She used her column as a podium to advance heretical challenges to southern pieties of race, religion, gender, and respectability. She rebelled most zealously against the ide-alized "southern lady" and in one 1925 column suggested propheti-cally that women's rights in the South would have been hastened by "a smashed window or two and a little arson."[24]

Seeming to heed her suggestion, the alleged Samarcand arsonists were immediately appealing to Lewis, who in the late 1920s had taken an extended break from journalism to become a lawyer.[25] When the court-appointed public defender neglected to mount a serious defense, she agreed to step in as defense attorney. Throughout the trial the press presented a glowing picture of Lewis as a fashionable modern woman who walked intrepidly where male lawyers feared to tread. Her presence in the case offered a version of modernity that was bold and stylish but ultimately asexual, professional, and respectful of the law. As such, Lewis posed a sharp and reassuring contrast to the law-lessness and sexuality of the young women she defended.

Trying to divert attention from her charges' disorderly behavior and shift blame for the fire from her clients to their keepers, Lewis played up public accusations of institutional neglect and cruelty. The mount-ing criticism forced the state's Department of Public Welfare to launch an investigation of claims that Samarcand staff administered brutal corporal punishments, failed to segregate venereally diseased inmates from noninfected girls (based on the belief that venereal disease spread through casual contact or airborne germs), isolated girls for weeks or months at a time in vermin-infested solitary confinement chambers, and generally failed in the goal of rehabilitation. After conducting extensive interviews, investigators issued a lengthy report exonerating the administration of all charges, despite sworn testimony from recently departed employees about routine brutality. The report did, however, make several suggestions, the most urgent of which was a call for the immediate abolition of corporal punishment.[26]

The voyeuristic, almost pornographic discussion of corporal punishment at Samarcand provides additional evidence of the uncertainty with which both state officials and the public viewed delinquent girls. While roundly condemning its use and abuse, most commentators nevertheless reveled in its detail. Reporters and investigators regularly inquired about the number and nature of the beatings, providing the public with graphic descriptions of mature female bodies forced to the ground, stripped, whipped repeatedly with sticks or straps, and left in a bruised and battered condition. These descriptions evoked both horror and hints of erotic interest, reflecting the public's ambivalence about adolescent bodies. Were they to be protected or punished? Who had the right to control and derive pleasure from them? And were these the bodies of children—thus subject to corporal punishment—or adults, for whom such punishments had been outlawed?

The confusion that characterized popular responses and official inquiries also appears in professional accounts of juvenile correction. Margaret Brietz, a city probation officer in Winston-Salem, North Carolina, who supervised former Samarcand inmates, had used their case records as the basis for her 1927 master's thesis in sociology.[27] Drawing heavily on contemporary psychological, sexological, and eugenic literatures, Brietz's elaborately drawn portraits of eighteen Samarcand girls reveal some of the tensions that characterized scientific and social-reform thinking on female delinquency during this period. Like her contemporaries, Brietz was especially uncertain about the relationship of delinquency to normal adolescence. Early in her 250-page thesis Brietz describes girls suffering from the "normal instability of adolescent years," typified by a youthful "craving for thrills and romance" and a sense of "great upheaval." That adolescent girls experienced "the desires and impulses of adulthood but only a child's self-control" could lead to an occasional "adolescent flare-up" and trouble with the law. In this sympathetic view, adolescence in and of itself could be a cause of delinquency.[28] Brietz echoed the thinking of psychoanalytically informed psychologists who saw "sexual desire and the wish for self-assertion (or the will to power)" as libidinal tendencies released in a girl's early adolescence "in half-conscious attempts to attract attention from the other sex." According to experts, it was precisely these girlish reveries of romantic love that created many of the difficulties faced by normal female adolescents.[29]

Brietz appears to lose sympathy with the notion of delinquents as normal but misguided adolescents as she proceeds through more difficult cases. Coming to view delinquency as typical of "subnormal" teens whose behavior indicates adolescent pathology, she grows more and more critical of her clients' "sickening backgrounds," "abnormal tendencies," deceitfulness, sexual obsessions, and "defective mental capacity."[30] Brietz's revulsion leads her further from modern views of normal adolescent compulsions to an assessment of hereditary depravity among "defective" adolescents who would soon add to the ranks of a degenerate white population. Her concern with heredity culminates in Brietz's analysis of sex delinquency as less a marker of adolescence than evidence of adult pathology among "degenerate" white women whose reputed lack of sexual inhibitions and morality had already begun to surface. Although a staple of four decades of American eugenics thought, views of hereditary degeneracy were losing scientific credibility by the late 1920s. Yet in Brietz's work they assume a modern scientific cast through her eager embrace of IQ tests to measure subnormal intelligence and of surgical sterilization as a eugenic corrective to the problem.[31]

In her conclusion, Brietz paints the dilemma faced by reformers, policy makers, and ordinary citizens of the state. She attests that the impulses motivating delinquency "are found to be those operating in the lives of the best of us." Reminding her readers that "we are all 'sisters under the skin,'" Brietz instructs educated citizens neither to punish nor ostracize the delinquent in any way that would "deny that she is our own."[32] Yet the high number of girls testing low in intelligence—"morons" in her parlance—leads Brietz to question her own guiding premise; by the end of the study she has come to doubt the entire enterprise of rehabilitating "subnormal" girls for a future of domesticity and motherhood. Considering the children borne by such

women, she exclaims, "What a price!" and concludes that "any program of 'Social Work' which encourages or permits feeble-minded individuals to 'become moral' by marriage and parenthood is of doubtful value" to the state.[33] Brietz wrote as a middle-class professional
and reformer coming to terms with young working-class females
whose independence, vulnerability, and spunk attracted her sympathy
while their sexual improprieties and grievous poverty discomfited and
sometimes repulsed her. Was the female sex delinquent one of "our
own" or did she belong, as Brietz feared, to a group of genetically inferior people whose costly immorality must not be tolerated?

Implicit in Brietz's narrative are questions of citizenship that re-
surfaced in popular debates about the Samarcand arson case. Who did
the state recognize as citizens? Were "immoral" and rebellious working-class white girls dangerous noncitizens who corrupted the body
politic, or were they "our girls" who through proper training could be
salvaged as productive members of a white citizenry? The contest between political inclusion and exclusion of white female delinquents
was not specific to the South of the 1930s. This issue, however, may
have held special resonance in the South, where long before the 1930s
white teenage girls had come to play a controversial and symbolic role
in regional events. Accusations of "unruly" or "disorderly" female sexuality reached back to the antebellum period, a time when the extramarital or interracial involvements of poor white women were perceived as especially threatening to a social order that depended on
white women's sexual purity for the orderly transmission of property
and racial identity.[34] These concerns intensified and shifted focus with
the advent of industrial development in the New South.

At issue now was the sexuality of the young white girls who rapidly
populated the paid labor force of mill towns and modern cities. The
infamous 1915 lynching of Leo Frank, a northern-bred Jewish factory
supervisor in Atlanta who allegedly raped and murdered his fourteen-
year-old employee Mary Phagan, reveals deep tensions in southern society over who would control the labor and sexuality of daughters
during the transition from family-based agriculture to individual wage
labor. Although framed as an issue of female vulnerability and victimization, reactions to the Phagan murder also exhibit an apprehensive-
ness about the possibility of daughters taking the initiative sexually

in direct defiance of traditional lines of gender and generational authority.[35]

By the 1920s, the revitalized Ku Klux Klan drew adherents by capitalizing on similar fears. Railing against youthful propensities for drink, dance, and sexual experimentation, the Klan exercised a violent brand of moral vigilantism aimed at restoring paternal authority and traditional sexual mores.[36] Progressive women reformers of the South, although they often represented the tendencies of modernity and elitism that the Klan abhorred, also embraced the vulnerability of poor white women to advance a set of reforms that included prohibition, moral reformatories, and other state-sanctioned "protective" measures. In an address to the United Daughters of the Confederacy, politician Rebecca Latimer Felton offered this justification for expanded public education: "Why do I particularly mention poor white girls? Because these girls are the coming mothers of the great majority of the Anglo-Saxon race in the South. The future of the race for the next fifty years is in their hands."[37]

By the 1930s, that future seemed to have arrived and it did not look promising. In an era of rapid but painful regional transformation, state governments fretted over how to allocate shrinking resources to ameliorate severe economic problems and hold together a racially tendentious society that now also threatened to split across class seams. In this context, it would seem unlikely that teenage girls would garner much attention, especially since new understandings of modern adolescents as sexually interested and active eroded the persuasive power of sentimental defenses of purity. Yet unusual circumstances could still throw teenage daughters into the center of public controversy. For example, in an incident both similar to and contemporaneous with the outbreak at Samarcand, charges of mistreatment and corruption at the Alabama Girls' Training School exploded in March 1931 into a public controversy that rivaled the Samarcand trial for sensationalism and outrage. Superintendent Ira Champion came under fire for her egregious mistreatment of inmates, including using as standard punishments physical beatings, head shaving, and the withholding of clothing. Well-publicized legislative hearings created a stage on which girls along with staff members got their "day in court" either to deny or confirm the charge against Champion, who after temporary exoneration was soon dismissed for lacking professional qualifications.[38]

A more devastating example is the Scottsboro case, in which nine African American teenagers in Alabama were charged and quickly convicted of the rape of two white women, Ruby Bates and Victoria Price, ages seventeen and twenty-one, respectively (though some accounts place Price in her middle twenties). Occurring less than two weeks after the Samarcand fire, the March 1931 incident once again placed poor white women—mill girls who perfectly fit reformers' description of the "rural girl in the city for work"—at the center of a trial that generated worldwide controversy. The two women, who were discovered riding freight trains illegally (most likely in search of work), claimed rape rather than face almost certain arrest for vagrancy or disorderly conduct. Although Bates quickly recanted and admitted that the two women were not even in the same car as the defendants, in this case the questionable sexual virtue of disreputable working-class white girls was trumped by cross-class white solidarity against an imagined and unproven threat of predatory black sexuality.[39]

Opinion was less unified in the Samarcand case. Although the white electorate generally agreed that the accused posed a danger to the state, they differed on the matter of how "salvageable" they were. It is possible that members of working-class or lower-middle-class communities who understood juvenile problems as part and parcel of growing up with limited resources may have been more sympathetic toward sexual delinquency.[40] But since the extant commentary comes largely from literate newspaper readers, interpretations of white female delinquency seem to have divided less along class lines and more at other points of cleavage—between fundamentalist Christian ideas of sin and more liberal religious views; between allegiances to "traditional" versus "modern" mores; and possibly between more permissive rural attitudes toward sexuality and more propriety-conscious views held by town and urban residents.

Yet if the lines of disagreement remain blurry, the Samarcand trial leaves no doubt that white North Carolinians saw the problem of sex delinquency as relevant to building a strong and moral white citizenry. The association between morality and whiteness appears most starkly in case records of inmates accused of associating voluntarily with African American men. Crossing racial lines was equivalent to crossing the boundary between lawfulness and delinquency, or good and evil. For the most part, though, racial implications remained muted, cloaked as a discussion about the motives, character, and ultimate social worth of the poor white girl, the future mother of the (white) citizens of North Carolina.

Through the press, the public wondered whether the alleged arsonists should be considered valuable citizens—"our own"—or members (and reproducers) of a class of poor whites not worthy of citizenship. An editorial in the *Raleigh Times* asserted that the question of "what causes a woman to elect promiscuity in youth . . . has to do distinctly with the abnormal . . . In the great majority of cases a woman or a girl given over to this worst of follies is, and always has been, a mental defective."[41] This author implicitly excluded Samarcand inmates from citizenship on the long-accepted grounds of mental deficiency. By contrast, a letter to the *Fayetteville Observer* made explicit a view that included delinquent girls as valued community members and potential citizens. Claiming that "we love our wayward unfortunate girls," the author contended that "as citizens and taxpayers" the public must assert its constitutional rights to intervene in mismanaged institutions like Samarcand because "our girls though unfortunate are too precious, too dear to our hearts to go to ruin."[42] Another sympathizer went even further, depicting the Samarcand defendants not only as the unfortunate daughters of citizen-taxpayers but also as spirited modern-day patriots. The author, "Citizen," asserted that the girls' repeated appeals for liberty demonstrated that they shared "the blood of our patriots."[43]

Other, less-sanguine observers confessed to being baffled by the rebellious defendants. A journalist reporting on the second jailhouse riot noted with puzzlement that the "five imprisoned little souls" who had moments ago engaged in riotous revolt now "seemed as gentle and demure as if they had never once dreamed of a mutiny."[44] Confusion could easily turn to suspicion, as it did when a more critical editorialist warned readers, "A chit may look as mild and sweet as you please—and yet be thinking in terms of the torch!"[45] Disturbingly, girls could at one moment seem normal and the next moment fiendish, one moment disarmingly childish and the next alarmingly adult.

The fear that one did not quite know whom one was dealing with in the case of delinquent females also carried over into the thinking of experts. In a rhetoric of "the masquerading mental defective," child experts became alarmed at the possibility of being tricked by mentally deficient teens who cleverly assumed the guise of intellectual normalcy. Probation officer Margaret Brietz, for example, made numerous references to Samarcand inmates, whose history of sexual immorality and low IQ scores classified them as "high moron types" but whose charm, verbal agility, and cleverness created a deceptive facade of intelligence. Describing one such "subnormal" girl as a "defective delinquent with special abilities," Brietz warned that her attractive personality and skills as a "verbalist" were deceptive. She concluded, however, that despite her unusual language and musical abilities, verbal fluency and cleverness—typical markers of intelligence—this girl's IQ score of sixty-seven made her "definitely feeble-minded" and therefore a good candidate for sterilization.[46]

Brietz was not alone in her fear that the difference between a sexually dangerous and apparently normal woman might be undetectable. In a feature essay on the North Carolina training school for feebleminded youth, the *Greensboro Daily News* cautioned readers against the girl who gave no outer sign of "inner lack" yet suffered from an "almost irresistible tendency to crime and immorality." The author described a female inmate who "of all the morons there, has an expression most benign" yet had a "record of immorality that is nothing less than appalling." As proof the reporter noted that the inmate had been discovered living with a "Negro man" and feeling "apparently entirely satisfied with herself and her estate." The article concluded that girls like this "who do not exhibit to the untrained eye the signs of their condition honey-comb the foundations of a state . . . [and] represent a menace which, if allowed to continue unchecked, cannot be overestimated."[47] Young sexually active women, whose premarital and interracial sexual relations served ipso facto as proof of "mental defect," threatened the foundations of a white supremacist state maintained, in part, through proscriptive controls on the sexuality of young white females.

The missing voice in the public discourse about female adolescence is that of the Samarcand inmates themselves. Although they were rarely given the opportunity to articulate publicly their own points of view, in their many actions and few words we can speculate about the experiences and self-understandings of white working-class southern girls caught in the institutional matrix of the state. Reporters were not far off in noting the "inner lack" of teenage inmates, but it seems they lacked not intelligence or moral scruples; rather, the girls missed a sense of security and ability to control their own lives.

Women of the early twentieth century used commercial entertainment, contemporary fashions, and popular narratives from film and dime novels to forge a modern sense of self, one marked by an expressive, affirmative female sexuality. This "new morality" was initially pioneered by urban working-class youth, especially girls who boldly insisted on the legitimacy of their sexual desires. These claims were not only condemned by parents and reformers but also pathologized by professional psychiatrists, who for a period in the 1910s and 1920s identified the assertive and charming allure of sexually active, white, working-class teenagers as symptoms of female "hypersexuality" in need of treatment.[48] Even as this diagnosis dropped from the charts, modern sexology continued to deny sexual self-determination to women by locating female passion in the mind's subconscious. Scientists believed that whereas men were rational, self-possessed sexual actors, women were driven by irrational passions unknowable at the conscious level—particularly during adolescence, a period noted for its stormy irrationality.[49]

Eventually the notion of female adolescent desire assimilated into modern sexual norms through "true love," a belief in a love so strong it could not be repressed. When true love was expressed through the conventions of romance, experts believed that love-struck teenage girls could be safely channeled along a path from dating to betrothal and marriage. Working-class adolescent sexuality, however, fell outside of this nexus; it was perceived as vulgar, unconscious, and often alienated by economic considerations, such as sexual favors exchanged for cash or the lure of gifts and free nights out on the town. As such, the working-class adolescent girl—portrayed in various guises as the hypersexual, the juvenile delinquent, the problem girl, or the mentally deficient girl—remained "a law unto herself" and subject to strict, often punitive regulation.[50]

Like their more urban, industrialized counterparts in the North, southern adolescent girls facing difficult economic and family conditions often saw in cars, cafes, dancing, and fashionable clothes the promise of self-expression and a better life. Yet it was the pursuit of such pleasures that typically led to incarceration. Most Samarcand inmates were arrested as they sought out the very realms of popular amusement that others found so useful in the making of the modern sexual self. Significantly, they did not enter this world from a position of economic or emotional strength.

Institutional records show that the typical inmate came from an impoverished family broken apart by death, violence, or illness.[51] Among the Samarcand defendants, for example, ten of the sixteen girls came from families separated by death, desertion, or divorce. In two of the remaining families, the mother was severely ill, and in a third the daughter lived away from her parents due to intolerable conditions at home. In only four cases were the girls' families described as having adequate economic resources.[52] Without emotional or financial support from relatives, these young women often entered the world of popular thrills illicitly, becoming involved in petty crime or simply in sexual relationships that others deemed immoral and blameworthy. While consensual sex in most cases made up one aspect of their experience, case records show the defendants also suffered from severe venereal infections, abusive and decidedly unromantic relations with men, constant mobility, and persistent poverty.

Under these circumstances it may have been particularly difficult for working-class inmates of Samarcand to develop or maintain a sense of self that combined sexuality and social respectability.[53] Cora Corman, for instance, served time at Samarcand in the 1920s. Cora was the youngest of seven children. Her three eldest siblings had died at young ages and her father died four years before her first arrest, forcing her mother to move into town and rent a small house in a neighborhood with many "jail-birds." Cora left school at thirteen to work in a cigarette factory, going out with "bad companions" after work to carnivals and movies, which she was reportedly "crazy about." After an initial arrest resulting in probation, she worked sporadically in different mills, counting the hours until her shift ended and she could go to cheap theaters. There she developed relationships with at least two steady boyfriends but also had sexual relations with other men until finally being picked up as a public nuisance and sent to Samarcand.[54] Several of the inmates on trial had similar interests in movies, carnivals, and cafes. Their lives took a turn for the worse when they ran away from unbearable home situations, often with a friend, to bigger cities. There they established casual sexual relationships with men who could offer money and protection from police as well as access to liquor, cars, and commercial entertainment.[55]

Incarcerated teenagers mirrored other adolescents in utilizing modern pleasures like travel, cars, clothing, and tales of romance to create themselves as "modern," fashioning hopeful narratives of love and adventure to counter the demoralizing drudgery of home and work life. Yet they lacked resources that might have enabled them to turn creative fantasy into a secure reality. Notably absent in their lives are education, intact and economically viable families, birth control, good jobs, and stable peer or residential communities. Troubled teenagers encountered instead a set of prejudices about poor, sexually active young women that denied their viability as knowing sexual subjects. Their tentative efforts to combine modernity, sexuality, and notions of "goodness" were met with charges of sexual deviance and mental defect. They then confronted a set of laws, public institutions, and state officials empowered to use this far more damning assessment to incarcerate them on the basis of their "delinquency."

The few adolescent voices that emerge from the records of Samarcand demonstrate that young inmates resisted such interpretations, attempting instead to piece together a positive if inchoate assertion of self that fused modern sensibilities with values absorbed from religion, family, reformatory staff, and peer culture. Self-assertion might simply consist of reckless acts of defiance that in their bravado demonstrate a crude, if self-defeating, expression of will. Other inmates articulated a concept of self based on compliance, a respect for God, and an end to transgressive behavior. An inmate at a similar institution, for example, wrote to her family about finally accepting Jesus. She initially resisted attending the prayer service and then made fun of girls testifying about Jesus, but soon "a feeling would run through me of unspeakable happiness and . . . the next thing I knew I was up confessing my sins and accepting Jesus."[56] Most often, though, we see a mixture of obedience and defiance through which inmates struggled to integrate an ignominious past with a bleak present and a hopefully more auspicious future.

Relying on a concept of self that was based on becoming a "good girl" or "lady," many delinquent girls apparently embraced the tale of sin and repentance laid out by reformatory supervisors.[57] In one awkward but seemingly heartfelt pledge to reform, an inmate wrote to her family: "I have done dirty but that is no reason I can not make a lady out off myself every lady hase had failures and [I] have had mine but it will come out all right some sweet day."[58] This teenager believed that neither her past nor her lack of education and means would prevent her from claiming status as a lady at some point if her behavior met the standards set forth by Samarcand Manor. Other girls, however, revealed more conflicted emotions through wildly inconsistent behavior. For example, one former Samarcand inmate who later found herself in the North Carolina Farm Colony (a reformatory for women sixteen and older) was described by staff as a "strange combination of apparent submission and great defiance." One month before parole she informed her parents that she had turned her life "to good from Bad." Explaining that she prayed nightly to the Lord for mercy, she wrote proudly that "I am being a good girl now." Yet within weeks of her parole this adolescent, who claimed "I am getting so I really love to be good," was convicted of larceny and sent to state prison. Her frustrated and perplexed caseworker wrote her off as an apparent "dual personality."[59]

Some heartfelt pledges of reform were most likely ruses designed to earn staff approval, privileges, or early release from Samarcand. But others demonstrate genuinely mixed emotions, that is, tension between a desire to embrace a "higher worthwhile life" and a fierce anger at those adults who seemed all too eager to judge and punish them. One paroled inmate had been baptized twice while in Samarcand, but upon her release and rearrest angrily informed officials that "she did not give a doggone what we did with her."[60] Like another inmate who simply "could not seem to feel that she had 'done much wrong,'" many Samarcand girls stubbornly clung to a sense of their past behavior as legitimate, if not commendable.[61] Although standard reformatory rules required that inmates bury their pasts, forbidding them even to mention their preinstitutional life, this did not prevent staff members from reminding them of their "immoral" history. Alabama inmates complained bitterly about the staff throwing "up to us what we are, why we are here, what our folks are," saying "we can never be anything" because "our people are nothing before us."[62] Some delinquent girls defended their past and demonstrated a remarkable determination to create a sense of self that did not sever past hardships from hopes for a better future. "Why should I be afraid of anything I've ever done?" asked one unrepentant inmate. "Although my background for the past three years hasn't been so very desirable, what does that count. It's very different now."[63]

Heartened by staff assurances that repentance and reform would produce an end to hardship and incarceration, most inmates looked forward to a more socially accepted life yet refused to view their past as reprehensible or their lives as divided into a dissolute "before" and a resolute and godly "after." For example, a woman who had spent much of her adolescence in Samarcand, given up a child for adoption, undergone forced sterilization, and been repeatedly arrested for drunken and disorderly conduct until placed in the adult women's reformatory acknowledged that at age twenty-one her life had "been spent in drunkness and immorality." With apparent sincerity, she wrote her superintendent that "I have fully made up my mind to do the right thing," resolving to live a life that would please God, her reformatory keepers, her mother, and, in doing so, herself as well. Yet she was unable to disregard an ever-present "blueness," writing in anguish that "I haven't been happy since I've been here or either before I came." She seemed fully aware that while her future happiness might depend on harmonious family and community relations, her past difficulties were rooted in those same relationships; at one point she complains bitterly that family members "haven't as much as took time to write hello's since I been here." The rhetoric of reform, however, left no room for informed skepticism or the recognition of contradictions, and she embraced the narrative of repentance offered by female reformatory staff as the only one that promised immediate release and a respectable future. Claiming that "I've never done a wrong but what I wasn't sorry afterward," she admitted her mistakes and sought redemption. Read another way, however, this inmate's simple declaration also acknowledges her lingering sorrow and steadfast wish to bridge past with present, suggesting a complex understanding of herself as a person capable of wrong and right, sorrow and hope, commitment to self and others.[64]

At their most powerful, these determined insights found expression as an aggrieved demand for justice and liberty. Samarcand defendant Pearl Stiles composed a letter to the governor of North Carolina that appears to have been intercepted and never delivered. In an appeal for her life, Stiles pleaded for herself and eight others being held in the county jail. To Governor Gardner she proclaimed: "The way we were treated was terrible. We were locked, beat, and fed on bread and water most of the time. Please give me liberty or death . . . We girls in Roberson County jail is just as innocent of this crime they hold against us as a little child . . . Please give me liberty or death . . . Mr. Gardner, this is Pearl Stiles writing and I am always trying to be good." Stiles closed her letter with another declaration of innocence followed by a wish from all the girls to send their love and then this ending: "Will close with good heart. From Miss Pearl Stiles to Mr. Gardner. Lumberton, North Carolina. Answer at once."[65] Employing a rhetoric of revolutionary patriotism, Pearl Stiles not only professed her own innocence and that of her cellmates, but also laid claim to a loving and "good" heart and to a set of rights to bodily integrity and justice under the law.

In the words of Pearl Stiles, along with those of other inmates claiming either to be wrongly condemned or righteously reformed, we can detect efforts to combine a traditional religious discourse with a language of human rights, the self-possessed body, and a romantic, loving heart—precisely the elements that formed the bedrock of modern political and sexual subjectivity. Twentieth-century political norms included shared notions of human rights, individual self-expression, and ownership over one's own body. Sexual norms assumed an ability to enter loving romantic relationships that acknowledged individual desire and personal satisfaction as basic to lasting relationships between distinct individuals. But Stiles and others in her situation sensed that such claims, coming from incarcerated sex delinquents, were precarious. She couched her innocence as that of "a little child," since innocence for a sexually delinquent teenager was presumably much harder to come by. Her sense of rights too is as tentative as it is bold, mixed with a claim to victim status and more supplicating declarations of love.

In the end, it was not through language that Samarcand inmates launched their most effective appeals. Rhetorical claims to rights or sexual self-determination succeeded far less often than protests enacted through rebellious behavior that stopped short of arson and the destruction of state property. From institutional records, it is clear that the quickest route out of Samarcand was not reform but defiance. Staff frequently judged the most difficult inmates as beyond rehabilitation and promptly returned them to their home communities.[66] Yet this form of protest, not supported by acknowledged rights or approved social identities, remained a dangerous one. The many expressions of public kindness and concern for Samarcand inmates did not prevent punitive incarceration, violent correction, and routine mistreatment at the hands of state officials. Underneath a rhetoric of sympathy and redemption, the state's actions spoke to an abiding distrust of and even revulsion for the adolescent minds and bodies over which it had assumed responsibility.

The Samarcand defendants found themselves prisoners in a legal system that mirrored the broader society's uncertainty over whether to classify female delinquents as children or adults. In the end the convicted arsonists experienced the harshest side of both the juvenile and adult justice systems. They were initially incarcerated for noncriminal status offenses like "running around," "incorrigibility," or being "in danger of prostitution" or "beyond parental control," and in one case as an incest victim whose father's conviction as the perpetrator left her without a legal guardian.[67] They were held under indeterminate sentences unique to juveniles and while incarcerated were subject to severe corporal punishment that had been outlawed for adult prisoners. Yet rebelling against the vagaries of the juvenile justice system landed them in court on adult arson charges that carried the possibility of execution.

With her clients' lives on the line, defense attorney Nell Battle Lewis devised a strategy that she hoped would avoid the penalties of adult criminality and steer clear of the culture's uneasiness about adolescence. She argued in court that the defendants must be understood as children on the basis of their low IQs. Through the claim of "feeblemindedness" she painted a picture of environmental deprivation that had left these girls in a state of mental, and thus moral, underdevelopment for which they could not be held responsible. To Lewis, feeblemindedness—in which immorality was seen as both symptom and proof of mental defect—offered the only potentially convincing defense. But too much about the defendants' behavior indicated either adult passions or adolescent compulsions, not childlike incapacity. The defense strategy failed and the teenagers received adult sentences. Authorities immediately transferred them to the predominately male state prison, where they occupied cells directly above death row, in the only fireproof wing of the prison.[68]

The judicial process, like the popular debate over the case, reveals a constant tug between sympathetic inclusion and punitive correction. The ambivalent response to female adolescent sexuality, especially that of white working-class girls, is not specific to the South of the 1930s. Rather, we can read the case as an unusually sharp articulation of persistent tensions that have surrounded adolescent girls, whose confident embrace of sexuality is as appealing as it is disturbing to adult society.

Yet we can also examine the Samarcand incident for the way in which experiences of female adolescent sexuality were demarcated by the class and racial fault lines of modern southern society. In this sense, sociologist and probation officer Margaret Brietz's claim that Samarcand inmates were "sisters under the skin" is revealing. It simultaneously portrays poor white girls as of another race—presumed to have a different skin—and as members of a white sisterhood whose physical and moral health held the key to the future of the state. How could white citizens of the New South maintain solidarity and social cohesion when confronted by working-class urban problems and sexual behaviors that so reviled middle-class modernists? And how would southerners deal with sexual modernity in girls who violated every tenet of both bourgeois respectability and a still powerful racial code of white female purity? Were these girls to be embraced as southern daughters or rejected as racial degenerates?

State authorities and reformers advanced a view that only through a maternal state institution, a reformatory staffed and headed by women but kept on course by paternal oversight and funds, could North Carolina hope to prevent its wayward girls—the future mothers of the state—from corrupting the moral or "racial" stock of current and future populations. The rhetoric of enlightened guidance and reclamation provided a veneer for much harsher policies that could, literally, cut like a knife. During the same years that they publicly debated the fate of rebellious daughters at Samarcand, state legislators quietly put in place sterilization laws and procedures used to control the fertility of poor women. Between 1929 and 1947, 79 percent of North

Carolina's 1,901 "eugenic sterilizations" were performed on females, half of whom were between the ages of ten and nineteen. Samarcand was one of the main cooperating institutions among various state schools, submitting at least three hundred inmates for sterilization.[69]

Meanwhile, white citizens of North Carolina remained torn. Some viewed Samarcand positively as a "training school" that could produce charm and refinement among rehabilitated poor and uneducated females. Skeptics, however, refused the suggestion that Samarcand was a working-class "boarding school," nor did they accept the incendiary acts of inmates as merely misguided demonstrations of "school spirit." They persisted in seeing the institution as a breeding ground for revolt and disease among the dangerous classes, a view that in turn sanctioned physical abuse and sterilization as state policies appropriate to the larger goal of shoring up a dependable white citizenry. Caught in the middle of contradictory public sentiments and state policies, troubled working-class white girls articulated tentative claims to social citizenship, moral worth, and personal dignity.

chapter three

"*Just as Much a Menace*"

Race and Sex Delinquency

$\mathcal{S}$amarcand Manor was not the only reformatory for delinquent girls in the state of North Carolina. As early as 1911, African American women activists in the state had begun work toward raising money and acquiring land for an "industrial school" for delinquent Negro girls. Years of fundraising allowed them to purchase land in 1921 and four years later open the doors to the North Carolina Industrial Home for Colored Girls in the Piedmont town of Efland. The reformers' efforts did not end there, however. For the next two decades they did battle with the government of North Carolina to obtain state funding for the institution so that it would become the African American equivalent to Samarcand Manor in the Jim Crow juvenile justice system.

Desperately in need of funds soon after opening the "school," in 1925 the North Carolina Federation of Colored Women's Clubs posted a plea for financial support. On the front, a bucolic image of Efland's grounds rests underneath an alarmed call to "SAVE OUR GIRLS." On the back the group directly addresses its audience: "How will you answer this great need? Suppose it was your girl who had gone astray? Would you want to give her a second chance?" The request closed with a statement of religious and racial mission, explaining that "in His name we are launching this effort to save Negro womanhood."[1] In the late 1930s, with the school on the verge of closing for lack of funds, the state federation issued another appeal, but with a dramatically different tone. Abandoning lofty references to a sympathetic God and good girls led astray, the clubwomen's "Open Letter to the People of North Carolina" contained a direct threat to white citizens of the state. "Members of no race can be hopelessly doomed to delinquency without eventually bringing a large part of the other race down to its level," warned the letter. "Records of the present inmates in our Home show promiscuity without regard to race."[2]

These two documents capture in a nutshell the complicated sexual politics of African American efforts to confront female juvenile delinquency, an issue that reformers of every race and region addressed in the first half of this century, but which had specially charged political meanings for black women and girls in the South. The first appeal bears the characteristic earmarks of middle-class black women's reform from Reconstruction through World War II.[3] Themes of "rescue" and "uplift" dominate, along with a shared sense of community among middle-class and poorer African Americans voiced in the expression "our girls." The reference to "His" name asserts a claim to virtue, godliness, and endorsement from a higher authority. More importantly, by presenting the effort as an action to "save Negro womanhood," the solicitation speaks to the centrality of sexual reputation to the collective plight and progress of black women.

The second letter introduces unexpected elements to the mix. Revealing black women's dependence on and involvement with white political constituencies, the letter expresses open frustration and dares to confront white North Carolinians with the consequences of their continued neglect of "hopelessly doomed" delinquent black girls. Despite the change in tone and tactics, these appeals have two claims in common: that adolescent girls would play a critical role in determining the future of black womanhood, and that at the heart of adolescent girlhood lay issues of sexuality.

In a struggle that lasted four decades—from the initial opening of Efland to the establishment of a state-funded Training School for Negro Girls in the immediate post–World War II years—African American activists confronted the issue of juvenile delinquency in their own communities. Similar efforts were under way in other southern states. Between 1910 and 1950, clubwomen in North Carolina, South Carolina, Florida, Alabama, Georgia, Tennessee, and Virginia made establishing reformatories for black girls a top priority.[4] As of 1930, only the northernmost states of Tennessee and Virginia had met this goal; other southern states had conspicuously overlooked black girls in their efforts to develop and maintain segregated "training schools" for white boys, black boys, and white girls. Implied in this neglect is the assumption that black girls were by nature sexually promiscuous, making any efforts at rehabilitation futile. As one North Carolina legislator surmised: "In my opinion it would take the United States army to correct the morals of all the negro girls in the state."[5] The demand for female reform schools was at once a claim on white supremacist governments to live up to "separate but equal" state laws and an act of self-defense against stigmatizing views of black female immorality.

Black clubwomen's efforts to police young women's sexuality originated in class and generational tensions within black communities that were intertwined with African American agendas for racial change and female sexual empowerment. In trying to secure their own class authority, disprove white supremacist beliefs, and develop protective strategies against sexual abuse and disrepute, clubwomen challenged notions of sexual difference rooted in scientific racism. Their reform efforts argued implicitly against claims of innate depravity by claiming that if some unfortunate black girls fell into sex delinquency, the majority did not. Similarly, if sex delinquents could be morally reformed, their condition was neither natural nor permanent. This logic shifted the terms of debate from sexual differences ascribed to "natural" racial instincts to social differences based on class and age. Attempting both to humanize the sexual delinquency of African American girls and underscore the dangers of ignoring it, activists made innovative arguments about the different and problematic sexuality of the poor, the young, and a certain sector of the southern black population. These claims had political implications beyond the subject of teenage sexuality. Through the issue of female reformatories, clubwomen challenged white supremacist ideologies, enlarged the political arena for black southerners, and shored up a middle-class politics of respectability threatened by the very girls they hoped to "save."

The movement to establish girls' reformatories was but one action in a far longer history of black women's efforts to defend against sexual exploitation and derogatory perceptions of black female "immorality." The history of African American enslavement is, among other things, a history of female sexual oppression. Slaveholders violated women's bodies in both sexual and nonsexual ways, subjecting them to rape, torture, and humiliation. As slaves, women had little control over when and with whom to have sexual relations, to form loving partnerships, or to bear children. Viewed and valued as "breeders" of additional slave labor, they faced not only the degradation of their commodified condition, but also the loss of their children, who at any time could be sold to a faraway owner.

Black women's opposition to sexual exploitation began during slavery, when mothers and female kin networks made concerted attempts to protect adolescent girls who, upon reaching puberty, became vulnerable to predatory acts of male slaveowners.[6] During Reconstruction, female sexuality remained central to African American resistance. Many black families tried to limit female field labor in order to allow women time for household labor and to remove women from public work sites where they remained vulnerable to male assault. Among those who could afford train travel, activists like Ida B. Wells fought for first-class seating in the "ladies car." This was both a symbolic claim to "ladyhood"—with its attendant sexual protection and implied sexual virtue—and a practical attempt to avoid mixed cars in which women had to endure unwanted verbal and physical advances from men.[7] In a similar vein, northern female educators offered their southern students lessons on deportment and morality so that, as "proper" ladies, they might receive better treatment from white southerners. These diverse efforts forged a "politics of respectability" that sought to bring African American sexual mores into line with dominant middle-class moral standards.[8] Respectability could discredit longstanding stereotypes of black promiscuity while strengthening claims to sexual virtue and, thus, status as fully and equally "civilized" beings.

This strategy, however, unfolded against a backdrop in which white southerners began to associate black men's threatening political and economic advances with pronounced sexual virility. They promoted a view of African American men as vicious sexual predators, which in turn fueled the rise of lynching and other acts of racial terrorism. The myth of the black male rapist hinged on an equally simplistic commitment to the idea of white female virtue and vulnerability.[9] Notions of white female purity had flourished in the antebellum period as well, but in its revised form the "purity" of white women now extended—at least in theory—to poor white women brought into the fold of a shared white virtue thought to be under siege by politically, economically, and sexually aggressive African Americans.

Black women were strangely absent from the triangular politics of black male assailants, white female victims, and white male avengers. Yet views about African American female sexuality underwrote each aspect of the discourse. Implicit in the notion of uncivilized or bestial black male sexuality was the absence of a civilized black female who could "tame" or contain male sexuality. Longstanding Euro-American views of women of color as lacking in domestic virtue and sexual restraint persisted into the twentieth century as a mirror to reflect the counterimage of endangered white purity in need of white male vengeance. The image of white men as aggressive and bestial in their defensive attacks on black men also implied the continued vulnerability of black women to assault. For if the vengeance of white men unleashed their deeper primitive instincts, unrestrained sexual aggression could be safely channeled into relations with reputedly promiscuous black women.

The paradoxical invisibility yet omnipresence of black women's sexuality in white racial discourse generated conflicting images of hypersexuality and, in a complete reversal, unattractive, unfeminine women unworthy of love, romance, and sexual intimacy. In response to this untenable position, African American women leaders adopted a stance of sexual dissemblance—a denial and avoidance of the sexual or erotic life—in favor of an image of female propriety. The first national black political organization, the National Association of Colored Women (NACW), organized in the 1890s around the issue of lynching. Launched to protect black males from fraudulent claims of sexual assault on white women, the antilynching movement was equally an indirect attack on black women's own sexual degradation. The NACW presented a desexualized image of absolute propriety to shield against further sexual scrutiny and to create a higher moral ground from which to speak.[10]

The politics of respectability cultivated by southern clubwomen took hold equally in women's church organizations, which comprised both elites and women of ordinary means. The national convention of black Baptist women tackled issues of temperance, education, fund-raising, social service, child welfare, and mother's training schools, occasionally in collaboration with white church women. In their constant emphasis on cleanliness, self-improvement, domestic skills, and sexual restraint, they used a rubric of religiosity to oppose common associations between black women and dirt, contamination, and promiscuity.[11] Baptist and Methodist women's organizations attempted simultaneously to shield themselves from a white American gaze and challenge that gaze's view.

From their earliest public efforts, black community leaders in church and secular organizations concerned themselves with the fate of adolescent girls. The establishment of the National Training School for Women and Girls in Washington, D.C., advocated vocational training as a way to professionalize black women's domestic employment while enhancing self-respect through work skills and a righteous morality. This pattern was repeated in many other settings. Because of the minuscule number of public black high schools in the South, educators and parents found common interest in creating residential seminaries and high school adjuncts to the many black colleges founded in the late nineteenth century. Girls far outnumbered boys at these schools. Parents could probably more easily sacrifice female farm labor than male and, since teaching was an overwhelmingly female profession and required a relatively short training period in this era, the financial benefits of girls' education were more assured and immediately remunerative. But parents also turned to residential schools, known for strict student supervision, to obtain for their daughters a level of sexual protection not available in their own communities, especially when parents and older children all worked long hours.

By the 1910s, women leaders began to speak not only of protection but also of corrective training for girls who violated community sexual norms. The beginning of the Great Northern Migration prompted the change in focus. The migration began as an internal one, with the proportion of urban blacks more than doubling in the South between 1870 and 1910. Over the next twenty years, the percentage of southern blacks residing in cities increased from approximately one-fifth to just under one-third.[12] Middle-class African Americans looked askance at the development of an urban culture that featured such modern pleasures as blues and jazz music, dancing, drinking, and socializing in "juke joints." Elite blacks, "pained by the Negro's reputation for wearing gaudy clothes" that they labeled "loud" or "flashy," spurned flamboyance for "quiet good taste."[13] Yet many young people—of all classes—preferred the more lively street and dance culture. In this setting, permissive rural sexual mores blended with the sexual possibilities of the modern city to create a sexual morality at odds with middle-class propriety and the religious beliefs of many working-class parents.[14]

The National Urban League, founded in 1911, addressed the manners and morals of young migrant women in cities throughout the country. Similarly, the newly formed National Association for the Advancement of Colored People used its national magazine, the *Crisis,* to support reformatories for black female delinquents.[15] In southern cities, activists like Norfolk's Janie Porter Barrett and Atlanta's Lugenia Burns Hope founded settlement houses that defined outreach to teenage girls as a primary objective.[16] After its 1908 founding meeting, Atlanta Neighborhood Union members surveyed the neighborhood for girls between ages eight and twenty-two who would benefit from activities offered through the settlement's "Moral and Education" department. In 1925 the Neighborhood Union still advertised its intention to save young girls "from evil courses by the touch of sympathetic neighborly hands."[17]

Janie Porter Barrett quickly shifted interest from her Locust Street Settlement to the founding and direction of the Virginia Industrial School for Colored Girls, a state-funded reformatory for African American delinquents. Barrett's efforts proved to be one of the earliest and most successful examples of a much broader trend among reformers who, during the 1910s and 1920s, mobilized black women's clubs throughout the South in campaigns to build "industrial schools" for "wayward" African American girls. In Virginia, the drive began in 1908 when Barrett, a member of the Hampton Institute faculty and married to a Hampton administrator, was elected president of the state's Federation of Colored Women's Clubs. After a successful fundraising drive, the first board meeting of the Virginia Industrial School for Colored Girls took place in 1913. In 1914 the state legislature appropriated money toward running the school, which opened its doors on January 1, 1915, in the town of Peaks Turnout, eighteen miles north of Richmond. Upon finding herself suddenly widowed in 1915 and facing strong opposition from white residents in the vicinity of the school, Barrett decided to leave her comfortable Norfolk home to assume the job of full-time residential superintendent of "Peaks," as it was called, a job she held for the next twenty-five years. Although the state Federation of Women's Clubs had purchased the land privately, under a threat of closure by the legislature the group turned over the deed to the State of Virginia in 1920. As a fully state-controlled institution, the school became the official parallel institution to the whites-only Virginia Home and Industrial School for Girls in Bon Air, which had opened just five years before the "school" at Peaks Turnout.[18]

In Tennessee, the legislature provided for the state-funded Vocational School for Colored Girls in 1921, six years after intensive lobbying by white women's clubs had led to the creation of a white reformatory, the Vocational School for Girls.[19] The parallel reformatory for African American delinquents first opened its doors in 1923. Inmates ranged in age from eleven to sixteen at the time of incarceration, with legal control extending to the age of twenty-one. The population averaged between seventy-five and one hundred persons, with an average annual total of 150 girls serving time in the Vocational School. State legislation that mandated the institution be under "the direct supervision and immediate control of a colored woman," who would in turn appoint a staff of "colored women teachers and assistants" for the purpose of giving the offender "a chance to make good in life," indicates the strong hand of black activists in establishing the reformatory.[20]

Clubwomen in Georgia and North Carolina met with less success. The Georgia State Federation of Black Women's Clubs began lobbying in 1913 for a training school for Negro girls but failed to raise adequate funds or win legislative interest for nearly three decades.[21] The effort in North Carolina initially seemed more hopeful. Educator and activist Charlotte Hawkins Brown commenced the campaign in 1908, several years after founding Palmer Memorial Institute, a private black school near Greensboro. The school initially provided basic education to poor rural blacks but later became one of the region's best private schools, renowned for the fine academic and cultural instruction it provided wealthier black children of the South.[22] Although still fully involved in the survival struggle of the Palmer Institute, Brown assumed the presidency of the North Carolina Federation of Colored

Women's Clubs and later presided over the Southeastern Federation of Colored Women's Clubs, an umbrella organization of southern black clubwomen. After a brief and successful campaign to found a state reform school for black delinquent boys, the federation turned to a similar plan for girls, drawing interest from white women's clubs, the state welfare commissioner Kate Burr Johnson, and the wife of the North Carolina governor. Brown and other activists began the drive as a private effort but fully intended to pressure the state government into taking over the reformatory, making it the African American equivalent to Samarcand Manor. In 1927 the North Carolina legislature agreed to contribute a token sum of two thousand dollars per biennium, a miserly amount compared to its allotment of $72,000 to Samarcand Manor for the 1927–1929 biennium.[23] For the next decade, black clubwomen appealed to the state for full institutional support, both to improve the reformatory's meager resources and to acknowledge an equal (if separate) concern for troubled black girls. Despite persistent efforts and a single dramatic meeting with the governor in which the federation's leaders presented him with the land deed to Efland as a gift to the state, North Carolina officials refused to recognize any responsibility for rehabilitating youthful female offenders unless they were white.

This mixed record of success and failure should not obscure the fact that in almost every southern state, organized black women focused on the same objective—creating state-run reformatories for neglected and delinquent girls of their communities. Like other Progressive-era reformers, clubwomen saw the high crime, death, and unemployment rates of poor black residents in rapidly expanding cities like Atlanta, Richmond, Chicago, or New York as undermining the stability and health of their urban community. They also viewed the sexual mores and leisure habits of the black working class as a threat to their own leadership. As good "race women," or activists for their race, they desired to set a standard for those less fortunate than themselves, at the same time linking their own well-being to the overall status of the wider black community, especially the poor in their midst.[24]

From another vantage point the creation of black female reformatories signals a clear departure from general trends in Progressive-era reform. The issue was one of the first around which African American and white women of the South coalesced in the budding interracial

Charlotte Hawkins Brown, circa 1930, dynamic educator and organizer, led black clubwomen in North Carolina and throughout the South in their efforts to win state-supported moral reformatories for delinquent African American adolescent girls. Courtesy of the North Carolina Office of Archives and History, Raleigh, North Carolina.

cooperation movement of the 1920s and 1930s. In Georgia, the reformatory movement stalled out until black leaders joined forces with white interracialist leader Jessie Daniel Ames in the 1930s. Working under the aegis of the Commission on Interracial Cooperation (CIC), black and white clubwomen organized a petition drive and lobbying campaign that by the late 1930s had succeeded in passing legislation for the creation of a state reform school for black girls.[25] Charlotte Hawkins Brown also engaged in interracial work, joining forces with

white clubwomen and political officials of North Carolina and participating in the CIC and the Interracial Committee of the Federal Council of Churches.[26] In Virginia, too, the state Industrial School for
Colored Girls had a board of directors "composed of white and Race
members" who worked in "harmonious cooperation."[27]

White clubwomen who had succeeded in establishing white female
reformatories were in sympathy with black reformers' wish to create
similar institutions for black delinquent girls. Moreover, as white
women worked their way into positions of responsibility through social welfare projects and growing state departments of public welfare,
they saw a chance to expand their realm of authority by extending
their rehabilitative programs to young black women. One welfare
publication warned that, if ignored, "the social problems among Negroes . . . will become a slow cankerous growth" resulting in "serious
maladjustments" affecting everyone.[28] Clubwomen and welfare workers of both races found common interest in keeping their cities free of
the crime and social disorder they associated with modern commercial culture, youthful leisure pursuits, and rampant sexual immorality.

The founding of the first black juvenile reformatories in the late
1910s and early 1920s had as much to do with labor as leisure, coinciding with the beginning of the massive exodus of southern black laborers to the North. Fears surrounding the availability of black male
labor and the protection of white property explain the willingness of
southern states to fund reformatories for black boys much earlier
than the equivalent for girls. Since male juveniles were almost always
arrested for crimes of property, vagrancy, or violence, the state had
an interest in policing black male crime and a further interest in making sure black youth did not become an undisciplined, unwilling, or
unruly adult labor force. The crisis and subsequent mechanization of
southern agriculture in the 1930s lessened white concern about the
out-migration of black farm labor. But by World War II, white leaders
again evinced concern about the availability of inexpensive black
domestic workers for white households enjoying a rising standard of
living.[29] It was at this time that longstanding efforts to establish state-
funded juvenile institutions for black girls in Georgia and North
Carolina finally succeeded—state finances had improved, federal
monies had become available, and out-migration had reduced the supply of black female domestic labor.

Black reformers warned that teenage girls could not resist the temptations of juke joints like this one in Clarksdale, Mississippi. As teenagers admire a couple's dance skills, the policeman in the doorway represents the danger of arrest and incarceration on charges of "delinquent behavior." Marion Post Wolcott, Library of Congress, LC-USF34–052479-D.

By designating black and white reformatories as "vocational," "industrial," and later, "training" schools, reformers' rhetoric seemed to offer promises of morally rehabilitated, productive, trained laborers. The reformatory discourse echoed that of a more generalized one among black educators who championed "industrial education" as a means to produce skilled, efficient, and responsible workers. Fitting well with the broader focus of black education in the South, the concept of industrial, training, or vocational schools served two additional purposes. It masked the correctional nature—and consequent stigmatizing effect on inmate-students—of the institution while hinting at the underlying function of the reformatory, turning unruly adolescents into a compliant, readily available labor force.

Some whites spoke openly of this function. Linking labor concerns with fears about the health and hygiene of black workers, a North

Carolina county official wrote in 1941, "Hardly a week passes that we are not forced to turn loose on the community one or more negro girls, who should be confined for a period of time in a correctional institution." Noting their high rates of venereal disease and sexual promiscuity, he concluded, "These girls might go into an institution and be trained principally along the lines of domestic work, which would fit them for better servants in our home."[30] A North Carolina lobbyist reminded state senators that the current situation allowed black female offenders to break the law with impunity since they knew there was no chance of long-term incarceration. A vocational training school, by contrast, "would train delinquent Negro girls for domestic work . . . In this way, they would become expert servants."[31]

It is doubtful that black clubwomen shared this objective, but they were not above catering to the white concern for labor in order to win needed support. When faced with strong opposition from whites residing near the new Industrial School for Colored Girls, Janie Porter Barrett won their cooperation by "permitting the school to launder their fine linens and clothing in order that the girls may get practice in laundry work." A contemporary also described Barrett's school as preparing her charges to meet Virginia's "constant demand for house girls."[32]

Like Barrett, black clubwomen fighting for female juvenile reformatories acted on a variety of shared concerns and capitalized on some they did not themselves hold. Anxious about the stability and welfare of their own communities, they also saw the issue of juvenile reform as a particularly productive one for making political alliances and inroads into state governments, in part because they could address their own cause while calming white trepidation about a compliant black labor force.

By exposing the state's failure to provide equal protection—or in this case, equal punishment—to black and white girls alike, middleclass activists attacked white supremacy on an institutional level, at the same time posing a challenge to widely held racial beliefs. Yet in order to do so, they had to confront the perceived sexual immorality of at least a certain group of African American women. In a seeming paradox, middle-class black clubwomen committed to a politics of respectability that eschewed all mention of adult female sexuality chose to focus on the sexual misbehavior of teenage girls within their communities. A certain degree of dissemblance remained possible, with middle-class reformers clearly separating themselves from the "immoral alley girls" they sought to reform.[33] Moreover, whenever possible clubwomen deemphasized the sexual nature of delinquency. Vague references to "vice" substituted for the detailed accounts of sexual experience found in contemporary discussions of white female delinquency. Charlotte Hawkins Brown, for example, cast the problem in general terms: "Young girls in their teens frequenting questionable places cannot long withstand the vice that stands with open arms to greet them." Brown's subtext of illicit sexuality is countered by an accompanying statement, "These girls, wayward as they seem, will be the mothers of tomorrow," through which she deftly shifted the frame of reference onto more respectable ground—mature reproductive sexuality.[34]

When they did confront sexuality, black reformatory advocates argued against racial difference by pointing to the similar needs and problems of all girls. Lugenia Burns Hope criticized southern white women who "have not been taught to think just GIRLS and as long as they can not . . . they can not think clearly for the highest development of the Colored girl."[35] By the 1940s, when black social workers had joined clubwomen in speaking for the interests of delinquent girls, the language of sociology and psychology helped advocates reframe the issue in terms of class, not racial, differences. One account described delinquents as coming from "the detritus of our economic and social processes," but defended them as "for the most part, normal girls . . . [whose] sordid circumstances are working to their disadvantage."[36] Delinquency did not by definition remove them from the "normal," but instead pointed to environmental conditions—unstable families; impoverished, overcrowded neighborhoods; commercialized dancing and drinking—that could affect any girl in a similarly "sordid" situation.

Social workers insisted that the psychosexual conflict and emotional tumult of adolescence applied to black and white teenagers alike. Wilma Loree McCleave explained, "Certain difficulties and conflicts related to the growth process and to the demands of present-day society . . . may be the cause of delinquency." Sexual delinquency, according to another researcher, was "essentially a pattern of adjustment, a way of resolving emotional tensions resulting from frustrations."[37] In extending the notion of developmental psychology to African Americans, black reformers insisted on a shared humanity and on the essentially psychological—rather than innately physiological—drives that caused delinquency. The difficulties encountered by adolescents in these stormy years of transition could, in this view, account equally for black and white female delinquency.

Yet activists also made creative use of racist assumptions, turning stereotypes of black promiscuity into subversive threats against an ignorant white public. In 1939 the editor of the African American *Carolina Times* theorized that "delinquency is delinquency and knows no race or color or creed." Alluding to the relationship between delinquency and interracial sex, he concluded ominously, "Negro girls are just as much a menace to the general welfare of the state as delinquent white girls."[38] Echoing this point, North Carolina clubwomen warned: "Disease and delinquency know no color . . . The races on the lower level find each other."[39] While black women reformers observed the rules of segregation, asking only for a separate girls' reformatory, they were quick to point out that sexually delinquent girls were not nearly as likely to respect racial boundaries. Neither their sexual relations nor the ensuing social damages would be limited to the black community.

By insisting that races on the "lower level" mixed, reformers pronounced themselves to be on a higher level, capable of observing and rectifying troublesome behavior among their social inferiors. Black women worked simultaneously both to "uplift" troubled, underprivileged girls to their own presumed "higher" standards and to affirm their class-based moral superiority by emphasizing the distinction between reformer and object of reform. They hoped, in the process, to shore up their position of moral authority within their own communities while reaching across racial divisions to enlightened, genteel white leaders who felt similarly burdened by a dangerous, mixed-race crowd of "incorrigibles."[40]

Activists working on behalf of delinquent black girls made their boldest challenge to the social order by forcing southern whites to reconsider the terms of sexual and racial difference. In the end, they turned African American women's emphasis on shared sexual virtue on its head; they argued for cross-racial similarity not on the basis of a shared morality but on the grounds of similar sexual immorality, bridging polarized notions of white and black sexuality through a mutual class bias against working-class and rural folk. The "us and them" of the politics of delinquency became an "us" of enlightened elites, who knew enough not to mix, and a "them" of dangerous "lower orders" whose promiscuity occurred "without regard to race."[41]

A weakness of this strategy was the presumption that white leaders would recognize this critical distinction. These hopes were sometimes disappointed, as in 1941 when a North Carolina governor's commission suggested converting Charlotte Hawkins Brown's Palmer Memorial Institute into the state reformatory for Negro girls. Brown responded by underscoring distinctions invisible to white politicians, explaining that the school's fine artwork and cultural splendor, used to educate the children of black elites, would be destroyed by the type of girl sent to a reformatory.[42] To a smaller group of African Americans she explained her indignant refusal, fuming that "after forty years of trying to help boys and girls with a desire to do something to go forward, to start now at the age of fifty-seven to turn my whole attention to incorrigibles was more than I could do."[43] The state's inability to distinguish between Palmer students and "incorrigibles" horrified Brown, who indefatigably touted the impressive accomplishments of the refined graduates of Palmer Memorial Institute.

We know far less about how teenage inmates accounted for their own "delinquency" and whether they shared the assessments of adults who sought to protect and rehabilitate them. There is, however, a slim historical record that gives some indication of the conditions surrounding African American female delinquency. Interviews with fifteen inmates of the Tennessee Vocational School (TVS), conducted as part of a sociological study of rural black youth, along with reports by social workers on early inmate populations in the North Carolina and Georgia training schools, permit a limited view into the lives and thoughts of convicted delinquent girls from the 1930s and early 1940s.

Case records reveal families disrupted by death, divorce, and separation, in many instances further weakened by poverty or debilitating illnesses. They show always rebellious and sometimes disturbed daughters with active sexual histories and an attraction to modern and disreputable forms of leisure. Much like the white inmates of Samarcand Manor, upon arrest and incarceration we see a familiar pattern of resistance and accommodation, in which frequent escapes and occasional acts of arson or violence alternate with heartfelt pledges to follow the moral path laid down by superintendents and staff. For example, after being orphaned at age five and shuffling back and forth between relatives living in St. Louis and Nashville, Novella Foster expressed her frustration by skipping school and running away. She entered the Tennessee Vocational School at age thirteen on a truancy charge. Her initial adjustment proved difficult: she got into "trouble" with a male work crew, aided other girls in a theft and escape, and upon her return spent two weeks locked in the lavatory with a bread and water diet as punishment. She eventually came to accept her fate, and after a four-year detention expressed her gratitude to the teachers and the "good Christian" lessons they provided. She also appreciated the school's certification in sewing, laundry, and cooking, which helped her obtain her current job. Her gratitude had its limits, though. As she concluded, "I can't say that the Vocational School had a bad effect on me, except for an inferiority complex."[44]

That Novella Foster came to feel inferior after four years of incarceration is not surprising, given attitudes like that of her teacher, Miss Stanley. Betraying an underlying bitterness toward "students" whose mercurial moods made her distrustful, Stanley described her charges as sometimes "as good as a normal child but other times [they] are stubborn as mules even if you would beat them all day."[45] The ambivalence of inmates like Novella Foster also finds a match in the attitudes of adult authorities, who oscillated between viewing inmates as "normal" girls capable of rehabilitation once removed from "sordid" circumstances and deriding what they interpreted as low intelligence, bedrock immorality, and unremitting stubbornness.

While this profile is similar to that of white reformatory inmates, the arrest and conviction records show a different pattern. For African American inmates of "training" or "industrial" schools in Tennessee and North Carolina, charges of larceny, fighting, truancy, and running away predominated—offenses that are not as explicitly sexual as are the charges of "immorality," "drunk and disorderly conduct," and "fornication and adultery" that recur in white inmates' files.[46] The difference in criminal charges can be explained in two ways. First, it is possible that the white policemen, welfare officials, and judges involved in the proceedings did not view premarital sex as unusual or specific enough to indict a particular African American girl on a morals charge, finding property crimes or more general charges of incorrigibility more consistent with their own views of African American criminality. And second, African American officials, especially truant officers or women involved with child welfare work, may have preferred less explicitly sex-based misdemeanors as a kind of protective measure against the compromised sexual reputation of all black women, in general, and their young charges in particular.

The criminal records of such girls can be misleading, however, since behind the variety of juvenile convictions often lay sexual and social behaviors deemed intolerable by adults. Sixteen-year-old Chinia Green of Memphis, serving a ten-month sentence for fighting, described her mother as a "nice" parent and revealed no serious family problems that would explain her conviction for fighting. But upon expressing her wish to return home and "to marry some day if I can find an honest man," she confided to her interviewer: "Once I thought I would like to stay away from home, especially after I had the misfortune of becoming the mother of a child." Although it was not reflected in her juvenile conviction, Chinia Green had had a sexually active past, a child out of wedlock at age thirteen, and family relations so troubled she wanted to leave home, conditions that almost certainly lay behind her conviction and incarceration.

Ella, sentenced to the North Carolina Training School, also had a history of premarital sex that preceded a conviction for larceny. By sixteen Ella had given birth to a child, been arrested for stealing a watch, run away three times from the training school, and cut her boyfriend, causing her "graduation" into the state women's prison. Her caseworker described her as being incorrigible despite having two working parents and a reasonably stable home.[47] Life histories like these led experts to view sexual delinquency as a frequent precursor to other kinds of juvenile crime. When girls allowed themselves to "indulge" sexual impulses, other forms of delinquency often followed. In fact, even the struggle against sexual urges or "mental conflicts about sexual ideas may lead to . . . other forms of delinquency, such as truancy."[48] In this view either sexual indulgence or sexual repression might lead to delinquent and even criminal behavior. The line between adolescence and delinquency grew hazy.

When criminal charges and case histories are viewed together, it appears that black female delinquency—like that of white girls—revolved around two interconnected issues, family strife and the pursuit of sexual and social relations deemed unacceptable or immoral by kin and other authorities. Conflicts between daughters and their parents, grandparents, or guardians spanned a full range of issues typical of twentieth-century family problems: adolescent defiance, family violence, incest, resentment of parental discipline, and conflicts over how and with whom a child spent her free time. These kinds of tensions were exacerbated by the emotional and financial strains of death, divorce, illness, or other disruptive events. When teenagers expressed their dissatisfaction and need for attention by seeking intimacy or excitement outside the family, their actions spurred angry parents or other adults to seek legal redress.

Some arrests illustrate the clash of values between two competing urban cultures, a hard-drinking, high-living, working-class culture and middle-class norms that truant officers and the law attempted to enforce. But intraclass discord also led to juvenile incarcerations. Adult diatribes against youthful immorality made reference to the rebellion of middle-class black youth as often as they did those from poorer backgrounds. Eight of the fifteen Tennessee Vocational School interviews leave clues that suggest better than average socioeconomic status, indicated by parental education, property ownership, and jobs as mechanics, Pullman porters, or barbers. Middle-class parents fearful of their daughters' sexual and social rebellions may have turned readily to the new social welfare services and institutions created largely by southern middle-class black reformers. The Tennessee Vocational School was popularly referred to as "Mrs. Pierce's school" after the director, indicating a kind of familiarity and confidence in Mrs. Pierce as a like-minded and trustworthy authority. A similar dynamic operated at "Peaks" run by Janie Porter Barrett, who corresponded regularly with friends she knew from her years at Hampton Institute. That the reformatories operated in a context of segregation and thus had an entirely black staff may have provided some sense of connection and accessibility.

Some inmates shared this view. Vera Furguson, described by her interviewer as from an upper-class family, went willingly to "Mrs. Pierce's vocational school" but once there found that many girls, committed for serious crimes, "weren't as good as they should be." She commented that at the beginning of her commitment the girls were "of a higher type" than toward the end of her seven years of confinement. Novella Foster agreed, complaining that too many serious criminals had been admitted to the reform school. Claiming that "we are all thrown together" and "never classed as we should be," she worried about the school's—and thus her own—bad reputation among the general public. Yet this evidence is particular to Tennessee and Virginia, where reformatories operated with a fair amount of independence from state supervision. Reports on the North Carolina and Georgia training schools from the 1940s, when state support and involvement finally kicked in, indicate that inmates came from predominantly impoverished backgrounds, with 80 percent already in the social welfare system as recipients of public assistance.[49]

$\mathcal{F}$rom the record of actions and reactions of adolescents, parents, and law officials, it is possible to discern some aspects of the subjective experience of girls, both before and during their incarceration. Three themes, often intertwined, run through the case records: the extremely painful situations that girls faced both before and during their reformatory stays; their determination to seek remedy or pleasure in the face of pain and suffering; and a tentative sense of self-worth and claim to justice mixed with feelings of uncertainty and isolation.

Narratives of delinquency often begin with stories of terrible conflicts or ruptures that sundered family relationships, leaving girls hurt, angry, and rebellious. For Vera Williams, conflict with her stepmother triggered a sequence of events that ended in her incarceration. Vera's mother died when she was seven, after which she lived with her grandmother for several years, until her death precipitated another move, this time back to Vera's father who had remarried. The transition was not a happy one. Accusing her father's wife of mistreatment, taking money meant for her, and disparaging her dark skin, Vera sought justice by stealing from her stepmother. Her father responded by bringing her to juvenile court where the judge sentenced her to time in TVS. Similar stories of escalating tensions and acting out fill the available case records, which differ only in their cast of characters and kinds of transgressions.

Conflicts frequently involved physical violence. While some girls initiated violence against family members, records more often report beatings by parents or guardians trying to rein in disobedient daughters. Ola Mai Hargrove's problems began with her alcoholic father's physical abuse of her mother, which led to the parents' separation and her mother's remarriage. Her stepfather, a kind and financially stable man, died when Ola was eleven. Unsettled by her mother's very strict rules and constant disruptions, including one year in which she moved fourteen times, Ola found friendship with an older and sexually experienced friend, Louise. Under Louise's tutelage she began to smoke, drink, go to picture shows, and have frequent sexual relations with boys in her home during her mother's work hours. Eventually neighbors informed her mother, who initiated court proceedings. Angry and frustrated at her mother's strictness and her sudden losses, Ola had literally tried to bring love and excitement back into a home life marred by violence, instability, and loss.

Incidents of coerced or nonconsensual sex occur as frequently as family violence in inmates' histories. One lonely girl described having sex with her friends' brothers, but could not remember ever consenting to these encounters. Ethel, in contrast, had a razor-sharp memory of a stepfather who beat her and then "started using me for himself" at the age of ten. Other inmates recounted having sex to please someone or when pressured by adult men. At age thirteen rumors started about Dorothy Widby's fast ways. She began wearing makeup to look more grown up, left school, and took a job offered by a family friend who soon asked her to "be his little girlfriend." A married twenty-seven-year-old man involved with a girl in her early teens constitutes statutory rape, but to Dorothy it meant feeling cared for and having someone to buy her anything she wanted. In the case of a North Carolina inmate identified only as Susie, two older family friends pressured her into having sex, threatening to tell her mother if she refused. When Susie's mother found out and brought her daughter's rape to the attention of the police, the two men received five-year prison sentences. But because both men had given Susie money, she was not treated as a rape victim; instead the court convicted her of sex delinquency and she too became a criminal.[50]

In almost all cases some form of tragedy or disruption—death, illness, frequent moves, rejection, violence, or coercion—created enormous pain, difficulty, or anger in adolescents not emotionally equipped to deal with such trauma. Girls' legal trouble often began when they refused to accept conditions they deemed unacceptable and tried to change the source of their unhappiness. The two most common forms of defiance involved dropping out of school or running away. Either could be a defiant statement or simply a way to avoid conflict, punishment, or violence. Anger, sexual relationships, theft, and bargaining were other means of expressing discontent and attempting to remedy intolerable conditions. Some girls fought back, physically or verbally, against family members they saw as too controlling. Others turned to people outside the family, often boys or men, for closeness, love, or material goods not available to them at home. Sexual relationships might develop casually, especially among peers for whom sex before marriage did not violate social norms. Other times sexual activity represented a dramatic rejection of family norms, whether conducted illicitly or in open defiance. If sex resulted in pregnancy, an act of provocation became a life-changing event often involving serious family rupture or giving up the child to older family members. Stealing, too, might be an act of defiance or a means of seeking revenge or some object of desire. Although girls' bold, resourceful actions in the face of hardship indicate a certain toughness and independence, many times their attempted remedy was the very thing that got them into trouble with the law.

Once incarcerated, some girls continued to use familiar methods of resistance: acting out, running away, having sex with workmen or other female inmates, and offering repentance in hopes of either obtaining their release or receiving gifts or visits from relatives. In the end, most inmates either professed or truly believed that they had committed terrible wrongs, adopting the moral code that reformatory staff proffered as the path to Christian respectability. Whether strategic or sincere, the change of heart could be interpreted as a submission to adult authority and a weakening of adolescents' independent and defiant spirits. Yet as conveyed to sociologists who visited the

Tennessee Vocational School, even inmates who had opted for reform exhibited a strong sense of justice and self-respect. Signs of strength, however, hung in tenuous balance with feelings of shame, rejection, isolation, and low self-worth.

Among the fifteen TVS inmates, a number of them made clear that they wanted to reclaim status as a "good" girl or respectable woman. Many talked of making their mothers proud once again or of not wanting "to do things that will cause people to criticize you." Such statements hint at a legacy of shame, but more positively establish the girls' claim to a valued status of black womanhood achieved through marriage, specific jobs, a higher standard of living, or independence from the correctional system. Varied as their hopes were, they shared a refusal to forget their past or see themselves as permanently tainted. Nor did inmates shy away from hard-nosed assessments of their current situation, including biting criticisms of family members and reformatory staff. While a few stated bluntly that being sent to TVS was the worst thing that had ever happened to them, others pointed to hypocrisy and injustice in their midst. After declining to join her local church because she was not ready to "give up the ways of the world," as her very religious mother insisted a good Christian must do, one girl acidly remarked that she did not think it was very Christian for her mother to have beaten her so much. Dorothy Widby turned her critical eye toward the staff of TVS, stating that she would like the school "if they'd only treat you like human beings. They work you like slaves and talk about you before everybody." TVS inmates, who were drilled to believe that they had disgraced their family by committing shameful deeds never to be repeated, expressed their own sensitivity to further disgrace, but they also retained a more subdued version of their former defiance, refusing to hold their tongues when invited to speak truth to power.

This same kind of honesty takes on a sadder cast when girls revealed vulnerabilities and sorrows that no amount of "good" behavior could erase. Two letters from Clara Willis to her Aunt Susie capture the hopes and disappointment of girls struggling with complex emotions and unresponsive adults. The first, dated May 18, 1939, informs her aunt that she and her sister Elizabeth, also at TVS, will be taking part in commencement exercises and celebratory events beginning in two weeks. She asks her aunt to send her pink organdy material so that she can make a dress for the upcoming fashion show. She also describes a play in which "Elizabeth is the Herald and I am the Spirit of the Dawn." At once a carefully calculated request for needed materials and an excited show of pride and expectation, Clara's voice becomes more cautious when she writes, "There will be something nearly every night and you are cordially invited." The next letter, dated June 27, begins, "My Dearest Aunt, It is indeed a great pleasure for me to write you," adding casually, "We looked for you commencement Sunday but failed to see you." The cool formality falls away as Clara's needs for approval, interest, and love spill over her initial restraint. She asks again for some material, in the next breath pleading, "Aunt susie eliz. and I are trying each day to be better girls but I haven't been doing so well in school, will you please come up here so I can tell you about it." Her emotional appeal turns formal again with a cordial ending: "I will close looking to hear from you soon." In a postscript she remembers to thank her aunt for a pair of shoes, remarking, "I liked them fine. I thank you very much they were just the right fit." Clara's two letters offer up pleas, hints, formal requests, thanks, and hopes—trying to find "just the right fit" that would cause her aunt to come visit, allowing the two sisters to demonstrate their progress toward reform and earn Clara the chance to confide in someone about her ongoing troubles and underlying sadness.

The delinquent girls at TVS exhibit independent will and thought, a keen sense of justice, and a belief that past wrongs did not indicate lasting inadequacies. Their histories reveal strength, defiance, and cleverness as well as poor judgment. Boldness combines with vulnerability, optimism with despair. African American "sex delinquents" are neither heroic rebels nor innocent victims of social control. While there is clearly a clash of sensibilities between a sexually permissive youthful working class and a middle-class and religiously based culture of respectability, we see as well an expression of intrafamily and intraclass disputes as older family members turned to new African American social welfare institutions to tame rebellious daughters. When their private family struggles merged with a larger political effort by African American community leaders to advance a particular view of racial progress against the restrictions of white supremacist state governments, adolescent girls pulled into this political drama pushed back.

*P*arents and even inmates may have taken to heart the ideas of reformatory leaders more readily than did white elected officials, who continued to stonewall the lobbying efforts of black clubwomen and their allies. The history of black female reformatories in the South is ultimately one of refusal and dereliction. Many southerners refused to see the problems of black and white female delinquency as similar in origin, significance, and treatment. And when state governments did create parallel reform institutions, they left a record of financial and human neglect that speaks volumes about the low official value placed on the moral condition and social welfare of black teenage girls in the South. Or more cynically, the record may indicate just the opposite—the high value placed on young black women's continued unofficial sexual availability and low repute in underwriting the status quo of southern race relations.

A significant sector of the voting South simply refused to believe that sexual delinquency among black teenage girls was an unusual or remediable condition. In response to intensified lobbying in the late 1930s for full state funding for the home in Efland, North Carolina, the *Charlotte Observer* explained public hostility to the proposal on the grounds that "such a large proportion of the negro girls might fall within the scope of such a correctional institution that the state would simply be overrun with inmates."[51]

Most southern states eventually responded in some measure to delinquency among black adolescent girls, but the pattern of institutional neglect remained the same whether the reformatories were small, underfunded schools run by black clubwomen or government institutions fully funded by the state. Observers deplored inadequate building facilities and fire protection; undertrained and underpaid staff; the lack of proper clothing, food, and medical attention to inmates; and scandalously low budgets. University of North Carolina professor George H. Lawrence wrote to the state's head of corrections after visiting Efland about the "rather shocking revelation of the total absence of just about everything essential toward the conduct of an institution for delinquent negro girls." Describing the school, as yet unfunded by the state, as "worse than useless," Lawrence added that at least in the county jail a girl would be assured of enough to eat.[52]

Not much changed once activists had succeeded in turning responsibility over to state governments. In Georgia, a sixteen-yard-long petition signed by women around the state in combination with intensified lobbying during the 1937 legislative session finally forced the state to assume fiscal responsibility and begin accepting inmates. Yet not until November 1943 did the state assembly actually appropriate the necessary funds. The Georgia Training School for Colored Girls in Macon did not open its doors until the mid-1940s, and ten years later consisted of only one building that served as dormitory, staff residence, recreation hall, kitchen, and dining area. Classes were held in girls' sleeping rooms.[53]

A similar situation developed in North Carolina. After the school at Efland closed in 1939 due to insufficient funds, the state did not replace it with a public institution until late in World War II, when an abandoned National Youth Administration camp became available. Opened in 1944 at Rocky Mount, the "school" operated in largely uncovered buildings and lacked a single desk; its chairs were borrowed from a local funeral home.[54] In 1947 the school found a permanent site at the former Dobbs Farm, a reformatory for adult white women that had been closed by the state. Despite the fact that until penicillin became readily available the institution had served primarily as a treatment facility for venereally diseased young white women, a consultant from the U.S. Children's Bureau reported after a visit in 1947 that venereally infected inmates at the new black school were receiving no treatment.[55] Even with this low quality of care, one study reported that members of the staff believed the girls were "overplaced" in their current situation, making the return to even worse conditions in their home communities difficult.[56]

In Tennessee and Virginia, surveys found equally abysmal conditions despite a much longer and more willing history of state support. A 1939 inspection by an independent penal reform organization, the Osborne Association, reported that the Tennessee Vocational School's budget had been slashed more than 60 percent between 1931 and 1939, from over $30,000 per year to an annual appropriation of only $12,000, compared to $50,000 received by the parallel training school for white girls in 1939. The authors described the school "as among the most forsaken and impoverished" of any in their study, offering the citizens of Tennessee "little but a monument of neglect and shame."[57]

The Osborne Association report on Virginia found the reformatory in Peaks Turnout more praiseworthy but still plagued by fire hazards so serious "that one must be in constant fear of a fire in which lives would almost certainly be lost, especially since the girls are locked in their rooms." The report pointed to the school's "lamentably inadequate" staff and physical plant as well as a "ridiculously low" educational budget. But the authors warned against the public's tendency to view delinquent girls of both races with an attitude favoring "sympathetic and kindly treatment" over "scientific" methods. Investigators singled out African American female delinquents as presenting "a highly complex problem, more difficult of solution than that presented by the boys of either race or by the white girls."[58] Offering little explanation for these views, the Osborne report seemed to confirm the belief that adolescent black girls and their communities presented a condition of immorality that was deeply rooted and not easily eradicated.

This entrenched view of black women's immorality and the slow pace of institutional change posed nearly insurmountable barriers to black women's clubs across the South. Almost completely disfranchised by the 1910s, southern African Americans shifted focus from electoral politics to the social provision sector in order to maintain a foothold in a shrinking political landscape. Party politics and electoral contests gave way to extended struggles with state and local governments over schooling, public health, child welfare, and public accommodations.[59] Black women activists found that any degree of victory required alliances with white women, who seldom overcame their own racial biases. That North Carolina and Georgia clubwomen persisted over three decades of rejection until finally meeting with a measure of success begs the question of why African American women struggled so tenaciously for this particular reform.

A 1943 exchange of letters between North Carolina activists who finally won a legislative commitment to a reformatory for delinquent black girls provides some clues, revealing both the cooperative spirit and the different vantage points of black and white women. In February, Lula Kelsey, president of the state federation of Negro women's clubs, responded to a letter of praise from Ellen Winston of the state legislative council. "I highly appreciate your comments on my feeble efforts on behalf of 'our school,'" began Kelsey. Referring to the upcoming legislative battle, she then remarked, "I only wish I was able to make a worth while contribution to the cause. If it is not asking too much will it be possible to furnish me with a copy of the bill as introduced in the legislature. Then I shall be pleased to know the progress of the bill."[60] Kelsey and Winston recognized their common interest and mutual dependency, highlighted by Winston's initial expression of thanks and Kelsey's reference to "our school." But Kelsey also reminded Winston that she was barred by race from further participation in the political process and dependent on white allies for whatever political gains black women hoped to make in the future. After the bill's passage several weeks later, Winston acknowledged her own debt, writing to Kelsey: "We fully realize that the efforts of the Negro women of the state were largely responsible for the establishment of the institution."[61] Winston found black women's political work crucial for the kinds of social welfare programs that facilitated white women's entrance into government positions, in particular her own appointment one year later as state commissioner of public welfare.[62] Applauding Winston's appointment, an officer of the state federation of Negro women's clubs reminded Winston that the organization "solicits your continued interest in the welfare of all the people of our state."[63] African American women chose their words strategically for two reasons: first, to articulate the difference in white and black women's access to political power and second, to forge ties of obligation that could be called on in the future.

The persistence of clubwomen's struggle for girls' reformatories indicates the importance of sexual reputation for the collective image and status of black womanhood as well as clubwomen's belief that middle-class respectability represented the best face of southern urban black communities. Their committed efforts to address delinquency also battled black political subordination by persistently demanding public services and representation from segregated and exclusionary state governments. Underlying these public battles were private ones in which adolescent girls struggled to find their own course amid difficult circumstances while older family members called on external authorities to bolster their own sagging command over rebellious daughters.

African American women's impressive fortitude in the struggle to create and maintain reformatories for delinquent black girls slowly wore down the political barriers posed by the Jim Crow South. Two years after finally finding a permanent structure at Dobbs Farm for the Negro Girls Training School, the North Carolina institution was filled to capacity in 1949 and receiving active support from the federation of women's clubs, wives of the Omega fraternity, a local PTA, a garden club, the Delta Sigma Theta sorority, and the Palmer Memorial Institute.[64] Leading black individuals served on the school's Negro advisory board, an unofficial advisory group that made recommendations to the state governing board. As early as 1948, within a year of the reformatory's opening, the advisory board began pushing toward its next goal—winning representation on the Board of Corrections and Training, an all-white advisory board appointed by the governor and responsible to the state's commissioner of corrections. Black representatives gradually voiced their dissatisfaction in stronger terms, asserting in 1952 that "the group is not satisfied with maintenance of its status, namely that of 'Advisory to the Board,'" adding that the North Carolina Federation of Negro Women's Clubs had endorsed their demand.[65]

As they challenged the reigning political structures and racial ideologies of the South, black clubwomen succeeded, eventually, in winning limited resources and space from governments that had systematically ignored the needs of black youth and denied the sexual vulnerability of black girls. Moreover, in confronting the issue of female delinquency they pressed southern society to redraw lines of sexual and racial difference. In the end, the advocates of female reformatories argued for racial similarity not on the basis of shared sexual virtue, but on the grounds of similar sexual problems among troubled youth. Yet the claim to similarity still hinged on a class distinction between virtuous respectable types and the "menace" of lower-class sexual immorality. In the class judgments that permeate reformers' treatment of "our girls," we see a desire to create distance as well as connection between respectable middle-class women and the sexually active teens they aimed to protect.

Ultimately, both black and white attempts to reckon with delinquent girls point to the political salience of adolescent female sexuality in this period. In each case, reformers addressed broader issues of citizenship and state power. White southerners debated the role of poor, sexually active white teenage girls in creating a strong citizenry capable of maintaining the avowed superiority and political dominance of the white race. Black southerners understood the state's refusal to support Negro female reformatories as revealing the lie behind a "separate but equal" legal system. In addition, reformers' faith in rehabilitation for black delinquent girls made an unwavering claim for shared humanity as the prerequisite to citizenship.

Yet the efforts of black southern reformers failed to win quick and significant concessions from stubbornly resistant white governments. In the end, this particular defeat may have been a blessing. For while southern governments were denying reformatory resources for black delinquent girls, these governments were passing sterilization laws that had especially harsh consequences for poor white teenage women. We can also see success in reformers' long years of labor. In their focus on sex delinquency, they shifted the explanation for delinquency away from the black body to childhood deprivation, a shared psychology of adolescent emotional crises, and the social provision obligations of modern government. Through the politicized subject of the adolescent sex delinquent, black elites expanded their claims to full citizenship. Their accomplishments both benefited and harmed incarcerated adolescents, who were themselves struggling for self-determination and justice within conflict-ridden families as well as within a white-dominated society that all too often treated them as beneath sin, without dignity, and beyond redemption.

chapter four

"*A Head Full of Diamonds*"

Fact, Fiction, and African American Girls' Sexuality

*I*n the late 1930s, sixteen-year-old Emma Graye told her interviewer that she was in love with her current boyfriend and might marry him since he was "as good as any." When asked about sexual relations, the North Carolina high school student hesitated, then responded, "We call that 'breaking.'" She explained, "You should have association with the boy" because "if you are going to marry a person you ought to know about them." Girls in her rural community did not necessarily wait for a marital prospect; they often sought immediate pleasure over permanence. Trying to convey to her African American interviewer that this was standard behavior, she reported, "Every one of the girls I know—'less they be real small, and some of them do [too]—breaks with boys."[1]

Emma Graye's initial hesitation and eventual frankness both tell a story. A truthful answer not only might hurt her reputation in the eyes of her interviewer but also could be misconstrued as part of a long history of so-called promiscuity among African American women. Stereotypes dating back to the antebellum South that characterized African American women as sexually wanton persisted long after slavery ended.[2] In 1937 John Dollard's renowned study *Caste and Class in a Southern Town* reported that "the image of the Negro woman in the white man's talk and fantasy . . . is rather that of a seducing, accessible person dominated by sexual feeling and, so far as straight-out sexual gratification goes, desirable." Southern whites made few distinctions based on age, informing Dollard that "there are actually no chaste Negro girls after the ages of fifteen or sixteen."[3] Such myths heightened black women's sexual vulnerability, forming the backdrop for every girl's transition from girlhood to womanhood.

Researchers have identified the sexualized black female body as being central to systems of white supremacy, with their accompanying patterns of devastating sexual violence and resulting psychological injuries.[4] We know much less about personal sexual practices, values, and desires that constituted black female subjectivity. But women's silence has not been absolute. Blues singers and authors of the Harlem Renaissance spoke eloquently of the sexual desires, satisfactions, and frustrations of young black women.[5] So too did ordinary teenage girls who, when questioned by researchers, gave compelling evidence of their many desires, dreams, and calculated attempts to enrich lives in which suffering, more often than not, commingled with satisfaction. These were not the "sex delinquents" targeted by reformers, yet in their day-to-day lives black adolescents of the 1930s and early '40s confronted issues of sexuality charged with possibility and risk. How these girls negotiated the terms of their own desires, both sexual and nonsexual, provides a glimpse into how sexuality formed part of every girl's coming of age. Moreover, it illustrates how sexual behaviors that moved to the center of racial politics and state policy in the years following World War II could, in an earlier era, generate only mild public interest and not a flicker of controversy.

In the 1930s the topic of adolescent sexuality emerged as a subject of importance to black social scientists, who formed part of a larger cadre of professionals newly interested in the category "youth," ages fifteen to twenty-four. Policy makers feared this age group might form a lost Depression-era generation that, due to chronic unemployment and poverty, would grow alienated from American economic and political ideals. In the worst-case scenario, they would lose faith in democratic and capitalist values, turning instead to socialism, fascism, or a disaffected apathy. Under Franklin Roosevelt's New Deal administration, federal leaders took up the cause of youth through a variety of agencies. While the Civilian Conservation Corps siphoned off unemployed city youth to military-like labor camps in rural and wilderness areas, agricultural extension agents reached out to rural youth through a variety of farm-based clubs that provided recreational activities and taught lessons in canning and hygiene. The National Youth Administration accepted a broader mandate of developing educational and employment programs for youth in need, a category that may well have encompassed a majority of all youth in the 1930s. Finally, under the auspices of the American Council on Education, a coalition of national educators, government administrators, and social workers formed the American Youth Commission (AYC) in 1935 for the purpose of gathering comprehensive data and then proposing a set of policy directives to guide federal and local assistance to the nation's youth.[6]

The AYC, which was funded largely by the Rockefellers and other major philanthropists (many with a record of past involvement in the South), paid special attention from the beginning to both southern and black youth because of their perceived greater risk of "social maladjustment."[7] The South as a region moved abruptly into the national spotlight when the National Emergency Council issued its 1938 *Report on Economic Conditions in the South.* The document identified the region as the nation's top economic problem, finding that fertility rates in the rural South far outpaced those of the rest of the nation and corresponded with the geographic areas of lowest average income.[8] For instance, while 24 percent of the nation's children lived in the southeastern United States, the region accounted for only 10 percent of national income. AYC researchers concluded that because of poor people's high birth rates, the nation recruited "each succeeding generation from the underprivileged elements in American life," creating the worrisome prospect that low-income, poorly educated southerners might crowd out other elements of the population over time and "actually lower America's innate capacity to learn."[9]

Although most experts appeared more concerned about white population trends than black, African American intellectuals made the most of this fortuitous convergence of fact and fear. Between 1936 and 1942 a predominantly black group of scholars researched and published five monographs under the auspices of the AYC, blending the study of social and economic conditions with psychological theories of adolescent personality development.[10] These included Ira Reid's *In a Minor Key: Negro Youth in Story and Fact,* E. Franklin

Frazier's *Negro Youth at the Crossways* about the upper South, Charles Johnson's *Growing Up in the Black Belt,* W. Lloyd Warner's *Color and Human Nature* on Chicago youth, and *Children of Bondage,* Allison Davis and John Dollard's case study of Negro youth in the urban South.[11] Using a combination of structured and informal interviews, case records from agencies and schools, questionnaires, and a battery of attitude and personality tests, researchers set out to investigate whether and how second-class racial status—the "socio-racial factor"—influenced the psychological and social development of Negro youth aged twelve to twenty-one.[12] Sexuality, which was understood as critical to adolescent development, figured prominently in the psychosocial profiles that these authors drew.

African American scholars struggled to refute myths of black promiscuity while coming to terms with sexual moralities that differed from the norms of white middle-class youth. Together they told a story of personalities that, on the one hand, were damaged by the legacy of slavery and the persistence of racial oppression yet, on the other hand, could be considered emotionally healthy if viewed in the context of black history and culture. An even more complex set of stories appears in the interview transcripts from Charles Johnson's AYC study. Black graduate students who had fanned out to communities in Tennessee, North Carolina, Georgia, Alabama, and Mississippi recorded stories that tell us less about the social adjustment of youth in the "black belt" than about the texture of daily life and the place of sexuality in adolescents' immediate lives and future plans.

Can we assume that teenagers imparted accurate information about themselves to relative strangers inquiring about their most personal and private experiences? Interviewers did occasionally relate their suspicions that certain girls told outright lies or tried to conceal the truth. Several girls affected an ignorance about sex that their interviewers suspected was more feigned than real. Typically, these instances involved self-reports of little or no sexual experience when interviewers had heard from teachers, other adults, or a girl's schoolmates that she was sexually active. Yet no researcher suggests that a girl claimed sexual knowledge or activity beyond what she had in fact experienced. The pressure that respondents felt, if any, was in the direction of concealing the extent of their sexual involvements. Since many girls abstained from sexual relations and thereby earned the respect of parents, peers, and community members, these teens had no reason to fake sexual knowledge or experience. Instead, out of concern for their reputation certain girls may have adopted a reticent stance, withholding information about past or present involvements. To the extent that respondents misled their interviewers, then, they most likely underreported sexual activity. But most teens had little reason to withhold information because they found support for their moral beliefs and sexual practices among friends, some family members, and at least a portion of the surrounding community. Because there were few disincentives for telling the truth, girls typically hesitated very little when discussing sex or other topics. In fact, they seemed eager to talk, feeling that the very interview process itself bestowed them with some importance.[13]

Although heavily mediated by the formatted questions and personal perspectives of the interviewers, the Johnson study allowed teenagers to talk about their lives in their own words.[14] As they answered queries about courtship, dating, sexual relations, and occupational goals, southern black girls delineated two contrasting sexual cultures: a restrictive code of conduct and a much more permissive one. These standards aimed at a balance of pleasure and protection, both of which many adolescents found sorely lacking in their lives.

Competing moralities operated in southern black communities of the late 1930s. One defined adolescent sexual activity as strictly out of bounds. Devoutly religious families raised their daughters according to an "old-fashioned" morality that limited a girl's contact with boys until the late teenage years and then carefully monitored her interactions with young men from "courting" until marriage. Parents typically set an age at which their daughter could begin "keeping company," requiring the boy to "call" at home or visit at church- and school-related functions only. By the time they allowed their daughter to go out walking, riding, or to movies free from adult vigilance, she had been thoroughly indoctrinated in the importance of avoiding sexual involvement and its possible consequence, pregnancy.

When asked about sexual relations Carrie Randolph, an eighteen-year-old Mississippian, surmised, "I wouldn't like it no ways, even if mother didn't tell me it was wrong."[15] Voicing her objections in explicitly religious terms, Randolph explained that she dreaded the possibility of unwed pregnancy because "I'd miss heaven and go to hell, and I'm working to go to heaven." Others worried that too great an interest in boys would interfere with educational and occupational ambitions. Having never had a boyfriend at an age that many other girls were actively courting or having sexual relationships, eighteen-year-old Stella Jenkins explained, "I do not care for any boy friends now . . . For I want to finish high school, of course." Shirley Motley viewed schooling as her lone ticket to a better life. On scholarship at a Memphis business school, she declared simply, "I don't think books and boys go together."

Many more teens referred to the social sanctions leveled against those young women who violated moral standards. They spoke often of the shame and disgrace that premarital pregnancies would bring to their families. As Eliza Drese put it, "Mama told me about girls who have babies without being married and how people look down on the mother and on the baby." Under this restrictive or "old-timey" code, young girls learned that delaying sex until marriage signaled respectability. Yet it is notable that adolescents did not so much condemn premarital sex as pregnancy out of wedlock. Contemplating the shame of having "a child without any name," Eliza insisted, "I would never disgrace my family like that."

Rural girls brought their restrictive moral code with them as they migrated to towns and cities of the South. Although sexual restrictions differed little in the two settings, urban girls often drew sharper lines between "good" and "bad" than did their rural counterparts. Dannie Freeman, a sixteen-year-old from Selma, North Carolina, described her own group of friends as not "rough like most of the girls here." Her parents praised her for disdaining the company of "fast girls" who slipped off to cafes and engaged in "raw dancing" and "all the vices," which included beer gardens, rough dancing, and frequent parties.

While urban teens could more easily access commercial recreation and the "fast life," cities also offered more recreational alternatives. Nannie Mary Hayes, an eleventh-grader living just outside of Nashville, listed her hobbies as tennis, hiking, embroidery, roller skating, and driving. She attended church weekly and belonged to both a church club and the Girl Reserves. While her social circles consisted of a "gang" of girls as well as several boys she liked, including one steady boyfriend from school, Nannie emphasized that she was "not fast." Fourteen-year-old Dorothy Harris engaged in numerous activities connected to her high school in Huntsville, Alabama, including studying piano, attending school football games, playing on the softball team, and participating in her school's class and home economics clubs. These organized activities, along with informal "social clubs" created by teens with similar interests and backgrounds, formed the day-to-day fabric of town or city life for girls committed to a more restrictive set of sexual norms.

Another sector of rural and urban black youth held to an entirely different set of norms, viewing premarital sex as within the bounds of customary and moral behavior. Among girls in this group, no single economic, religious, or educational background predominated. Some came from extremely poor tenant families with little formal education, while others were the children of landowners who expected their daughters to finish high school and possibly college. A few expressed no interest in religion, but most attended church and Sunday school regularly. A large number taught Sunday school or were involved in their church's youth or service organizations, finding no conflict between their religious beliefs and sexual activity. In fact, having sex in the fields on the way home from church was a popular way to transition from the sacred back to the secular.

Within this group, sexual experiences varied greatly. Some girls reported beginning sexual activity as early as age eight or nine while others in their late teens had only recently become sexually active. While some spoke of having had only one or two partners and infrequent contacts, others reported having sex with numerous partners on a frequent basis, with "having sex" or "sex relations" understood by both interviewers and their subjects as heterosexual intercourse. A few teenagers made reference to the fact that some people thought this was "bad," but others explicitly described sex as a positive good in their lives. Still others referred to sexual relations as simply a customary and, in some cases, necessary part of dating, courting, or peer relations.

After hearing friends talking about sex, seventeen-year-old Ethel Lee Sanders decided to try it with her current boyfriend. Although she did not enjoy her first experience, she continued because "I reckon it's just the custom" in her Mississippi town. Fifteen-year-old Ophelia Hamilton agreed, having been sexually active since the age of eight. Although her unknowing mother discouraged her from dating because she might become pregnant, Ophelia proceeded without fear: "I tell the boys not to make me pregnant . . . I don't see nothing wrong 'bout it, so long as they don't mess me up." Many of her peers agreed, seeing sex as perfectly acceptable for a girl as long as she did not "get caught," or pregnant.

Mothers cautioned daughters about pregnancy but often did little to intervene in their sexual lives, suggesting either a tacit approval or a belief in either fate or an adolescent's right to make her own decisions. In other instances, however, teen frustration with adults points to generational tensions. Twelfth-grader Vivian Lowe derided the old-fashioned attitudes and hypocrisy of neighbors who had "as many faces as a brick," speaking nicely to her face then gossiping about her "fast" ways behind her back. Adolescents also ridiculed sanctimonious preachers who condemned youth for their "sinful" ways while engaging in sexual affairs themselves. Students bristled against school authorities too, using their wits and wiles to evade the prohibitive rules of teachers who supervised them closely and forbade any intimate heterosocial contact.

Although social scientists frequently described nonmarital sex as a holdover from patterns developed during slavery, young and old alike labeled the sexually active behavior of young people as "modern," that is, associated with the newer ways of town and city. The context, if not the content, of youthful sexuality had changed by the 1930s. Young people themselves identified strongly with the idea of "modern," a notion encouraged by participation in a "fast" life of urban pleasures and sexual possibilities. Fourteen-year-old Rosa Mae Harding, for instance, lived in an area of Nashville known for its roughness and revelry. She and her gang of five girls regularly went to taverns to drink, smoke, and gamble or danced to the "rockola" jukebox in Rosa Mae's home. Entranced by this urban sensibility, Pauline Nesbitt looked forward to leaving her rural home for Memphis. "I like movies and dances and they don't have them things here. In Memphis I can have a good time," she explained—which in Pauline's mind also included meeting attractive boys.

These cases reflect the "rough" side of a rough and respectable divide between poor and middle-class black communities, yet some better-off adolescents maintained a definition of respectability that did not preclude sexual involvements. Agnes Jackson, a tenth-grade student at Nashville's Pearl High School, described herself as part of a group of girls who "are all nice and they are not loud." She dated a boy who had already graduated and now worked, owned a car, and took her often to the Paradise Ballroom or for romantic drives in the countryside. They had frequent sex, either going to "a house" that rented rooms by the hour or using the back seat of his car. Although her great-aunt, with whom she lived, threatened to kick her out of the house because of her sexual activity, Agnes believed she could manage sex without her aunt's knowledge while finishing school to become a stenographer.

Although youth at times clashed with their elders on matters of sexuality, an equally significant gap existed between adolescents who adhered to a restrictive standard, opposing premarital sex and pregnancy, and those embracing a more permissive standard that defined sex as a customary part of adolescent leisure and sociability. Yet just as attitudes between adults and youth were not uniformly polarized, the behavior of young people did not always divide neatly into two opposing camps. A majority fell toward one end or another of a spectrum that spanned permissive to restrictive sensibilities, but their own decisions and those of their friends led them into gray areas.

In a few cases girls, usually from farm- or business-owning families of higher economic standing, chose not to associate with peers known to be sexually active. Fifteen-year-old Emma Lee McCullen reported that other girls saw her as stuck up because she refused to socialize with "fast" girls who would "run around with boys." More frequently, teenagers spoke casually and not very critically of girls whose sexual behavior differed from their own. Larrine Perry revealed that she once had sexual intercourse "when I was real small" but "I don't do it now 'cause it's bad." Aware that many of her peers chose not to refrain, she adroitly articulated a subtle moral distinction. "I don't think the girls are so bad that do it with boys," she maintained, "but they are bad when they are doing it." Larrine's distinction between bad character and bad behavior exhibits a commonplace tolerance of dissimilar sexual choices. Adolescent girls proved themselves fully capable of working out complex moral codes that established parameters for their own desires and those of the boys or men they dated.

Frequency of sex operated as one such moral measuring stick. Earselle Mayo told her interviewer, "I don't know why I do it . . . just like to, I reckon," but added immediately that she had sex only infrequently. Vivian Lowe, a high school senior, also drew a line based on frequency, informing her interviewer that when her previous boyfriend had become too sexually demanding she ended the relationship, not wishing to appear "common." Others drew a moral distinction based not on the number of encounters but on the number and type of sexual partners one had. Nineteen-year-old Hazel Jones told her interviewer she had been having intercourse with boys since age sixteen, adding, "It's always with the boy I'm going with, though. I don't go to bed with just any boy." Jeanette Whitley agreed: "All the girls I know and go with have relations with boys and I don't think it's wrong if you do it only with your boyfriend." Ethel Oliver of Mississippi, by contrast, claimed that girls earned bad reputations not from multiple partners but by dating married men.

Still others invoked mutuality as the standard for ethical behavior. When asked about sexual relations, Mamie Philpot of Alabama responded, "I reckon I have," reasoning that if she liked the boy, the relationship was acceptable. In this calculus, sex was "moral" if it involved either mutual affection or physical pleasure. Sara Eason judged "running around" with lots of men and having sex as wrong, but believed, "If a girl and a boy should be going together for some time and they cared about each other it would be alright." A steady man willing to marry and take care of his girlfriend if she got pregnant fell on the side of decency, while she found reprehensible boys who "will take rounds" by visiting a different girl each Sunday with no emotional commitment. For Eason, respectability derived from mutual affection and male intentions rather than any specific behavior of girls.

The importance of shared feelings between partners did not, however, imply a commitment to marriage or exclusivity. Sex involving some kinds of material exchanges could also be considered moral as long as the exchange was voluntary and relatively equal. Girls mentioned, in particular, the exchange of sexual favors for car rides. Lillie Odell Scruggs, for example, attended high school in town and maintained a relationship with a former classmate now in college, but also kept a boyfriend in the country. He was a farmer with "a good looking car" and a crowd of girls interested in dating him. Although she had no interest in marrying him, to keep him interested she disclosed, "I go with him that way about once a month." Although not stated as an explicit exchange, Lillie seems to have valued her boyfriend's car and popularity, for which she was willing to consent to sex once a month but not to marriage.

Implicit in this view is that a lack of mutuality—in the form of exploitation or deception—made sexual relations immoral. Adolescents consistently described two situations in negative terms: unwanted overtures from white men and voluntary sexual relations resulting in pregnancy. A number of girls described fending off white men who pressured them for sex, especially employers, policemen, and men cruising the street in automobiles. While some feigned deafness to roadside solicitations, Hazel Jones of Louisiana took a different tack: "[When] white men . . . want me to go riding with them, I tell them to go to hell and why don't you get your own women?" Annie Florence Holder spoke with particular anger about a white policeman in town known for "always pinching and hitting the colored girls, and calling himself being very friendly and playing." Holder makes the absence of mutuality clear when she describes the officer as "calling himself being very friendly," pointing to the disparity between an image of jocular sex play held by white harassers and young black women's contrasting view of such sexual overtures as aggressive, hostile acts. Yet despite frequent and fearful encounters with white men, none mentioned these incidents when asked by interviewers about sexual relations. As unwanted advances they fell outside a self-determined framework of mutuality.

Teenagers described pregnancy as another form of unequal sexual exchange between girls and boys or men who "fooled them." Despite in most cases entering into these involvements willingly, the fact that upon finding themselves pregnant young women claimed to have been fooled suggests a moral distinction between intended purpose and unintended results. Savola Lee, an eighteen-year-old mother, recalled: "We was in love and just couldn't wait to get married . . . Well we just got caught, that's all." She quickly amended this to "at least *I* was the one that got caught. I had to quit school . . . I can't have no more pleasures like I used to." Savola's description hints at the meaning of common terms for out-of-wedlock pregnancy—getting "caught," "in trouble," "messed up," and "in misery." The term "getting caught" referred less to being found out—exposed to the community as committing "sinful" or "immoral" acts—than to getting caught up, or ensnared, in undesirable circumstances. Unwed teen mothers typically had to leave school for work in the fields or as a domestic servant, also losing the freedom to date, dance, and go to parties with their peers. These conditions comprised the "trouble," "misery," and "mess" of pregnancy much more than the disapproval that accompanied the discovery of their condition.

Teens who engaged in premarital heterosexuality did so within an ethical framework based on an (apparently movable) line between the type and number of allowable sexual encounters. Although most girls positioned themselves on the side of less rather than more, a few claimed being "fast" as a badge of distinction. Morality offers one view into sexual decision-making, yet people make decisions for many reasons that do not involve personal ethics or social mores. These decisions open a window onto the tangled relationship between sexuality and desire in adolescent lives.

In a number of cases girls spoke openly about their own sexual pleasure and interest as a compelling reason for sex. Agnes Jackson described the pleasure of sex with her current boyfriend, remarking, "You know, I get such a sensation out of the affair." Other girls referred to custom when queried about sex. Lula Strange, a teenage farm laborer and domestic worker, reasoned, "You don't love if you don't do that," explaining that among her peers couples typically had sex after parties or "sometimes after church suppers . . . on the way home." In Lula's eyes, the very definition of love included sexual intimacy.

Besides physical pleasure and social custom, another explanation for sex involved pleasures more social than physical. Doris Brown wrote on a questionnaire that the best things that ever happened to her were "petting" and "playing games of love," suggesting an overlap between physical pleasure and the social involvement that came with love "games." Mattie Lester, a twelfth-grader, described the place of sex among her close female friends: "Lots of times we get together and start talking about our sex experiences." For Mattie and others, sex figured into a social world of peer relations, not simply a private world of dyadic intimacy. Sexual knowledge contained its own pleasures, generating a sense of worldliness that some girls craved. Four-teen-year-old Rosa Mae Harding shared a sense of sophistication with her five girlfriends who as a group discussed sex and enjoyed drink-ing, smoking, and gambling at taverns. She told her interviewer that this lifestyle fed her desire for adventure and what she called her "craving for sex experiences and thrills."

The excitement of the "fast" life could also be linked literally to movement or mobility. Lula Ward, an eighteen-year-old from rural Mississippi, had sex about once a week with her boyfriend and occa-sionally with other boys if, she explained, they had something she wanted. Her terminology leaves it unclear whether the "something" she wanted was sex or some material object or social event to which she could gain access in exchange for sexual intimacy. Boasting that she enjoyed sex even if it did give her a reputation with adults as a "fast" girl, she used "fast" not as a term of reprobation but as an adjec-tive describing her tastes, style, and ambition: "I am the fast type . . . I believe in having a good time and as soon as I can, I am going to leave this place." To Lula, "fast" signaled her orientation toward a "good time" as well as mobility—her wish to leave Mississippi as quickly as possible.

Although Lula Ward only hinted at the practice, a few adolescents explicitly mentioned entering into sexual relations in exchange for economic benefit. Ethel Oliver told her interviewer that girls in her Mississippi community most often got pregnant from dating married men who, unlike single boys, rarely used condoms but could "give them a better time," elaborating, "You know girls like money." Older married men might offer adolescent girls the "good times" that money could buy, but often at the cost of pregnancy and single motherhood. Dorothy Widby, for example, took up with the husband of a family friend when she was barely into her teenage years. After he asked her to be his "little girlfriend," an older cousin advised her to agree in or-der to get money from him. Dorothy at first refused intercourse, but then he made her so "hot" she assented. At twenty-seven, twice her age and willing to buy her anything she wanted, her married lover's power made his pressure hard to refuse, muddying any notion of Dor-othy's self-reported "consent."

Only one young woman reported a direct exchange of sex for money. Everline Waters, a twenty-year-old eleventh-grader from Louisiana, lived with her siblings in town after their mother died and rheumatism had disabled her father. She acknowledged having sex relations with five men, all of whom paid her from twenty-five cents to a dollar for each act. She had become pregnant twice but aborted both times through the use of strong drugs. Although Everline Waters's case suggests the possibility of casual prostitution entered into without immediate physical coercion, her circumstances raise the possibility of sexual activity compelled by peer pressure, economic need, or the kinds of emotional manipulations possible within relationships.

Although such pressures to have sex were more transparent in relationships with older men, a number of adolescents spoke frankly about the sexual pressures they felt from boyfriends close in age. Agnes Jackson generally enjoyed sex, yet qualified her approval, saying, "I don't always want to have an intercourse, but my boyfriend will get mad if I don't, so I just go on and have it." Other teenagers suggested a subtler form of coercion: their understanding that the only way to keep a boyfriend was to have sex with him. When asked about sex, Pauline Nesbitt answered: "You mean do I let him love me? Oh, Yes'm, sometimes I won't but I don't s'pec he'd bother with any girl if he couldn't." Jeanette Whitley of North Carolina echoed this sentiment, reckoning, "If you want to have a beau you have to [have sex] or the boys will go with girls who do." Phrases like "let him love me" and "you have to" suggest that sexual intercourse was something a boy "did" to a girl and not, for some adolescent girls, a mutual and pleasurable activity.

In the worst scenario, sexual relations had nothing to do with either pleasure or maintaining a desired relationship. Myldred Dunn showed signs of great distress when telling her interviewer that she had engaged in more sexual encounters than she could count. None had been with a "sweetheart," but rather with the brothers of her friends, encounters that "just happened" without her active consent or, in her memory, any pleasurable sensations. In addition, a number of interviewers recorded rumors of incestuous relations between girls and their fathers or other male relatives. Adolescents remained mute on this subject, conveying little about sexual violence or trauma in their lives. Nor did they mention sexual relations with white men, even though they spoke freely about harassment. Sexual relations that violated the norms of the community and that exhibited a pattern of clear exploitation or abuse rather than mutual exchange may have haunted African American adolescent girls, but these were feelings they chose not to articulate to interviewers probing about daily life and "ordinary" teenage experience.

The contrast between the silence maintained around issues of incest, rape, and interracial sex and the openness with which informants addressed issues of premarital sex with boyfriends or casual acquaintances suggests that intraracial, nonincestuous, heterosexual sex constituted an acceptable topic of discussion and, at least for some girls, a legitimate activity. Adolescents who opted for abstinence also saw sexual desires—their own or those of men—as feelings to be reckoned with and an area of their life in which they made meaningful decisions.

Teens adhering to a restrictive morality most often presented their desire as social rather than sexual—the desire for social approval and respect. Others gave as their primary reason for sexual abstinence their lack of sexual desire or active dislike of earlier sexual encounters. Mable Holden and Mattie Pearce mentioned their own awkwardness with boys and their perception that boys and men showed no interest in them. But more often teens related the feeling that dating and sex had little appeal for them. At eighteen, Rachel Smith summarily dismissed the subject of sex and men: "I just don't like them—that's all." Nancy Irene Sales told her interviewer that the possibility of pregnancy did not explain her unwillingness to "fool with boys," insisting, "That ain't why I don't do it. I'm telling you the truth, I just don't want to."

Whether they felt free and inclined to engage in sexual relations or lacked either interest or a sense of permission, adolescent girls made decisions about sex that involved a level of complexity not often captured by historians.[16] The Johnson study challenges the ubiquity of middle-class courtship norms and suggests that there were not only competing moral codes among African American southern teens, but also a complex set of incentives and disincentives that girls weighed when they opted to engage in or refrain from sexual relations.

In making decisions about sex, girls had to deal not only with their own expectations and those of adult authorities, but also with those of the boys and men in their lives. A sample of fifty male interviews from the Charles Johnson study confirms that black youth across the South saw sex as a pleasurable activity, one talked about among boys and to be negotiated with girls. Even more than their female peers, adolescent boys described premarital sexual intercourse as common, even expected, for both genders.[17] A few boys stated that they were either too young for sex, uninterested, did not like girls, or girls did not like them. Two others abstained from sex because they believed it was immoral or sinful. The remainder articulated a norm that sex in one's teenage years was not only acceptable but absolutely predictable. Seventeen-year-old Nathan Johnson recounted, "I began having girls when I was fourteen. All the boys I know have them regular."[18]

Teenage boys named three locations as the most common sites for sexual liaisons: the house, the car, or the outdoors. This set of locations, referred to by urban and rural youth alike, interestingly has no connection with the world of vice or commercial pleasures that adults condemned as sexually dangerous. Although some urban teens brought girls to juke joints, dives, and other sites of disrepute, sexual encounters took place most often in areas and during times identified with safety or moral health: the home, the fields, the woods, and during the day, after church or while school was in session. The automobile had a more controversial reputation, having long been identified as a site of sexual iniquity. Yet by the late 1930s cars had lost much of this connotation, having become a necessity of rural life and common in urban life, associated with work, travel, and wholesome leisure rather than a scandalous immorality.

The commonplace locations for sexual encounters reflect the commonplace nature of sex in adolescent boys' lives. Former childhood evangelist Jessie Henderson recalled that even as a young preacher he had been sexually active for the simple reason that "we all do it. I ain't never thought of there being anything wrong to it." Only Joseph Lowry, child of a middle-class businessman, felt plagued by his conscience. Worrying over the morality of sex, he concluded, "I really think it's wrong, but I go on and do it anyway." J. Fernandez Holmes agreed on the sinfulness of sex, but justified his own involvements on the grounds that "I see how everyone else does and there's no use in me being different." The belief that virtually all girls were sexually active, and thus available, also pervaded boys' testimonies. Mark Peters, for instance, doubted if you could find a "girl what don't know noth-ing about men . . . nowadays" to marry. Several boys did make moral judgments, stating their preference for "good girls" who had "nice ways," but this distinction did not rest on sexual experience. Jessie Henderson, for example, explained that he would marry a sexually active girl who was "well thought of" but not one who "had a name for it."

The distinction boys drew between "nice" and "regular" girls some-times, but not always, corresponded to another distinction, an assess-ment of how difficult or easy it was to persuade girls to have sexual intercourse. Lacking moral overtones, this evaluation reflected a kind of cost accounting for how much and what kind of expenditure it took to induce girls to "give it to" a boy. As Charlie B. Hurt explained, "Some girls is easier than the rest. Some you have to talk your head off to make them say yes. And some of them will ask you." Other girls demanded more than talk. "We just give the girls candy, sometimes beer," elaborated John Jackson. "When we have some money they will 'come across.'" The acceptability of premarital sex did not neutralize inequalities based on gender, age, or access to money. The assumed availability of girls, in fact, made bargaining—using whatever leverage one had—a central dynamic in heterosexual relationships.

The notion that girls "gave" sex to boys in exchange for various goods comes through in the testimony of even a shy, unassuming boy smitten by his girlfriend. Roland McJunkins began dating his first and only girlfriend by taking her for ice cream. When his older brother found out that Roland had not even received a kiss for his efforts, the brother teased him until finally he began to ask his girlfriend for more intimacy. Two weeks later, Roland reported, "she gave it to me" in her house when no one was home. A greater degree of coercion is implicit in the account of John Phillips, who described having sex regularly with his friend's sisters while his friend watched out for intruders. He added that his friend also had sex with his own sisters sometimes, presumably while John stood guard. Though he did not report resis-tance on the part of the sisters, the fact that it occurred with more than one sibling, in a house with his brother keeping guard, and sometimes included incestuous sex, indicates that the sex acts may well have been nonconsensual for the girls.

For most boys, sexual access to girls formed a kind of improved fortune or good luck, even when having sex required calculation or pressure. Boys expressed apprehension in only two matters. The fear of sexually transmitted disease formed a threat for boys similar to that of pregnancy for girls. Thomas McDowel approached girls cautiously, believing, "You have to be careful, if you don't you can mess yourself up or mess them up." His statement hints at the gendered meaning of the term "mess." For boys getting "messed up" or "ruined" referred to venereal disease, a messy problem requiring medical treatment and periods of abstinence. But the acceptable act of "messing with" a girl might also lead to "messing her up," the other situation adolescent boys feared.

Fred Holland, a thirteen-year-old from Nashville, explained the risks of sex for boys: "Sometimes you liable to get the girl messed up and she'll have a baby. Then her people are gonna want you to marry her and take care of her. I wouldn't marry her though." Joseph McLaurin also looked reluctantly on the prospect of marriage. He had been dating the same girl for over three years, having sexual relations on a regular basis with the expectation that marriage would follow. At least his girlfriend expected it. He explained, "We're supposed to be co'tin but I don't think I'm gonna marry her." Condoms, for the boys who used them, offered protection from disease and from the likely event that if a sexual partner got pregnant, he would face pressure to support her.[19] In either case, being "messed up" for boys referred more to a temporary loss of a carefree sex life than the permanent loss of freedom that girls ascribed to unwed motherhood.

Girls understood the mess of pregnancy and expressed an almost uniform desire to avoid conception. Yet only twenty-five of the nearly two hundred transcripts contain any discussion of birth control devices or practices. Because some interviewers seem to have asked pointed questions about contraception while most did not, this small sample is not representative of black southern girls in general nor does it indicate the extent of knowledge and use of birth control even among the study's participants. It does suggest something about range of knowledge, however. Nineteen-year-old Hazel Jones, who hoped to attend West Virginia State College and become a teacher, insisted that her partner wear a "merry widow," or condom, because "I don't want a baby and I don't want any disease either." In stark contrast, Agnes

Jackson did not use condoms, yet still did not fear pregnancy because "I just don't feel that anything is going to happen." These opposite approaches offer tantalizing hints about fertility control as understood and practiced by young women of the South at a time when courts had only just legalized the dissemination of birth control devices and information through the mail and when contraception was available in only a tiny number of birth control clinics around the country.[20]

Fourteen-year-old Bettye Watson, who was planning to avoid premarital pregnancy, appeared confident that despite having sex on a daily basis she could prevent conception by refraining from sex during menstruation, the time she believed insemination occurred. When informed that she had misunderstood the "safe period," Bettye rejected the new information as false. Fortunately she did not rely solely on the rhythm method, reporting as well that her boyfriend sometimes used condoms and at other times practiced withdrawal, which she described as telling "him to stop just before he gets ready to mess you up." Watson's references to condoms, withdrawal, and rhythm point to the three forms of birth control named by the teens who mentioned contraception. Besides Watson, eleven girls reported either personally relying on condoms or knowing other teenagers in the community who did. They referred to condoms as "rubbers," "merry widows," "a little round thing" used by boys, "protection," or having men be "covered up." Although this form of birth control depended entirely on their boyfriends' willingness to use a contraceptive device, adolescent girls had some say in that they could insist on this practice or, short of that, at least know whether they were engaging in safe or risky sex.

Coitus interruptus, or withdrawal, left girls more dependent on their partners' active interest and good timing in preventing conception. Despite her concern about possible pregnancy, sixteen-year-old Pauline Nesbitt explained that there "ain't no chance of getting a baby 'cause what makes the baby all goes in the handkerchief." Vivian Low, a twelfth-grader from Nashville, repeated a common saying that "it's a lazy man who gives a girl a baby," explaining that men who were not "lazy" did not need condoms because they withdrew before ejaculation. Low and several others knew of women who had undergone abortions, yet felt confident that they would not face this choice since their own sexual partners would act responsibly to avoid pregnancy.

If condoms and withdrawal left teenage girls dependent on men to protect them, the rhythm method gave girls more control in the sense that they themselves made decisions about when to engage in sexual relations and when to refrain. It had the distinct disadvantage, however, of depending, first, on a girl's access to correct information and subsequently on her ability to keep accurate track of her cycle and then to say no in the face of either her own desire or that of her partner. In the two cases where adolescents mentioned this as their method of birth control, neither girl operated with accurate information. While Bettye Watson believed that conception occurred only during menstruation, Eleanor Williams understood the "safe period" for sex to extend from the middle of her cycle to just before menstruation.

Lacking reliable contraception, a number of teenagers turned to the riskiest possible method of pregnancy prevention—an alchemy of hope, luck, and denial. Ophelia Hamilton, a fifteen-year-old from rural Louisiana, told her boyfriends that she did not want to become pregnant, but after that single act of self-assertion relied on them to honor her request. As she explained, "I tell the boys not to make me pregnant. I don't know how they do it, but they don't make me that way, so they must keep from it some way." Other young women relied purely on chance or their own sense of invulnerability. Sixteen-year-old Frances Reed reported that despite having had numerous lovers she did not fear pregnancy because "I just don't think nothing's goin' to happen to me."[21]

If luck and hope spelled the least reliable types of pregnancy prevention, the method of contraception that birth control advocates championed as most effective for women, the diaphragm, appears nowhere in these accounts.[22] Just as they faced profoundly restricted educational and occupational opportunities, black girls in the South had little access to quality medical care, in general, or reproductive health care in particular. This fact, however, may not have set them apart from the larger set of unmarried American teenagers who, whatever their economic background, did not have the legal right to contraceptive information or to utilize existing birth control clinics designed to assist married women only.[23] Similarly, girls from all backgrounds paid a steep price for pregnancy, financially, socially, and morally. The effects of contraceptive failure may have been in some respects less severe for black girls than white, since at least some sector of African American communities did not stigmatize children born out of wedlock as "illegitimate" or condemn their mothers to permanent disrepute. Black teens' use of terms like "messed up" and "caught" suggests that in comparison to the white girls "ruined" by unmarried pregnancy, black adolescent mothers suffered relatively milder consequences. Yet African American girls had on average fewer financial resources and found themselves excluded from social services like maternity homes or adoption programs that offered unmarried white girls the option of giving birth and then returning to "normal" teenage life followed by conventional marriage and motherhood.[24] References to pregnancy as being "in misery" suggest that even without lasting social stigma, early childbirth for teenage black girls carried long-term hardships and the loss of already limited opportunities.

In the end, the little information we have about birth control use among black adolescent girls is most compelling as further evidence of the varied meanings of sex in their lives. The use of contraception, like sexuality in general, could be part of an adolescent girl's struggle to create a more desirable life in the immediate present or the distant future. Certainly the insistence on condoms or withdrawal illustrates the ability of some teenagers to act pragmatically and proactively in their effort to find pleasure in the moment and still preserve opportunities for education, work, or mobility. Expressed reliance on luck and chance struck some interviewers at the time—and may appear today—as a reckless denial of the consequences of unprotected sex that foolishly sacrificed the future for momentary pleasure. Yet in fact, most black teenage girls in the South had very little control over their futures regardless of their sexual behavior. Most could not afford to finish high school, much less attend college. The gender- and race-stratified southern labor market limited their job opportunities almost exclusively to farm labor or domestic work. And marriage, which did not customarily depend on premarital virginity or the absence of children, rarely brought upward mobility even under the best of circumstances.

Without a stroke of luck an adolescent's hard work, self-denial, and

Many African American girls who grew up picking cotton and observing their mothers' lives of unrelenting toil conceived of marriage in pragmatic rather than romantic terms. Repeated statements like "Before I marry a farmer I wouldn't marry at all" expressed their greatest desire–to escape farm labor. Ben Shahn, Library of Congress, LC-USF33–006218-M3.

determination would probably not create a future that differed much from her present life—that is, depending on "luck" and "fate" in sexual matters was not likely to significantly change lives already severely constrained by racism and poverty. At its worst, sex without protection signaled pressured sexual involvements, forming part of the mesh of obligatory and unsatisfying relations that marred the lives of poor southern girls who dreaded picking cotton, found little pleasure or opportunity in school, and saw few prospects in marriage. At its best, sexual activity offered some immediate enjoyment in otherwise difficult lives, forming part of the fabric of a life oriented toward enhancing available pleasures without becoming too invested in a future beyond one's control.

African American scholars worked hard to secure a better future for the youth of their communities. With this objective in mind, they struggled over how to relate their findings to a largely white audience conditioned by commonplace sexual stereotypes and inaccuracies. A report from the Negro Youth Study to the American Youth Commission described the continuing need to disprove "the earlier supposition that the Negro child differs racially, that is biologically, from other children in temperamental qualities and general aptitudes."[25] AYC authors adopted a two-pronged approach, attempting to refute scientific racism and myths of black women's promiscuity while coming to terms with sexual moralities that differed from the stated norms of white middle-class youth of the era (and their own).

They wrote in conversation with John Dollard's very influential 1937 study of southern caste and class relations in the Delta. Dollard described a black "folk culture" characterized by indulgent behavior, unrestrained by middle-class inhibitions against sexual and physical aggression. Consequently, the typically "disorganized" Negro family placed fewer controls on children than white families did, especially in late adolescence. The Negro personality developed, then, with greater "impulse freedom," giving black Americans more access to the "pleasure principle" and "libido outflow" than a repressed white society allowed. Although written with a certain amount of envy at the Negro's freedom from "impulse management," Dollard's references to family disorganization, dependence, and lack of control evoked images of pathology already familiar in academia and popular culture.[26]

Dollard elaborated his "caste and class" framework when he teamed up with the African American anthropologist Allison Davis in *Children of Bondage,* a 1940 study of thirty black teenagers in Natchez, Mississippi, and New Orleans. Despite their claims that "lower-class" children of both white and black races exhibited similar kinds of behaviors, since the project did not include any data on white adolescents, the personality problems analyzed by the authors seemed to characterize black youth alone. For instance, Davis and Dollard chose to portray lower-class girlhood through the story of sixteen-year-old Julia Wilson, described as a "tigerish Amazon" whose "insatiable aggression" toward men made her an embittered but "clever and unrelenting exploiter of men."[27] In the end, given their claim that three-quarters of black Americans fell into a lower-class category characterized by a "relative lack of socialization" and an unwillingness to renounce direct impulse gratification, even occasional examples of "well-adjusted" teenagers did little to alter the impression of sexual pathology among southern black youth.[28]

Charles Johnson's study of rural southern youth, *Growing Up in the Black Belt,* drew on the relativism advanced by the "culture and personality" school that came to prominence in the interwar period. Theorists like Johnson used a nonjudgmental pluralist framework to analyze differences in human behavior and values as the product of particular social environments and group cultures. He suggested that characteristics of black sexuality that might signal immorality in the dominant culture made sense and could even be considered an asset in rural black culture. He saw, for example, the relatively greater freedom of sexual expression among rural Negro youth as an alternative form of self-expression for teens suffering from feelings of racial inadequacy and the reality of blocked social and economic ambitions in the Jim Crow South.[29]

Yet Johnson could not escape the language of cultural pathology. Despite finding that women headed fewer than one in five of the study's 916 participating families, he nevertheless described the key features of Negro family life as female independence and male irresponsibility. Suffering consequently from a "defective cultural inheritance" and the "handicap of imperfect organization," southern Negro youth exhibited a matter-of-fact attitude about premarital sexual behavior and a lack of reticence or embarrassment about sex compared to the "rigid sex regulations" that characterized the dominant American culture.[30]

In contrast, he saw middle-class black youth as valuing discretion over sexual expression and moving gradually closer to white standards of sexual repression, values held in absolute reverence by the much smaller stratum of upper-class Negroes. The fact that Johnson characterized the development of stricter sexual standards as an index of cultural advancement suggests that no matter how sensible and appropriate were the sexual standards of lower-class blacks, who comprised 82 percent of the adolescents in his study, their behaviors represented the opposite of cultural advancement—cultural backwardness and deficiency.

E. Franklin Frazier's *Negro Youth at the Crossways* came closer than other AYC studies to rejecting all notions of black adolescent pathology. Observing that among lower- and middle-class black youth "heterosexual activity seems to be one of the few unrestricted sexual outlets," he argued that such sexual laxity or "promiscuity" reflected ordinary personality development in a permissive culture. Furthermore, he warned his readers against "projecting most of our privately condemned faults" onto black Americans simply because they had failed to adopt the nation's "historic puritanism."[31] Insisting on a pluralist cultural framework, Frazier rejected any attempts by white academics and audiences to find in black sexual behavior a foil of promiscuous immorality for an opposing image of white morality.

Yet Frazier's use of value-laden terms like "promiscuous people" and sexual "laxity" gave nod to the maxim that a certain degree of sexual repression characterized well-adjusted individuals and a well-functioning society. By contrasting the generalized sexual behavior of black youth with the "historic *puritanism*" of the dominant culture, Frazier's findings support Charles Johnson's claim that within the parameters of black rural society the sexual mores of African American adolescents were both internally consistent and no more or less "moral" than the mores of the dominant society. Yet in their efforts to condemn racism while affirming black culture, Frazier, Johnson, and other AYC authors found themselves caught in an intellectual trap and the web of their own nagging ambivalence.[32]

On the one hand, they argued that black children and adolescents followed the same developmental process as any other group of children. But on the other hand, they also believed that "caste-like barriers" to opportunities, success, and prestige marred the "adjustment process" of Negro youth, whose behavior merited "special concern." This problem begged a deeper one: What would constitute a healthy adjustment to racial inequality? The Committee on Negro Youth argued, "The very necessity of becoming accommodated to an unequal relationship is itself problematic." Yet this is what they found themselves trying to measure. And though the authors argued that the "number of distorted personalities" surprised them less than the number of youth who had achieved a "survival type of accommodation" to their circumstances, in the long run they committed themselves to an assimilationist project in which black youth would overcome their personality "distortions" by acquiring personalities that resembled those of well-adjusted white youth.[33]

With this goal in mind, sympathetic social scientists cast the more restrained sexual codes of black middle-class and upper-class society as ultimately more desirable than the "promiscuous" or "distorted" patterns observed among some, but not all, rural and working-class African Americans. References to promiscuity and laxity lent credence to commonplace accusations of black female immorality. Moreover, in their ambivalent response to their own findings, the AYC scholars missed the well-articulated moral system that guided the sexually active teens they studied. Then, applying the axiomatic view that female (rather than male) premarital or extramarital sex denoted sexual "laxity," their findings ascribed to adolescent black girls the very qualities of cultural deficiency and troubled personality they intended to dispel.

Historians have faced a similar conundrum when evaluating adolescent sexuality. Although aware of diverse norms that governed dating, courtship, and sexual behavior, most have emphasized the predominance of a "rating and dating" system that from the 1920s through the 1950s comprised the experience of a majority of teenagers.[34] They have described white middle-class sexuality as operating along two intersecting axes: the axis of popularity and pleasure in the present balanced against the axis of sexual reputation and social and economic opportunities for the future. Assuming that boys would always push for as much sexual pleasure in the present as possible, girls carried the responsibility of finding the balance point between maximum social popularity and sexual pleasure in the here-and-now and maintaining their chances of long-term success and happiness through marriage. Since women's economic well-being corresponded closely to the class standing of the men they married, decisions made as a teenager had long-term effects that could determine the course of a woman's life.

Or so the story went. When looking at African American adolescent girls of the South, the picture is not so neatly drawn. If the generic portrait of white teenagers of the 1920s and 1930s is one in which adolescent dating, "petting," and romance led gradually toward "true love," marriage, and monogamous sexual intimacy, black girls told a different story, one in which love and romance did not necessarily lead to marriage, and sexual intimacy had no necessary connection to love, romance, or marriage. Pragmatism far more than romantic love guided a young woman's decisions about sexuality and marriage, which significantly often remained separate from her fantasies of marriage and mobility.

Like other teenagers, southern African American girls sometimes spoke of an idealized form of marriage that promised the possibility of long-term sexual and emotional intimacy, material comfort, and economic security. But the premium placed on virginity as the exchange medium for marital success and happiness struck many black adolescents as nonsensical. First, while some members in their communities held that sex should be reserved only for marriage, another sector of the population believed that premarital sex or even having a child did not disqualify a woman for respectable marriage. According to this view, marriage—not sex—was the rare commodity, held in reserve as a special relationship entered into only at the right time, under the right conditions, with the right person.

Many teenage girls, however, expressed a far less sanguine view of marriage. For example, marriage appeared to offer little in the way of pleasure or security to Sadie Barnes, a fourteen-year-old from North Carolina who viewed wedlock as a loss of pleasure and an end to freedom. She alluded to the twin dangers of dependence and subordination: "I don't want to lose my pleasure, my freedom . . . I don't want anyone to boss me." Fifteen-year-old Salome Hinton also saw "no sense in letting a man boss you around and you have to do what he says just because he's your husband and has you. I want to be free to do the things I want to." Others spoke even more bluntly, declaring "husbands do their wives bad around here" or, simply, "There ain't no good men."[35]

Having witnessed close-up their mothers' hardships, teenagers knew that marriage required of wives a significant amount of unpaid household labor, almost certainly performed in addition to—rather than instead of—paid labor outside the home. With the unerring logic of a twelve-year-old, Geneva Gardner calculated, "When you marry you have to work hard and I don't like to [work] hard. I guess I won't marry." This sentiment rang especially true for rural girls who saw the life of married farm women in their communities and wanted no part of it. Carrie Randolph and Mamie Philpot made this point emphatically, declaring respectively, "Before I marry a farmer I wouldn't

Private homes, along with cars and the outdoors, were the most frequent sites for teenage sexual liaisons. At the same time, impoverished girls fantasized about improbable marriages to professional men who would provide homes far removed from their own—houses with windows, multiple rooms, new furniture, and a painted exterior. Walker Evans, Library of Congress, LC-USF342–008016-A.

marry at all" and "I sure ain't going to marry a farmer, and there don't be nothin' else here." Hoping to avoid this cycle of endless toil and poverty, rural teens envisioned alternatives. Mable Holden hoped to marry "an educated man so that he would know how to make a living and I would not have to work in the fields all my life." Carrie Randolph also imagined a rich husband but, in a less optimistic moment, indicated that she would probably end up marrying a poor man "because he will be just like I am."

African Americans like Carrie Randolph were not immune to notions of romantic love and wedded bliss. Yet marriage operated in the teenage imaginary less as a fantasy of romantic love than as a romantic fantasy about material well-being, security, and comfort. Ida Lee Barrett's avid reading of romance magazines like *True Stories* fueled fantasies about marrying into wealth, to "a man that has something," while Ethel Lee Sanders hoped to marry a lawyer, doctor, or mail clerk and not work outside the home. Fourteen-year-old Earnestine Walker, who earned seventy-five cents a day doing farm labor, was even choosier, picturing marriage to a doctor who would provide two children and a home in town.

Adolescent girls used movies, popular magazines, or simply their own imaginations to create fantasies about future occupations as well as marriages. After reading *True Confessions,* fourteen-year-old Gertrude Hallon imagined working as a nurse "'cause I don't want to be picking cotton all my days." Hazel Woodard hoped to continue her education then move to New York and become a beautician, allowing her to "make money so I can have a real nice home and go with nice people and buy mother pretty clothes." She planned eventually to "marry a settled man who is kind of old because they won't run off and leave you." Romance infused Hazel's fantasies about jobs and migration, while marriage seemed less a romantic proposition than a possible means of achieving security and stability. Romance appears only rarely in black girls' accounts of actual dating and sexual relationships. Instead it fueled fantasies of plenitude that bestowed an abundance of clothing, food, comfort, leisure, travel, and independence, as well as love.

Sex, in this scheme, might be part of a fantasy of romantic marriage to a wealthy professional or one's "true love." Then again, it might be one element in a girl's pragmatic approach to finding what pleasure and opportunity she could in a harsh life and circumscribed future. Although many teens viewed sex as inappropriate before marriage, neither these girls nor those embracing a more permissive standard cast sexuality in highly romantic terms. Sex represented a set of possibilities for love, affection, adventure, or material goods. But it might also represent an obligation, a medium of exchange, or a source of danger, whether in the form of unwanted pregnancy, unwanted touching, or illicit relations that resulted in disrepute or punishment. These potential meanings of sex developed against the backdrop of white male sexual overtures and assaults, which occurred in tandem with cultural condemnation of black women as promiscuous perpetrators, rather than victims, of illicit interracial sex.

The fact that black girls' sexual desires sometimes merged with romantic dreams and marital hopes reflects an ideal of adolescent romantic love pervasive in twentieth-century U.S. culture. The fact that sexual desire and romantic fantasy also operated in every possible combination with pragmatic calculation and shrewd maneuvering speaks to the way teenagers balanced copious fantasies with common sense. The contradictions lie less in their minds than in the circumstances of their lives. Black girls lived in a culture of consumption that promised abundance and personal gratification to those who looked and acted "right" (or white); yet more immediately, this culture consumed the energy, money, and hopes of their mothers and other women whose lives they hoped not to replicate. Living in conditions too often characterized by a poverty of goods, opportunities, and sometimes love, sexual desire formed part and parcel of material and emotional desires for a more nourishing and exciting life that would afford a degree of control and respect found largely in their imaginations.

The stated expectations of poor teenagers struck sociologists as disconcertingly improbable. Over and over again, girls described their fantasy future as either securing a job that guaranteed a good income, mobility, and independence or marrying a doctor, businessman, or other professional who would provide a nice house and wardrobe, limit family size, and whose income would enable her to remain at home or at least not work "too hard." Because these imagined futures failed to mesh with adolescents' day-to-day lives, interviewers for the Johnson study judged teen fantasies as unrealistic, silly, and even harmful, declaring the gap between expectation and reality "so great to suggest that the expectation itself borders on fantasy."[36]

But there is another way to approach such fantasies. Grace Dorothy Pinson at sixteen wanted to be a blues singer, piano teacher, or stenographer. She entertained the possibility of marriage, but specified, "I want to marry a man that's got a good job so I'll be somebody." Such "wish images" were moments of utopian imagination important not because they might come true but because they enabled young African American women to envision themselves as capable of, and entitled to, having more—more money, candy, or love; more security or adventure; and most of all, more power to shape their lives.[37]

Grace Pinson's statement that through marrying a rich man "I'll be somebody" indicates, sadly, her understanding that in 1930s America a poor rural black girl from the South did not have much societal value. But it also expressed her sense of entitlement to both the goods of society and her own personhood. That African American teenagers recognized themselves as "somebody" by envisioning a future that had no basis in "reality" speaks not to a failure of practical planning but to the success of their imaginations; having a "head full of diamonds," as one blues singer described his teenage girlfriend's childish dreams, could create an even more important reality—a realization of self.[38] Its significance lay not in the likelihood of a dream come true but in the hope, the wish, the impractical vision that affirmed a girl's worth by insisting that her value as a person did not derive from her current material worth, marital prospects, or devalued status in society, but rather inhered in her very being and thus could transcend present circumstances for an imagined, much improved, future.

In a society that imposed harsh judgments on the poor, the uneducated, the rural, the sexually vulnerable, and African Americans, black adolescent girls understood that in the larger picture their lives were worth less than those of others, a recognition that, when fully internalized, could quickly change to feelings of worthlessness. When deprived of material goods and social worth, imagining oneself as deserving of something better registers as an act of survival. For a girl to maintain a sense that she deserves what she did not get in the past and may not get in the future—and that she herself can be the agent of change—is a profound act of subjective affirmation in the face of objective difficulty.

chapter five

"*Living in Hopes*"

An Economy of Desire

By the 1930s, a modern southerner was defined, in part, by his or her participation in the cash economy. Mollie Goodwin, the eldest daughter of poor white tenant farmers, measured her life in terms of access to cash and material goods. When living at home, lack of money and her father's strict rules constrained her social life. Unable to buy clothes and not permitted to join friends at rural parties for ice cream and kissing games, she feared her life would mirror that of her mother, whose constant labor had destroyed her health and made her old before her time. Mollie's luck turned when a relative offered her the chance to board in town. She ran away from home and for four months worked at a factory making twenty dollars a week, sharing meals and conversation with other young working women while delighting in purchases like store-bought food and factory-made coats, hats, shoes, dresses, and jewelry. Entry into the world of goods expanded her marriage options as well. She dated a worker in a nearby cigarette factory who asked her to marry, but she rejected the proposal, reasoning, "Why should I marry and keep house and have babies when I've got such a good job and can buy myself such fine clothes?"[1] For adolescents like Mollie, the shift from country to town and from nonwage to wage labor created a thrilling range of choices that included not only the kind of shoes to buy, but also when, whether, and whom to marry.

Experiences like Mollie's led reformers and social critics to define country girls who migrated to the city as a serious social problem linked to sex delinquency. The young migrant worker and "problem girl" shared mobility, freedom from adult oversight, a small wage that nevertheless allowed some consumer purchases, and a greater range of sexual and marital options than available at home. Yet Mollie appeared not in the records of social workers or reformatories but as a portrait in Margaret Hagood's *Mothers of the South.* Published in 1939 as a study of the ravages of the Depression on white female tenant farmers, Hagood presented Molly, initially, as a temporary ray of hope in an otherwise gloomy prognosis.

Molly would not have recognized herself in the portrayals of either reformers or social scientists. Where experts saw relative poverty and limited opportunities, Molly described herself as fortunate to work in a factory, eager to consume modern merchandise, and hopeful that she could create a life different from her mother, who did fit the image of haggard, worn-to-the-bone tenant mothers. Even though young wage earners commonly turned over all or most of their earnings to the family, employed girls—especially if living away from home—had some disposable income to spend on items like clothing, jewelry, hats, shoes, hair styling, and entertainment. Their participation in the consumer economy contributed to the economic changes and urbanization of the South. But even more important, those purchases that critics condemned as frivolous and wasteful, wage-earning girls viewed as the building blocks of pleasure, independence, and self-transformation. In the early to mid-twentieth-century South, an adolescent girl's sense of self, her romantic fantasies, and her image of the future commonly incorporated a world of material goods like clothing, makeup, shoes, and home furnishings such as curtains, linens, or beds.

Southern girls typically acquired their first cash and opportunities for consumption in early to middle adolescence, when they were also experiencing physiological changes related to sexual maturity and, perhaps, their first stirrings of sexual interest and desire. As adolescent girls entered into a culture of consumption, their encounters with material goods stimulated desires, prompted actions, and evoked feelings that related, directly or indirectly, to their sexual desires and decisions. When asked about spending money, girls almost always mentioned clothing first. Store-bought clothes and other consumer

Girls typically acquired their first cash and shopping opportunities in early to middle adolescence. Typical purchases were store-bought clothing, shoes, and items like makeup or hair products. Here, Louisiana girls relax while applying fingernail polish, probably bought with their own money. Ben Shahn, Library of Congress, LC-USF33–006214-M5.

goods played a very concrete role in determining an adolescent's class and racial status, in forming peer relations, and in delimiting opportunities for dating and courtship. But consumer purchases also fed romantic fantasies about life and love beyond what most girls' current circumstances allowed. Adolescents used the possibilities of material goods to nourish a sense of self-worth measured in terms that frequently offended older, privileged southerners quick to pass judgment on girls attempting to turn cotton bolls into raiments that could outfit their strongest desires.

As they took factory jobs, sold cash crops at market, and entered into other forms of wage labor, southerners of all types had more money to spend. They also had more places to spend it, from small-town general stores to big-city department stores, mail order catalogues, and popular forms of commercial entertainment. In these locations the number and variety of objects for purchase also expanded from rudimentary household staples like sugar, cloth, and coffee to factory-made clothing, hats, movies, magazines, furniture, restaurant food, liquor, and automobiles.[2]

This transformation did not signal progress to all southerners. In their 1930s antimodern manifesto *I'll Take My Stand,* conservatives like Allan Tate and John Crowe Ransom attacked consumption as one of the primary evils of industrial society. Advocating a return to agrarian self-sufficiency, intellectuals known collectively as the "Agrarians" assailed cash-based commodity consumption as "the grand end which justifies the evils of modern labor." As one of industrialism's "false prophets," consumption, like labor, became "brutal and hurried." It deceived the farmer into purchasing mass-produced goods, depriving him of the honest product of his labor, leading eventually to a condition of "satiety and aimlessness."[3] This reasoning would not have convinced Mollie Goodwin, whose purchases were anything but aimless, conducted with the intent to enjoy a life she could never live as a rural tenant.

For Molly, consumption represented a small rebellion in which goods and shopping signaled the end to a childhood marred by poverty and desperately few options.[4] Yet the connections between goods and freedom remained tenuous at best. Her luck ended when after four months in the city she returned at her father's urgent request to help tend to her younger siblings. Illness in the family and a sense of obligation kept her from running away when her father refused her repeated requests to go back to the cigarette factory, which he saw as an improper place for women. Instead she married an older man, admittedly one who did not excite her like younger boys did. She then settled into a life she found dull and disappointing except for a cherished daughter in whom she invested her faded hopes for a different, more modern, kind of life.[5]

In Molly Goodwin's story and others like it, the purchase of mass-produced goods not only defined the line between old and new in the South, but also contributed to demarcating the divisions between social classes, races, and genders. Consuming—shopping, purchasing, owning, and displaying or using—is most obviously a practice through which wealthier people mark themselves as different from, and often better than, poorer people through the accumulation of goods. Civil rights activist Ella Baker came of age in the South during the 1910s and early 1920s. Her father's job as a waiter earned the family middle-class status in their community, a status Baker defined as meaning that "you had all the things that people bought."[6] Home furnishings such as sewing machines, dining room furniture, and silver provided the internal signs of a middle-class status signaled on the outside by the size, condition, location, and ownership of a home.

Beyond the home, the body served as the primary carrier of class distinctions. Through dress, gesture, and manner of speaking, people communicated to others their actual, or sometimes desired, place in the social order. The importance of clothing as a marker of class is in no way limited to the modern South, as evidenced by much older sumptuary laws and more recent uses of designer fashions. Yet as both cash and consumption became essential to the lives of more and more southerners, and as geographic mobility reduced the significance of one's "name" as an immediately recognizable indicator of class status, the purchase and display of consumer goods, and especially clothing, grew in importance as a method of marking and assessing class within the region.

Modern practices of racial segregation and consumption developed together as fundamentally interconnected forms of social relation. While white domestic space remained "integrated" by black servants and electoral politics operated to exclude African Americans, public commercial space formed the ground on which white southerners constructed the edifice of de jure and de facto racial segregation known as Jim Crow. Government entities such as schools, libraries, and parks tended to divide completely into separate "white" and "colored" facilities (if any were provided for African Americans). Commercial services like trains, buses, streetcars, and waiting rooms proved more difficult to segregate given the constant inflow and outflow of customers. They instituted Jim Crow through maintaining separate sections within a shared space, dividing off white and black seating areas with lines that often shifted according to the flow of people.

Places where people bought and consumed goods proved the hardest to segregate and thus took on added importance for both advocates and opponents of Jim Crow. Saturday afternoons in any small town or big city's central commercial district produced an integrated scene of black and white shoppers walking the same streets, looking in the same shop windows, and lining up for purchase at some of the same store counters. A white man from Columbus, Mississippi, recalled the shopping district of his boyhood, where on Mobile Avenue "dozens of bargain-merchandise stores" were patronized by a racially mixed clientele of "customers mainly from the plantations, cotton factories, and sawmills."[7] Against this tendency to mix freely, store owners installed separate water fountains and restrooms, served all whites before any black customer, and often designated racially specific credit terms and policies for trying on or returning merchandise.[8]

Segregation took multiple forms in consumption, but always operated in tension with business's ultimate goal of sales; white merchants, valuing the color green more than distinctions between black and white, still sought African American customers. Furthermore, segregation was made more difficult by the very nature of shopping, which involves a certain amount of wandering through aisles, touching of products, intimate contact between sales clerk and customer around items like clothing or toiletries, and a loosely defined, constantly shifting use of space as lines form and reform. Thus commodity culture's racial divisions proved the least stable of the various forms of segregation in the Jim Crow South, and is one of the reasons that midcentury African Americans targeted downtown shopping districts, lunch counters, and public transportation for the boycotts and sit-ins that launched the modern civil rights movement.

A more informal kind of segregation developed along gender lines. When large department stores first dotted the northern urban landscape in the last third of the nineteenth century, the presence of women shoppers disturbed a longstanding male monopoly of public urban space. In the early decades of the twentieth century, the gender divide faded as throngs of women workers and consumers moved through the city with ease. "Shopping" acquired an association with women's labor and leisure, reflecting both female domestic responsibilities and a feminine fantasy world that offered escape from household drudgery.[9] By the interwar period, these connotations held true for southern towns and cities as well, although in rural areas farm women still commonly allowed men to "tote the pocketbook" and do most of the family purchasing on trips to town.[10]

As a female activity, shopping has helped define not only what women do but also who they are and imagine themselves to be. Because of women's second-class status in the labor market, class mobility or maintenance has for women typically depended on marriage to a good provider. Material goods have served as both a means to this end—with clothing, makeup, and hairstyles being used to attract a "good" husband—and the reward for success. For relatively poor teenagers, their own lack of goods led to an envious awareness of "how the goods of that world of privilege might be appropriated, with the cut and fall of a skirt, a good winter coat, with leather shoes, a certain voice; but above all with clothes, the best boundary between you and a cold world."[11] The material boundaries of privilege corresponded to psychic boundaries. Owning little or having less easily turned into a sense of being less; this often translated into a perceived boundary between self and other, or between groups of "haves" and "have-nots." A girl's subjective responses to her desires and disappointments spawned emotions that were in one sense individual. But comparable responses among teens similarly situated in the hierarchy of southern society led to shared structures of feeling—a class-conscious subjectivity that girls carried with them as they moved toward adulthood and made decisions about labor, leisure, and love. Identity, desire, and economic privilege or privation did not form separate compartments of experience. Rather the labor, adventure, romance, and pain involved in acquiring "things" as well as erotic or emotional gratification together constitute an economy of desire. In their fused longings for both material and emotional "goods," southern teenage girls used simple items like clothing to fuel a consumer economy, remake regional courtship traditions, and fashion their own identities.

Clothing is, along with shelter, a literal boundary between a person and a cold world. For many working-class girls—rural, town, and urban adolescents living near subsistence—clothes were a necessary but not-taken-for-granted commodity that could figure into the family economy in several ways. The scarcity or shabbiness of clothing at a time of growing self-consciousness might signal to a girl her poverty and vulnerability within a distressed kin network. Many parents and children of poor farm families in the 1930s reported that threadbare or insufficient clothing was one of the primary obstacles to continued school attendance, especially in consolidated rural schools where the sartorial signs of poverty were in visible contrast to the greater quantity and quality of clothes worn by "town kids."[12] In such families, an adolescent's first move toward economic independence involved taking responsibility for clothing. White tobacco-farming tenants often gave older children their own "patch" to farm along with their regular chores, with any money earned allocated for clothing.[13] In African American families, girls frequently stayed out of school in the early fall to earn money for clothes by picking cotton. The purchase of clothing represented a daughter's independence and her contribution to a family's basic subsistence.[14]

A girl's entrance into wage labor might also mean a transition from bare adequacy to something better. In these cases, adolescent earnings represented improved living conditions and a new measure of independence. After moving frequently among the homes of a grandparent, aunt, and stepmother during the worst years of the Depression, Mozelle Riddle's life improved when she joined the stream of white teenagers who began working in the mills in their early to mid-teens: "I felt better. I felt like I could have a little something . . . I did have a little money to buy me clothes, and I didn't have nothing [before]."[15] Other teenagers from farm or mill villages also referred to the desire for new clothes as a determining factor in the decision to leave school for work. Annie Viola Fries recalled that as a young girl she wore dresses her mother sewed from flour sacks. Then as a teenager, "I felt like I should help out . . . Then too I was old enough that I wanted things too, like clothes. I wanted to have my own things and didn't want to be begging somebody all the time for stuff . . . So I just told Mama that I'd quit school and go to work."[16]

Whether she kept part or all of her earnings for herself or turned them over to her parents, a girl's wages represented more than a contribution to the family economy; they meant a new semi-adult status often symbolized by the new clothing she purchased or that parents bought for a working daughter. Factory work especially encouraged a new commercial outlook among teenage mill workers, since on the farm girls were the least likely to share in cash earnings. Upon receiving her first paycheck in Dalton, Georgia, a girl typically bought not only an outfit for herself but also a dress and shoes for each younger sister, an act of generosity that signaled her new status as earner and consumer.[17] A fine store-bought dress or coat conveyed the subtle shifts in family relations that accompanied teenage wage labor. With cash wages, a daughter's labor might become more valuable or essential, even as her actual or potential earnings made her more powerful and independent. This could translate into greater pressure from parents to contribute, or conversely a weaker parental command of a teenager's education, labor, and leisure time.[18]

Middle-class girls also described clothing as a matter of central concern, but their interest was more social than economic. In autobiographical essays written by white Alabama high school students in the 1940s, one girl recalled buying her first evening dress for a junior high school music recital, while another marked the occasion of her first date by wearing her first "formal" gown. Others mentioned clothes in relation to hobbies. One daughter of a wealthy farmer wrote of "cowgirls clothes" she wore to show her prize-winning cattle, another mentioned sewing as her favorite summer pastime, while a third wrote that she liked to help her mother rearrange the furniture and plan her clothing for summer and winter.[19] Clothing and household goods entered a realm of middle-class leisure that existed apart from working-class adolescent economic activities like wage labor or self-financed consumption.

As important as clothes were to the material aspects of teenage economies, they were probably more powerful as a reference point for strong emotions. Feelings of shame, pride, and envy stand out among the emotional resonances of clothing. Shame derives from an awareness of absence, lack, or deficiency relative to others, although recognizing such a difference does not in all cases produce shame. Gladys Griffin, a white mill worker from North Carolina, recalled that she and her eight siblings "had a rough time coming up, we didn't have things like other families . . . I went to work when I was ten . . . We helped support the family this way. Mother would buy what we wore and everything, and she provided good for us. We didn't have fancy things."[20] Griffin's sense of lack—indicated by "rough time" and not having "fancy things"—is countered by her sense of adequacy, represented by store-bought clothes and a mother who "provided good." These words evoke ambivalence more than pain. But in other settings, relative lack carried with it the sting of humiliation. Edna Yandell Hargett, a mill worker in Burlington, North Carolina, discussed the self-described "inferiority complex" that mill children developed relative to better-off teens who stayed in school, explaining: "We didn't have the conveniences that other people had. We were very conscious of that . . . [and] we felt like we wasn't dressed as nice, because most of our clothes were made out of gingham."[21]

Clothing figured prominently in memories of shameful childhood episodes of peer ridicule, patronizing charity, or humiliating comparisons among classmates. Fifteen-year-old Amanda Hayden bitterly recalled how after her parents' illness led local teachers to collect clothes for the family, her classmates ridiculed her when they recognized Amanda's dresses as their own cast-offs.[22] Shame touched middle-class girls as well in times of declining class status. In a memoir about her Arkansas childhood in the 1930s and '40s, Shirley Abbott describes her feelings after her father's financial troubles forced the family to move from their middle-class home in Hot Springs to a rundown farm in the country. She continued at the same junior high school, but the loss of status, visually represented by the hand-me-down dresses she now wore, led her to quit the sorority she had pledged and withdraw from her former peers. "I burned with rage and sorrow," she recounts. "What was I doing here, cast backward into medieval squalor, when so lately I had worn ribbons and a long dress, had been launched into nice-girl society?"[23] The shame that adolescent girls felt at their relative lack could feed a sense of self defined as less than or worse than others.

Notions of deficiency rooted in material distinctions extended beyond the visible surface to encompass less tangible attributes. The community of haves marked the have-nots as lacking not only in clothes, but in cleanliness, morality, and civility as well. Several wealthier African American teenagers interviewed by sociologists in the late 1930s mentioned that girls with fewer clothes were "rough" and "loud," terms that referred doubly to physical qualities and to an imputed lack of morals and manners.[24] Similarly, in her memoir of growing up in a white landowning family in the Mississippi Delta, Margaret Bolsterli describes how she learned to tell the difference between "common" and "nice" women: "Common women let their slips show and their stocking seams remain crooked and, given a choice, would have two cheap sweaters instead of one good one."[25] Even more pejorative than "common" was the term "tacky," which sounded nearly like "trashy," the most severe insult used to describe poor whites.[26]

Adults made similar judgments. When the social scientists who worked on the southern Negro youth project made notations about the state of a girl's clothing, they often commented on her cleanliness and respectability as well. Even a simple statement that a girl had nineteen or twenty dresses in a variety of fabrics, "enough" dresses, or nine dresses with six of them "bought" carried with it a nod of approval from purportedly objective researchers.[27] White social workers made their own critical distinctions, noting for example that one former delinquent girl now working in the mills "spends much money for beautiful clothes, which look out of place in her sordid environment."[28] Since to be working class was to the social worker by definition sordid, beautiful clothes did not bestow respectability but signaled a suspect form of striving in which the girl stepped "out of place." Because the tendency of wealthier southerners to note the "loud" and "cheap" clothing of the poor signals not only a judgment against their taste, but also the disgust and visceral intolerance evoked by class differences in taste, differences in clothing—an external sign of taste—stood in for presumed inner properties such as moral character, personal cleanliness, or sexual virtue.[29] For adolescent girls on the receiving end of such reactions, feelings of shame converted an externally imposed social stigma to an interior branding of the self as being somehow "wrong" or less than desirable.

Yet clothing could also be a source of pride and a realm of female agency, a way to become "somebody" and express one's self-confidence, dignity, and either assent or dissent. Icy Norman, who began factory work at age thirteen in the mid-1920s, remembered the excitement of her first job and pay envelope, which she turned directly over to her father: "Of course I didn't make nothing but I thought that I was rich when I got that five dollars and a half."[30] Norman's new stature as "wealthy" was captured in a memory of the new dress, shoes, hat, and spring coat her father bought her with her earnings.

Dress provided a simple yet powerful way to mark oneself as special or of value. Sometimes overtly expressed in campaigns for homecoming queen or class office, the striving for status could also occur underneath a veneer of feigned nonchalance, a display of indifferent ease that cloaked what writer Robb Forman Dew describes as an "arduous and strategically planned battle" for popularity. She recalls a day in the 1950s when she and several friends, all white upper-middle-class fourteen-year-olds from Baton Rouge, traveled downtown for lunch in the local department store followed by a movie: "We wore stockings and low heels to match our leather handbags, and we were carefully blase, but I don't believe it was only I who was filled with exhilaration at the notion of our fashionable singularity among the Saturday shoppers . . . I don't like to remember how lovely and superior I imagined we were in our short, boxy suit jackets over our matching dresses." Such ordinary pleasures of dressing up had high stakes, according to Dew. "It was absolutely crucial to be counted among the current crop of attractive girls," she noted. "How else could we attract men? If we did not learn how to be lovely, how to be charming, why should we expect to marry well or to marry at all?"[31]

In her rural black community of Mississippi, Anne Moody had no such expectations of profitable romance, but the competition over clothes and status carried the same fierce resonances of pride and shame. Chosen through a competition as her junior high school's homecoming queen in the early 1950s, Moody recounts the enormous pride she felt as she looked in the mirror, seeing in her lacy blue gown, curled and teased hair piled high, and full makeup a surprisingly beautiful young woman. Her pride rested in part on a comparison between herself and the girls serving as her attendants. Moments earlier as they had prepared to dress, Moody let out a laugh of pure pleasure that Dorothy, the girl she had defeated for the position of queen, mistook as mockery. Dorothy's friends challenged Moody to unpack her dress and reveal herself: "Without saying a word, I walked slowly over to one of the two beds in the room, placed the box on it and carefully opened it, folding back the tissue paper. They all crowded around, as if I was unveiling a newborn baby. As I lifted the gown from the box and held it against me, they all went 'ooh' and 'where did you get *that?*' and I could see that not one of them thought her own gown was pretty any more."[32] The unveiling affirmed Moody's momentary self-satisfaction, all the more important because she struggled from year to year to earn the money for a daily wardrobe of school clothes.

Working-class pride in dress appears as highly self-conscious and often in uneasy proximity to feelings of shame and envy. For example, Tessie Helms Dyer began mill work as a teenager in the mid-1920s. She describes the pride she felt when she took her savings of seventeen dollars and "went to town, and I bought me a dress, and a coat, and a pair of shoes, and I believe I bought me a hat . . . and oh, I thought I was dressed up. I never will forget it, it was a black and white checked coat. It was pretty, it was made pretty, and I just loved that coat." Such pride rested on a tenuous foundation, however, as became evident in Dyer's memory of another incident, a day when she and her sister boarded the street car wearing lovely black gabardine coats. At a later stop workers from a different mill got on visibly covered with lint. Responding with admitted scorn, she recalled thinking that no wonder she and other mill workers were mocked as "lintheads": "When I got to town, I was just about covered in cotton, and my sister too . . . We liked not to ever got those coats clean." She added that she and her coworkers always stayed fixed up "nice."[33] Implicit in her recollection is the fine line Dyer walked between pride and shame, between gabardine and cotton lint, between the clothes she could purchase as an independent young working woman and the fibers that stuck to a low-status textile worker.

The desire among have-nots to have things could produce the flipside of shame—envy, an emotion born of resentment and desire. Salome Hinton, a North Carolina teenager whose family lived in dire poverty in the late 1930s, told an interviewer that she wished for a house with no leaks, smooth floors, nice things inside, enough to eat, and clothes like other girls, in particular like her schoolmate Madge Johnson, whose pretty shape, hair, and clothing made her the envy of all. "Everybody loves Madge. I love to see her walk . . . Yes'm she have pretty clothes," explained Salome, displaying both admiration and envy.[34]

The oldest of five children, sixteen-year-old Earselle Mayo lived on an isolated farm with her father, whose meager earnings barely provided for the family and whose violent temper and suspected sexual abuse left his daughter feeling tyrannized and trapped. Earselle explained that she quit school because of her embarrassment at owning only ragged clothes and, indeed, a visiting sociologist described her as dirty and unkempt. When the well-dressed professional returned for a second interview, Earselle reported that every night since the first visit she had dreamed that the older woman had taken off her nice dress and given it to Earselle to keep.[35] Envy could feed fantasies based on the knowledge that fine clothing carried with it the possibility of respect, self-sufficiency, and mobility. No less forceful an insight for its simplicity, to Earselle and other poor adolescent girls, possessions represented self-possession.

Some teenagers turned their envy into actions such as leaving school for work; pursuing or opting for men who could offer money, presents, or other material benefits; or stealing what one could not otherwise obtain. In records of female reformatories, although young women were overwhelmingly incarcerated for sexual offenses, the rare cases of larceny typically involved clothing. Young women convicted on other charges such as prostitution, adultery, or lewd behavior also mentioned that their actions were motivated by interlocking desires for affection, glamour, and material goods.[36] In 1942 a young white inmate with the initials N. J. wrote to the warden of the North Carolina women's reformatory trying to explain her tangled motivations. She told of how she had been married at age fourteen (mentioning only later and in passing that this was an attempt to escape her father's incestuous pursuit), separated within a month, and then became involved with a married preacher for whom she was working as a housekeeper. "I was just down and out when I met him. He was a married man and I knew it was wrong to go with him, but he spent lots of money on me and took care of me." Now at age nineteen, she communicated her own uncertainty: "I don't know what I want. One time I want one thing and then again at other times I want something different. At times I want to be good and at other times I don't care. It is in those times when I don't care that I do something wrong. I do try at times and at others I don't try at all."[37]

Adolescents like N. J. were caught in an internal war between the desire for the goods and attention lacking in their lives and the desire for the higher status granted to "good girls" and respectable women. They also understood that as working-class teens this was not a simple choice. The ridicule and disrespect they encountered as children without wealth taught them that clothing and appearance were essential to gaining access to the middle-class world of "nice girls" and nice things. Yet pursuing the goods carried its own risks. Especially if the path entailed making calculated decisions involving men, money, and sexual relations, an adolescent risked not only a loss of reputation but also her physical safety and freedom. The stigma of poverty and accompanying assumptions about working-class immorality taught girls that there was no virtue in poverty; yet they knew equally well that there might indeed be all too much poverty in conventionally defined virtue. This knowledge prompted some teenagers to take bold actions in dress, spending, or sexual behavior that only further marked them as "low-class" women.

For poor and working-class girls in the South, feelings of pride, shame, and envy converged around dress, accented by other emotions like scorn and admiration. This emotional landscape coupled a very matter-of-fact desire for clothes as necessary goods or the fruits of one's labor with a more intense longing for clothing as a means of escape or a talisman of material security. In a volatile southern society destabilized by urban migration, the decline of agriculture, the rise of manufacturing, and the rapid penetration of commercial goods and leisure into an increasingly cash-based economy, clothes functioned as obvious signifiers of class and modernity. Peers, parents, and teachers assessed clothing and drew conclusions about class and character. Social workers and reformers also took inordinate interest in the clothes of adolescent girls, evaluating them to determine economic and moral standing. Even more importantly, through her own knowledge of such judgments a teenager learned how to recognize something about herself in the clothing she wore, for example in the meaning of a gingham dress, of home-sewn versus store-bought clothing, or the difference between tired-looking hand-me-downs and crisp, up-to-date fashions. These recognitions and their emotional reverberations entered into self-understandings, underwriting adolescent identities rooted in class and gender experiences.

Yet we stop short if we see dress primarily as a symbol of class, a representation that when read by others marks a person as belonging to or striving for a certain class position. For dress also involves an array of practices by adolescent girls that produce class identity in its gendered and racial forms. The deceptively simple acts of buying and wearing clothes joined in the ongoing process of creating the categories and relations of class as teenagers regarded each other and formed distinct peer groups on the basis of their evaluations.

Dannie Freeman, a college-bound sixteen-year-old, announced that her group of three African American girlfriends stood out in high school because "I guess we dress better than any of the other children. We all have nice clothes and extra spending money." Along with not running the streets, these attributes made them "not rough like most of the girls here." Oglena Kennedy, an eleventh-grade black student living outside of Nashville, related a similar experience, explaining that "rough girls" criticized her for thinking she was better than the rest. These girls "don't like me since I change my clothes every other day and they wear a dress the whole week."[38] In these accounts, middle-class teens report firsthand the way that "nice clothes" produce "nice girls" and the feelings of relative superiority that accompany that status. The clothed body bore the signs of class out of which certain teenagers recognized an affinity and created a sense of sympathetic "us." Together they reinforced the category of an inferior "them," designated through paired oppositions of bad / good, common / nice, ugly / attractive, and rough / respectable.

This process worked in reverse as well. While a working-class teen might feel the hurt and shame of being singled out for her poor dress and appearance, she too might bond with her peers and criticize wealthier girls for the attitude that accompanied their fine dress. Labeling them as "biggity" or "stuck up," less-privileged girls stigmatized "snobbish" girls who broke with peer-established norms, thus reassuring themselves of their own worth. Retired textile worker Mabel Kinney Summers recalled a humorous response to her exclusion from middle-class status. She and her friends attended "tacky parties" in which young mill workers purposely dressed as "low-class" or "tacky" as possible.[39] This ritual established the youthful revelers as ordinarily above tackiness—since this was a form of playful dress up (or dress down). Tacky parties may have subtly ridiculed the notions of middle-class respectability that made dress such an important designator of status and, at the same time, distinguished "respectable" working-class adolescents from poorer people judged to be truly "tacky." As with middle-class girls, working-class girls marked class distinctions

For adolescent girls, nice clothing represented not only material worth but self-worth. Here, three Arkansas teenagers proudly display stylish hats in front of their church, where Sunday services doubled as religious event and fashion show. Ben Shahn, Library of Congress, LC-USF33–006025-M4.

and created affiliations on the basis of dress, reproducing both the categories and antipathies of class.

Through clothing girls also learned the bodily lessons of class. For middle-class girls this often consisted of instruction in control and propriety. Shirley Abbott describes how as a child she endured her mother's efforts to keep her perfectly groomed: "my dress perfect, every curl coaxed into a perfect blond sausage . . . she believed that every part of me, from hair to bowels to cuticles, would respond eventually to her discipline and patience."[40] Her mother's own adolescent journey had taken her from farm to town, where she worked as a maid cleaning tourist cabins until she met and married a traveling man whose gambling bought the family a precarious middle-class status. The fierce maternal attention to detail stemmed from her desire that Shirley be like other girls, thus ensuring acceptance in the middle-class society that she herself had only recently entered. Recalling her Georgia childhood, Rosemary Daniell describes a similar relationship with her mother around clothes and bodily discipline. To defend against "tackiness," Rosemary's mother focused inordinate attention on her daughter's dress, demanding perfection in every detail. In the ensuing struggle, Daniell's mother asserted her personal power while teaching lessons about class and gender to a white middle-class daughter who well into adulthood had "never imagined . . . being admired for anything but my body and/or its coverings."[41]

Daniell's and Abbott's adolescence occurred in the late 1940s in families that had a tenuous claim on middle-class status. Coming of age a decade later in a wealthier family during a postwar era remembered for its elaborate culture of femininity, Robb Forman Dew writes of the techniques of self-discipline she had learned by her early teens. "We worked so hard at being appealing!" she remembers. "We had bedrooms that looked like beauty parlors, with storklike hair dryers . . . We slept miserably with enormous, bristly rollers wound into our hair and got up at six in the morning to unwind them . . . We applied makeup base, eyeliner, mascara, lipstick, and a final dusting of loose powder which we had read would *set* our makeup for the day. This was in order for us to go to *school!*"[42] Through this regime of bodily care, girls worked to earn acceptance and popularity, understood as the prerequisites for white, middle-class courtship and marriage to a man of "quality."

Discipline involving the body and dress could take other forms as well, administered not by oneself or family members but by other adults in positions of power. This process is most transparent in evidence from reformatories for delinquent girls in which school authorities used clothing as part of the reward and punishment system. Staff members typically locked up a girl's everyday clothes upon her incarceration and took additional garments away as punishment for institutional infractions. The link between punishment and clothing in reformatories serves as an extreme example of the broader point that clothes are the layer of protection between our naked or revealed self and the self we expose to others. In more subtle ways, failure to possess the proper clothing might have punishing effects. Mary Mebane, for example, grew up in rural North Carolina in the 1940s, working summers in tobacco factories to save money for school. She eventually attended a black college in Durham where her class background made her an object of scrutiny. She recalled being admonished by one teacher for wearing a mismatched skirt and blouse, an incident that only heightened her self-consciousness among well-dressed, wealthier classmates who reigned over campus social life.[43] Incidents resulting in public shame provided a lesson in feminine obedience and class stigma to all participants. Privately, shame disciplined the body in what to wear and how to act, training the mind as well in what to want.

The mind, however, proved harder to discipline than the body. A girl might learn to dress appropriately for her class, or to work hard to save money to buy school clothes. But her exposure to the world of consumer goods might also stimulate desires for a life well beyond her material means. Oral histories and sociological interview data provide ample evidence that poor and working-class adolescent girls fantasized about improving their material lives and expanding their social horizons by escaping the limits of their economic circumstances. Clothing and well-built, finely furnished homes supplied the substance of these dreams. Marriage often, but not always, figured into the fantasy as the means to the end.

Doris Brown, a fourteen-year-old African American from Smithfield, North Carolina, imagined marrying a rich, good-looking person so she could get all the pretty clothes she wanted and travel all over the world, while her schoolmate Annie Lou Thigpen envisioned marrying a rich man who could ensure that she have pretty clothes and plentiful candy. Marriage to a wealthy man could sound like an acquisition in itself. Fannie Maxwell, a nineteen-year-old Alabaman from a hard-working, home-owning black family, described her vision of the future as having a well-fixed house with a nice husband, a car, plenty of nice clothes, one or two children, and some household help so she could keep her job and play music as a hobby. The husband, in this view, seemed more like a household fixture than an intimate relation.[44]

It could be argued that southern adolescent fantasies reified existing class relations even as girls envisioned an escape from them.[45] In their desire to marry businessmen, doctors, or other professionals, teenagers reproduced existing occupational hierarchies, romanticizing and exalting elite occupations for the promise they offered of rare wealth and security. Moreover, the contrast between actual conditions and imagined futures replicated the very real inequalities between poor and rich. Ruby Low Outlaw, a white thirteen-year-old, wrote in her 1948 autobiographical essay that she lived on an eighty-acre farm in Alabama with a seven-room house that was neither painted or papered inside. Asked about her future wishes, she replied, "My greatest wish that I want to come true is to have our home painted and a dinning room suit in it, and a living room suit. The worst job I hate to do is pick cotton and shell peas."[46] The disconcerting juxtaposition of her "worst job" and her "greatest wish" parallels the disparity between her present conditions and desired future.

The distance between imagined futures and present circumstances often played out in the difference between the men whom girls dreamed of marrying and the ones they chose to marry. Eva Hopkins began work in 1932 at the age of fourteen when her father became ill with tuberculosis. Working with other white teenagers in a North Carolina textile mill, they discussed their current romances and their dreams of marriage. "I was going to marry somebody that was rich [so] that I wouldn't have to work," recalled Hopkins. "I could have a nice home and beautiful clothes." At seventeen Hopkins married a man six years older than she who also worked in the mills. They eloped to South Carolina on a Saturday night, returned home, and went to work on Monday morning. Adolescent dreams of a better life transformed into the hope that her children would not work in the mills and would have "nicer homes, more conveniences, nicer cars and everything than we had. Dreams like that."[47]

The fact that adolescent girls who had little access to material goods and social status turned, of necessity, to their imagination for the richness lacking in their lives speaks powerfully to the social divisions underlying the dream; the gap between the have-nots and haves was often as big as the difference between real life and the imagination. The particular forms of adolescent longing may have even reaffirmed some of the very class distinctions that operated against working-class teenagers in the broader society. There is something sadly ironic, after all, about adolescent girls who worked in cotton fields or textile mills trying to imagine themselves in a position of actually possessing the clothing that their labor helped produce. But the self-valuing that their desires permitted also offered a critical resource to young women as they pursued aspirations of material and emotional fulfillment, and quite possibly provided a legacy of self-respect for their children or other loved ones.[48]

As southern adolescents worked for, shopped for, and dressed in ready-made clothing purchased from a consumer economy, their dress stitched together class and race relations into a weave of social meaning. To be black in the South usually also meant being very poor.[49] To whites, the poverty of African Americans proved their inferiority, whereas to blacks it symbolized racial oppression. For the relatively small number of blacks in skilled jobs, business, and the professions, middle-class status represented not only an economic accomplishment, but also a significant racial achievement. To whites with middle-class or elite standing, economic advantages represented the "natural" outcome of white racial superiority. For working-class and poor whites, segregation along with relative advantages over African Americans in wage rates, hiring, credit policies, or rental agreements compensated for mere subsistence earnings. These arrangements supplied both the material "wages of whiteness" and a psychological wage—a reminder that though poor, they still held superior caste status in the South as members of the white race.[50]

For these reasons, not only the jobs people worked but also the goods they purchased carried pointed racial meanings in the South. In his 1932 study *The Southern Urban Negro as a Consumer*, economist Paul K. Edwards argued that because of "social segregation" in the South, blacks and whites in similar economic conditions tended to purchase differently, with the Negro consumer buying relatively better quality goods at higher prices. The small black middle class, Edwards suggests, viewed such goods as critical to establishing its respectability and prestige. In addition, the greater proportion of black "commoners," including an "upper-lower class," invested in consumer goods that marked the difference between its members and those of lower standing. At all economic levels, Edwards discovered that African Americans based their purchases not solely on price or credit availability, but also on the degree of respect shown by white clerks and owners and the absence or presence of offensive stereotypes in racialized advertising.[51]

Hortense Powdermaker's 1939 study of Indianola, Mississippi, found that the purchase of clothing in particular combined both class and racial meanings. She noted that for the majority of poor African Americans in the area, participation in the cash economy was still minimal, preventing families from purchasing needed clothing and household goods. For those who could afford to buy, clothing formed a key index of social status, with all classes striving to keep up with the latest fashions. Powdermaker then described a popular form of church fundraising, "style shows" in which black participants simultaneously assumed and mocked middle-class white manners by parodying fashion shows. In these events, women contestants donned their finest dresses, paraded into the room, and then sat down for tea at small tables served by younger girls dressed as maids. Combining the usual runway display of fashions with the role of female observers at fashion shows, the style-show contestants then watched a short musical program while indulging in loud conversation full of affected speech and concerned talk of "the banking crisis," all for the benefit of the amused audience who then awarded prizes to the best contestant at each table.[52] Participants enjoyed both the spectacle of consumption and the mockery of white society airs, at once joining in a common commodity culture and signaling a critical stance toward the whites who controlled it—and so much else—in southern society.

For black teenagers, racial consciousness about consumption rested on the knowledge that to be white was often to be wealthier. According to thirteen-year-old Louise Graham, the difference between "white" and "colored" was simply that whites were richer. For adolescents, the potential of consumption to stimulate racial pride could easily be undercut by its more damaging tendency to evoke racialized class shame. When asked about color preferences, Louise responded, "I'd rather be white," because "then I'd be rich and have a fine house."[53] If wealth equaled whiteness, then the negative connotations of poverty could just as easily signal the inferiority of blackness.

Conversely, white southern teenagers could embrace consumption as a sign of their own racial superiority. Adolescents need not be consciously aware that in shopping for dresses, trying on shoes, or wearing a store-bought hat they participated in—and benefited from—a consumer culture that privileged whiteness. They simply had to walk downtown, take a drink from a "white only" drinking fountain, and be served by an attentive clerk as they browsed through aisles of products, many of which carried labels displaying caricatured Mammy and pickaninny images like "Aunt Jemima" and the "Gold Dust Twins."[54] Whether spending hard-earned wages or charging items to a parent's line of credit, both working- and middle-class white girls reaffirmed their racial privilege through ordinary acts of consumption. Not only the goods purchased but even the act of shopping signaled white privilege. The exclusion of African Americans from arenas of consumption like restaurants and certain "white only" stores, separate bathroom and drinking facilities, and rituals of deference expected of black customers in dealing with white clerks or managers created a set of racist practices described by Lillian Smith as "ceremonials in honor of white supremacy."[55]

The symbolism of consumer goods extended beyond the body to the visible surface of the home. Here the color white conveyed class information that in its explicitness about color must also have communicated racial meanings. In an essay she titled "My Life," a white Alabama high school student recounted her family's economic climb by describing the homes in which she had lived. "The house I first live in had four rooms," wrote Emmie Lou Sheffield. "The second house had four rooms and a porch. Then we move up in the middle of Coy and bought us a home. The house had eight room and a hall. It is 'Painted white.'"[56] The significance of whiteness is emphasized by her use of quotation marks and capitalization. The house does not simply happen to be white, in town, large, and purchased rather than rented; it has been "Painted white." Margaret Bolsterli learned the same lesson when she moved from a small rural elementary school to a larger school in a nearby Mississippi Delta town. As a new student, she gained acceptance only after her classmates ascertained that she lived in a nicely painted white house and descended from a family of reputable background. Favorably distinguished from the "common" kids, she became a candidate for private high school parties and country club dances. These lessons became inured in what Bolsterli calls the "the Delta of the mind," those habits of thinking that were all the more powerful for their lack of conscious attention.[57]

Children coming of age in the South learned that owning a white home, shopping in the right stores, and wearing the best clothes communicated middle-class standing, with all its social benefits. When

Louise Graham told interviewers that naturally she wanted to be white because then she would be rich and own a nice house, she may have failed to consider the actual economic status of all white and black southerners. But she spoke the larger truth that in southern society, racial meanings underwrote class relations; symbolically, wealth and whiteness belonged together.[58]

For teenage girls in the modern South, dress figured heavily in a psychosocial drama important for its ability to produce the markers, stratified relationships, and emotional identifications of class. This social drama also contained within it a more overtly economic framework of production and exchange. Teens faced decisions involving such measured exchanges as quitting school for work; spending meager savings on stylish clothing to "become somebody" or marry well; forgoing courtship to pursue an education; or trading sexual "virtue" for sexual relations in the hope of escaping a difficult home situation. For example, a working-class teenager who obtained the money to buy a fashionable dress with a new pair of shoes and just the right hat may also have been purchasing entry into new settings—schools, sites of leisure, new social groups, a better job. This purchase would provide some immediate satisfactions but might also be considered a down payment on a desired future, whether it be one of independence, higher earnings, or marriage to a good provider.

The connection between labor and love, or commerce and sex, was not news to teenagers.[59] Modern dating developed within a consumer economy in which a "date"—both person and event—was understood to be a commodity with a measurable value. From the 1920s through at least the 1950s, this implicit economy regarded a man's value as equivalent to the size of his wallet. Since a woman acquired value according to the price she could command from her male escort, she herself became an item of consumption. Yet she was also a trader on the market of love and romance, investing in production costs like fashionable clothes and well-styled hair that she then parlayed into "popularity," higher-priced dates, and a promising future on the marriage market.[60]

Female sexual desire, a defining characteristic of modern youth, was tamed in this economic calculus and masked by a new popular ideology of passionate teen romance. According to psychologists, marriage counselors, and advice columnists, girls' sexuality was expressed through and contained by romantic fantasies and relationships that eventuated in modern companionate marriage.[61] In this model, adolescent female sexuality proceeds in orderly progression from peer culture participation; to increasing interest in dress, appearance, and boys; to dating that is heavy on romance and theoretically light on sex; followed by more serious dating (and heavier petting); until finally, like linked cars on a track, female romance, desire, and femininity arrive at the wedding day (with its bridal train), where sexual desire is licensed for use as long as it remains within marriage. Girls who did not pay the price of the ticket—who tried to ride for free or have sex before marriage—were labeled, appropriately enough, "tramps."

In the system of "rating and dating," the structures of opportunity available to middle-class adolescents—high school and college educations with their attendant peer activities, well-made and attractive clothing, opportunities to develop social graces and confidence, the good health that money can buy—meshed with the emotional structure of romantic femininity, with all its desires, fears, and affirmations, to produce a relatively smooth journey for middle-class white teenage girls. At least if all went well, an adolescent girl could move along a well-worn path from dating to marriage, unscathed by barriers like racial discrimination, financial need, or sexual exploitation.

This does not accurately describe working-class experiences in which clothing, desire, sexual attraction, and attractiveness were fluid elements in a complicated chemistry of love, money, romance, need, and imagination.[62] Historical understanding of adolescent sexuality can be broadened and complicated to include the full range of working- and middle-class experience by turning from the notion of "sexual economy" to the broader concept of an "economy of desire." This is an economy in which sexual desire mingles with the desire for clothes; for adventure; for a more secure livelihood; for education or work; for friendship, love, and joy; for an end to cotton picking; for a house with no leaks; and for money or things of one's own. These desires fueled adolescent decisions about work, love, marriage, sex, and money not in any singular predictable way but in numerous and contradictory ways. Sometimes the economy of desire featured conventional notions of romantic love, but in other cases adolescent female desires, especially in working-class contexts, led to decidedly unromantic relationships and calculated decisions about love and money. At the heart of these exchanges lay desire—desire to escape the past, for a better future, to be somebody or to have something. Shame, pride, envy—the emotions of class—figured into this economy as much as did hard cash, sexual exchange, or the emotions of love.

Unlike the dominant cultural scenario where a construct of feminine romance could encompass the many desires of adolescent girls and channel them safely along a course of dating to marriage, the economy of desire most prominent among southern working-class teenagers features, paradoxically, both hard-edged, unromantic calculations and utopian dreams that almost surely went unrealized. From one angle, such desires can be read as evidence of deprivation and absurdly unrealistic fantasy. Yet in the envy of a working-class adolescent girl, her many and conflicting desires, or the decision to pursue—even if only in her imagination—something beyond her reach, we can also find evidence of self-affirmation.

In the late 1930s fourteen-year-old Carlottie Jones, from a struggling African American farm family, told an interviewer that she feared not being able to go to school for lack of clothes but still imagined herself living in town with lots of money, clothes, and a fine car, adding that she hoped to be a music teacher or a secretary despite having no training in music and no apparent way to further her education.[63] In such adolescent fantasies we can recognize naive desires that are discomfiting for the ignorance and impracticality they reveal. But in Jones's longing, and in the sometimes calculating, often improvident desires of other black and white southern teenagers, we can also see an expression of self, an insistence on having or imagining a desired future, or simply a way to soften the barrier between one's self and a cold world.

For southern adolescent girls in the interwar and immediate postwar period, participation in the region's modern consumer economy was a formative experience, helping to constitute young women both as economic actors in their society and as social subjects whose sense of self developed from a web of gender, racial, class, and sexual identifications. Depending on her particular location in southern society—rich or poor, black or white, rural or urban, and a range of other vari-

able factors—an adolescent encountered a given, but probably changing, set of structural opportunities around work, residence, education,
entertainment, friendship, and love. From within these parameters,
teenage girls formulated and acted on desires for both the material
and immaterial goods of their society. As workers, daughters, lovers,
students, inmates, and peers they calculated their chances and imagined their futures, behaving in ways that made them important social
actors. Their participation as laborers and consumers in the southern
economy fueled the region's growing commercial sector and changing
public life. In the early decades of the century, alarmed adults saw
sexual danger and social decay where girls saw opportunity. In the
1950s, when girls passionately consumed rock 'n' roll music and
imagined romances with white and black performers, the connection
between female consumption and sexuality would precipitate another
regional backlash. Yet long before this and without controversy, adolescent girls assumed an important public economic role as workers
and consumers. As they influenced the public culture of the South,
they also acted privately as agents in their own lives, managing their
day-to-day existence in the present and, as one teen described it, "living in hopes" for the future.[64]

chapter six

Sex, Science, and Eugenic Sterilization

"Lily Daw and the Three Ladies," a short story by Eudora Welty published in 1936, opens with the news that Lily Daw has been accepted into the Ellisville Institute for the Feeble-Minded of Mississippi. Lily, a simple-minded girl whose mother died and whose father once attempted to slit her throat, has been taken care of by the townsfolk of Victory, Mississippi, for some years. Concerned that "Lily has gotten so she is very mature for her age," three of the town's leading "ladies" have solicited Lily's entrance into the school and agreed to pay for her transportation there. Lily, however, announces she has made her own plans, having just the previous night attended a tent show and met a traveling xylophone player who has proposed marriage. When the three ladies find Lily, she is packing her trunk in preparation for the musician's return. Alarmed by Lily's obvious sexual interest and independence, they try to persuade her that life at Ellisville would be far superior to married life, bribing her with offers of food, a personalized Bible, and a pink lace brassiere. She at first stubbornly resists, but finally agrees when assured that she can bring her hope chest to the institution. As she boards the train, hope chest in tow, the town's band strikes up a number in a grand send-off. Just then, however, a stranger on the platform inquires after Lily; the xylophone player has returned to find his date, although it remains uncertain whether his marriage proposal stands. Lily is then pulled off the train, confused and whimpering that "I don't want to git married . . . I'm going to Ellisville." The three ladies overrule her, hustling Lily and her beau off to get married by a preacher while the band plays the Independence March and the train pulls away with Lily's hope chest still aboard.[1]

Eudora Welty's story ends ambiguously; Lily escapes institutionalization but with no clear indication of her will. Her hope rolls away while the band plays musical homage to an independence she has never known. What drives the story is not Lily's own desires but the desire of her community to put her safely away—whether in an institution or in marriage—before her budding sexual interest brings disrepute or chaos to the town. Welty's short story alludes to a much wider phenomenon in the South of the interwar years: the fear of unrestrained sexuality among girls presumed to lack the mental and moral capacity to govern their own actions. While the three ladies handled Lily Daw's situation informally, their petition for institutionalization points to a far more typical pattern of official intervention. Beginning in the late 1920s and lasting through the 1960s, southern states aggressively regulated the sexuality of young women charged with criminal offenses or with mental incapacity. Nationally, numerous reformers committed to "girls' work" had developed remedies for increasingly assertive adolescent sexuality. When these failed, state governments turned to incarceration in criminal reformatories or colonies for the feebleminded and insane. But soon they resorted to a more cost-effective measure: the surgical sterilization of young women whom the state deemed "mentally defective" and "socially inadequate."

Sterilization represents the cruelly logical endpoint of efforts to gain control over threatening changes in sexual mores by distinguishing the criminal and pathological adolescent, labeled a "racial degenerate," from an emergent notion of sexually interested "normal" teenage girls. We might suspect that racial issues played a central role in such policies, and this is indeed true. By the 1950s African Americans formed a disproportionate share of women sterilized by southern states. But they were not the first targets of southern officials. The racial practice and discourse of sterilization formed first and most explicitly around young white women, whose victimization on the basis of race and class formed a precedent for later sterilizations of young black women. In each case, public officials argued that the mental and social inadequacies of sexually active young women posed such a threat to the welfare of society that the state could justifiably force them to sacrifice the right to bear children for the greater interest of the body politic.

In the South, widespread concerns about white supremacy, class conflict, and public finance infused sexual politics. Consequently, the attack on teenage girls' sexual and reproductive freedom occurred within the context of a broader assault on the sexual and reproductive freedom of poor women and men, both black and white, who could be labeled mentally unfit.[2] Employing age-inclusive discourses, state officials rarely admitted publicly that adolescents formed the easiest and most desirable group to sterilize. Nevertheless, southern sterilization policies succeeded in imposing draconian restrictions on thousands of young working-class women. The state acted as a formidable sexual authority that, by fusing scientific expertise with traditions of patriarchal and racial domination, practiced violence and deception under the guise of protection.

The first southern teenager to make this sacrifice under state law was a white Virginia girl named Carrie Buck. Adopted by Mr. and Mrs. J. T. Dobbs of Charlottesville, Buck grew up in a family that treated her more like a domestic servant than a daughter. In 1924, the seventeen-year-old found herself pregnant as a result of rape, she claimed, by her visiting cousin. The disbelieving Dobbses committed Carrie to the state institution for the feebleminded, although she had attended school regularly and advanced with no apparent difficulty. Once there, the superintendent decided to use Buck as a test case for Virginia's recently enacted law permitting the sterilization of epileptic, feebleminded, and insane individuals judged a danger to themselves or to the public. In 1927 the U.S. Supreme Court ruled eight to one in favor of the State of Virginia and its constitutional right to terminate Carrie Buck's ability to bear children. Drawing on expert testimony that Buck, her infant daughter, and her biological mother belonged "to the shiftless, ignorant and worthless class of anti-social whites of the South," Chief Justice Oliver Wendell Holmes ruled that "three generations of imbeciles are enough" to justify the state-man-

Carrie Buck and her mother, Emma, the day before the 1924 Virginia *Buck v. Bell* decision that, upon appeal, reached the Supreme Court in 1927. The Court ruled that the
low IQs of Buck, her mother, and her infant daughter–all officially classified as imbeciles–qualified Carrie Buck for state-mandated eugenic sterilization. Arthur Estabrook
Papers, M. E. Grenander Department of Special Collections and Archives, University at
Albany Libraries.

dated sterilization of Buck and similar individuals who threatened the
welfare of the state.[3]

The court's decision sanctioned sterilizations not only in Virginia,
but also in a number of other states with untested sterilization laws as
well as in the approximately one dozen states that passed new laws
soon after the *Buck v. Bell* ruling. By the mid-1930s, the number of
states with sterilization laws on the books had jumped from seventeen
to thirty, with state officials applying them more aggressively than
ever before. The national rate of between two and four sterilizations
per 100,000 people in the 1920s jumped to twenty per 100,000 by the
end of the 1930s. Virginia alone accounted for one-seventh of national
sterilizations, while the South as a region became the leading proponent and practitioner of eugenic sterilization over the next three decades.[4]

Carrie Buck's tragedy also marks the increased frequency with which state governments targeted young single women under gender- and race-neutral laws. While males had made up 53 percent of steril- ized persons up until 1927, in the next five years women constituted 67 percent of those sterilized, a percentage that rose steadily in suc- ceeding decades.[5] Through 1944, women were 59 percent of all per- sons ever sterilized in Virginia, 73 percent in Mississippi, 77 percent in North Carolina, and 90 percent in South Carolina.[6] In the only state reporting data by age, North Carolina performed 50 percent of all its eugenic sterilizations between 1929 and 1948 on women under twenty years of age.[7] Through most of the 1930s and 1940s, the typi- cal southern sterilization victim was a single, sexually active, working- class white teenage girl with one or no children and a low IQ score. Why would the state target this group?

For several decades the behavior of working-class adolescent girls had raised concern among older, "respectable" middle-class southern- ers concerned about preserving the social order as they knew it. The rapid growth of modern cities and mill towns in the New South had spawned a new morality that broke with Victorian codes of restraint and modesty. Reversing the usual southern tale of (typically black) male aggression and (always white) female victimization, white re- formers began to focus on poor, sexually active white girls as danger- ous sexual aggressors in their own right. This group of adolescents posed a double threat to white elites. While their sexual involvement threatened to produce offspring of illegitimate birth and low aptitude, enlarging the number of "inferior" whites in a population that claimed superiority, their very sexual activity suggested an inversion of the ideology of white female purity. They exposed the southern myth of virtuous white womanhood, toppling a longstanding pillar in the de- fense of white privilege and racial segregation.

A growing number of reformers clamored for an end to assertive adolescent sexual behavior in the interests of racial purity and social stability. They were joined by professionals in medicine, psychology, psychiatry, social work, and public health who found eugenic theories compatible with their own professional interests and beliefs. Eugenic sterilization, today associated with the genocidal policies of Nazi Ger- many and its later widespread use against Native American and Puerto Rican women in the United States, initially appeared to many as a progressive reform in step with the most current scientific knowledge and enlightened social planning. Building on recent scientific developments in genetics, surgery, and psychology, it was embraced by doctors, social reformers, women's groups, public officials, and other individuals concerned about ensuring the good "stock" of American citizens.[8]

Yet the rhetoric of "progressive" science and social planning only thinly masked a much more reactionary set of sentiments against immigrants, the poor, racial minorities, and people with mental disabilities. Anti-immigrant feelings among native-born Americans had risen steadily in the post–Civil War decades, reaching a frenzied pitch in the 1910s and early 1920s. Nativism grew from an even more general middle-class fear of the poor, who appeared to be growing more unruly and aggressive in urban slums and in radical labor organizations. The discomfort with poor and in immigrant populations contained as well a strong racial prejudice against people of darker hues, whether African American, Mexican, Indian, Asian, or "swarthy" Europeans of Italian or Greek heritage.

As racial violence and xenophobia peaked in the early years of the twentieth century, a seemingly distinct fear of the "feebleminded," a group more recently known as mentally retarded or developmentally delayed, also reached new heights. Popular opinion held that bad heredity set in motion a disastrous slippery slope that led from inferior intelligence to sexual immorality and drunkenness, high rates of illegitimacy, and repetition of the cycle through generations of feebleminded offspring. The national panic over "the menace of the feebleminded" provided a catch-all category of danger, allowing well-to-do white Americans to articulate their fear of social disorder erupting from the masses of unpredictable strangers in their midst.[9]

These fears gained intellectual credence as evolutionary theory spurred inquiry into the science of heredity. Eugenic science sought to apply the latest scientific knowledge of heredity to population policies designed for the best possible social outcome. Such theories gained many adherents among scientists and the general public during the first two decades of the century. Two big research institutes, the Cold Spring Harbor Eugenics Records Office on Long Island, New York, and the Chicago Psychopath Laboratory, spent years training field workers and collecting data that became the basis for scientific publications and popularized studies that traced the lineages of genetically "defective" families. As these studies built interest and incited fears, eugenics clubs sprouted in cities around the nation, while popular magazines published over 120 articles about eugenics in the five-year period between 1909 and 1914. The strongest advocates created national organizations like the American Eugenics Association and Human Betterment Foundation to proselytize for a cause funded by some of the nation's leading philanthropists.[10]

By the time the southern states jumped on the sterilization bandwagon in the 1920s and 1930s, many scientists had already disputed the credibility of eugenic theories. As knowledge of mass sterilizations and genocide by the Nazis reached the public, few experts could defend the claims that justified state-mandated sterilization, and northern states gradually restricted or halted their eugenics programs.[11] Yet scientific criticism did little to slow the momentum of such programs in the South. Professional and political interest in eugenic solutions to the problem of mental and social "defectives" remained strong, untouched by more sophisticated scientific discourses. By the late 1950s, the states of Georgia, Virginia, and North Carolina were responsible for three-quarters of all U.S. eugenic sterilizations.[12]

The late onset of sterilization policies in the South can be explained by the comparatively later development of activist state governments, so-called progressive reforms, and strong academic communities in the South. When southerners did embrace sterilization, traditions in racial thought and regulation contributed to its long duration. Southern slavery entailed the first and most widespread embrace of eugenics in America. Some slaveowners tried to match their strongest male and female fieldhands for the purpose of breeding stronger, healthier slaves. Others operated with a somewhat lighter hand, but still attempted to influence mate selection and childbearing among enslaved African Americans. Moreover, slaveowners regularly intervened in reproductive matters, rewarding women who bore many children, separating children from mothers, and producing children of their own through rape or other coercive sexual liaisons. Thus from the beginning, elites of the South viewed intervention into procreation as a worthy and rational practice.[13] The continuing strength of white supremacist thought combined with the tradition of eugenic intervention helps account for the receptivity of southern legislators and their constituencies to eugenic sterilization.

*Y*et paradoxically it was exactly this tradition that justified policies that at first sterilized a disproportionate number of white women. National proponents of eugenic intervention focused from an early date on the danger posed by young mentally and socially impaired women. In a classic statement of the problem, Walter Fernald of Massachusetts told an audience in 1904: "It is well known that feebleminded women and girls are very liable to become sources of unspeakable debauchery and licentiousness which pollutes . . . the minds and bodies of thoughtless youth at the very threshold of manhood."[14] Southerners followed this lead. A 1919 state survey conducted in Florida found that the feebleminded girl, "always a child," was "vastly more dangerous to the community than the feebleminded boy."[15] Experts and commoners alike understood adolescent boys to have a strong sex drive that they would more than likely fail to contain. Girls, however, were thought primarily to desire male attention and approval, not sexual fulfillment. To the extent that they did feel erotic stirrings, their natural reserve and training in feminine modesty were expected to hold them back.

The surprising lack of sexual inhibition among some adolescent girls prompted a search for explanations. Feeblemindedness offered one answer. According to this view, such girls, who were both mentally and physically defective, had a weak biology that gave birth to a weak mind and even weaker moral compunction. Experts so conflated mental with moral weakness that they referred to the feebleminded as "moral imbeciles." The figure of the moral imbecile was powerful precisely because it explained away violations of conventional morality as not a social phenomenon but a biological one, reducible to a set of inferior genes. By this reasoning, "normal" girls would never engage in sexual relations outside of marriage. Those girls who did were products of their genetic inferiority. Feeblemindedness thus offered a scientific demarcation between "normal" and "defective" young women at a time when adolescents' shared embrace of modern culture and sexual morality threatened to blur the social distinctions that traditionally divided rich from poor, white from black.

Concerns about sexual immorality never lay far from the most pressing problem of the South, race relations. During the Carrie Buck case, the head of Virginia's Western State Hospital testified that feebleminded women would come to the institution "having had children, and, brother, worse than all, white women come there having negro children."[16] Such direct reference to interracial sex as a cause for eugenic concern was rare, however. The far more common rhetoric emphasized the internal weakening of "the race," that is, an imperiled white race. The head of Mississippi's feebleminded colony, for instance, argued for more attention to the feebleminded girl because with her more than others "the preservation of the intelligence of the race" was at stake.[17] Without sterilization, said Louisiana activist Jean Gordon, "our nordic civilization is gone."[18] Since the evolutionary troublemakers, in this view, resided squarely among the class of poor white southerners, issues of race and class became inseparable. In 1937 a Georgia medical journal claimed that the "South's 'poor white trash'" would choke civilization "in a wilderness of weeds" unless sterilization reduced the ranks of such "human rubbish."[19] Another expert stated that without action, this population would "continue to pour defective genes into the State's bloodstream to pollute and degrade future generations."[20]

Working-class girls moved to the front of this debate precisely because of their very active role in social and sexual transformations. Standard definitions of adolescence as a time of heightened passion, unrestrained by mature judgment, contributed to a belief that teenagers lacking a "proper" upbringing could not be relied on to exert self-control in matters of sexual expression. The presence of more and more "loose" young women, who had gathered in towns and cities to work, shop, socialize, and seek adventure, made this a particularly dangerous cohort in the eyes of the state. Freewheeling adolescent girls, both as women claiming sexual independence and as youth asserting their will over adults, posed precisely the kind of challenge to the South's traditional patriarchal structure that conservatives predicted would lead to social chaos. Consequently, a North Carolina rural county reported that "most of the operations were performed upon young single girls" whose behavior had raised concern "about actual or potential sex delinquencies which might result in children being born out of wedlock."[21] Simply giving the impression of sexual activity might land an adolescent girl in a hospital bed for sterilization.

Although moralists criticized the behavior of both African American and white adolescents, a combination of factors led southern states initially to concentrate more on white teenage women. Few whites expected black girls and young women to refrain from sexual activity, assuming sexual involvement as the norm and therefore impervious to corrective action. Moreover, "illegitimate" offspring posed little problem to local authorities as long as black communities absorbed these children into their kin networks. They cost the state nothing, since it rarely extended welfare payments to African Americans. Furthermore, because biracial children assumed the racial status of "Negro," they did not threaten to weaken the "racial stock" of southern whites. By contrast, eugenicists believed that the genetic purity of "the race" rested on the sexual purity of young white women, who were responsible for the future of "nordic civilization."

Allegations of the feebleminded girl's pernicious influence on sexual morality, racial heritage, and economic welfare spoke to the most divisive questions in southern society: the region's ambivalent embrace of modernity, the struggle over white supremacy, and the possibility that economic stagnation would produce class fissures deep enough to ruin the racial compact shared by poor and wealthy whites, an alliance on which elite control rested. The combination of these issues and fears of adolescent sexuality ensured that when state officials and reformers sought remedies for social problems, sexually active teenage girls often held center stage.

Confronting "sexual delinquency" raised problems of definition for officials implementing sterilization laws. What distinguished the normally sexed from the oversexed female adolescent, and among those who deviated, who should undergo the operation? Feeblemindedness at first appeared to resolve the conflict; girls of normal capacity refrained from sex, while girls who pursued sexual relationships by definition exhibited mental defect and "subnormal" intelligence. The fact that a majority of incarcerated delinquent girls tested in the feebleminded IQ range further linked sexual immorality to low intelligence. For example, the North Carolina Farm Colony during the 1930s assessed two-thirds of its inmates as having IQs below seventy, the typical cut-off score for feeblemindedness.[22]

To strengthen the correlation, experts used both intelligence and "social adequacy" to distinguish average individuals from the feeble-minded. Mental defect, according to this view, inevitably accompanied social inadequacy, defined by one leading eugenicist as "any sort of defect or condition" that left people "unable to maintain themselves according to the accepted rules of society."[23] In this circular logic, if idiots, imbeciles, and morons were genetically incapable of conforming to social norms, then people who failed to live according to those norms were most likely feebleminded.

Confusion arose, however, when some sexually active girls seemed not to lack intelligence or reason. The notion of "borderline intelligence" captured the phenomenon of individuals who could not immediately be classified as feebleminded but who nevertheless struck observers as dull, immoral, or both. This group, often referred to as "dull normal," muddied the line between crude categories of normal and defective, and implicitly of virtue and vice. A North Carolina sociologist wrote that the institutionalized feebleminded posed a far smaller threat than "those dull and stupid individuals, of borderline intelligence, yet not sufficiently abnormal to require community care, who constitute the greatest menace to the preservation of sound and healthy human stock."[24]

The Human Betterment Association agreed, noting that contrary to popular belief, only a small percentage of "morons" or "high-grade defectives" lived in institutions, with over 90 percent mingling freely with the rest of the population. Even worse, most people held the mistaken notion "that you can tell one by looking at him. That just isn't so. They don't look bright to be sure, but many look like thousands of us good solid citizens in our more discouraged moments."[25] Some might even look more attractive than solid citizens. A North Carolina journalist reporting on "The Case for Sterilization" commented that compared to "idiots" or "imbeciles," the true evolutionary danger lay with the "moron group which includes a host of physically attractive individuals whose IQ's are lower than a January thermometer reading. Among other things, they breed like mink."[26] This writer feared that normal people might unknowingly find themselves attracted to a "moron" and be contaminated by "lower" orders who rejected the dictates of middle-class morality. As "mental defectiveness spreads abroad among the normal and into unrestricted increase,"

Virgie Corbin, described as a sixteen-year-old mountain girl with the "mentality of a child of seven," typifies the kind of adolescent targeted by eugenics programs in the 1930s—single white girls perceived as a threat to "the state's bloodstream." By the 1950s southern sterilization programs targeted young African American women thought to drain the state of economic resources. Arthur Rothstein, Library of Congress, LC-USF33-T01–002179-M4.

cautioned another journalist, it "gravely threatens a none-too-stable society."[27]

The fear that "morons" might escape detection and cause eugenic havoc extended beyond concerns about young women, but girls seemed especially capable of deceiving through their charm and physical allure. A social worker described one reformatory inmate as a real charmer with an attractive personality and special abilities in language and music. Despite being "a coquettish type, and somewhat of a verbalist," the young woman tested with an IQ of sixty-seven and therefore qualified as "definitely feebleminded." The same social worker described other cases of teenage morons who were "quick, keen, [and] alert" with "charm of personality and conversational ability." They posed a greater social threat than more obviously disabled persons since their very attractiveness would lead to more opportunities for illicit sex or marriage and, thus, the likelihood of starting "a family of future liabilities to the State."[28]

The conundrum of adolescent female sexuality as articulated through the problem of feeblemindedness remained compelling, in part, because the masquerade of the deceptively ordinary "moron" captured southern doubts about the relationship between traditional and modern morality. Who, among modern girls, represented the best of the New South? Who, in contrast, presented a liability to the present and future welfare of the region and, consequently, should be recommended for sterilization?

*C*ase records of the North Carolina Farm Colony, a reformatory for women age sixteen and older, offer evidence of the kinds of personal histories that brought one under the surgical knife of the state. In most cases, sterilizations occurred when institutional directors and county public welfare officials conferred about troublesome individuals and petitioned the state's eugenics board to authorize the operation. But what made one girl a more likely subject for sterilization than another?[29]

The absence of a strong parental figure to act in their interest made some daughters particularly vulnerable. For example, in the mid-1930s nineteen-year-old Evelyn O'Hara got into trouble with the law after her father died and mother became very ill. Her brother's work in the Civilian Conservation Corps provided the only income for the family and brought the family to government attention. Evelyn's caseworker believed she came from "defective people" with a "distaste for work" and recommended sterilization. With a deceased father, a terminally ill mother, and a brother dependent on the government for his job, no adults could intercede on Evelyn's behalf.[30] In another case from the 1930s, the law accused Reba Carter and her sister of running a disorderly house supplied with illegal whiskey by their brother and father. After their father had been arrested and convicted and with no mother ever mentioned, the court committed both sisters to the Farm Colony. Prior to incarceration, however, a doctor treating Reba for a severe gonorrheal infection surgically removed her tubes and appendix without authorization by the eugenics board; the sterilization occurred, ostensibly, as a medically necessary treatment for venereal infection.[31]

The case of seventeen-year-old Emma Suggs suggests two other conditions that led to sterilization—unusually severe emotional problems and out-of-wedlock pregnancy. Emma had spent her childhood shuffling among the homes of her aunt, her mother and stepfather, and her father and stepmother. Deeply unhappy, she regularly ran away. After an arrest and attempted suicide, the state released her to live with her mother in Florida. Problems followed, however, and Emma returned to North Carolina by train in the custody of her county welfare worker. At one point during the trip, she became so enraged that she kicked out a window of the rail car. After another incident, the court sentenced her to the state reformatory. Emma had no record of sex delinquency and, despite being labeled "unmanageable," officials did not suggest sterilization at this time. She served her time and, after being paroled in 1940, Emma wrote to Superintendent Elsa Ernst that living at her aunt's without any friends or a job made her very lonely and unhappy. No response followed, with Emma apparently left to fend for herself emotionally until three years later a county official reported that Emma was seven months pregnant. The welfare department now searched for prior test results that might indicate a "mental condition" to justify sterilization at the time of childbirth.[32] The record ends there, but it appears that for Emma Suggs, the combination of emotional problems and the absence of any adult defender left her vulnerable to state-mandated sterilization after she became pregnant in what could well have been an attempt to end the loneliness that had plagued her for years. The case also demonstrates the long arm of the law, which followed Emma from North Carolina to Florida and from her first legal scrape to a pregnancy years after her final release from the reformatory.

Not only government authorities but also parents sometimes initiated the process that eventually led to sterilization. A parent might act out of genuine concern to protect a daughter with serious mental or emotional problems, but a more typical scenario involved parents turning to the state out of frustration, fear, or anger. In the mid-1930s, reformatory officials were contacted by the mother and younger brother of a nineteen-year-old parolee, Grace Corbett. Their letters described enraged, drunken outbursts in which Grace threatened to kill anyone who attempted to commit her again. While the mother questioned whether Grace's "mind is right," Grace's twelve-year-old brother asked only that the superintendent please come "get her and keeper for ever." This level of violence and conflict called for some type of intervention, but family members rarely received the kind of help they needed. In this case, the superintendent did not revoke parole but instead petitioned for Grace's placement in an institution for the feebleminded—a condition for which there had been no previous mention—and recommended sterilization. She failed to address how tubal ligation would solve the problems of domestic violence and alcoholic rage that prompted the plea for help.[33]

Typically, girls recommended for sterilization had long histories of "running around" or "loitering" near places of low repute like juke joints, tourist camps, or filling stations, which led to arrests for vagrancy or lewd behavior. Seventeen-year-old Olla Mae Carter, for example, had a reputation for wild sprees of drinking, lovemaking, and arrests. When Olla Mae and her partner in crime merely laughed at a judge's stern lecture, promising "to turn the damn town upside down and sow it in peas," he committed them to the reformatory where officials threatened the girls with sterilization if they did not "adjust satisfactorily."[34] But even compliance and remorse could not guarantee exemption from the procedure. Sixteen-year-old Annie Price served time for forgery in 1932 until her parole a year later. Subsequently, the county welfare officer informed Superintendent Ernst that Annie was living in a wholesome manner and had an "apparently respectable" boyfriend. Ernst nevertheless advised sterilization "as soon as possible" since with "a girl of Annie's type one can not say with any degree of certainty how long this will last."[35] Once marked as feebleminded and immoral, even acquiescence could not override suspicions of permanent sordidness and genetic danger.

Sexuality entered the decision in a more subtle way as well. When psychiatric professionals assessed the mental state of delinquent girls, they sometimes commented on their attractiveness. In one instance, a psychologist described sixteen-year-old Adele Gorman as "a nice looking girl with a ready smile" who, for her own protection, should be institutionalized because "she will never be able to cope with the temptations of civilian life." Farm Colony officials then tried to arrange for her sterilization and transfer to the school for the feebleminded.[36] The psychologists in this and similar cases may have projected their own sexual responses onto girls undergoing "scientific" assessment, with their personal attractions contributing to a recommendation for sterilization.

The actions of state officials appear to have been motivated by a mixture of dislike and attraction, the desire to help and simultaneously to retaliate against working-class girls who led troubled lives and exhibited troubling behaviors. Interpreting these surgeries as a form of state violence against the right to bodily integrity and self-determination does not preclude the possibility that state officials saw themselves as acting ethically and even in the interest of the chosen individual. Perhaps those who passed and applied the laws acted out of conscious intent to improve their society through eugenic population control, but underlying their good intentions were other, less conscious feelings of repulsion, class resentment, and anger. That they believed in the worthiness of their actions, however, does not explain the state's power to act.

Teenage girls along with other selected women and men underwent sterilization because state and professional leaders believed in their authority to do so and encountered limited resistance along the way. A convergence of political and professional interests enabled sterilization advocates to pass and implement laws without demonstrated support from a majority of southerners. To the extent that the public knew or cared about sterilization, experts relied on pseudoscience, racial fears, and dire economic predictions to win support for their programs. Constituencies that might have contested the policy—teenagers, African Americans, poor whites—lacked the political strength to wage effective opposition. It took large numbers of citizens and solid economic backing to defeat sterilization legislation, as Catholic voters did in Louisiana. Having secured a position of unchallenged authority in Mississippi, Georgia, Virginia, South Carolina, and North Carolina, state medical authorities carried out sterilization orders there with impunity.

Yet the absence of organized opposition did not translate into a lack of resistance at the individual level. Despite the imbalance of power a number of parents refused consent, preventing an intended sterilization. One mother, for example, dodged the request from reformatory officials by explaining that she was so fed up with the daughter's "sauceness" that she would sign nothing that required further involvement: "I have gone my limit in trying to correct her . . . She will be eighteen years old [soon] . . . and then she will be her own boss as she has tried so hard for to be."[37] Another mother took almost fifteen months to come to a decision after the welfare department advised sterilization for her daughter, expressing uncertainty about interfering with "God's plan." When delaying tactics no longer sufficed, the mother flatly refused consent, claiming that it would be better to care for an illegitimate child than to prevent its birth.[38] Whether through indirection, stalling, or flat-out refusal, parents with very little societal power sometimes managed to prevent their daughters' sterilization. Commenting on parental resistance, one county welfare officer defended himself against charges of weak compliance by reminding the state corrections commissioner that "the law requires that the parents sign consent papers . . . and we have found parents who refused to sign these."[39] A survey of North Carolina county welfare departments listed "resistance of client and relatives" as a major obstacle to eugenic sterilization.[40]

At least one black community shows evidence of collective resistance to government attempts to identify sterilization prospects. In 1950 the state superintendent of welfare, Dr. Ellen Winston, sent letters to county welfare superintendents asking them to identify feebleminded African American children who could benefit from being institutionalized. The Caldwell County agent informed Winston that while she believed numerous feebleminded Negro children resided in the county, her efforts to get ministers and teachers to provide names had proved futile. When approached, "ministers were unable to furnish us names of any such children," while teachers either "did not respond to our inquiry" or "could not furnish us any information."[41] It is possible that black communities suspected that eugenic sterilization motivated these inquiries. The state welfare department kept a typed list of names provided by other counties. Faint pencil marks next to children's names recorded information such as "sterilized," "petition has been filed," "sterilization ordered," or "operation approved."[42] While the South's weakest citizens could not in the end halt the process, they mustered enough resistance to force the state to disguise both its practice of and motives for sterilization.

The widespread use of deception by government officials suggests a concerted effort to deflect expected criticisms of eugenic policies. One form of deception occurred when state officials compelled "consent" by making institutional release contingent on agreeing to the surgery. For example, a letter sent to parents of a reformatory inmate in 1944 explained that the superintendent had recommended their daughter "for release but prior to her leaving that she should be given a sterilization operation." The letter then summoned the parents to the county welfare office "so that you can sign a Consent for the operation."[43] In this and many similar cases, officials gave the strong impression that a daughter's release depended on her sterilization.

In another deceptive practice, social workers or medical professionals steered likely candidates into the hands of the few officials empowered to authorize sterilizations. State laws permitted eugenic sterilizations only if conducted under the aegis of state custodial institutions or, in North Carolina, through the Department of Public Welfare. Officials found it easy to evade this statutory restriction, however, through interdepartmental referrals. If a poor woman or pregnant teenager went to a public clinic for birth control, prenatal care, or an infection, a public health worker might evaluate her as a prospect for sterilization and then refer her to the welfare department, which could legally arrange for the procedure or for institutional commitment.[44]

State governments also misrepresented the number of mandated sterilizations they performed by labeling a significant number of them "therapeutic" rather than "eugenic." If judged necessary for the individual's health, a "therapeutic" sterilization could be performed by a physician without involving the state eugenics board. Dr. Albert Priddy of the Virginia State Colony, for example, performed seventy-five to one hundred sterilizations on young women with "pelvic diseases" despite some victims' claims that they had not experienced any illness whatsoever.[45]

State officials concealed information most immediately by preventing young women from learning about the procedure in advance. At Samarcand Manor, the superintendent arranged for inmates to be sterilized between the time of their institutional release and their return home to ensure that sterilization did not become common knowledge among inmates. The state corrections commissioner reasoned, "It certainly would not be well to have these operations performed while the girls are at Samarcand as tonsillectomies are, there would be too much talk."[46] Some authorities purposely misled individuals about the nature of the operation. In one common ruse, doctors informed the patient that a medical condition, especially gonorrhea, necessitated the surgery. Alternatively, physicians used the event of childbirth or nongynecological surgeries, like appendectomies, to perform a tubal ligation. By the 1960s, these operations had become so common in Mississippi that they were nicknamed "Mississippi appendectomies."[47] Tragically, not everyone understood that the procedure would end their reproductive capacity. The State of Virginia sterilized Mary Frances Corbin Donald at age eleven, a surgery that left her in a coma for almost two weeks, telling her simply that it was "for your own health." Only as an adult did she discover the purpose of the surgery.[48]

Sterilization advocates also concealed information from the public. The eugenics board in North Carolina decided to limit its "educational work" to those public officials involved in the referral or petition process on the grounds that "an outspoken propaganda campaign would be distrusted as tending to stir up opposition, not hitherto manifest."[49] When states did inform the public, educational materials consistently portrayed the typical sterilized subject as an adult married woman, suffering from poverty, overwork, multiple pregnancies, and poor health, who gratefully accepted the state's offer of sterilization as an answer to her many problems. A University of North Carolina research report from 1949 hailed the "popularity" of the operation with a folksy passage summarizing a typical enthusiastic response: "Ah'm proud of mine . . . Ah think it's a great thing for poor folks to have."

The claim that "relief from worry and anxiety was everywhere expressed" by many older women who underwent the surgery may have indeed been true.[50] One study of North Carolina found that not all women who underwent eugenic sterilization felt victimized; some in fact appreciated the state's interest in limiting family size.[51] But teenage girls were not in such a position to use eugenic sterilization for their own benefit. Adolescents did not seek out the operation, exhibited no desire to end their child-bearing capacity, and attempted to resist the operation in the rare instances when they had foreknowledge or power in the situation.

This pattern of deception and coercion, allowing for the fact that some women understood and chose surgery as an option, suggests that eugenic sterilization never received widespread acceptance, even in states that used it extensively. Yet as long as it met with favor among a select group of professionals and administrators, the state required no other support—only a lack of organized opposition. Once politicians enacted the original law, its implementation became part of an administrative state that remained largely invisible except to those whom it directly affected. Middle-class and poor southerners untouched by the policy had scant knowledge of the practice, since officials made little effort to publicize it. And those subject to eugenic policies encountered a paternalistic government that viewed them as a mass of ignorant, backward folk whose judgment paled before the superior insights of state officials who thereby gained the right not only to regulate the public behavior of citizens, but also to intervene in the most private space of their bodies.

$\mathcal{E}$ventually, however, southern states did alter their eugenic policies in response to changing public opinion. Subtle changes in the demographics of sterilization that began in the 1940s had, by the 1950s, produced a significant shift in both the discourse and application of eugenic policies. Public discussion of the "defective delinquent" faded before a castigating gaze on the "welfare mother," who unlike her predecessor was now figured as a black woman "cheating" the state out of its money rather than its precious racial heritage. Underlying this transformation were new understandings of adolescent female sexuality and changing dynamics of southern class and race relations.

Several related social transformations underlay this shift. Nationally, class and ethnic conflicts subsided in the 1940s, partially resolved by a booming wartime economy and diminished as well by efforts to forge a unified nation in a time of crisis. The fear of the feebleminded menace faded from the national scene as leaders focused first on the Depression and then on what every American could contribute to the war effort. The discovery and availability toward the end of the war of penicillin as a rapid cure for syphilis also had an effect. Incarceration of sexually active, infected women became less important for public officials, who tempered their anger toward diseased and delinquent young women. These changes produced a new, more sympathetic view of sexuality in the average adolescent girl—a view that theoretically extended to African American and other young women of color, but in practice was much more likely to include only white teenagers.[52] In the South, this tendency only amplified a preexisting pattern of racial differentiation and contempt.

A chilling example of this phenomenon occurred in 1954 when an eighteen-year-old black girl named Eleanor Rush met her death in the North Carolina state prison for women. Serving six months for forgery, Rush died after prison staff forcibly restrained her with leather straps, iron claws, and a gag. Although a coroner's jury found that Eleanor died "due to her own violent efforts against necessary restraints," further investigation determined that guards dislocated her neck during gagging, which caused her to die minutes later with a crushed spinal chord.[53] What is significant about this case is not the shocking mistreatment of an adolescent girl with a history of delinquency and incarceration—an all-too-common occurrence for many black as well as white inmates. The important difference is that unlike the Samarcand arson case, which led to a lively public debate about the causes and nature of delinquency in girls, the surrounding furor in the Eleanor Rush case rarely, if ever, considered her—even in death—as a sympathetic figure with a troubled but unfortunate past. North Carolinians learned only that she was a domestic worker who, according to the white press, "never was important to anybody except as a nuisance at best and a trouble maker at worst . . . She was an almost worthless person."[54] One editorial defended the state's possible use of excessive force, unexpectedly introducing sterilization into the debate. "Her parents should have been sterilized," wrote the enraged author. "All such vicious, mean and dangerous pests should be exterminated."[55] Eleanor Rush, in this view, never deserved to be born, and once born, did not deserve to live.

The author's mention of sterilization in reference to black women is significant, for although it was unlikely that her parents would have been sterilized, it was entirely likely that under slightly different circumstances the state would have sterilized Eleanor Rush. As part of New Deal relief programs, federal law required southern states to extend welfare payments to all of its needy citizens, not just poor white families. At the same time, by the late 1940s and 1950s the percentage of whites in need of social provision declined as the healthy postwar economy lifted many white southerners out of poverty. Consequently, by the 1950s Aid to Dependent Children programs had more black women on the rolls than ever before, a presence that made them increasingly vulnerable to social criticism and state action.

African Americans in the postwar South demonstrated greater determination than ever to challenge the undemocratic racial hierarchy of their region. The revival of southern NAACP chapters, the Montgomery bus boycott, and successful legal challenges to segregated schools launched the modern civil rights movement. These actions also provoked an angry backlash of violent reprisals, organized political resistance, and punitive government actions. Although black welfare recipients did not organize as a constituency and the movement did not yet address issues of public assistance, this cohort of predominantly single mothers formed a population vulnerable to racial retaliation. The growing enmity of white southern leaders toward assertive black citizens helps account for the growing hostility directed at poor black mothers "demanding" welfare from the state.

This mix proved dangerous when added to the already punitive nature of state eugenic programs. By midcentury, southern sterilization policies were specifically targeting African American women between the ages of fifteen and thirty. In North Carolina, from the mid-1930s to 1950 only 21.5 percent of sterilized women were African American, despite their constituting roughly 30 percent of the population. But from 1950 through the mid-1960s they comprised 50.7 percent of sterilized women.[56] Evidence from South Carolina is even more extreme. Of the 104 persons whom South Carolina sterilized between 1949 and 1960, 102 were African American women.[57] Among sterilized women, the number of adolescents remained high. While North Carolina sterilized 843 ten- to nineteen-year-olds between 1936 and 1950, the number increased to 1,029 between 1950 and 1964.[58]

Although rarely discussed publicly, subtle clues signaled the shift in racial orientation. In 1946 the *Chapel Hill Weekly* described mental defectives as heavily dependent on public relief and including a "higher proportion of Negroes than whites."[59] Several years later a study of North Carolina sterilizations noted that "the feeble-minded Negro woman, often with illegitimate children, is a familiar and recurrent problem to health and welfare agencies."[60] This last comment is all the more important because of the state's increased reliance on welfare offices and health clinics to identify candidates for sterilization.

The turn toward welfare departments accompanied a shift from eugenic to economic rationales; economic dependency now replaced mental deficiency as the main criterion for sterilization. By 1960, the young, black "welfare mother" with out-of-wedlock children occupied the position formerly held by the poor, white, feebleminded adolescent girl. Yet advocates of sterilization avoided explicitly racial language. The pattern of government deception established in earlier years continued, probably heightened by the discredited status of eugenics in a post-Nazi world.

Instead, attention shifted to the linked questions of birth control and welfare, where the allegedly vast numbers of young black women on welfare held center stage in public debate. Issues of illegitimacy, welfare, and birth control assumed a highly racialized form as concern about a worldwide "population explosion" of darker races mushroomed and, closer to home, southern political officials vented their anger at African Americans who dared to challenge white supremacy. When the State of Alabama passed a 1959 statute cutting off aid to mothers of more than one illegitimate child, more than a few legislators admitted to local journalists that "if the question of segregation had not been involved they would not have voted for the measure at all."[61]

Midcentury public policies and racial rhetoric directed at poor young black mothers in the South laid a foundation for a future nationwide debate: the recent furor over African American "teenage mothers" and "welfare queens" who are held responsible for larger problems of social disorder and economic decline. In the intervening years, thousands of young black women, along with white and Native women, suffered sterilizations under a policy that continued to operate without public oversight until the 1970s, when black civil rights workers joined forces with Native American, Puerto Rican, and feminist activists to publicize and demand an end to sterilization abuses.

A number of ironies mark the history of eugenic sterilization in the South. From the 1910s through the 1930s, the decades in which legislators first proposed and implemented sterilization laws, white intellectuals identified the regional culture of "simple" white rural and mountain folk as the most "pure" form of Anglo-Saxon heritage, worthy of preservation and celebration in "folk" schools and folk festivals developed throughout the mountain South.[62] Yet scientific experts and political reformers of the period identified the same group of poor white southerners as a source of racial degeneracy dangerous enough to justify compulsory sterilizations. Of even greater irony, records show that in numerous cases reformatory officials sterilized inmates as "unfit mothers" only to turn around and parole them to domestic jobs in which their primary responsibility was to care for middle-class children. In a bizarre twist of logic, after condemning sterilized wo-men as too feebleminded to bear and rear productive citizens of their own, the state judged them perfectly fit to help rear the children of well-to-do parents.

A more profound inconsistency involves the relationship between adolescent women and democratic government. Teenage girls stood at the border of not only sexual and social maturity, but also full female citizenship. A political system that had historically defined female citi-zenship in terms of motherhood had, by 1920, recognized women's capacity as independent citizens guaranteed the right to vote and the right to individualized personhood apart from fathers and husbands. The sterilization of thousands of southerners, most of them women and from one-third to one-half of them teenagers, denied women a po-litical role as mothers of the state and rescinded their individual lib-erty, violating principles of bodily integrity and reproductive choice. The modern southern state assumed the role of firm but benevolent patriarch, positioning itself as the head of a single white family with one shared bloodstream. White women held a subordinate position that nevertheless bestowed the great responsibility of maintaining the "purity" of the body politic—through premarital virginity followed by eugenic procreation. Black women's procreation served, as it did in slavery, a more economic purpose of providing laborers and contribut-ing to, not subtracting from, the public coffers.

When adolescents admitted to sexual relations, ran away from home, got pregnant, or turned to the state for support, they shrugged off the private authority of southern white men. At this point, public officials stepped into the breach. State governments first singled out poor, young, white women who violated sexual norms, designating them as "not-mothers" at a time when most white women were val-ued as "mothers of the state." Southern states treated black women differently in the beginning, ignoring most sexual violations in favor of maintaining high fertility rates that ensured a ready supply of cheap agricultural labor. But when labor demands shrank and elites perceived black women's fertility as costing rather than enriching white taxpayers, state governments turned their attention to terminating the reproductive capacity of those single black women receiving welfare or other state services.

Positioning itself as a paternalistic provider acting in the best interest of women and children, the state demanded a far greater service in return. The *Buck v. Bell* judicial opinion concluded that the "principle that sustains compulsory vaccination is broad enough to cover cutting the Fallopian tubes." Reasoning that "the public welfare may call upon the best citizens for their lives," the opinion continued, "It would be strange if it could not call upon those who already sap the strength of the state for their lesser sacrifices . . . in order to prevent our being swamped with incompetence."[63] The Supreme Court's analogy with vaccination fails to hold up, however. Introducing a tiny amount of a virus to protect against future contagion does not mirror the process of sterilization, in which the state commanded young women to sacrifice future life not in an effort to fight against an external danger, but to eliminate the ostensible threat that they themselves embodied.

Adolescent girls exercising social and sexual autonomy threatened both individual family hierarchies and the authority of paternalistic state governments. At times they successfully challenged parents and other adults who imposed restrictions that daughters found unpleasant or unjust. But when their accumulative actions began to challenge a social order that empowered white over black, male over female, and rich over poor, southern governments intervened, committing violence and deception under the guise of social protection and scientific progress. State officials condemned thousands of young black and white women to a publicly stigmatized status as mentally and morally defective, then cut privately into their bodies to prevent them from ever enjoying the sexual independence and social autonomy they had once tried to claim.

chapter seven

The World War II Pickup Girl and Wartime Passions

As the U.S. government mobilized for war in the early 1940s, the nation focused anxious attention on the young men who would defend American democracy against foreign aggression. Soldiers had to be protected against not only injury and death but also disease. Public health officials frequently recounted the horrible price in lost manpower and lives caused by the prevalence of venereal disease (VD) during World War I, when 400,000 men suffering from VD missed almost 7.5 million days of service, the equivalent of losing six infantry regiments for an entire year.[1] Moreover, evidence from World War II induction exams revealed an alarmingly high rate of syphilis and gonorrhea among current draftees.[2]

National leaders developed a number of responses to this danger, ranging from the educational to the harshly punitive. The armed services created instructional programs for soldiers, as well as "pro stations," short for prophylactic stations, which offered free and easily available condoms for military men. Even as officials tried to steer soldiers along a healthy path, they tended to locate the source of the problem outside the military, finding an easy target in the young women who traded sex for cash in the vicinity of military camps and defense plants.[3] One army investigation estimated that among soldiers, 15 percent abstained from sex, another 15 percent were "incorrigibles," and the remaining 70 percent fell somewhere in be-

tween, suffering from "occasional lapses of virtue" exploited by enterprising prostitutes.[4]

But officials soon realized the problem had spread far beyond red
light districts and professional prostitution. Journalists, military leaders, and social service providers complained, "Today, the hard and fast
line between prostitute and non-prostitute has been blurred," pointing
especially to the great number of female minors who acceded to the
sexual and financial temptations of servicemen looking for a good
time.[5] Seventeen-year-old Mertie, for example, moved from Mississippi to Memphis, found employment as a waitress, and shared a
cheap room at a boarding house with her coworker. After closing time
the two girls regularly arranged dates with servicemen, often ending
up back in their room. One night police arrested Mertie and her
friend for loitering in an uptown alley with two soldiers. In a similar
sweep police arrested fifteen-year-old Lou, who had left home for
Memphis to visit a sailor she knew, arranging to stay for a week's
visit. After making friends with another girl at the bus station, she
stayed in Memphis and began double-dating servicemen, often going
to a local tourist camp for semi-private assignations. She also went
with men to a city hotel, where local police arrested her one night for
sex delinquency.[6]

The wartime press named such teenagers "pick-up girls," or the
"amateur girl," in contrast to experienced prostitutes who worked for
cash only. Also called "Victory Girls," "Khaki Whackies," and "Good
Time Charlottes," they charged little or nothing for their sexual encounters, seeking instead the company of soldiers, a night on the town
paid for by their date, excitement and adventure, or the pleasures of
sex. White working-class girls like Mertie and Lou spawned a widespread public discourse on the phenomenon of the pickup girl. African American girls garnered far less public attention, although their
pursuit of social and sexual freedom generated concern among family
and community members. For example, Ruth, a fourteen-year-old
from Portsmouth, Virginia, found herself equally drawn to the economic and social opportunities of wartime. She found work as a soda
jerk in a "colored" USO club and at the same time began dating local
boys and soldiers, all against her father's orders. Still living with her
family, Ruth faced not the law but a violent confrontation with her
wrathful father, who condemned both her dating and nightclub job as

immoral.[7] Although black protective agencies used stories like Ruth's to lobby for job opportunities and improved social services for black youth, the public panic over wartime promiscuity ignored black youth for an almost exclusive focus on the white teenage pickup girl, who became a focal point for home-front anxieties.

Newsweek described "the moral breakdown among teen-age American girls" as "what may well turn out to be the gravest home-front tragedy of the war."[8] Condemned for their role in spreading venereal diseases and moral chaos, the adolescent sex delinquent complicated the issues of prostitution and promiscuity. In both popular media and professional literature, the pickup girl raised fundamental questions about how to draw the line between "normal" and "deviant" sexuality, between good girls and bad.[9] Placed in the national spotlight, sexually active girls provoked a widespread discussion about a topic that at first glance seems far removed from the exigencies of war—the nature of female adolescent sexuality.

Although understood as national in scope, the problem of sex delinquency near military bases and defense industries focused initially and disproportionately on the South, since the region played host to more than two-thirds of domestic army and naval bases. As fertile ground for new defense plants, southern towns underwent dramatic population changes. Between 1940 and 1944, Mobile, Alabama, grew more rapidly than any other American city with a 65 percent increase, from 141,947 to 233,891 residents.[10] Norfolk, Virginia, and its surrounding towns grew by 45 percent, while the population of Charleston County, South Carolina, jumped by 38 percent.[11] The influx of hundreds of thousands of newcomers in the military and defense industry jobs drove venereal disease rates in the South, already the highest in the nation, even higher. In one study of six southern states, syphilis rates for white soldiers ranked second among eleven national regions, with rates for black soldiers the highest in the country.[12] In a study of cities with the worst rates of infection among Army personnel, forty of the eighty-one identified cities were in the South. The small city of Columbus, Georgia, reported 647 infections during 1944, a number higher than that reported by the much larger cities of Chicago, Boston, Detroit, Dallas, and Houston.[13]

Social critics frequently linked high syphilis rates to sex delinquency in young girls. After *Washington Post* reporter Agnes Meyer took a cross-country tour to investigate wartime conditions, her 1943 book, *Journey through Chaos,* named juvenile delinquency as a prime culprit in wartime chaos, with its "most distressing" aspect the sexual delinquency of very young adolescents. Reporting on army maneuvers near Leesville, Louisiana, Meyer attributed venereal disease to both the "slatternly prostitute" and "that new war product, the 'amateur' or 'pickup girl.'" Moving on to Mobile, she found that residents named sex delinquency among eleven- to fifteen-year-old girls as the city's worst problem.[14] Meyer believed the greatest trouble lay in girls who hailed from "very primitive, ignorant" backwoods people, "the like of which I have never seen anywhere else." Yet she noted with surprise, "Even the highest type of children are getting into serious trouble."[15]

The federal government responded to problems of disease and delinquency by creating the Social Protection Division (SPD) under the Office of Community War Services (OCWS), headed by Eliot Ness (later depicted as the hero of the popular television show *The Untouchables*). By the war's end, the agency's depiction of prostitution blended seamlessly into a scenario that could just as easily describe conventional teenage dating. Leo Wilson, the SPD's regional representative in Georgia, complained in late 1945, "I find it difficult to draw a line between the girl who grants her favors for a certain sum of money and her sister who will indulge in identical activities for a T-bone steak." Or less than a steak, since he also found it "difficult to draw a line between the promiscuous female who has as her price a good meal, and her less-exacting sister whose only price is that of a couple of hamburgers or bottle of beer or an evening's entertainment." In depicting these "sisters," Wilson's account of illicit nights on the town sounds remarkably like typical scenarios of teenage dating. He asked, "How can we say that the girl who expects money or a meal is much different from the one who has as her price a ticket to the movies, a ride in an automobile, or an evening spent in dancing?"[16] In light of this slippage, Wilson concluded that the Social Protection Division must redefine prostitution in very broad terms.

In fact, the wartime sexual activities of adolescent girls did less to expand the concept of prostitution than to make concepts of "normal" adolescent sexuality more elastic. By the late 1940s, teenagers, experts, and popular media recognized sexual desire and its expression, in some form, as within the bounds of ordinary adolescent girl-

During World War II the increased social and economic autonomy of teenage girls–and their avid interest in soldiers–made it harder to distinguish between illicit "pick-up girls" and typical teenage "bobby-soxers." This 1938 photo of Louisiana girls enjoying themselves in a cafe presages the independence of wartime adolescents, who looked to peer groups–rather than adults–as their primary source of guidance. Russell Lee, Library of Congress, LC-USF33–011661-M3.

hood, represented by the newly popular figure of the teenage "bobby-soxer." Whether labeled a "delinquent" or a "typical" teenager, southern adolescent girls altered the meanings of sex, romance, and love in ways that would have long-term implications for American teenage culture and southern sexual politics. Their actions prompted changes in law enforcement, social services, and expert opinion, in the process throwing into question highly valued distinctions—between rich and poor, white and black, and mind and body—that undergirded southern society.

Government officials developed policies to reduce prostitution and pickups in military areas while testing, treating, and hopefully preventing venereal infections. Demanding that "social hygiene" organizations and public health experts act quickly to eliminate "vice" in nearby military encampments, federal agents also pressured local law enforcement and politicians to close down red light districts and drive commercial prostitutes from the city limits. Despite their success in reducing the number of visible vice districts, the problem of venereal disease persisted and the federal government turned to other solutions.

In 1941 Congress passed the May Act, which enabled federal law enforcement to intervene in those cases where local authorities had refused to attack prostitution aggressively. Although only enforced twice—in Tennessee and North Carolina—the May Act served as a stick over the head of local officials, employing the threat of federal intervention. As a result, standard prewar red light districts declined measurably, civilian areas were policed, and women suspected of transmitting syphilis and gonorrhea were detained.[17] In addition to stepping up arrests and prosecutions, public health officials initiated compulsory testing programs. In the most drastic example, the state of Alabama required every person between fourteen and fifty to undergo blood tests for venereal disease and submit to mandatory treatment if positive.[18]

Expanding the police powers of the state, the federal government funded quarantine hospitals "for segregation and treatment of prostitutes and other recalcitrant persons capable of spreading syphilis."[19] Quarantine camps incarcerated women for periods of several weeks to months, ensuring a full course of treatment and preventing any additional contacts while contagious. Treatment for venereal disease became quicker and more effective over the course of the war, especially with the availability of penicillin toward the war's end. The government replaced long-term confinement with rapid treatment centers that treated and released women within a week; but as before women were forcibly held for treatment under the law.

In response to stepped-up arrests, prosecutions, and compulsory testing, critics accused government agents of detaining women without criminal evidence and coercing "confessions" to justify forced testing.[20] The Social Protection Division denied coercion but admitted, "We *do* encourage police departments . . . to pick up women and girls who are found in situations where they are obviously *in danger of becoming* pick-ups or promiscuous." Young women suspected not of actual sexual or criminal activity, but of potential future sexual activity, became subject to police detention, invasive medical procedures, and possible incarceration in female reformatories.[21]

The public outcry over female delinquency as a potential drain on the armed forces set the war years apart from the Depression, when the condition of unemployed male youth in their teens and early twenties had sparked the greatest concern. In wartime, young men of this age were not casting about for something to do; they were serving in the military. And young women in their early twenties joined the throngs of women entering the labor force, enjoying higher pay and a greater range of job opportunities than ever before. In their stead, children in their early and middle teens drew the lion's share of attention. The FBI, national media, and child experts issued report after report of skyrocketing rates of juvenile delinquency. In the first six months of 1943, American magazines published 1,200 articles on juvenile delinquency, while J. Edgar Hoover issued panicked press releases about the severity of the problem.[22] The press talked constantly about damaged, neglected children, the result of working mothers and fathers and husbands gone to war. Commentators bemoaned the loss of stable community life caused by mass migration as well as the cultural clash and personal anomie that followed in its wake. As conditions of war disrupted patterns of daily life and eroded established mechanisms of social control—the family, schools, church, and informal community oversight—what was to become of family life, peacetime values, and the social order?

The pickup girl stood at the conjunction of these troubling questions, collapsing problems of delinquency, disease, and sexual deviance into a single villainous figure. Journalists as well as public health and law enforcement officials condemned the pickup girl as a vector of disease, the transfer point from immoral females to "innocent" soldiers following their natural sexual urges. Though many such "girls" were women in their twenties, the public outcry centered on teenagers, especially those under sixteen. As legal minors, they symbolized dramatic and frightening change, a time when the "normal" ways of life had been pulled out like a rug from underneath the feet of surprised adults—older persons who had long imagined adolescence as a time of gradual character formation under the influence of their own "good character" and wise guidance. And though public health and social workers typically described pickup girls as uneducated, impoverished migrants lacking in basic moral and intellectual capacities, they also fretted over the pleasures that might lure any teenager into the pickup scene. One reformer worried that "many youngsters from all walks of life" now indulged in promiscuity and, even worse, that they believed "this type of behavior is not wrong."[23] Such girls found the attractions of a night out on the town, small gifts, thrilling adventure, instant romance, and the possibility of marriage worth the price of some form of sexual exchange (which significantly also held the possibility of physical delight). At the same time, in pursuing pleasure they risked being "picked up" not by a date but by police. They then faced forcible detention, invasive medical procedures, and possible incarceration for weeks, months, or in rare cases, years.

*E*xperts struggled to analyze this disturbing turn of events. Why had sexual delinquency become so widespread as to include girls who in all other respects seemed "typical" or "normal"? What had gone wrong, in society or in these individuals' development? They discovered the roots of sex delinquency in two locations, one specific to the war and the other hardwired into the body's transition from childhood to adulthood.

Social workers, psychologists, and recreational specialists pointed first to conditions of war that had disrupted healthy adolescent development. Huge wartime population shifts meant that just under 15 percent of civilians moved from their native county or state at some point during the war.[24] Individuals and families faced a series of dislocating and disorienting changes including the shift from rural to urban life, the loss of family members and familiar routines, and the absence of a known, reliable community for both material and moral support. Absent fathers and working mothers created a vacuum of adult oversight and authority, leaving teenagers more on their own than ever before.

Adolescents had not only time on their hands, but also money in their pockets. Labor shortages for war production prompted a rapid, extensive increase of teenage workers. In 1940, a total of 872,314 teens between the ages of fourteen and eighteen were in the labor force. By April 1944 an estimated three million in this age group held paying jobs.[25] About half of teenage workers balanced employment with school. The other 1.5 million left high school or never attended in order to take advantage of the chance to earn decent money while also contributing to the war effort. After years of increasing enroll-ment, the number of fifteen- to eighteen-year-olds in high school dropped by 24 percent during the war.[26]

Greater social and financial independence resulted in a premature autonomy that experts dubbed a "rush to maturity." Teenagers de-pended not on adults for guidance but on each other. A "group in-stinct" developed among insecure adolescents who reassured them-selves by conforming to the crowd, making peers far more influential than parents or other adults. Accordingly, thirteen- and fourteen-year-olds took on the behavior of fifteen- and sixteen-year-olds who, in turn, modeled themselves after those in their late teens, who for their part now assumed the responsibilities of military service and labor usually reserved for young adults. Children who rushed into maturity, in this view, overestimated their own abilities to handle money and to exercise proper judgment in choices of leisure, friendship, and sexual-ity. When their precocious personalities leaped far ahead of their emo-tional development, the mismatch spelled trouble.

Trouble often came in the form of objectionable sexual behavior, es-pecially among girls. Defining the female rush to maturity as a sexual phenomenon, experts used sex delinquency and juvenile delinquency as interchangeable terms. In the past, professionals had characterized sex delinquents as a small population whose troubles signaled some kind of psychopathology or "mental deficiency" that distinguished them from "normal" (sexually inactive) girls their age. But in the 1940s, a new interpretation of female adolescent sexual behavior took shape. Alice Scott Nutt described how "new stresses and strains and the quickened tempo of life accentuate and complicate for adolescents the inevitable problems incident to the growing-up process." Such strains too often led girls into sexual problems, euphemistically la-beled "Patriotism Gone Wrong."[27] Professionals now deemed sexual temptations and difficulties "inevitable" for girls.

Yet the effects of war did not strike experts as a sufficient explana-tion for increased delinquency. Psychologists and other social scien-tists looked to their own fields for theories of adolescent psychosexual development that probed beyond immediate circumstance. They ar-gued that such teens could best be understood as an extreme example of difficulties inherent to the transition from childhood to adulthood. Adolescence, in this view, involved physical, emotional, and social disturbances; it was a harrowing transition that even under the best of circumstances could result in serious behavioral and emotional problems.

Experts articulated basic developmental tasks of this stage that contributed to adolescent confusion, unhappiness, and instability. In a special issue of *Annals of the American Academy of Political and Social Science* devoted to the influence of war on adolescents, James Plant informed readers that the three stages of childhood—infant, child, and adolescent—corresponded to three different "reflex" responses that the child must develop and master. In infancy babies gained sphincter control, in early childhood they learned to speak, and in adolescence teens developed their "physical sexual expression." Since children typically manifested emotional disturbances through the "most recently established reflex," Plant determined that sexual delinquency was the logical expression of teenage problems rooted in these physical developmental processes.[28]

Others focused on developmental tasks not directly rooted in somatic experience. One crucial task involved the transition from the natural bisexuality of early childhood to solid identification with one's own gender. Psychiatry equated mature gender identity with exclusive sexual desire for the "opposite" gender, arguing that successful development as a feminine woman or masculine man required unwavering commitment to heterosexuality. *Parents Magazine* cautioned readers that many individuals failed to achieve heterosexuality "in the broad psychiatric sense." Explaining that adolescence represented the only chance that average boys and girls would have to establish their heterosexuality, the article warned that if failure occurred at this stage, "there is a question whether it can ever come out naturally and normally again."[29]

Since a mature normal adult was by definition a heterosexual adult, the professional literature of the 1940s featured a subtext about the dangers posed by homosexual alternatives. An essay on adolescence in wartime asserted that the war's tendency to unleash emotions and destabilize gender arrangements aggravated psychosexual problems, causing "queer people, with all kinds of mental twists and quirks" to reveal "even more clearly the vagaries of their behavior."[30] Lesbianism represented one such queer twist, described as an incapacity to realize femininity. This "maladjustment" might result from insufficient inner controls—a condition that plagued adolescents in general. But experts warned it could also arise from a teenager's overreaction to sexual prohibitions and consequent failure to develop sexual interest in boys.[31] Although few explicit references to homosexuality appeared in popular discourse about female adolescent sexuality, the threat of lesbianism as the worst possible outcome reconfigured the terms of adolescent "maturity." Professional opinion stated that girls must establish their heterosexuality as a visible, consistent desire, yet at the same time stop themselves from acting on those yearnings. In wartime, with emotions running high and external controls weakened, "instinctual urges" might get the better of an adolescent, who then might become "a victim of his own inadequate inner controlling mechanism," especially if "he" was a girl fourteen to seventeen years old.[32]

As wartime social workers and psychologists emended theories of adolescent sexuality, they expanded their sense of which kind of child might become diseased or delinquent. Earlier beliefs had been derived from a set of core assumptions about racial and class distinctions, in particular the supposition that African Americans tended toward immorality and disease. Based on a long history of representing the black body as a degenerate opposite to the naturally healthy and moral white body, many white Americans interpreted extremely high syphilis rates among black draftees as confirmation that disease and promiscuity were the natural state of African American bodies.[33]

In contrast, scientists saw venereal disease as the exception among whites, endemic only to "the lowest classes of society" for whom "syphilis has become . . . a disease of the ignorant, the careless, the criminal and the social outcast."[34] Regional SPD supervisor Arthur E. Fink reported that training camps and war production areas had "acted as magnets" attracting "hordes of girls" from rural and semi-rural areas who were running from their past and thought little about their future, caring only to live in the present.[35] Assumptions about impoverished rural whites and African Americans helped well-to-do southerners conceive of themselves as healthy, sophisticated, and beyond moral reproach in relation to a group of "other" southerners who were bringing scorn on the entire region.

Although biased assumptions about the class and race of female delinquents by no means disappeared, by the war's end they had started to evolve into a new belief among social scientists and child experts: a suspicion that delinquency and disease were becoming pervasive among youth of all backgrounds. The Office of War Information issued a press release on juvenile delinquency stating that the average age of girls picked up by vice squads had dropped from between eighteen and twenty to a new low of sixteen or younger, and "frequently of good family."[36] In a *New York Times Magazine* report on postwar sexual dangers, Dr. Walter Clarke claimed that youth between fifteen and twenty-five years old comprised close to 60 percent of new venereal disease cases. More alarming yet to Clarke, this group did not consist "exclusively of boys and girls from 'the wrong side of the tracks.' Reflected in these grim statistics are the case histories of the boy around the corner and the girl from the house on the hill . . . Young people are in danger everywhere—in the silk-stocking districts and in the slums."[37]

Parents Magazine reported a similar trend among amateur pickup girls from "good" families: "A new type of girl was discovered drifting into an old type of delinquency—the result of uniform hysteria."[38] While "uniform hysteria" referred to girls who went "boy crazy" over young men in military uniforms, the term hinted at a deeper problem. Sexual delinquency was moving in the direction of becoming "uniform" across class lines, no longer caused by material and moral poverty but rather by unconscious processes in which teenage psychic crises found expression through the body, a displacement Freud had labeled "hysteria." Environmental explanations of sex delinquency persisted, but a newer psychological interpretation that potentially encompassed girls from all backgrounds moved into the forefront.

This etiology, which combined wartime distress and "normal" adolescent difficulties, paralleled broader developments in psychology. World War II proved to be a boon to clinical psychology and allied fields of psychiatry, research psychology, social work, marriage and family counseling, and trained youth work. The U.S. Armed Forces and federal intelligence agencies drew heavily on the knowledge of psychiatrists and psychologists to screen draftees for poor mental health and low intelligence and to treat combat-related emotional problems. Social psychologists scrutinized the collective mind, or national character, of both Axis countries and the United States and then designed strategies to undermine enemy morale or, conversely, bolster

American civilian and military morale. Involvement was extensive, with one-third of professional psychiatrists and one-fourth of trained psychologists contributing their services to the military during the war.[39] Yet even this large group did not begin to meet the need for thousands of clinical workers capable of evaluating personnel and treating wartime casualties. As a result, the government instructed thousands of other workers to perform clinical assessments and provide psychological counseling. The number of trained professionals increased geometrically, creating a plethora of experts on matters of individual and group psychology ready to turn their newly gained respect into postwar prestige and profits.

New clinical approaches accompanied the profession's unprecedented rise in numbers and status. Psychiatrists had long been interested in expanding from their narrow client base of "insane" patients hospitalized for severe mental illness. Answering the military's call to meet the needs of the common soldier facilitated a professional shift from treating acute mental illness to promoting mental health for the general population of Americans. New approaches included preventive measures—evident in the extensive advice literature to parents on child rearing and potential problems of adolescence—and the diagnosis, treatment, and cure of less severe mental health problems that ordinary or "normal" people might encounter. Viewing mental health and illness as moving along a continuum, psychology attributed emotional disturbances to a combination of immediate circumstances and deep-seated neurotic tendencies that may have remained dormant under less traumatic conditions.[40]

Just as wartime clinical psychologists had determined that any GI could suffer short-term mental health problems when the extreme duress of war triggered psychic conflicts, experts on adolescence pointed to the combination of dangerous wartime conditions and the "normal" stress and strain of adolescent development to explain high rates of delinquency among girls and boys from seemingly "good" families. After 1945, the normalizing project of psychology found that even in the absence of war the ordinary trials of adolescent development could, in the presence of detrimental family dynamics and weak ego development, account for temporary psychic crises that might lead even the "girl next door" into stigmatized sexual behaviors. The exponential increase in clinicians, the shift from treating severe mental illness to ordinary neuroses, and the ascending cultural status of allied psychological professions laid the groundwork for a postwar interpretation of sexual delinquency as a failed adjustment to the naturally destabilizing effects of adolescence.

In the absence of international conflict, adolescence itself became defined as a warlike psychic struggle between overpowering emotional and physical impulses and imperfectly developed powers of reason and moral judgment. Most professionals trained in adolescent psychology employed a "stress and strain" model of adolescent development pioneered at the turn of the century by G. Stanley Hall. The basic conditions of adolescence included intense emotional turmoil, instability, and anxiety, all of which contributed to mercurial moods and rash action. Theorists located adolescent sexual impulses and inner conflict in two primary contradictions. Teens felt torn between the strong urge toward independence and the fact that in most cases they remained physically and emotionally dependent on adults. They also experienced a lag between the physical maturity achieved in adolescence and the slower process of emotional maturation. In both interpretations, one common denominator linked physical drives, emotional needs, and developmental achievements: desire. Earlier experts had nodded to female desire but assumed that a majority of girls experienced eroticism less intensely than boys and, for this reason and because of social expectations, could hold back from premarital sexual activity and channel erotic desire into appropriate longings for marriage and motherhood. Yet in wartime and postwar America, the intensity of young female desire struck some experts as not only commonplace, but to some degree uncontainable.

Psychologists, psychiatrists, social workers, and recreation specialists believed that female desire sprang from several sources. As girls' bodies became more sexually developed, they experienced a physical quickening of the entire body, "an intensification of feeling responses, even to sensory stimuli, a growing attraction for members of the opposite sex, and the appearance of strange and disturbing erotic sensations."[41] In the social realm, adolescent girls desired acceptance and recognition, love and caring, adventure and independence—all part of the gradual process of separating from one's parents and shifting to a peer-based society and more individuated self. A new emotional intensity, too, accentuated the adolescent's need for friends, romance, and a sense of belonging. Theorists described promiscuity as the harmful outcome of a girl's struggle to feel connected through sexual intimacy. The emotional need for love became inseparable from a troubled girl's efforts to find sociability and excitement. Thus "normal" desire for erotic fulfillment, social adventure, and material goods might catapult girls into a whirl of soldiers, sex, and commercial nightlife so immediately satisfying it blinded them to the likelihood of infection, psychic damage, and social stigma.

The accounts of experts in many ways echo the narratives of teenage girls themselves. Working-class adolescents conveyed to social workers, reformatory staff, and sociologists a complicated set of needs and wants that included erotic fulfillment within a broader set of desires for material riches, romantic pleasure, travel, and a yearning to "be somebody." Professional explanations differed from teenagers' own accounts only in that these desires impressed experts as highly problematic. Where teenagers dreamed of pleasure, and sometimes found it, social workers and psychologists saw disturbing behavior that muddied the line between the psychologically normal and deviant. The fantasies and sexual behavior of adolescent girls upset professionals' own sense of what was realistic, socially normative, and sexually respectable.

In response, midcentury experts endeavored to normalize and assimilate female sexual desire and activity into common scenarios of adolescent development. Yet they continued to use premarital intercourse as the criterion that differentiated between mental illness and health, social adjustment and maladjustment, the sexually normal and the deviant. In "Does Your Daughter Think She's in Love?" Gladys Schultz described the urge for sexual intimacy as quite normal, part of a biological mechanism connecting nerves to the sexual organs, with feelings gaining in intensity "the closer they are to the genital regions." Schultz saw sexual responsiveness and interest as "normal" to adolescence, even among "good girls," yet she did not offer approval, only understanding. After arguing that "it's nothing to be ashamed of" since the "best man and woman on earth could be carried away by these emotions, given certain circumstances," she nonetheless forbade petting—at all—because "it gets both parties to the point where they want to go further" and might very well cause them to make "mistakes" that would ruin their lives.[42]

Theorists like Schultz articulated a new standard in which premarital sexuality crossed into the realm of understandable behavior while still differentiating the "bad" girls from the "good." This perspective, contradictory as it appears, permitted professionals to address and finesse troubling questions about the sexual desire and behavior of adolescent girls. They familiarized sexual desire without shedding dualistic categories of illness and health, the intellectual framework that conferred their authority as experts. Depicting premarital sexual desire as part of the normal process of adolescent maturation, theorists at the same time isolated sexual activity as a product of exceptional conditions and failed personal adjustment.

Psychology employed a second maneuver to bring teenage female sexuality into range of normalcy, relocating the "problem" from the body to the psyche. Prior to the war most experts understood sexual delinquency as rooted in mental deficiency or poor economic and moral environments, viewing promiscuity as an innate tendency among the poor and incompetent. By the 1940s, authorities supposed that the potential for promiscuity resided in all girls, rather than in the genetic or moral predispositions of the poor and nonwhite. Whereas earlier descriptions pointed to failures of moral development and physical control, midcentury social scientists began to focus on psychic conflicts as the unconscious motivation for sexual misconduct. A 1945 Social Protection Division pamphlet warned that many "highly promiscuous 'pick-ups' . . . are sick, mentally and physically," adding that the "reasons for promiscuity are much more complicated and even neurotic than simple sensuality."[43]

In the past, attributions of "simple sensuality" centered around poor white and black, Mexican or Native American girls suspected of having "simple" minds and "simple" means. Accounts of middle-class adolescent promiscuity, however, focused on psychic conflicts—neuroses—rather than conscious desire. The SPD's "Challenge to Community Action" pamphlet, aimed at a majority white readership, stressed that sexually active girls could no longer be classified as "oversexed" since some "seem to be totally frigid and even to dislike sex relations."[44] Desires were primarily psychic, and never fully conscious, finding only indirect expression through the body. In this sense, teen-age girls remained alienated from their own eroticism even though midcentury ideologies more often acknowledged the power of adoles-cent sexual desire.[45]

Studies of unmarried mothers in the early to mid-twentieth century point to important racial distinctions in professional discourse. While white experts of the 1940s still viewed black illegitimacy as a sign of cultural pathology or ingrained immorality, they asserted that unmar-ried pregnancy might happen to the (white) "girl next door" as a con-sequence of neurosis and maladjustment. The psychic conflicts of ad-olescence, especially failed adjustment to femininity and unresolved parent-child conflicts within the family, created unconscious desires that some middle-class white girls acted out through sexual activity and pregnancy. Psychiatric social workers treated the pregnancies of white girls as symbolic declarations of unmet needs or unexpressed anger, deemphasizing the sexual activity that unquestionably pre-ceded pregnancy.[46]

Such theories accounted for an apparent rise in sexual activity among white middle-class teenagers, part of the perceived wartime and postwar epidemic of female sexual promiscuity. Notions of cul-tural pathology, impoverished environment, and genetic propensity persisted, especially in explanations for commercial prostitutes and working-class pickup girls, but receded before psychological theories that could explain increased sexual activity and boldness in teenage girls from a wide range of class or racial backgrounds.

*B*lack social scientists were conversant with psychological theo-ries, but continued to insist on social, as well as psychological, expla-nations for young people's sexual behavior. Alarm over juvenile delin-quency and declining morals ran the gamut from individual parents to educators, youth workers, and community and national leaders. Speaking before a wartime rally of twenty-five thousand people in Madison Square Garden, Charlotte Hawkins Brown described a gen-eration of Negro youth drawn to "riotous living" as "a sort of defense mechanism" against the pain of racial discrimination.[47] Brown's men-tion of defense mechanisms clearly draws on psychiatric discourses. But African American social scientists refused to see the problem in terms of either wholesale moral decline or individual psychic crises.

Community leaders and academics insistently put forth psychosocial explanations of sexual promiscuity linked to poverty, lack of recreational facilities, and the cumulative effects of decades of racial discrimination. They attempted to rebut white social protection agents who understood Negro sex delinquency as one expression of rampantly promiscuous behavior common to all black southerners. (For example, one Louisiana study located teenage black prostitutes within "the entire Negro promiscuity problem in New Orleans."[48]) Black social protection boards, set up in conjunction with social protection committees headed by white agents, enunciated the problem and its solution in quite different terms.

In Augusta, Georgia, the Negro Coordinating Council of the Committee on Social Protection argued: "In view of the fact that our 'teen-age' boys and girls frequent 'jook' joints, hang around corners and create disturbances in other public places as a means of entertainment because they have no other place to go, we believe that provision of properly supervised public parks in the densely populated areas will aid in the solution of the playgirl [and] zoot suit problems and reduce petty thievery, and venereal infection." Calling as well for a swimming pool and other recreational facilities, the council resolutely defined delinquency and venereal disease as problems of "juveniles," "adolescents," and "teen-agers" rather than a characteristic of the larger community.[49] Black leaders not only disputed white interpretations, but also used the widespread concern over delinquency and disease to seek political leverage, asking local and federal governments for redress against segregationist policies that left black youth with separate, unequal, and inadequate services and facilities.

Delinquency, moreover, was just one concern among many that black communities sought to address through discussion of war-related social problems. Number one on the list of black leaders was violence, whether racially motivated attacks on black soldiers by white vigilantes or the age-old problem of white men's sexual assaults on black girls and women. Discriminatory racial policies also featured prominently in African American leaders' complaints, spawning campaigns against inequality and mistreatment in the military and defense industries. Rather than bemoaning the pickup girl's lack of moral resolve, most activists expressed greater interest in defending the sexual reputation of black girls and young women, especially those contributing to the military effort as volunteers at USO functions, trainees for defense industry jobs, or members of the newly created Women's Army Corps.[50]

These concerns remained primary during the war and immediate postwar years. Only around 1950 did the black press pick up the theme of shocking immorality among teenagers. In a lull between wartime protests and the grassroots struggles initiated by the Montgomery bus boycott in 1955, *Ebony* magazine ran a string of alarmist articles about teenage sex clubs and the aggressive sexual behavior of adolescent girls. Articles like "Sex in High School," "Teen-Age Love Clubs," and "Child Brides" told of high school girls engaged in "shocking sex orgies" and "so-called non-virgin clubs," resulting in pregnancy and marriage among girls in their early teens.[51] In a poll of female college students, the best-educated and most respectable group of young women, "How Moral Are Our Coeds?" found that 72 percent of female college students favored premarital sex.[52] In response to the rueful question of journalists "What has happened to our youth?" they themselves provided three typical answers: parents and schools had failed to provide needed sex education; the path to popularity at school had become "confused with commonness" by girls; and finally, that this problem, while severe, mirrored what was already happening among white adolescents and was therefore not particular to black communities.[53] In the same way that wartime concerns about sex delinquency had been one among many, the "sex-club" scandal raised eyebrows but did not dominate the discourse on youth in the black press, which continued to focus on broader problems amid a new sense of heightened possibilities, especially for middle-class black youth.

*W*hether voiced by journalists, community leaders, or professional experts, alarmist commentary on adolescent sexual behavior did not develop simply in response to statistical data, although these helped state the problem in stark numerical terms. While the overall increase in female juvenile delinquency hovered around 100 percent, the percentage reached such heights in part because the original number of female delinquents was so small compared to boys, who still accounted for the vast majority of juvenile arrests. Moreover, venereal disease rates actually declined during the war.[54] Both the initial alarm and the expert theories that followed developed in direct response to an emerging teenage culture of the 1940s. The term "teen-ager" first came into use in the early 1940s, signaling the distinctiveness of adolescents' joining together in a shared culture created by and for themselves. Teenagers appeared—to themselves and their observers—as a group apart, no longer adults in formation but an autonomous, highly self-conscious group with its own distinctive rituals, values, and activities. Music, dance, and dress styles formed the primary markers of a youth culture based in the common experiences and milieu that most teens encountered as high school students.

One development that contributed to the distinctive teenage culture was "swing," which emerged around 1940. The music, which was a style within big-band jazz music, had stirred teenagers into a wildly enthusiastic music "craze" accompanied by its own form of dance, the jitterbug. Swing music featured a hard-driving brassy beat made for dancing. Young people flocked to concerts and jukeboxes to hear black artists such as Duke Ellington, Lionel Hampton, and Cab Calloway, as well as white favorites Tommy Dorsey, Harry James, and Glenn Miller.[55] In 1940 Frank Sinatra burst onto the scene with a sweeter, more romantic style of crooning that thrilled adolescent girls especially. Large crowds of female fans, like the twenty-five thousand teens who blocked the streets of Manhattan before a 1944 Sinatra concert at the Paramount Theater, created pandemonium as they shrieked and swooned over their young idol.[56]

The music itself did not depart radically from other kinds of popular jazz and orchestra music of the period. But the accompanying dance, the jitterbug, struck many critics as too wild and sexual for the ranks of the respectable. In jitterbugging, partners danced together hand in hand, swinging each other forcefully around in a high-paced, intense set of maneuvers that brought the two together for an instant and then flung them apart in crowd-pleasing athletic moves like swinging a girl through a boy's legs or over his back and around his waist. Defenders of the jitterbug argued that it was no more sexual than other kinds of popular dance, especially because it involved little face to face contact and hardly allowed the slow, close movement conducive to caressing or kissing. Critics did not buy this argument, claiming instead that the dance was fundamentally sexual and often linked to juvenile delinquency. Although girls dressed in loose, wide skirts or dresses, revealing far less skin than the streamlined flapper

Memphis teenagers gather in a juke joint to show off their jitterbugging skills. The war-time moral panic over juvenile delinquency led the government to support "teen can-teens," clubs designed to lure teenagers away from "sordid" dance halls into teen-only sites where adolescents could dance and socialize in a "wholesome" environment. Marion Post Wolcott, Library of Congress, LC-USF34–052590-D.

of the 1920s, when they swung around or jumped, their skirts lifted to reveal thighs and underpants. Moreover, the rapid, hard movements of the jitterbug, the intensity and energy it required, and the ecstasy it produced struck observers as both simulating and stimulating erotic activity. In this view, music and dance "crazes" might further incite the emotional and sexual disturbances of adolescence, weakening restraints already diminished by the inherent instability of the teen years.

The older generation feared swing music and dance because youth claimed these styles as their own. Teenagers responded to the music as a group, creating a "jive" culture—borrowed from African American "hipster" culture—with its own lingo and dress. Adopting slang like the terms "hep," "swell," "solid," or "catsy," they also demarcated themselves through dress. Popular styles of the early 1940s included zoot suits and then letter sweaters, khakis, and rolled-up dungarees (blue jeans) for boys. Girls wore flared skirts, dirty saddle-shoes, rolled-down ankle socks called bobby socks, and large, baggy sweaters called Sloppy Joes.[57]

By the late 1940s, marketers eager to pull teenagers into a booming consumer economy embraced youth culture for reasons of profit. But during the war years, teenagers created a collective culture in response to their own needs and not market incentives. They often complained of being marginalized and left out of the war, but in fact the war created new social spaces and possibilities for teens. By the early 1940s adolescents were finding camaraderie in school, at work, on the streets, or in juke joints, theaters, and dance parlors. This sensibility took unique institutional form in newly created wartime clubs for teenagers. Called teen canteens or teen towns, these recreation centers sprang up in response to the demand by students and young workers for an inexpensive place to gather for dancing, games, and socializing. Typically, the founders cleaned, outfitted, decorated, and named the club site. As a group they also established ground rules for membership, including age limits, opening and closing times, dues, and rules governing club members' conduct.

Teen canteens carved a new space for sociability, this time sanctioned by adult approval. Between five hundred and seven hundred centers were identified across the country, including many in southern cities like Richmond, Shreveport, Raleigh, and Jacksonville.[58] Segregation operated routinely in these centers, with most canteens designed for white youth only, although in a few instances sponsors funded separate teen centers for African Americans.[59] In addition, canteens respected local class divisions. Leaders designated recreation sites as for either high school students or out-of-school teenagers. By placing them in targeted neighborhoods or school buildings, centers typically brought together a group of teens already familiar to each other and excluded a wider range of teens with more varied backgrounds.

In Raleigh's "Teen Age Club for white youth from age 13 to 19," operated by the city's recreation commission, attendance figures averaged 250 out of a total membership of three hundred. Teens joined by paying dues of fifty cents per month and agreeing to follow rules laid out by an elective junior board of governance.[60] While Raleigh's club began with a demand by teenagers, in Shreveport parents from the Methodist church initiated a plan and secured funding for youth recreation centers in three different parts of the city. Here too, members agreed to rules of conduct enforced by their elected "recreation police."[61]

Even as they touted teen canteens as youth-organized and operated, adult authorities attempted to control them with a soft and somewhat invisible hand. Civic organizations or government agencies typically provided the primary source of funding. The Office of Community War Services used federal money allotted through the Lanham Act, which provided aid to communities facing facility shortages in childcare, recreation, and health. At the local level, organizations such as the community chest, recreation departments, school boards, and parent-teacher associations typically authorized the founding of a teen town, then provided ongoing financial support and social approbation. The same agencies formed supervisory boards and hired an adult director to oversee the purportedly independent, self-governing clubs, ensuring that the behavior and decisions of teenage members did not stray far from adult expectations and standards.[62]

Mark McCloskey, the innovative director of OCWS youth programs, genuinely supported teenage initiative and independence, believing that anything less would be a sham and lead to failure.[63] But adults involved at the local level rarely adopted this approach or granted anything beyond rhetorical license to teenagers. One survey found that of 178 teen centers in thirty different states, only 2 percent operated without adult involvement.[64] Lip service to teenage autonomy in conjunction with adult control reveals a deep ambivalence toward teenagers on the part of their elders. In one sense, teen canteens acknowledged the very separateness and cultural distinctiveness that adolescents craved. The enterprise officially condoned the music and dance of 1940s youth culture and a measure of adolescent autonomy. But as they seemingly accepted the culture and desires of the new aggregate called teenagers, adults continued to fear the dangers of an independent teen culture figured in the image of the bobby-soxer, a singular symbol of the midcentury adolescent girl.

Why did adults find cause for alarm in the middle-class bobby-soxer who, in retrospect and compared to the wartime pickup girl, seems to epitomize wholesome, "normal," fun-loving teenage girl-hood? In large part because of the lurking issue of sexuality. Journal-ists and experts investigated teenage dating habits, dance styles, and "petting" customs. A *New York Times Magazine* piece on "Boys, Girls—and Dates" explained that because the social interests of girls matured more quickly than boys, they tended to date older boys whose inter-ests had "advanced" to dating.[65] The age difference between partners in turn made girls more likely to "yield" to male sexual advances, es-pecially from soldiers cast in the romantic glow of war and patriotism. Observant adults, however, more often posed the problem as one of adolescent girls who, as participants in an increasingly sexualized youth culture, yielded not to external pressure but to their own de-sires.

Discussions about music and dance revealed anxieties about adoles-cent sexuality. Upon supervising a community center dance, an anx-ious adult reported that as "boogie-woogie music" blared, the gymna-sium "filled with couples, barely sixteen years old, twisting and contorting themselves into backbends, twirls and gyrations that gave the atmosphere a frenzied aspect." The author intimated the sexual content of the dance when he observed "a nervousness—a restless-ness" in the jitterbug that led to "quick impulsive actions and . . . im-patient moves," a veritable "orgy of leg throwing."[66] In describing a horrifying and contrived "Frankenstein-like" maturity "born out of frenzy," the author noted that "it isn't all Johnnie's doing." He con-cluded that Johnnie's female contemporaries were as frank and ag-gressive as Johnnie, and wiser than their mothers or grandmothers in "that special sex-wise sense of understanding men."[67]

Some authors reassured readers that the erotic dynamism of teen culture did not ultimately pose a sexual danger to girls. Popular bandleader Paul Whiteman explained that adolescents were only re-sponding naturally to an irresistible rhythm. Jitterbugging might strike like a contagious illness among early teens, but the dance itself merely allowed "kids . . . to give free and public rein to their impulses." It in-volved no "cheek to cheek" dancing and did not require more than momentary contact between partners. Moreover, by the late teens the jitterbug contagion resolved on its own as "Joe Jive" began thinking about a serious job and "Susy Shag" began searching for a husband.

"They revert," claimed Whiteman, "to normal," a condition that apparently needed no explanation.[68]

But other authors confirmed parental fears of teenage sexuality as a pressing danger. Popular titles like "Are Girls Becoming Pursuers?" framed the question specifically in terms of female aggression. Marriage and family expert Dr. Henry Bowman answered in the affirmative, explaining the issue as largely based on the postwar shortage of available men and women's consequent fears of spinsterhood. Taking the initiative in the hope of securing a husband, girls were "becoming the hunters and the boys the hunted," a situation Bowman deemed ill-advised.[69] The anxious "overforward girl" adopted a boldness that might repel future mates and, if she crossed that hurdle, "leave a residue of female dominance" likely to prevent a successful marriage.[70] In addressing the issue of the "overforward girl," Bowman raised a second issue—the unsettling shift in the power dynamics of heterosexual relationships. He associated female sexual self-assertion with a loss of male dominance, a prospect made more frightening by the social, economic, and sexual independence exhibited by both adult women and adolescent girls during the war.

Calling for Americans to "re-enshrine chastity and continence" in the face of "super-charged sex emotions," the *Ladies' Home Journal* described the prototypical teenager as suffering from the stresses of modern-day life. By converting her worries into undischarged "sexual and nervous tensions," a girl's mental worries paradoxically might find expression in a "direct drive into sexual hyperactivity, and even sexual abnormality." Concerned about role reversal, author Mona Gardner cited a contention by a foremost expert on syphilis that women had now become "the sex adventurer, . . . the sexual seeker, the aggressor of the male-female combination," causing a "rampant restlessness in all social groups" more "malignant" than any virus.[71] To both Bowman and Gardner, the rules of sex reflected the hierarchy of gender, freighting the issue of adolescent sexual self-assertion with consequences far beyond the fate of an individual girl.

Disturbed by the idea of aggressive, self-interested females in sexual pursuit, experts confirmed the prevailing ideology that girls must act as the brakes—not the accelerator—of sexual passion, their own and that of boys. When this standard failed, some commentators linked uninhibited teen sexuality to larger social fears of instability and chaos in Cold War society. But in a literature addressed largely to concerned parents and advice-seeking teenagers, professionals most often emphasized the personal danger that sexuality held for a girl's mental health and social future. Ernest Groves, a professor of marriage and family relations at the University of North Carolina, posed the question "Too Much Kissing?" and answered with a definitive yes. Kissing, Groves maintained, often led to "mismating." Because "kisses had destroyed the capacity for sound judgment these girls had been tricked by biological reactions" into "sordid intimacies" which they mistook for "true love." "The average nice girl," professed Groves, "would rather not pet unless she is in love."[72]

The contradictory implications of Groves's analysis gave experts pause. On the one hand, his North Carolina research demonstrated that petting and necking had become rampant among teenagers. On the other hand, nice girls preferred to kiss only in instances of romantic, "true" love. If the line between casual involvement and "true love" divided illegitimate from legitimate petting, what did it mean that so many girls engaged in premarital sexual involvements? Did it mean that nice girls were becoming obsolete, or, more likely, that when the "normal" teenager engaged in heavy petting, she believed she was in love? But if biology tricked girls into confusing sordid intimacy for true love, what would stop them from acting on sexual desires?

Adolescent girls could no more answer this question than professionals. A column geared toward African American teens, "Naomi's Advice" in the *Norfolk Journal and Guide,* illustrates the way romantic love confounded girls, at once justifying sexual intimacy and causing sexual jeopardy. A fifteen-year-old informed Naomi that for six months she had been in love with an older boy of nineteen, but he suddenly seemed to lose all affection for her. The problem, she wrote, is that "I have been intimate with him and I am in trouble. What must I do?" She ended her letter, "I love him more than life itself."[73] Another fifteen-year-old wrote of having been in love for eight months with her twenty-two-year-old boyfriend who wanted to marry her. Besides not wanting to wed at such a young age, her feelings had recently become clouded after meeting "a fine looking boy from New York who says that he loves me." Although this man was married, separated, and a father, she insisted "I am sure that I love him. Please tell me what to do."[74] Being "sure" of one's love could undermine certainty about other matters, especially decisions around relationships. If girls could not easily discern true love from false, or found love to be as fleeting as it was forceful, how could they make good judgments in the heat of emotional and biological reactions?

According to experts, they could not; girls too often lost their hearts and heads to attractive, persistent boys who promised love in exchange for sex. Yet this did not sour professionals on the importance of romance. Paradoxically, even as romance presented an immediate peril, it also augured the promise of marriage and postmarital sexual satisfaction.[75] In "Does Your Daughter Think She's in Love?" *Reader's Digest* advised parents of adolescent daughters: "Chances are she's in love—or thinks she is, which amounts to the same thing—with someone in the services." Complaining that "too many good girls are getting in trouble" under wartime stresses, author Gladys Denny Schultz urged parents to discuss "petting" with their daughters before the illusion of romantic love caused a misstep. Yet she also believed that falling "really and truly in love" ennobled otherwise "cheap" sex based on "mere sense and stimulation."[76] Three years later, Schultz's sense of danger further diminished in favor of a thoroughly positive view of teenage romance. In 1947 she cautioned parents against looking "with alarm upon dating and the other manifestations of the romantic urge." She explained: "If parents could understand more clearly the function served by romance in a teen-ager's life, they would view the matter very differently . . . The romances and dating of the adolescent years are a youngster's schooling for a wise marriage choice, which after all lies not very far ahead."[77] The greater danger, she believed, lay in the possibility that "overstrict" parents would cause girls to shun contact with the opposite sex and ultimately fail to accomplish a complete transition to heterosexuality consummated through marriage. Without romance during the teen years, Schultz intimated, a girl faced life as a "sexually immature" lesbian or an abandoned old maid.

The shift toward greater acceptance of adolescent romantic passion evident in the popular advice literature of the immediate postwar period did not solve the sexual riddle of true love. The acceptance of natural sexual urges did not extend as far as intercourse and pregnancy. Believing that if love were "true," sexual intercourse could wait, experts used true or romantic love as the marker distinguishing between "nice girls" who waited and others who lacked either restraint or lasting, deep feelings. Yet romantic love also helped account for this sexual behavior when it did occur. True love, or its illusion, served as the untamed force that could induce a good girl to succumb to passion.

In a matter of years, a class of morally and mentally deficient sex delinquents—the initial view of wartime pickup girls—had grown to include middle-class girls whose natural adolescent problems and passions could lead to "patriotism gone wrong." As new explanations normalized the kinds of problems that could lead a "nice girl" astray, middle-class white teenagers became victims of unconscious wishes rooted in family conflict rather than female sexual desire. Significantly, a public discourse that first created the adolescent sexual subject as an aggressive "amateur" or pickup girl, and then generalized the problem to one of girls becoming pursuers in heterosexual relations, ended with a reversal of roles: the "promiscuous" teenage girl suffered from being a victim of romance. What began as a response to the astonishingly bold initiative of teenagers actively pursuing sexual relations reverted to a view of girls conquered by the power of illusory romance, swept away by desires beyond their control.

*W*ar brought romance, sex, and adolescent girlhood into the same orbit. For the first time since the flappers of the 1910s and 1920s, teenage girls moved to the forefront of national concern, forcing adults as well as teenagers to acknowledge the centrality of sexual desire and activity to the experience of female adolescence. Pragmatic government officials responded with federal, state, and local programs designed to reduce venereal disease and prevent or treat delinquency. Social critics and frightened parents responded with anxious condemnation.

Southerners found the issue even more pressing as wartime migration, training camps, and defense industries magnified the problems associated with sexually delinquent girls. Because a majority of U.S. military training occurred in the South and the region suffered from astronomical rates of syphilis, the issue of sexually assertive girls was brought into sharp relief. Further heightening tensions was the time bomb of race relations during wartime, when direct confrontations between black soldiers and white supremacists grew increasingly common. Because the foundational myth of unblemished "southern womanhood" rationalized the region's racial and gender order, if white girls abandoned chastity for the pursuit of sexual intimacy or pleasure, whether by their own design or from unconscious motivations, one stanchion of white supremacy would fall. When teenage girls of all ranks and races insisted on the validity of their interests in love, romance, and sex, it threatened the everyday practices of racial segregation, male dominance, and black subordination that constituted the "southern way of life."

In the South and across the nation, parents, social workers, and experts in psychology denounced the sexual involvements of the pickup girl and bobby-soxer, even while summoning empathy for such deplorable behavior. Emphasizing both the situational conditions of war and the "natural" dynamics of adolescent development, contemporary explanations maintained the boundary between permissible and forbidden sexual behaviors even as they explained its erosion. The line still hovered around a longstanding categorical divide between black and white working-class teens and the white, middle-class "nice girl" or bobby-soxer. Crucially, however, this demarcation no longer held firm, especially in the charged atmosphere of the wartime South. How different, indeed, were "nice" white girls who aggressively pursued sexual relations from "low-class" white and black girls presumed to be promiscuous?

In the 1940s fears of social and sexual "mixing" shifted from an initial focus on pickup girls who frequented defense towns and military training areas to the ordinary practices of adolescent dating. Social scientists, government officials, and youth service providers responded by expanding the powers of the state and reexamining prevailing theories of adolescent sexuality. But adolescents had their own point of view. They gathered together in high school hallways, around jukeboxes, at canteens, and at other sites conducive for socializing and dating. The broader public could not ignore the distinctive passions and practices of "teenagers," especially girls whose sexual and social assertiveness blurred prevailing views of difference—between boys and girls and between girls from "good" and "bad" homes. Theorists responded by expanding the category of promiscuous girls to include those from middle-class as well as working-class backgrounds, looking to unconscious psychological conflicts and drives to explain—away— the behavior of sexually active bobby-soxers.

But this reformulation did not erase popular concern. The romantic passions and sexual desires of the war era had, by the late 1940s, become central to the day-to-day sexual culture of high school. The formal and informal curricula of postwar southern high schools offered countless lessons on heterosexuality. Changes in high school culture loosened the hard-packed foundation of the South's gender and racial order, preparing the ground for the seismic shifts of the late 1950s and 1960s.

chapter eight

School Days

Reading, 'Riting, 'Rithmetic, and Romance

In a 1942 "imaginary letter" addressed to a fictional high school girl in Nazi Germany, a student at Atlanta's Commercial High School wrote that girls in her school intended to get jobs and "make our own money." Abruptly shifting to the subject of love, she pronounced: "We fall in love over here. We have wonderful romances here and culminate them to marriage to our 'one and only' . . . What kind of marriage do you have?"[1] In less romanticized terms, a 1941 poll at Atlanta's elite Girls' High School found that while the immediate ambition of a typical student was to graduate from high school, her chief ambition was to "get her man."[2]

When girls of the 1940s spoke of delicious romances, getting a man, and marriages based on a singularly powerful love, how did those ambitions enter into everyday coming-of-age experiences? Wartime "pickups" or "Victory girls" unnerved adults with their alarmingly bold sexual behavior and willingness to sacrifice premarital abstinence for immediate pleasures. Similarly, starstruck female rock 'n' roll fans of the next decade would cause mayhem with their seemingly sudden and peculiar outbursts of romantic and erotic longings. But what about noncontroversial, or "normal," teenage girls like the Atlanta high school students? Clearly, they also had men and romance on their minds. By midcentury, subtle changes in ordinary life had shifted the patterns of sociability and structures of opportunity in which sexual desire and adolescent dreams take form. The years from the early 1940s to the mid-1950s reveal what dating, romance, sex, and marriage had come to mean to girls presumed to be healthy, well-adjusted teenagers.

A teenage culture, embryonic in the teen canteens and swing dancing of World War II, grew stronger and more institutionally rooted in the decade after the war. It revolved around the everyday sociability and extensive recreational opportunities of the high school. An educational trend toward "comprehensive" or "consolidated" high schools brought students of different class (but similar racial) backgrounds and educational trajectories together in large, geographically based schools that provided multiple opportunities for friendship and romance. The same period brought significant change in the culture of sexuality. Panics over homosexuality, imagined as an invisible contagion eating away at American moral fiber, occurred in conjunction with Cold War political hysteria over the menace of communism. The panic heightened awareness of heterosexuality as an achieved goal necessary for the "social adjustment" of the individual and collective strength of the nation.[3] Heterosexuality infused not only the discourses of politics and social science, but also everyday behavior. The intensified focus on dating, sexuality, and marriage that spawned the 1950s phenomena of rock 'n' roll, teenage marriages, and the baby boom had already been embraced in the 1940s by adolescents of high school and college age.

This heterosexually oriented youth culture of the 1940s and early 1950s can be traced through the high school newspapers and yearbooks of Harding High School in Charlotte, North Carolina, along with publications of other urban southern high schools.[4] Sexual interest and romantic drama formed a part of everyday student interactions. The "search for a man" by girls looking forward to financially and emotionally fulfilling romantic marriages blended seamlessly into the rhythm of high school life. There is nothing particularly southern about the romantic turn of high school culture except, perhaps, that because of the South's lower rates of college enrollment, dating and marriage considerations may have felt more pressing during high school. Casual and serious dating thrived in the mix of formal dances, proms, homecomings, and more informal gatherings at sporting or other organized activities. In addition, sex education courses, usually

By the 1940s and '50s, when high school attendance was near universal, the "three R's" (Reading, 'Riting, and 'Rithmetic) had to compete with a fourth 'R'–Romance. The periods between classes offered opportunities for teens like these Keysville, Virginia, students to create a high school culture in which casual or serious dating, sexual activity, and prospective marriage became predominant themes. Philip Bonn, Library of Congress, LC-USW3–033453-E.

under the rubric of "family life education," became commonplace in school districts across the country.[5]

But just under the smooth surface of high school culture lay more intense, yet often ambivalent, desires indicative of fissures in the highly structured, seemingly contained sexuality of adolescence. In the context of the South, these small tears in the social fabric contributed to larger rifts that fueled the violent eruptions of the late 1950s and early 1960s over segregated schools and interracial youth culture. Looking at the fourth "R" of postwar high school life—romance—reveals nonthreatening sexual changes that occurred in day-to-day life, outside of a politicized rhetoric, that nevertheless had significant unintended consequences. The changes in high school culture, unremarkable at the time, formed the necessary antecedent for subsequent changes that rocked high schools and colleges in the 1960s, when students challenged the fundamental hierarchies of southern society.

The academic training of secondary education was indeed often secondary to the social and sexual dramas that unfolded in this setting. Students regularly participated in casual dating and serious romance, oriented toward both eventual marriage and immediate pleasure and recreation. A strong heterosexual current developed mainly through informal student interactions between and after classes, yet the new dynamic also manifested itself in organized, formally endorsed high school activities like "sock hops," "formals," proms, school beauty contests, and a focus on heterosexual pairs in school publications.

Harding High School in Charlotte, North Carolina, opened its doors in 1935 as an alternative to Central High, a citywide school that had formerly served all of Charlotte's white students enrolled in secondary education. Harding taught the eighth through the twelfth grades under a state plan that began secondary education in the eighth grade. The city system also included two black high schools—Second Ward High School, opened in 1923, and West End High School, which opened three years after Harding did, in 1938. This sequence reflects the historical development of southern secondary education, which in the 1920s served elite, middle-class, and a trickle of working-class white students. Southern black communities fought and won separate and—in theory only—"equal" high schools that received minimal funding from state and county governments. As the system expanded, additional white schools always preceded any additional black schools and retained the lion's share of public resources.[6]

By the late 1930s, and even more so in the postwar period, a large majority of teenagers attended high school, prompting school building programs throughout the South to serve a more geographically and economically diverse student body. Charlotte built Harding High School in light of such changes, locating the new building in the city's northern sector, an area populated by mill workers and other working-class and lower-middle-class residents who had achieved stable family economies without much money to spare. Early school photos show students dressed in plain dresses, shirts, sweaters, and jackets that appear well-worn and sometimes frayed around the edges. Although for many Harding students financial resources were scarce, references to dances, movies, and casual trips to the drugstore soda fountain indicate that most teens had access to some pocket money for dating and entertainment expenses.[7]

Compared to Central High, where students spoke often about high school as a prelude to college and professional careers, Harding High School students expected less from their schooling. Only a small number mentioned continuing their education beyond high school, while as many as one-half of the students from a given ninth-grade class did not go on to graduate with their senior class.[8] College-bound or not, working-class students viewed their years in high school as a special time of life. To graduate from secondary school represented a significant achievement for this generation, especially among working-class teens whose parents had left school for work at ages as young as twelve. Socially, high school provided a short window between childhood and late adolescence—when most working-class youth would begin full-time employment, often taking on the responsibilities of marriage and parenting in their late teens or early twenties. By the 1940s, students had more leisure time than they would in their later working years and more cash than they did as young children, a trend that continued through the prosperous 1950s. They spent much of this time and money with each other.

Annual school yearbooks of the 1940s and early 1950s establish high school as the centripetal force of teenage life, pulling students into a school-based culture that revolved around the rituals, dreams, and disappointments of heterosexual love. This trend began in the late 1930s and early 1940s, despite the fact that high dropout rates and the draft severely skewed school gender ratios, making girls a large majority of the student body.[9] Prior to this period, same-gender or nonsexual activities—like girls' homemaking clubs, boys' religious service groups, or coed subject-oriented French or Math clubs—generally stood at the foreground of student life. By midcentury this held true only for elementary and junior high school children who typically played in single-sex groups. Teenagers, in contrast, frequently gathered in mixed-sex groups. Girls and boys dated as lone couples, but even more often gathered to socialize at football games or skating parties, casually as couples or in a mix of friends including both genders. Heterosocial recreation, new high school rites, and a consuming interest in dating, couples, romance, and marriage created the elements of a romantic heterosexual culture. The May queen of early twentieth-century school pageantry, floating ethereally around the May pole surrounded by other "maidens" attired in gauzy white flowing gowns, had become the prom queen who couldn't wait to date and dance.

*O*ne institutionalized heterosexual rite was the formal dance, whether a prom or a celebration of fall homecoming, Valentine's Day, or the coming of spring. School dances had a history of controversy, with religious critics questioning their morality. Opponents argued that even when chaperoned, dancing was the first step on a hellbound slope toward drink, irresponsible carousing, and sinful sexuality. As late as 1945, a pamphlet issued by the Southern Christian Life Commission described dancing as "of pagan origin . . . and withal a road to hell." Oklahoma minister J. M. Gaskin condemned dancing on a number of accounts. First, even if a girl was escorted by a young gentleman, the practice of "cutting in" meant that she would have to "dance with anything," even boys lacking in manners or morals. The "base, animal nature" of modern dancing proved especially dangerous, in Gaskin's view, because it broke down necessary social boundaries, unleashing in white girls a sexuality as "base" as that of boys and men, or worse, as that of "the only American who does not have to learn to dance . . . a negro."[10] In condemning the sexuality of the dance, white critics pointed to the deeper risks that dance posed to the social order, in general, and racial segregation in particular.

Despite continuing objections from conservative religious quarters, black and white, by midcentury schools increasingly held dances as a matter of course. African American students at Atlanta's Booker T. Washington High held their first prom in 1943, even though yearbook photos indicate that boys formed at most one-quarter of the student body.[11] Charlotte's Second Ward High School announced that the 1946 student council's initial act would be to plan the first school dance.[12] In rural black schools where resources were scarce, dances were fewer but, as a result, charged with singular significance. Mary Mebane, a student in rural Durham County, North Carolina, recalled working for weeks with other committee members to plan her class prom in the late 1940s. On the fateful night, dressed in a store-bought green gown with a rhinestone-studded waist and long white gloves, hair fixed in an elegant upsweep, her date never arrived to escort her. He chose to go to the dance alone, where her noticeable absence made the insult obvious to all her friends, leaving a memory of indelible shame.[13]

High school students in towns and cities invested time, money, and hope in proms and other big dances. Two white high school seniors from Camden, Alabama, described their work on the junior-senior prom in autobiographies they wrote for a 1948 senior English essay assignment. Compared to previous grades where "nothing very exciting happened," Ann Perry described eleventh grade as eventful because of her class's year-long project of raising money for the junior-senior banquet and prom. Similarly Peggy Acker described her junior year as "the busiest I ever spent." As class treasurer she felt a special responsibility for fund-raising activities, stating proudly, "After a year's hard work and cooperation, we reached our only goal, the Junior-Senior banquet and prom," receiving praise from both "patrons and faculty."[14]

In Birmingham, Alabama, adult approval went beyond parents and faculty to city government officials. In the autumn of 1943 the city began sponsoring free dances after Friday night football games in an effort to provide "wholesome" wartime recreation for students from the city's five white high schools. The idea originated with Police Commissioner Eugene Connor (who as "Bull" Connor gained national notoriety twenty years later for his violent opposition to civil rights demonstrators, which included using hoses and dogs on protesting schoolchildren). Connor, aided by local civic groups, arranged student transportation to and from the municipal auditorium, and in 1945 supported capping the fall season with the first annual junior-senior prom for white students.[15] The tradition continued through the late 1950s, with at least nine participating schools and as many as six thousand white students attending the January prom.[16] Throughout the region, proms and other formal dances became more frequent and elaborate during the 1950s. Charlotte's Central High School held five dances during the 1951–1952 school year: a fall dance, a Christmas

Snowball, a leap year dance, a semi-formal spring dance, and then the season finale junior-senior prom. Each dance had its own theme, dress regulations, and color schemes.[17]

Another heterosexual rite often accompanied school dances or celebrations: the selection of a queen. Like the homecoming queen, who led off the homecoming dance with the captain of the football team, these royal figures were selected on the basis of their beauty and popularity, then placed at the forefront of important school rituals. Many black schools tied the selection of a queen to competitive fund-raising projects in which the class that raised the most money earned the right to choose the queen from among their own numbers. In the 1940s and '50s some schools added a strictly photographic beauty contest. A committee of male yearbook staff reviewed photos of female classmates in order to select and rank the great "beauties" of the year, who would then be featured in full-page layouts in the yearbook. Sometimes male classmates served as judges, but at other times schools engaged outside "experts," such as modeling school directors, whose professional and impartial judgments authenticated the school's final selections.[18]

The appreciation of good looks and alluring charm was not in itself new. Students of earlier decades recognized beauty through accolades, homecoming events, and printed commentary that marked individual girls as pretty, good-looking, or beautiful. But students of the 1920s and '30s typically balanced their appraisal of personal attractiveness with an assessment of other attributes like responsibility, intelligence, and loyalty. Central High School's 1926 yearbook, for example, described the attractive senior Elenor Lorraine Ward with a poem: "At the boys she often flirts / But still she never duty shirks."[19] Duty, responsibility, loyalty, and character were considered to be equal in value to beauty and charm. As heterosexuality became more central to school life in the late 1930s and 1940s, beauty contests did too. Although only girls participated in the contests themselves, these competitions revealed some of the central dynamics of a heterosexual peer culture. Girls stood as the objects at which boys gazed, valued for their appearance and allure. Boys assessed girls, ranked them in order of attractiveness, and made their selections accordingly. The ritual did not involve heterosexual coupling, but it did lay out some of the terms on which girls established their worth in the "marketplace" of dating and eventual marriage.

In this environment, heterosexual couples occupied an increasingly prominent place in the life of the school, especially when postwar gender ratios evened out. One visual clue to this development comes from a change in the photographic conventions of high school annuals. For decades schoolmates had honored outstanding members of their class through a series of "superlatives" that recognized the talents and qualities most valued among students, such as most intelligent, best dressed, wittiest, or most likely to succeed. Earlier yearbooks typically photographed the winners individually, granting each one some portion of a page. But in 1942 Charlotte's Central High School initiated two changes. The *Snips and Cuts* staff made the accolades identical for boys and girls, so that students competed to be the most intelligent girl and boy, or the best dressed or the most athletic of each gender. The only superlatives lacking a semantic match were for the "best looking" boy / "prettiest" girl and for the "best bull shooter" (male) and "biggest heart breaker" (female). The first pair nodded to gendered ideals of beauty in which "pretty" would be an insult rather than an accolade for a male, while the latter pair acknowledged the role-specific behavior of boys and girls as they sought to begin or end dating. In a second change, Central's annual began photographing the winners in each category as couples. Whether the winners even knew or liked each other, the yearbook staff appropriated the visual language of heterosexual coupledom to present seniors noted for their individual accomplishments.[20]

Harding High School and other southern schools of the 1940s elaborated this pattern of heightened attention to heterosexual couples. The *Harding Hi-Lites* school newspaper of 1946–1947, for example, published a crossword puzzle that tested classmates' up-to-date knowledge of current couples. The author directed students to unscramble jumbled names and then "try to match the true lovers."[21] In the paper's "Hearts and Flowers" gossip column, the author commented on the expansion of the three r's to a fourth: "Reading, 'riting, 'rithmetic, AND romance—that's the curriculum for the would-be slick chick or swoon bait around these parts."[22] Not only had couples come to dominate extracurricular activities, but the "slick" girls and boys perceived the couples scene as the curriculum itself. And in a way, the author was right. New psychology or family life courses imbued the formal curriculum with an orientation toward dating and marriage. According to one report, while the first Harding psychology class in 1946 covered topics from personal development to group behavior and leadership, it proved especially useful to girls: "Why? Because they get their tips on how to 'get their man!'"[23]

Tips on husband hunting seemed all important in a postwar culture that represented marriage as a woman's most valuable achievement, her proof of femininity, and her contribution toward reestablishing stable family life in the aftermath of Depression-era and wartime disruptions. While during World War II women received praise for their independence and willingness to sacrifice personal life for the public good, during the postwar era there was a renewed emphasis on marriage and domestic life accompanied by increased ridicule of unmarried "spinsters" as heterosexual failures or mannish lesbians.[24] In this context, dating, romance, and marriage occupied center stage in high school discourse, exhibiting girls' interest in the process of "man getting" and their confident assumption that, with the right knowledge and experience, they would indeed find a man to love and marry.

This pattern developed first in urban areas and in white high schools, which typically had more resources than black or rural schools. To form a semi-autonomous teen culture operating within and around the high school, students needed a central location, school resources devoted to social events, and access to cash, free time, and transportation. The resources available to African American youth varied along a continuum, with urban schools in thriving cities having more and rural black "county training schools" (a term intended to signal a vocational emphasis) the least. White rural schools fit somewhere along the same continuum, but in all cases received more public funds to support their activities than did black schools. In North Carolina, for example, during the 1945–1946 school year, the assessed total value of school property at white schools reached $217 per pupil compared to a miserly $70 per pupil at schools for African Americans.[25]

Large urban schools like Birmingham's Parker High School, which in 1950 had the highest enrollment of any black high school nationwide, and Nashville's Pearl High School offered students a plethora of after-school activities like academic and hobby clubs, newspaper and yearbook staff, interscholastic sports, band, choral groups, dramatics, and debate.[26] Students also formed informal cliques and clubs that socialized on or near the school grounds during and after the school day. Urban school terms ran longer as well, with a nine-month term in Birmingham compared to terms as short as five or six months in some rural areas. A 1947 study of Macon's two African American high schools found that each offered many of the activities of larger schools, but that most students, and especially boys, pursued recreational interests beyond the confines of school and adult-sponsored organizations like Girl Scouts or the YMCA.[27] The limited resources of Charlotte's two black high schools in the 1950s heightened the importance of the "Queen City Classic" football game between the rival schools because, according to students, "there wasn't much to do so we made a big deal out of it." Significantly, the female student who sold the most tickets to the game won the title of Miss Queen City Classic, suggesting that despite limited resources, black students created their own heterosexually oriented culture.[28]

Rural schools might also hold one or two large events like dances or parades, but had far fewer resources than urban schools and thus a less developed school-based culture. Many rural southern counties into the 1950s still failed to fund any secondary education for black students, forcing teens to attend private academies, usually dismally poor, or to board with friends or relatives in another county that did have a high school. More typically, counties like Caswell County, North Carolina, tacked on higher grades to an existing poorly funded rural school. Caswell County Training School, near Yanceyville, North Carolina, produced its first graduating senior class—of seven students—in 1934, with each subsequent class larger than the previous. The county finally approved a separate high school in the 1940s, but then failed to build it until the early 1950s. For its part, the school offered some extracurricular activities, but required all clubs to meet during the last class period of the day so that participants would not miss the school bus, their only means of transportation home. When interscholastic athletic competition began in the early 1950s, the school still lacked a gymnasium, substituting a smoothed-out dirt floor in an old, partially demolished school building next door. Beyond club activities, larger school events occurred at night so that working parents, who thought of Caswell County Training School activities as being events for the whole community, could attend. Not only were parents involved in the school, but the school's principal and teachers resided in the black community as well, interacting with children informally from a young age through their teenage years, creating a level of adult supervision and intervention that surpassed that of larger more anonymous urban high schools.[29]

Although limited funds and greater adult involvement stifled the kind of flourishing heterosexual culture of urban, especially white, high schools, this did not mean the absence of peer culture or romantic and sexual relationships between students. Greater adult supervision on campus often meant less supervision outside of school, at off-campus locations, and over long summers. Friends still formed cliques, gossiped about who was dating whom, and discussed "how far" certain girls "had gone" sexually. After riding the bus home, friends or lovers could gather at someone's home, often unsupervised since adults were away at work. Mary Mebane remembered how after each summer and over the course of the school year certain girls stopped attending her rural county school, having dropped out due to pregnancy. Mary and several others who were excluded from the more "popular" crowd formed a social club of their own based on a shared vow of celibacy to ensure that they, unlike other girls they knew, would graduate from high school.[30]

Comparing black high schools to white, or rural high schools to urban, shows that the sexual culture of midcentury high schools was not uniform or pervasive, but rather existed to different degrees in different settings, varying according to resources, location, and the relative independence or supervision that students experienced. The trajectory of change, however, followed the kind of autonomous school-based peer culture evident at the Charlotte and Atlanta high schools. Especially as rural schools underwent consolidation and as the Supreme Court's 1954 *Brown v. Board of Education* decision led southern school districts to build newer, much improved black high schools to avoid court-ordered desegregation, more and more high schools resembled Harding High School by the late 1950s. In Charlotte and elsewhere, a not-so-hidden curriculum of dating, romance, and teenage sexuality thrived in formal classroom settings, at school events, among informal

In rural black high schools like Holcomb School in Mississippi's Grenada County, over-crowding and greater adult supervision (note the adults stationed around the room) discouraged a school-based culture of romance. But rural students took advantage of unsupervised time and open spaces to cultivate teenage romance and sexual relations beyond school boundaries. John E. Fay Collection, 1955, Southern Media Archive, Special Collections, University of Mississippi Libraries.

peer groups, and in school publications like literary magazines, school newspapers, and especially yearbooks.

If official school publications hinted at the importance of love and marriage in adolescence, this was the featured topic in the informal handwritten inscriptions that classmates wrote to each other in their school yearbooks' last section, which usually consisted of several pages of advertising and another few blank pages. Students crammed their messages into every available space. Written at odd angles, sideways, and upside down on pages already crowded with advertisements, they inserted their own handwritten messages in the margins or sometimes directly over the ad copy. Most inscriptions consisted of two or three lines of good wishes for the future, fond commentary on the recipient's personality, or thanks for shared "good times." Other students, however, scrawled their communiqués across a full page, scribbling heartfelt messages that attempted to convey their feelings to a schoolmate whose friendship they valued.

Yearbook inscriptions offer a snapshot of ordinary student relationships, a capsular statement set down on the self-conscious occasion of the school year's end, when students departed for the summer or possibly forever. The practice of exchanging yearbooks for reciprocated messages had its own ritualized conventions; certain forms of address, words, expressions, and kinds of commentary predominated, which lent a formulaic quality to most entries. Nevertheless, yearbook inscriptions offer a rare window into informal student culture and ongoing student relationships. The annuals of three Harding students within the span of a decade—Bob Weddington in 1943, Alice Nivens from 1946 to 1950, and June Platt in 1952—illustrate the ritualistic exchange of high school annuals and the deeper meanings they held.[31]

Strikingly, the inscriptions say almost nothing about academic activity, revealing instead the range of social activities that students enjoyed during and after school. Some wrote about academic classes as a location for mischief, hilarity, brushes with authority or, less often, the occasion for a near failure, funny in retrospect. Classmates in 1949 reminded Alice Nivens about our "hard times in World History" and "our good times in 'English.' Big joke." Beyond classroom experiences, the yearbooks preserve a record of day-to-day social activities in an adolescent world revolving around the high school. Students recalled after-school trips to the river, the local drugstore, or the movies; planning or attending school dances; telling jokes; enjoying parties and occasional gatherings at a skating rink or beach; and going to classmates' homes to listen to music. For Charlotte teens in the 1940s and early 1950s, consumption and commercial entertainment did not yet dominate adolescent culture, as it later did.[32] Students might buy a soft drink at the drugstore, go to the movies, or take a date to a dance or a local cafe, but informal noncommercial fun still lay at the center of teenage social life as classmates walked, talked, or relaxed at a nearby river, attended school dances and football games, or simply laughed together during daily classes and hallway interchanges.

In commemorating their "good times" together, students created a collective narrative about their high school days focused around shared fun or intimacies. This narrative would form the basis of later memories, recollections of a distinct peer world and the formative role it played in their adult lives. Within this shared narrative, classmates also asked friends to find a place for them in their individual memories. Instructions to Bob, Alice, or June to "remember our good times" or "never forget the fun we had" in some specified activity served to lodge the inscriber in the mind of the yearbook's owner, weaving a more personal memory into the fabric of the collective memories being forged. A girl named Joyce, for example, thanks Bob Weddington for "being around when I've had 'mostest' fun. Remember the sailboat ride (don't forget me either)." Both the yearbook itself and the inscribed messages linked the present transitional moment to the future by creating a common past of fond, lasting memories.

The most formulaic entries wishing the best of luck to a "cute guy" or a "great gal" might indicate that some students did not invest great meaning in the annual commemorations. But yearbook entries that went beyond banal greetings display a liveliness and occasional intensity that suggest a greater significance. While lightness and humor set the mood, an undertone of seriousness seeped through remarks made by seniors to either fellow graduates or younger students remaining at Harding. Since in the early 1940s nearly every boy was destined to enter the military upon graduation, there was a sense of an unknowable, dangerous future in which life itself could not be guaranteed. When friends wrote to Bob Weddington, "You and I will soon be leaving in some part of the armed forces. I . . . will always remember you" and "I certainly hope we will get to stay in the Navy together. Let's not let anything come between our lovely, wholesome friendship," they betrayed a nervousness about imminent departures and possible losses.

Harding classmates also addressed the uncertain future by issuing pointed recommendations. Girls, especially, instructed friends to "always stay the same" or "keep that personality and those fine looks and you'll be tops" in order to ensure their happiness and success. The most promising future would resemble the present, as if by etching the here-and-now into the future the student might remain a known entity whose constancy would not impede—but rather improve—her ability to succeed in life. Boys rarely received this advice, although they sometimes issued it to girls. This curious piece of advice might simply express the desire for friends to maintain a resemblance to their teenage self so they would remain in some sense familiar or "known." Yet the explicit link to success might also suggest that for girls not going on to higher education, the high school years were meant to cultivate the qualities—as a finishing school would—of charm and personality that would make her marriageable, thus guaranteeing that she would "be tops" in the race for a "good man."

Advice offered toward future achievements served another more immediate purpose; it prescribed desirable behavior in the present. Typically students addressed qualities of personality and physical appearance. Bob Weddington, who seemed to be well known, liked by all, and very involved in school activities, received acclaim as a "fine," "cute," or "swell boy." Classmates also employed superlatives like "the nicest boy," or in one entry, the "nicest, swellest, sweetest boy I know." June Platt, a Harding sophomore in 1952, found herself appreciated for some of the same qualities—her cuteness, sweetness, and niceness. Similarly, contributors to Alice Nivens's eighth- and ninth-grade annuals described her as sweet, cute, nice, swell, and darling, or, in the words of one older classmate, as "really one cute 'n' sweet gal." Both boys and girls used these words in praise of female friends and acquaintances, with girls using them as well to address their male friends. In contrast, Bob Weddington's male classmates referred to him as a "swell" or "fine" friend, addressing him affectionately as "son" or "you kid!!!" They abstained from phrases that referenced physical appearance, like "best looking," or words expressing endearing attributes like sweetness or cuteness.

Stock phrases like "nice boy" and "cute gal" appear so frequently that one wonders if they contain any meaning. In one sense the answer must be no, since they were interchangeable terms used by almost everyone to describe almost everyone else. But this does not make these phrases devoid of all meaning. The stock platitudes suggest commonly valued qualities and a common lingo of high school culture that informed recipients that they not only were appreciated but also had met the standards of their peers. The absence of such stock inscriptions for a particular student might have communicated disapproval or some kind of outsider status that would change only if the student in question conformed by adopting a swell, cute, or nice demeanor.

The yearbooks of Alice Nivens contain more extensive personal commentary in which students move beyond brief or standard inscriptions to reveal more about the social and sexual dynamics of adolescence. Classmates appear to have found conventional platitudes and advice inadequate to the task of describing Alice. Boys in particular qualified their praise by designating her as "very sweet but crazy," "very beautiful and changed," and as a "swell (I guess) girl." In these entries, we can begin to see some of the complexities lying just beneath the surface of more patterned remarks, indicating ambivalent feelings and multivalent relationships. Boys who wrote in Alice's yearbook displayed a variety of emotions, from love and interest to resentment and anger. Some wished to date her, others fondly remembered going out together, while still others voiced regret about a soured romance. Such inscriptions suggest that the different needs and perspectives of girls and boys could spark gender conflict, yet they confirm that heterosexuality formed the storyline of high school life.

Alice's ninth-grade yearbook includes an entry from classmate Gerald, who begins with a standard line: "You're a swell 'gal,'" followed by a more personal entreaty: "I like you and always have. I hope your feelings toward me have changed because I think you're very cute." Another would-be suitor, George, communicates his continuing availability, despite Alice's apparent lack of interest, reminding her, "The next time you get stood up all you have to do is 'buzz me!'" While these two entries walk the line between feelings of interest and rejection, a boy named Sandy expresses unqualified satisfaction, commenting, "It has been nice knowing you and dating you. Remember me, if you will." In the dating system boys had the power to initiate, determine the frequencies and the activities of dating, and by paying for the date created some sense of obligation for the girl who "owed" him for his financial investment.[33] These entries, however, speak to the vulnerability of boys in the dating system. Although girls had to wait to be asked and might suffer the rejection of not being approached, boys who received refusals experienced a more public kind of rejection by having clearly stated their interest only to be rebuffed. While Gerald states his hopes that Alice will one day reciprocate his feelings, George stoops to offering himself as a stand-in if Alice ever finds herself "stood-up" and in sudden need of a date, any date. Even Sandy's apparent contentment as a former date expresses some tentativeness in his request to "Remember me, if you will."

Still others signaled much greater ambivalence. Don Little, for instance, writes admiringly of Alice in her sophomore yearbook yet defends against his own vulnerability by assuming the voice of an authoritative guide. "Always wear high-heeled shoes to Sunday School," he counsels, "and there will be more than girls looking at you. No fooling! Lots of luck to a swell (I guess) girl." Don commends Alice on her attractiveness, reassures her of boys' interest, and takes on the role of heterosexual adviser. In instructing her to wear high heels, he refers to her desirability while also reminding her that boys are looking and judging in ways that might determine her future. Extending his wishes for a lucky future, he again also questions her reputation as a "swell (I guess) girl." The uncertainty of his approval may refer to some of Alice's less desirable qualities or possibly to his own frustration with their relationship; perhaps he "guesses" she is swell because he missed the chance to find out for himself by dating her.

A classmate named Walter also mixes regret, frustration, and lusty esteem. Beginning "Dearest Alice!!!" he continues, "Another year has passed and I still haven't got you as my girl. But life is life." He then substitutes a drawing for words, sketching a headless torso with curvy breasts, waist, and hips, with the explanation: "That [drawing of body] of yours oh!!! is enough to kill me, but really you are swell in every way that's the truth." Walter depicts himself as the victim of her sexiness—her body is killing him—but restores himself to power as her admiring assessor, evaluating her as "swell in every way" despite her unavailability.

Boys conveyed both admiration and judgment by mixing their compliments with criticism. Don Payne wishes Alice success at the end of tenth grade, praises her as a "sweet girl," then quickly follows with a caveat that she should be "a little more careful how you talk though, and you can hold your own." Don warns Alice that her "talk" is somehow inappropriate and that only by following his cautious standards will she be able to "hold her own" in the world—an ambiguous phrase that could refer to holding her place in the world or holding her own loved one. A boy named "Duck" assumes a similar gatekeeping role by following a complimentary remark with a stern warning: "You are a real spark. You could even start the world turning. Don't try it." Alice's "spark" is attractive, yet her sexuality appears threatening too, something Alice should not unleash. Duck's concluding remarks return to Alice's sexuality, but this time Duck holds the initiative and presents his own availability as reward for her compliance. Wishing her luck and success, he then vows that "I might some day 'rock' you to sleep—you will succeed." In her own hands Alice's "spark" is dangerous, but Duck declares that in his hands "rocking" (a sexualized slang term soon applied to a new style of "rocking" music) is the very definition of success. Duck's bravado reveals his view that only a boy's assertive sexuality could safely contain but also gratify the tinderbox of adolescent female sexuality.

Hints of hostility and gender antagonism did not in every case remain veiled. In the eighth grade Bill "Curly" Helms dated Alice, a relationship that led to heartbreak and bad feelings. Her 1946 yearbook contains a message from Betty, who predicts that "someday a certain guy will come along. One who won't make you cry like Billy did," then adds, "Wish my man would hurry up and come." The romantic struggle between Bill and Alice continued; two years later Bill's full-page entry in Alice's annual expresses abiding interest, accompanied by somewhat belligerent and threatening remarks. Wishing her "the best," Bill continues: "(getting serious now!) Is my name still listed in your matrimonial files? (I hope so.) Stop running away from me—hear—you better stop. Don't say you don't [run away] or I'll sock ya." Bill then calls Alice a "mankiller," thus reversing the direction of violence and conceding her power over him. He quickly returns to his gruff commands, telling Alice she had better come to next year's football games, "all of them—hear." Vacillating between submission and aggression, Bill ends with a drawing of himself, labeled "ME," down on one knee, arms extended forward so that he appears either to be begging for something or proposing marriage. Alice stands before him, face impassive, dressed in a sweater, skirt, and clownish shoes, clearly giving nothing away easily.

The following year the conversation continued along a similar path, although without as much fire. Bill writes with some appreciation, "Say Gal—Thanks for writing in my annual. I was surprised." Making reference to their ongoing problems, Bill's next sentence is a plea couched as a demand: "How about speaking to me." Then under the guise of advice he warns, "You better watch your step around school, you're always getting into too much trouble," followed by the more supplicatory, "What you say to us being friends?" He ends with a humorous critique of her aggression, again in the form of advice: "You ought to play football next year—you'd make good, I'm sure." Although no other entries match the emotional jaggedness of Bill's, more subtle tensions surface in a number of well-wishing comments from boys who nevertheless refer to some history of conflict. Johnnie Salem writes after Alice's junior year, "We have had our fights etc. but we've always apologized. I have enjoyed knowing you and it has really been a pleasure dating you." Another boy, Joe, wishes Alice luck followed by an expression of fond regret: "I sure wish we could have agreed on a few things. But I still love you."

The range of sentiments in boys' written comments to Alice point to the centrality and complexity of heterosexual relations for teenagers in high school. Dating appears as both a casual affair and an early stage of courtship for marriage. Statements like "it has really been a pleasure dating you" establish some kind of special relationship but one without great significance—a pleasant experience among many. The enmity of a boy who hopes "your hate for me will die as Father Time puts gray hair into your head" suggests more intensity, yet still contains a joking quality. The ongoing exchange between Bill Helms and Alice, however, reverberates with tension, speaking both to the intense heartbeat and heartbreak of adolescent love and its significance as a prelude to marriage, stated plainly in Bill's mention of Alice's "matrimonial files." Bill's oscillation between hostile threats and acquiescent pleas is echoed by other remarks from boys who clearly wish for Alice's attention yet feel painfully vulnerable to her sexual allure and refusals. From this uncomfortable position, they convey their desire but at the same time protect their masculine authority by assuming the role of adviser and critic. Boys seem to have wanted casual dating with the possibility of more serious love, as did girls, but resented girls' power of initial refusal or later rejection. Caught between assertive desire and humbling rebuffs, high school boys exhibited a mix of anger, kindness, and criticism, employing as well a mix of sometimes cutting, sometimes self-mocking humor—all of which were designed to declare the boys' feelings while protecting both their masculine pride and power.

The importance of heterosexual relationships shaped same-sex friendships too, as girls served as confidantes, advisers, consolers, and cheerleaders for their friends' involvements with boys. In Alice's tenth-grade yearbook, for example, Gwendolyn "Blondie" Harris remembers a variety of fun times but then remarks, "I'll remember most of all the talks we have had about our troubles and our boyfriends." Wishing Alice well with her new "darling" boyfriend Lorence, she then reassures her that in two years, as a senior, "the person who gets you will be mighty lucky." This prediction implies that "our troubles and our boyfriends" are simply a prelude to marriage, which is expected to occur around the time of high school graduation when some lucky man will finally "get" Alice for keeps.

A year later, when Alice is a junior, friends continue to share information and express hope about Alice's love life, which now centers around a boy named Donald. An entry by Jeanne wishes that "you and Don can patch things up, 'cause from reliable sources, I think the guy likes you," while another friend writes, "Hope you have everything in life your little heart desires including Donald." Her close friend Bette expresses a sense of solidarity and shared suffering around heterosexual relationships, thanking Alice for being there "to tell my troubles to." She wishes she was writing the note "when I was not so blue," but anticipates better times, hoping, "Maybe someday we'll find the right one (and let's hope that we'll have enough sense to *realize* that)." Anticipating their next year as seniors, Bette concludes, "I can hardly wait till school starts again. Then our big times will really come."

Although dramatic heterosexual plotlines frequently formed the main text of same-sex friendships, female friendships did not revolve solely around boys. Friends of Alice Nivens and June Platt bring up good times shared between girlfriends, ranging from raising "heck" in school, to parties, day trips, and adventures ending in confrontations with the police. Friends also thank Alice and June for sharing "things you have," including home and family life, money, and the "kindness you have given me." Along with thanks, acceptance, and advice, friends offered criticisms as well, usually softened by humor. Alice's friend Gloria remembers their fine times together during sophomore year, but adds that she and Alice can remain good friends only "as long as you don't hang up on me every day," concluding with a plea, "Be good just for me." In their regular comments on Alice's fine figure, cute looks, sweet temperament—as well as her sharp tongue and unpredictable temper—Alice's friends choose words that speak to the immediacy and depth of their relationships. Rather than detracting from the closeness of female friendship, animated interest in boys fueled homosocial intimacies. As girls talked among themselves about boys, dates, and marital possibilities, they reinforced the centrality of heterosexuality while drawing closer to each other.

Entries by girls form a large majority of the inscriptions written in the yearbooks of Bob Weddington, June Platt, and Alice Nivens. Adolescent girls communicated to boys their fond feelings, at the same time using praise to instruct the boys in expected male behavior and attitudes. With each other, they shared the most heartfelt experiences of female friendship by weaving their deepest gratitude and anxieties into a plotline of dating and romantic pursuit. The yearbook represents adult-sanctioned, official high school culture. But girls especially appropriated the blank pages, the advertising section, and the edges as a space of their own. Having little public voice, they commandeered the margins to communicate their feelings about both the mundane and intensely emotional aspects of high school life. And although they often revealed their vulnerability, through the very act of utilizing an official document for their own purposes they gained some control. Girls had, at least temporarily, the last word about heterosexual relationships that, on the one hand, might have been playful and short-term but, on the other hand, seemed to many teens a prelude to all-important marital decisions that would determine their adult destiny.

The collected yearbooks of Alice Nivens speak to the drama of heterosexual adventure and love performed on the stage of "ordinary" high school life. They provide a log of shifting female friendships and of the boyfriends who moved in and out of Alice's mercurial love life during her five years at Harding. Her annuals mention dates with Sandy, Bill, Donald, Walter, "dear ole" Carl, Monk, Johnnie, and Lorence, as well as a host of other would-be suitors. In her junior year, while bemoaning her up and down relationship with Donald, she also began dating two sailors who wrote entries in her yearbook. Alice cared enough about the first, Jackie, to reserve a space in his name, but she had a more serious relationship with another named Barry, whose yearbook missive speaks with heartrending earnestness about his hopes for the future. He implores Alice, "Please just believe in me," pledging that "I'll always believe in you." About to ship out, Barry then begs, "All I ask is that you wait until I'm out of the Navy and you are through school. Until then, let's not change a bit." To Barry's misfortune, Alice was nothing if not changeable and did not honor the sailor's request for commitment. Instead, Alice's high school career combined not only numerous boyfriends but also a variety of types of dating. She dated for casual fun, for serious romance, and by her junior year moved outside Harding to date sailors who would be unfamiliar to family and friends and thus represent both danger and excitement.

In the formula of "reading, 'riting, 'rithmetic and romance," the nonacademic "R" took priority at Harding High. Alice Nivens's yearbooks reveal romance to be ordinary and fully integrated into mid-century teenage life, providing adolescents with some of their deepest thrills and spills. The tension, competition, theatricality, and happiness hoped for, gained, and lost made for a roller coaster with its own dips, lulls, gradual ascents, curves, and perilous drops—a ride that students experienced for themselves and observed in others as a spectacle of adolescent drama. In some ways high school romance flowed along predictable channels, even as it added to the playfulness, suspense, and excitement of everyday life. But the seemingly safe, contained world of high school heterosexual culture did not prove as predictable as promised. Girls got pregnant, dropped out to marry (pregnant or not), or made other rash decisions about sexuality and marriage that were often paid for with later misery. High school romances, as routine as they were, might also presage a precarious future.

Romance, then, promised both danger and delight to students of the 1940s. Two girls at Charlotte's Central High School addressed the uncertainties of romance in short fiction pieces they published in the 1940 edition of Central's literary magazine, *Lace and Pig Iron.* The short stories, one a suspenseful drama and the other a parodic comedy, suggest both the ardor and the tentativeness with which students approached the paradoxical experience of romantic love. The first story, "Fifteen," reflects on the dangers of romantic deception, while the second, "Trudy at the Sea Shore," comments on the crudeness and inappropriateness of marriages built on any foundation other than "true" romantic love.

"Fifteen," told in the first person by fifteen-year-old June, begins with the protagonist reflecting on her embarrassing experience at the Fairview Academy's January prom. After traveling alone by train to the distant private school, June's date, Charles, meets her at the station but is immediately pushed aside by a tall charming boy named Porter who "smiled a look that made my toes tingle." June floats through the prom that evening, aglow as the dreamy Porter breaks in and out of each dance despite Charles's official claim on her attention. As the dance is about to end, Porter breaks in one more time and whispers to June to meet him in an hour and a half at the campus's landmark oak tree. Sneaking away from the girls' residence, she dashes through cold and snow to get to the giant tree. As she awaits her secret date, June hears voices approaching. Seconds later a girl exclaims, "And she believed you?" and bursts into laughter with Porter about a silly girl, gullible enough to take his bait. Stung by humiliation, June runs blindly down the hill and stumbles, only to be caught by another unseen presence. Charles had sensed the situation and followed her to the oak tree as a silent protector. Steadfast and true, he rescues June and solicitously instructs her to button her coat as they walk off into the blustery night.[34] If experts warned that teens were especially susceptible to bad sexual judgment given the explosive mix of physical maturity and emotional immaturity, "Fifteen," a story of female vulnerability to deception, presents an adolescent's confirmation of this view.

"Trudy at the Sea Shore" presents an entirely different scenario of love and marriage, told through the genre of working-class adventure stories. While still a mill girl from the mountains, Trudy Trueheart marries the disfigured "Hunchback Ben" and lives happily for a year until a train hits and kills him. When her boss at the rayon factory gives Trudy a week off to recover from the shock of her husband's death, she spends Ben's insurance money for a week-long visit to a seashore resort, where she decides it is time to "git" another man. Meeting a series of available men at the resort, Trudy inadvertently repels them with her lack of manners and sensitivity. But when she hears about a local resident, "Clubfoot Joe," who spends his days at the shore, alone, soaking his foot in the salty ocean, she perks up and begins to pursue the disabled prospect. Trudy, looking "lovelier than ever" for having washed her hands and run a comb through her greasy hair, approaches Joe with an offer of marriage and life in the mountains with Trudy supporting him. She leaves Joe to ponder the proposal, but before she can return for his answer catastrophe strikes and Joe drowns when he is run over by a yacht. Trudy prepares to return to her mountain home, inconsolable about the loss of her future husband. The story ends on a positive note, however, when Trudy suddenly remembers an available man back home, a thread-winder at the mill named "Deaf-and-Dumb Dan."[35]

Trudy represents everything most girls at Central High, and Harding as well, wanted to avoid—relative poverty, rurality, millwork, unattractive and unclean appearance, total lack of manners and sophistication, brazen pursuit of men and marriage, and foolish ignorance about "real" love and middle-class courtship. Trudy's repeated social gaffes tag her as a stock figure of southern ridicule, a poor rube unaware and unconcerned about proper etiquette or "good taste." She uses a paper bag for a suitcase, alternates a pink chiffon dress from a rummage sale with a remaindered purple and blue rayon dress, eats an entire bucket of shrimp and plate of biscuits for her supper, and neglects to wash her hair or hands on a regular basis. Trudy represents a despised kind of womanhood who, by serving as a figure of mockery, might reassure adolescent female readers that they were not that dreaded type. Yet curiously her name is "Trueheart."

The two stories present diametrically opposed romantic debacles, first in the form of upper-middle-class starry-eyed credulity, followed by a parody of bumbling, crude, and benighted love attributed to poor, rural hayseeds. Together they admit to a nervousness about the process of identifying and wisely following one's "true heart," even as they reassure high school girls that they can safely pursue their own romances because they resembled neither the tragic June nor the parodic Trudy. The stories act as object lessons to Charlotte high school girls, most of them neither mountain "rubes" nor society debs, who were trying to embrace the romantic possibilities of real love while remaining wary of potentially shameful mistakes.

$\mathcal{A}$dults, too, had by the mid-1940s become concerned about the inability of teenage girls to distinguish between true romance and the immediacy of momentary infatuation and sexual temptation. But by the late 1940s and 1950s, professionals had established new mechanisms for guiding youth. Especially in the fields of psychology and education, experts believed that their sophisticated understandings of adolescent social and sexual "adjustment" could be successfully communicated to parents, teachers, and even directly to teenagers.

Sex educators, who through World War II had gravitated toward a fear-based model emphasizing sexual sin and disease, replaced morbid scenarios with an affirmative language of "family life education" that stressed the importance of sexual intimacy and fulfillment to modern marriage and healthy families. The Cold War era viewed strong nuclear families as the bedrock of a stable, democratic nation populated by well-adjusted, patriotic citizens. In this context, sex educators laid claim to an expertise regarding sexual adjustment, marriage, and family that made them important players in postwar society. While the much larger fields of psychiatry and psychology made far-reaching gains in the medical field, private therapeutic practice, the military, and college curricula, sex educators made their biggest inroads in developing "family life" instruction for students ranging from the upper elementary grades through college.[36]

During the same years, panic erupted concerning homosexuals, who were viewed as insidious agents corrupting American virtue, and male sexual predators, who were accused of molesting innocent children in unprecedented numbers.[37] Law officials and the media often lumped the two groups together in the single category of sexual psychopaths. The images of the secretive gay man and the child molester formed the antithesis of the positive image of healthy, happy heterosexual families enjoying life in a democratic consumer society. While law officers and the courts dealt with sexual offenders, who represented "failed" sexual adjustment, sex educators focused on positive outcomes secured by teaching children the basics of reproductive biology and more. They instructed vulnerable teenagers how to navigate "successfully" the path from puberty through dating, romance, marriage, and child rearing.

Sex education caught on as a topic of national interest, with popular magazines like *Time, Life, Parents Magazine,* and *Ladies' Home Journal* publishing a spate of articles on the subject in the late 1940s. Yet the nation did not embrace sex education as an urgent public health measure like the syphilis campaigns directed by the U.S. surgeon general in the late 1930s. Rather, individual schools, school districts, and sometimes states gave their approval to sex education programs in a piecemeal fashion. This led sex educators to take a cautious approach, deemphasizing sexual acts and eroticism in favor of more general discussions of emotions, social adaptation, personality, and "healthy family life," which subsumed the topic of sex. The strategy worked; the question seemed to shift from "whether" to "how" sex should be taught in the schools.[38]

The South, as a region, showed some reluctance to embrace this educational trend.[39] But numerous school systems adopted some version of sex education, like Georgia's "character education" program or Charlotte city high schools' psychology courses focused on marriage and family life. This trend fit into a more general approach to gearing secondary education to practical knowledge, since the majority of students did not continue on to college. High school, in less elite areas, became the last, best chance for adult guidance. Sex education, along with civics classes, consumer education, and vocational training, aimed to socialize students as citizens, consumers, and well-adjusted individuals who would marry, have children, work, make purchases, vote, and remain loyal to their country.

The official curriculum of sex educators operated, for the most part, in synch with the unofficial lessons that students taught each other about sex, dating, and romance. Teenagers may have allowed for more extensive petting or sanctioned premarital intercourse, under some circumstances, against their teachers' recommendations. The informal culture of high school sexuality visible in yearbooks and school publications did not provoke adult alarm or social controversy. Its relatively calm surface, however, hid much rockier undercurrents. The greater autonomy of postwar teenagers and the heightened emphasis on both love and lust in teen culture created opportunities for adolescents to make decisions, or fail to take precautions, that might result in unexpected pregnancies, hurried marriages, or unwed motherhood with its resulting social disrepute.

Alice Nivens may not have taken a family education course instructing her on the necessary precautions to take with boys, but she had received frequent warning signals from friends who cautioned her about her temper, impulsive "craziness," and rebellious nature. These unheeded warnings and Alice's evident preoccupation with finding excitement and romance appear to have caught up with her much sooner than her classmates had predicted. Her junior yearbook is filled with comments from casual acquaintances and close friends, all pointing toward the heightened drama of their senior year when they envisioned "our big times will really come." Yet of the many pages of advertising and blank end pages of her twelfth-grade annual, only one bears any inscription, and this from a single person. The message begins with the customary, if more hyperbolic, acclamation: "I think that you are the most beautiful, sweet, understanding, kind, lovable, thoughtful, helpful [girl] and other things which I can't think of right now." The author asks Alice to "Please stay the same way as you are now because in my opinion you are perfect," then promises, "I'll always love and cherish you forever." Boyfriends had written such ardent words in the past, but this entry ends on a different note, concluding that these are "just a few of the reasons why I love and married you." Signed, "Yours forever, Wayne."

On the title page of the 1950 *Acorn,* Alice's name is handwritten in pen. "Alice Nivens" appears in blue ink, followed by a parenthetical "(Bradley)" in black. Alice Nivens, or an Alice Bradley, does not have her senior picture in the yearbook, and her name appears nowhere but on the front page in her own handwriting. Nor does Wayne Bradley appear by picture or name in this annual. Alice does not seem to have graduated, and Wayne remains a shadowy figure. Not a Harding graduate in 1950, he may have dropped out also because of marriage, may have attended a different school, or may have finished or left school years before. The mystery raises unanswerable questions. We do not know the explanation for, or outcome of, the abrupt end of Alice's high school career and apparent entry into married life. Moreover, her story is but a single case of a single girl at a single high school.

Yet the story is both gripping and illustrative. Alice's active dating life suggests that the heterosexual desires at the heart of high school culture were, in one sense, casual and capricious. For girls as well as boys, high school dating involved a certain amount of gamesmanship, entertainment, competition, and see-saw emotions that energized everyday adolescent life. But girls also saw the "game" of dating as a high stakes one that could easily determine their adult future. Frequent references to "getting a man" or "finding the right one" represented, for many girls, a utopian daydream that enlivened daily life.

Yet girls also used school romances to prepare for and take steps toward marriage, a goal fully supported by the formal and informal curricula of midcentury high schools.

Alice's abrupt exit from high school reflects the postwar trend toward a younger marriage age. But it speaks as well to a historical development underlying that trend—the increasing centrality of heterosexuality to high school culture and to the world that teenagers created and inhabited. High school involvements provided a pool of experience and men from which girls might choose a husband and attempt to secure a future, especially if they had no immediate plans for life after graduation. In the case of Alice Nivens, an indifferent student who invested more in her social life than in her academic pursuits, heterosexual momentum built from junior high school toward her last year at Harding High, when a relatively casual world of fun, dating, rivalry, and romance came to a crashing halt in a sudden and mysterious marriage.

Alice's story hints at the impelling force of sexual and emotional desires. Oddly, however, by 1950 popular media was featuring minimal discussion of the sexual interests or behaviors of adolescents, in sharp contrast to the public blare around teenage pickup girls in World War II. At the war's end, uncertainty prevailed as the popular press took up the issues of girls' aggressive pursuit of boys and lack of reticence in petting and necking. But by the late 1940s and early 1950s, experts evinced far less concern about unrestrained female sexuality than about male juvenile delinquency. Public discourse around sexuality entered a broader Cold War rhetoric committed to the strategic "containment" of both international and domestic threats to American democracy. While U.S. foreign policy aimed at containing communism to the Soviet Union and its Eastern European buffer states, domestic policy attempted to contain sexuality within permanent monogamous marriages and tight nuclear families, which were assumed to have the moral fortitude to resist subversive sexual and Communist threats.[40]

Southern high schools of the late 1940s and early 1950s exemplify the apparent containment of adolescent sexuality in a high school culture that structured sociability, dating, and the search for romance. Beyond formal sex education, instruction focused largely on family relations and psychological adjustment, not sexual behavior, and school administrators rarely confronted sexual issues. Instead, heterosexual interest, pleasure, and temporary "craziness" over boys were integrated into an emergent teen culture that normalized and routinized intimacy and adventure within the society of working-class and middle-class high schools. The kinds of romances that grew into true love appeared to be judiciously paced and safely contained in an academic setting in which students lacked great autonomy and were not likely to suddenly assert their full social or sexual independence.

High school students monitored themselves through their own peer culture, a process made visible in high school yearbooks where students utilized written and photographic conventions to set normative standards of behavior. We do not know from these sources what girls and boys talked about privately or whether discussions of crushes, romances, and dating included explicit references to sexual practices and desires. This kind of information is not something that official records and formal publications typically expose. The records, then, make it hard to gauge whether sexual desire and activity fundamentally changed in this period. We know only that explicit talk of sex was not part of middle-class student discourse and did not become a point of public controversy among adults. Although sex most surely remained a topic of concern and contention between parents and their own teenagers, in the immediate postwar decade the dangerous, unreliable aspects of romance appeared safely contained by high school peer culture. With sexual interest absorbed into a starry-eyed view of romantic love and imminent marriage, cruder calculations about sex, money, and men—far more obvious among wartime pickup girls—disappeared under a shield of tightly regulated high school rituals like homecomings, proms, and Friday night football games.

Yet if midcentury peer culture submerged explicitly sexual female desire, these feelings did not remain buried for long, nor did their potential to rend the social fabric of southern society. In the later 1950s, sexual interest exploded into public view with the development of rock 'n' roll music. Its lyrics, rhythm, and dance styles screamed out the presence of female adolescent desire and adults screamed back in opposition. Moreover, controversies over rock 'n' roll coincided with furious political debate over racial desegregation in southern high schools, ending the temporary calm of the immediate postwar years and ushering in a decade of unparalleled cultural and racial conflict in which teenagers held center stage.

chapter nine

Would Jesus Dance?

The Dangerous Rhythms of Rock 'n' Roll

*I*n April 1956, Asa E. (Ace) Carter, a leader in the White Citizens Council movement of Alabama, launched a public campaign against rock 'n' roll and other types of "Negro music." Citizens councils were famous throughout the South for organizing in fierce opposition to the 1954 Supreme Court ruling *Brown v. Board of Education,* which had resolved that a "separate but equal" educational system was inherently unequal because it perpetuated inferior conditions for black students as well as reinforced an ideology of white superiority and black inferiority. Given the massive political resistance to school desegregation in the years following the *Brown* decision, it seems strange that an Alabama citizens council would take a cultural detour to focus its efforts on banning rock 'n' roll music.[1] But Carter linked jazz, bebop, rock 'n' roll, and all "Negro music" to an NAACP "plot to mongrelize America." He informed reporters that citizens council subcommittees would pressure jukebox owners, radio and concert sponsors, and music promoters to stop targeting teenage audiences with rock music, which he claimed "appeals to the base in man, brings out animalism and vulgarity."[2]

The media presented Carter as something of an oddity for putting his highly publicized political efforts into these two fronts at once. But in fact, many other religious leaders, politicians, and ordinary white southerners agreed with Carter in identifying two simultaneous and interconnected threats to the South's social order: the teenage music craze sweeping the nation in the mid-1950s, and the Supreme Court's mandate to desegregate schools. At the center of each controversy stood southern high school students. On their own initiative, white and black adolescents had begun to share a common interest in the new musical style called rock 'n' roll, a fusion of black rhythm and blues and up-tempo white country music that had originated in the South. And if the federal government had its way, black and white teenagers would soon be attending the same southern high schools, engaging not only in shared learning but also in the shared social life that lay at the core of adolescent high school culture.

Adult southern whites exhibited special horror at the prospect of their children, who had already fallen prey to a form of black-influenced sexually evocative music, attending school with black children. They feared that the shared classes, school dances, and other extracurricular activities could lead directly to a social mixture of the races and the potential for sexual "mixing," intermarriage, and a "mongrelized" generation of biracial children. Political and religious leaders in the South made constant reference to this possibility in their attacks on desegregation as well as in their damning statements against rock music.

High schools and dance floors had two things in common. Each constituted a shared physical space that teenagers—black and white—had claimed as their own, forging a heterosocial youth culture beyond the control of adults. Moreover, both high schools and the culture of rock music formed social spaces that beat to the drum of adolescent sexuality, whether through the literal beat of rock 'n' roll's stimulating rhythms and erotic lyrics or through the heartbeat of love, romance, and sexual possibility that coursed through the everyday life of coed high schools.

As sexually charged physical spaces, the high school and the dance floor threatened to undermine another kind of southern place—the place each southerner occupied on the social and economic ladder of southern society. Southerners customarily spoke of "knowing one's place," referring to one's assigned social status and its expected behavior—for example, whether to enroll in a dilapidated understaffed black high school or a well-built white high school with new books, new sports uniforms, and well-paid teachers. They also used location—that is, a person's place of origin—to identify family names and social connections that enabled people to recognize social status and to "place" even unfamiliar people in the hierarchy that was "southern society." When infused with the disruptive potential of racial "mixing," the democracy of the dance floor and the local comprehensive high school, which enrolled students from all ranks of life, threatened to dramatically alter longstanding notions of people's place in southern society.

The shared teenage spaces created by rock 'n' roll and potentially integrated high schools highlighted the sexual tensions and possibilities of the midcentury South. For adults invested in maintaining prevailing norms, adolescent sexuality suddenly presented an inordinate danger, a fire hazard set in the hothouse environment of an upstart teen culture. But the dangers they envisioned did not apply equally to all teenagers. The central and unpredictable character in this 1950s high school sexual drama was the white teenage girl and, implicitly, her black counterpart. For when rock 'n' roll first jumped into the limelight the most surprising element—to journalists, promoters, artists, and critics alike—was the intensely sexual nature of the music and the ardor with which teenage girls responded. Described as crazed and hysterical, female fans rushed the stage, screamed from their seats, wet their underpants, and lusted after male rock idols like Elvis Presley, Bill Haley, and Chuck Berry. The press reported similar behavior among black and white girls: throwing caution to the wind, girls of both races willfully cast aside the passivity and restraint required of the white southern "lady" or middle-class "respectable" black woman.

After more than a decade of gradual, uncontroversial change in postwar teenage culture, in the 1950s there was a "coming out" of teenage girls' sexuality, with rock music at the conspicuous center. Adolescent female sexuality seemed to be an independent, unpredictable force no longer controlled by adults or self-policed by well-trained young ladies standing at the threshold of their mothers' worlds. With rock 'n' roll in their midst and school integration looming on the horizon, white adults faced the stark reality that it was their own emboldened daughters who might well initiate sexual "mixing" or "integration" in choosing boys to date or marry. Similarly, black girls involved with white boys could conceivably demand sexual acknowledgment, forcing the legitimation of such relationships in the peer world of high school dating and, eventually, in marriage. Judging from their response to rock 'n' roll, teenage girls were ready and willing to take the initiative, challenging racial shibboleths and parental authority.

*Y*outhful music and dance fads had come and gone before, and the most recent, swing music and the jitterbug, had caused a minor uproar. Even the fervent response of adolescent girls to male stars signaled nothing new: Frank Sinatra, for example, had been adored. Yet both contemporary and historical portrayals of rock 'n' roll in the 1950s have revolved around the sexuality of adolescent girls and their uninhibited responses to male performers. Although not cast as sexual actors or decision-makers, the girls nevertheless became the center of controversy because of the complicated and subversive dynamics of race and class in Cold War America, especially in the South. How do we understand the connections between rock 'n' roll, adolescent girls' sexuality, and a youth culture that blended African American and white working-class influences?

The origins of the revolution in music lay in the major demographic and cultural changes that occurred around World War II. As over 15 million civilians migrated out of their home counties and 10 million military personnel traveled the nation and the world, often settling in new towns and cities after the war, music followed its own migratory path.[3] Southerners who moved north to factory towns or left rural areas for cities like Mobile and Memphis often rejected the bland popular standards of singers like Bing Crosby or Patti Page, seeking a sound that reminded them of home yet reflected something of their new experience in a sped-up world of city traffic and factory assembly lines. They also looked for new places of entertainment to replace the local country store or illicit juke joint of rural life, finding a lively world of urban bars, dance clubs, or "honky tonks" where patrons avidly talked, fought, and drank away the day's frustrations—and sometimes, wages.[4]

New styles of music satisfied both needs. Among black audiences, a sound dubbed "rhythm and blues" became popular as it moved away from slow, haunting country blues with a traditional chord and lyrical structure toward the up-tempo electrified "jump blues." Other black performers originated a very different sound, blending the smooth harmonies of southern gospel music with the themes of love and romance found in popular mainstream songs. Groups like the Orioles, Ravens, Platters, and Drifters produced a sound that evolved into 1960s "soul" music. During the late 1940s and the 1950s, that sound shared space with hard-driving bluesy numbers on *Billboard*'s new "Rhythm and Blues" (R & B) chart (which in 1949 replaced the older category of "race music").[5]

White southern migrants embraced a different musical style. Bluegrass music, although presented today as southern "traditional" or "roots" music, was pioneered in the 1940s by artists like Bill Monroe and his Bluegrass Boys to meet the need for a faster, hard-driving rhythm boisterous enough to move the patrons of noisy, rowdy honky-tonks. By the end of the decade another new sound emerged, this time blending rhythms from black R & B with the cadences and lyrics of popular country music. This sound, called "rockabilly," fed directly into what soon became "rock 'n' roll" music.[6]

None of these musical genres could have gained commercial success without contemporaneous developments in the industry and technology of music. Weakened by the success of television, network radio lost its powerful hold on national media, and the number of nationally syndicated radio shows declined. In addition, the number of radio stations more than doubled between 1945 and 1949, with network affiliates losing ground to locally owned stations that could identify and cater to specific audiences, often defined by age.[7] With the breakup of network monopolies, even mainstream radio began offering afternoon and late-night radio shows aimed at young audiences. Simultaneously, small, independently owned black radio stations sprang up, backed by black musical entrepreneurs who, along with white newcomers, invested in record companies that capitalized on new technologies and lowered production costs. Pioneer labels like Stax, Chess, and Sun Records opened the market to a range of new musical sounds.[8]

As a result, the innovative sounds of R & B and country performers gained airtime on small—and sometimes large—stations across the country, filling the airwaves with music that defied the conventions of mainstream pop. Soon African American station managers noted that young people of both races were tuning into their stations, finding in rhythm and blues a beat and intensity that appealed to their own search for musical passion and meaning beyond the staid styles of mass-marketed entertainment. The sounds of black church and secular music held special allure for poor white youth like Elvis Presley, Jerry Lee Lewis, and Johnny Cash, who soon melded black and white musical influences into their own syncretic styles.[9]

By the early 1950s, then, a dramatically different world of commercial music presented itself to a burgeoning teenage culture. As a small but significant cadre of white adolescents became faithful fans of black rhythm and blues, new technologies made the dissemination of commercial music easier than a generation earlier, when music had entered the home through a single family radio, sheet music, or 78 rpm records spun on the family Victrola. With transistor radios, car radios, portable record players, local record shops with listening booths, and inexpensive 45 rpm "singles" with one song on each side, teenagers could purchase and transport their favorite music with relative ease, integrating it into a teen culture of dances, record parties, automobiles, and jukeboxes that attracted adolescents of all types.

Disc jockeys played a crucial role in this transition. As African American deejays tailored R & B shows to teenage audiences, which were predominately black but included a significant minority of white fans, white pioneers like Alan Freed began promoting black artists to teenagers on radio shows in Cleveland and New York City during the early 1950s. His success forced more conventional disc jockeys to fall in line, gradually mixing black R & B into shows featuring white pop. In addition white deejays, benefiting from access to local television stations, created afternoon teen dance shows featuring talented white youth moving to the latest hits by both black and white artists.

As a result, rhythm and blues artists achieved some crossover success in mainstream markets, making it onto *Billboard*'s pop charts with increasing frequency and gaining even greater popularity when white stars "covered" their songs. These covers tended to be toned-down versions of the originals, tamed to fit the less adventurous tastes of mainstream white audiences.[10] Yet black R & B acts also drew white listeners, not just to the airwaves but to live performances. Whites sometimes attended predominately black music clubs, usually as a small minority seated in the balcony—in a reversal of the Jim Crow movie-theater seating that restricted black viewers to remote balcony sections. Club owners occasionally tried to draw integrated audiences by stretching a rope down the middle of the auditorium to comply with segregated seating requirements. Increasingly, however, promoters began hiring black bands to perform for white audiences, especially at high school or college dances. Ironically, one of the most racially and socially conservative institutions of the South—white fraternities—consistently employed black bands, creating, in effect, a fraternity circuit of black artists traveling across the South to successive engagements.[11]

By the mid-1950s, the flourishing racial exchange in musical styles, tastes, and audiences crystallized in a variation of R & B called "rock 'n' roll," a phrase coined for the new genre by Alan Freed but long recognized in black secular music as a euphemism for sexual relations. Early hits include classics like "Hound Dog" by Willie Mae Thornton, the Orioles' "Crying in the Chapel," "Sh-Boom" by the Chords, and Joe Turner's "Shake, Rattle and Roll," all songs by black performers. Rock music broke through to national audiences when in 1955 "Rock around the Clock," performed by the white band Bill Haley and His Comets, became the theme song for the hit movie *Blackboard Jungle,* which kicked off a multitude of 1950s movies about juvenile delinquency that featured rock 'n' roll scores.

Rock music gradually expanded from its southern roots to a national audience, drawing attention from the press as a new and controversial phenomenon sweeping the teenage world. Yet the most important factor in the explosive takeoff of rock was still to come—the discovery of a white star who could transpose the sounds of "black" music into an equally audacious, powerful style but who, unlike black R & B stars, could reach the white youth market en masse. The singer who accomplished this feat was still a teenager himself, a nineteen-year-old recent high school graduate named Elvis Presley.

Originally from Tupelo, Mississippi, Elvis Presley moved to Memphis with his parents at age twelve. As a shy teen, Elvis learned to play the guitar and performed mostly for friends and neighbors. After high school he started a more serious search for recognition, developing relationships with well-known gospel bands and with local record producer Sam Phillips, who founded Sun Records. Elvis persuaded Phillips to record him, issuing his first 45 record in 1954. An instant success, his initial record captured beautifully the new blend of black blues and white country that underpinned rock 'n' roll: Side A covered African American Arthur Crudup's "That's All Right Mama" and the B side covered Bill Monroe's signature bluegrass song, "Blue Moon of Kentucky." Upon hearing "That's All Right Mama," many listeners called the station wondering whether its singer was black or white. Phillips, and soon an array of other promoters, knew they had found their ticket to success: a white singer who could sing "black."

Why did Elvis need to be white? The record industry did not believe that a black artist would draw the sizeable number of white fans necessary to make big profits, nor would print media or television pay the kind of attention to black performers necessary to turn a hit-maker into a national celebrity. Sam Phillips, Presley's first producer, explained that while R & B drew white radio listeners, "There was something in many of those youngsters that resisted buying this music. The Southern ones especially felt a resistance that even they probably didn't quite understand. They liked the music, but they weren't sure whether they ought to like it or not. So I got to thinking how many records you could sell if you could find white performers who could play and sing in this same exciting, alive way."[12] Phillips's hunch proved correct; Elvis Presley's first recordings produced chart-topping bullets. Myriads of white teenagers purchased his records and mobbed his performances, even as Presley maintained a sizeable popularity among black youth.

The record industry's success in marketing Elvis Presley to white audiences should not suggest that Presley represented white norms. In fact, Elvis vaulted into fame as a highly transgressive figure, appealing to teenagers seeking out the wilder side of life. Moreover, his white fans did not restrict their enthusiasm to white performers alone; they were excited equally by African American stars like Fats Domino, Chuck Berry, and Little Richard. As the collective success of Presley and other rock 'n' roll performers gained attention, the eyes of the nation turned toward them in an effort to understand this new teenage passion.

*P*arents admitted to being baffled by rock 'n' roll, unable to understand the music and surprised at the lack of adult influence on teenagers' choices, values, and cultural tastes. *Life* magazine reported that for teens "the music is theirs and theirs alone—most adults don't dig it."[13] *Down Beat* looked with nostalgia at "the old days" when "adults handed culture down to their children, shaping their tastes according to their own mature judgment. Today adolescents dictate musical culture, so to speak, to the rest of us."[14] While the *New York Times* inquired simply, "Is this generation going to hell?" another critic described his experience at a rock show as "like attending the rites of some obscure tribe whose means of communication are incomprehensible." Furthermore, "teenagers of all races have fallen under its spell . . . Rock 'n' roll is their own, and they love it."[15]

Although adults found rock 'n' roll confusing, many worried that teenagers found a message not only comprehensible but reprehensible as well, with performers and audiences communicating a willingness to disregard conventional rules of propriety. Alarmed music critics, industry insiders, parents, local civic groups, ministers, and political officials registered their opposition in numerous ways. While music critics issued scathing reviews, denouncing the music as monotonous and crude and the performers as untalented shouters completely lacking in talent, other experts tried to untangle the social pathology they heard in the music.

They pointed first to rock 'n' roll's black roots. Described as having a "jungle strain" that appealed to all races, rock 'n' roll raised hackles about racial mixture in the music and its fan base.[16] *Time* magazine described rock 'n' roll as "based on Negro blues, but in a self-conscious style which underlines the primitive qualities of the blues with malice aforethought." The malice, apparently, consisted of "violent" sounds that struck the listener like a "bull whip" or a "honking mating call," eliciting in fans "rings and shrieks like the jungle-bird house at the zoo."[17] The references to malicious violence and primitive animal sounds echoed many other assessments that linked rock to "primitive" Africa or its African American descendants, even when performed by white musicians. Elvis Presley, who appeared to dress "black," sing "black," and dance "black," represented the kind of racial mixing that most white, middle-class southerners opposed, intellectually and viscerally.

Presley's own white roots did not improve his reputation. Middle-class whites mocked the new sound as "hillbilly" music associated with "white trash" culture. Presley and other white stars like Carl Perkins, Johnny Cash, and Jerry Lee Lewis, all of whom came from poor rural or working-class backgrounds, found themselves depicted as figures of musical and material excess, where excess signaled not abundance but garbage, the disposable remains of consumption exceeding the limits of necessity.[18] Upholding middle-class ideals of refinement and moderation, the press regularly reported on the flamboyant clothing of white stars along with the luxury cars and lavish homes their fame afforded them. These class violations hinted at a fear of white stars acting "black," as journalists issued accounts of similar excess among black performers like Fats Domino, reported to own "200 pairs of shoes, several Cadillacs and 30 suits for his road trips."[19]

Accusations of excessive desire point to another perceived transgression, violations of a sexual nature. Rock 'n' roll's mixture of black and white sounds, musicians, and audiences invoked sexual possibilities and metaphors in the minds of many observers. A publicist at Sun Records described the revolutionary new music as "like a giant wedding ceremony. It was like two feuding clans who had been brought together by marriage."[20] A metaphor of feuding races brought together in a "mixed" marriage certainly did little to ease the fears of white critics wary of the music's sexualized beat. Accounts of Elvis Presley's suggestive movements as just "short of an aborigine's mating dance" suggest sexual "mating" among primitives or "natives"—categories associated with people of African descent, American Indian descent, and at times poor and rural white southerners.[21]

Moreover, the music itself communicated sexuality. When critics described the "jungle" sounds of rock they referred not only to the music's rhythmic origins but also to its "primitive," "uncivilized," and "throbbing" sexual beat. Accurately noted links between rock music and its origins in African (American) rhythms almost always carried racist connotations rooted in stereotypes about not only black music but black sexuality and incivility as well. If the beat wasn't enough, rock critics also blasted the music for its lyrical content, castigating the music's "frequently suggestive and occasionally lewd" lyrics, or "leerics."[22] A reporter for *Look* magazine, for example, denigrated rock's "simple-minded often sexy lyrics" as a "reversion to savagery."[23]

Beyond noting the sexual nature of rock performance and lyrics, critics found the accompanying dance styles equally vulgar and uncouth. One critic renamed Dick Clark's *American Bandstand* show the

"Zombie Hour," featuring "teen performers togged out in erotic costumes." The dance floor included "adolescent Americans of all creeds and colors, jitterbugging with dead pan and trancelike movements, regular and lifeless as clockwork."[24] Other moralists worried that rock's dance style was far from lifeless. The controversy surrounding Elvis Presley focused most of all on his body movements. Scandalized adults watched aghast as Elvis spread his legs wide, thrust his hips about, placed the microphone between his quaking legs, and gyrated his lower body in a motion suggestive of sexual "bumping" or intercourse, earning him the derisive nickname Elvis the Pelvis.

Critics were disturbed not only by Presley's "vulgar" gesticulations, but also by the erotic feelings his presence stirred in young fans, particularly girls in their early to mid-teens. Opponents assailed Presley and other rising stars for creating scenes of wild frenzy, eliciting "high-pitched squeals of females in fanatic teen-age packs."[25] Although a few experts defended the new stars on the grounds that rock music gave teens a relatively safe outlet for emotional and physical desires that "couldn't be expressed through channels that nature provided," the general consensus was that rock 'n' roll music offered audiences an unrestrained, crudely erotic display that evoked uninhibited, and heretofore unseen, wild sexual responses from teenage girls who screamed, tore their hair out, and cried while proclaiming their undying love, and sometimes lust, for a favorite rock star.[26]

The media relished such scenes. After a 1955 concert in Orlando, the local press pronounced that Presley had stolen the show, proving to be "a real sex box as far as the teenage girls are concerned. They squealed themselves silly over this fellow." While one reporter likened Presley's performance to a "strip-tease with clothes on," a 1955 account from Jacksonville, Florida, described Presley's involuntary "strip tease" when hundreds of girls stormed his dressing room, tearing pieces of clothing off their hero until security guards restored calm.[27]

Presley's sexual appeal raised eyebrows in the black press as well. Local deejay and music critic Nat Williams described the scene at a Memphis concert: "A thousand black, brown and beige teen-age girls" raised their voices "in one wild crescendo of sound that rent the rafters . . . and took off like scalded cats in the direction of Elvis." Williams raised the question of interracial sexuality when, speaking in the street vernacular of "Beale Streeters" he wondered, "How come cullud girls would take on so over a Memphis white boy . . . when they hardly let out a squeak over B. B. King, a Memphis cullud boy?" Returning to his own voice, Williams asked "if these teen-age girls' demonstration over Presley doesn't reflect a basic integra-tion in attitude and aspiration which has been festering in the minds of . . . women folk all along?"[28] The possibility of interracial sexual longings moved both ways across racial lines, causing surprised con-cern among black and white observers, especially in the South. Pres-ley's manager, Colonel Parker, made a similar point, describing Elvis as "*dynamite* in personal appearances, affecting southern girls, white and black—as Sinatra once had."[29]

The appeal of Elvis and other white rock stars did not shut the door to black R & B artists, who were also famous for arousing young female fans. Observers of Sonny Til, vocal star of the Orioles, de-scribed his performances for predominantly black audiences as affect-ing "the girls like an aphrodisiac. When he bent over . . . and leaned to one side, sensuously gyrating his shoulders and caressing the air with his hands, the girls would shriek, 'Ride my alley, Sonny! Ride my alley!'"[30] As with Elvis, it was not Til's own sexuality as much as the response he drew from teenagers that proved most notable.

Singers like Fats Domino, Chuck Berry, and Little Richard stand out as some of the original African American stars of rock 'n' roll who captivated both white and black teenagers, especially in the South. Their crossover appeal added to the racially and sexually provocative nature of rock 'n' roll. Fats Domino reportedly "draws a mixed audi-ence wherever he goes. His attraction is as strong with a white audi-ence as it is with a predominantly Negro audience."[31] A segregated Fats Domino concert in Houston attracted four hundred white and a thousand black fans, organized in separate seating. "Rioting" broke out when "the offays" unexpectedly joined the black youth on the dance floor.[32]

Little Richard's fame grew from a series of hits in which he used nonsense words to soften bawdy lyrics—but in a way that left the sex-ual connotation implied. For instance, in his original version of "Tutti Frutti," Little Richard's title and refrain, "Tutti Frutti," referenced a raw, easy form of sexuality that included anal sex and did not specify

Elvis Presley became the first white star to transpose the "black" sound of R & B into the audaciously sexual music called rock 'n' roll. While his tremendous appeal spanned the entire youth market, disapproving adults worried most about his effect on love-struck teenage daughters, likening it to sexual "dynamite." Library of Congress, NYWTS Photo, Elvis Presley (1956).

gender. Upon recording the song for a popular audience, he sanitized the lyrics by replacing the original explicit references with a milder heterosexual narrative about a girl named Sue who loved to rock and knew exactly what to do to please him. Beyond his raucous lyrics and performance style, Little Richard openly explored gender ambiguity in his appearance and public statements. Prior to his fame as a rock singer, Richard Penniman had worked as a teenage drag artist in the circuit of southern black drag shows that flourished in the postwar years. Sanitizing his act for national consumption, Little Richard retained some of the hallmark outrageousness of drag performance, with his foot-high pompadour, facial makeup, sequins, and gender-bending claim to being the self-pronounced "King and Queen" of rock 'n' roll. Presenting a less conventionally masculine persona may have made him less of a sexual threat in the eyes of white critics, but his ambiguously gendered, sexually suggestive performance defied white standards of respectability and sexual propriety.[33]

More than any other artist, Chuck Berry used his talents as a songwriter to recreate the experiences of high school and teen culture. Cars, dancing, teenage love, and romance formed the basic themes of hit songs such as "Maybellene," "Sweet Little Sixteen," and "School Days." Berry's unique mixture of country, rock, and R & B influences drew acclaim from white and black teens alike, even though for white listeners this meant that their sexual interlocutor was a black man addressing white girls on matters of love and desire. Berry initially drafted "Maybellene," his signature song about a car race, as an open expression of his desire for the pretty girls who typically dated football heroes. Berry describes himself enviously watching pretty girls riding up and down the street in his dream car, a Cadillac Coupe DeVille, while he is stuck sitting inside the classroom. The chorus, addressed to the title's dream girl, Maybellene, reiterates his desire that she become his girlfriend. The romantic allusion shifts to sexual fantasy when he wishes that she "be true" by letting him do, sexually, the same things she allows boys on the football team to do to her.

Though based on his own earlier segregated high school experiences, by the 1950s such lyrics addressed to white as well as black girls suggested nothing less than interracial relations. Berry himself commented that among the black and white fans who rushed the stage after every show, mingling with and hugging the performers, "I noticed the friendliness of the white females more than that of the white males, going beyond normal musical appreciation to wanting to personally meet and associate with the singers, something I never expected to occur."[34]

The presence of black stars with crossover racial appeal and white stars who drew on black musical forms (and, in some sense, performed blackness itself) exceeded the limits of what many southern whites could accept. Racial markers, differences, and barriers were disintegrating just at the time when conservative white southerners felt more desperate than ever to shore up lines of difference and separation. The question of racial delineation overlapped with similar uncertainties about lines of class. *New York Times* critic Gertrude Samuels protested that the "children themselves come from all economic classes and neighborhoods . . . Outside the theatre they seem to become one class—rocking the neighborhood with wild and emotional behavior."[35] Under rock 'n' roll's influence, formerly well-established social stations grew murky, raising uncertainty and anger.

Sexuality presented the single biggest threat in this racially and economically ambiguous context. With federally mandated school desegregation on every southerner's mind, the interracial sexual appeal of rock 'n' roll music struck many observers as a portent of things to come. A reporter for *Look* magazine kindled this anxiety when he explained, "Rock was born in those border Southern areas where Negro and white populations are evenly mixed, causing the musical forms to 'integrate.'"[36] If teenage slang labeled rock 'n' roll as positively "dynamite," apprehensive adults saw a far more dangerous kind of sexual dynamite in this nefarious "integrated" music.

Although ministers regularly joined in the chorus of opposition, church leaders faced a tougher job than simply denouncing rock 'n' roll and the dancing it inspired. As clergy, their job included persuading youth to follow a religious path and resist sinful worldly pleasures. Southern Baptists, for instance, had long opposed dancing as a sinful activity on the grounds that "sex and the dance are inseparable."[37] As early as 1945, a pamphlet called "The Modern Dance on Trial" previewed the criticisms of rock 'n' roll when it condemned swing and blues as music "spawned in the jungles" by "natives" prone to "heathenish orgies" and "sinful debauchery." The author rated the world's best dancers as "the most uncivilized people on earth," proven by the fact that only the Negro did not have to learn to dance since "it is natural with him." Worse still, the dance violated gender norms of female modesty and sexual restraint since, "on the whole women are as fascinated by the fiendish sensuality of the dance as are men. The dance makes 'loving' appear respectable."[38]

The new breed of 1950s "rockers" surpassed their musical predecessors in making "loving" appear respectable. Rock 'n' roll culture served as an arena for teenage exploration of young love, saturating the airwaves with songs about the difficulties and joys of teenage love, romance, and lust.[39] Compared to the 1940s youth culture, in which sexuality formed the submerged underside of a high school social world of dating, gossip, going steady, proms, and early engagements, by the late 1950s teenagers were in open rebellion, at least in matters of music. In an effort to win teens back to prescribed religious morality, the Southern Baptist Christian Life Commission published pamphlets, sermons, and articles to provide guidance to youth on how best to live a Christian life. Along with advice on dating, kissing, going steady, and selecting a marriage partner, the commission's publications issued commentary on the relationship of dancing to Christian living. Adolescents could read tracts like "Teen Talk: What about Dancing?" "Shall We Dance?" "Teen Talk about Rock 'n' Roll," and "Dancing: Right or Wrong?" presented as open-minded considerations of dancing (since nowhere did the Bible directly prohibit dancing or designate it as sinful). Although labeled "teen talk," this discourse featured the opinions of adults who invariably arrived at the same conclusion: dancing either constituted or paved the way to immorality and sin.[40]

Religious leaders posed a number of arguments to convince adolescents to adopt recommended behavior. They warned of "the danger of inflamed sex emotion" caused by sensuous intoxicating rhythms.[41] Another danger lay in the power of peer pressure to seduce young Christians down a treacherous path. In one didactic pamphlet, a son asks his father if a teenager could be both "hep" and a Christian. He explains that rock 'n' roll "sends me! . . . After all, it's something we [teens] can call our own . . . [and] kinda gives me a feeling of being unhinged." Not surprisingly, the father responds with a definitive "no," insisting that, even with his son's best intentions, secular teen culture would open his body and mind to "the mud of the world" and cause an inevitable breakdown of moral standards.[42] In such a breakdown, sexual impulses meant "only for high and holy purposes" would be exploited for profane physical pleasure.[43]

Ministers also employed a slippery slope argument, noting, "Where there is a great deal of dancing there is frequently also a great deal of drinking, heavy petting, and 'going all the way' in sexual adventures." They stressed that even if one Christian youth could withstand the temptations associated with dancing, friends with weaker Christian convictions might be unable to resist the pull toward immorality. Thus even the "uncorrupted" teenage girl or boy who remained pure of purpose would likely encourage un-Christian behavior among others.[44]

Literature addressed to Christian youth primarily took a "just say no" approach, but occasionally proposed active alternatives to the temptation of dance. One suggestion encouraged young people to contact their local disc jockey with requests to "play music with more class," in addition to purchasing more wholesome records to "help channel your interests to something which is not associated with the questionable and the vulgar."[45] The other proposed solution urged teens to seek out alternatives to dance "like miniature golf, raking leaves in the fall, making fudge together, . . . [or] church work activity." As if aware of the absurdity of exchanging the pleasure of rock music for the joys of raking leaves, advisers returned to the matter of individual choice and will, reminding youth that it was his or her decision "to dance or not to dance."[46] Religious tracts recommended making this decision by asking whether Jesus would dance if alive today. In case young Baptists answered in the affirmative, the denomination supplied its own interdiction. In November 1957 Baptist state conventions voted to ban dancing at all Baptist-funded schools. The decision sparked at least one protest movement: students at Wake Forest College staged a chapel walkout in order to dance to their favorite rock songs blasting from the snack shop jukebox.[47]

Although southern ministers developed the most thoroughly prescriptive literature addressed to youth, other adults got involved in the movement to discourage rock 'n' roll, combining persuasive efforts with scare tactics and outright censorship. Law officials' frequent accusation that rock music contributed to skyrocketing juvenile delinquency prompted a federal inquiry. A 1958 Senate subcommittee investigation heard testimony that rock 'n' roll stirred the "animal instinct" of teenagers through its "raw savage tone."[48] Even J. Edgar Hoover jumped on the antirock bandwagon, authorizing an FBI investigation of Elvis Presley. The investigation concluded that adolescents "are easily aroused to sexual indulgence and perversion by certain types of motions and hysteria—the type that was exhibited at the Presley show."[49]

This view found abundant support within the music industry and among parents. Some radio stations banned particular songs thought to cross the line from bad taste to immorality, while other stations eliminated any and all rock or R & B programming. Businesses too took up the call, creating ritualistic record-breaking ceremonies, much like book-burning events, in which merchants smashed 45 rpm rock 'n' roll singles to demonstrate their vehement dislike of the music. Angry parents engaged in similar protests in cities like Nashville and St. Louis, where they gathered in public to burn effigies of Elvis Presley.[50]

*G*iven the tremendous attention paid to the sexual provocativeness of rock music, one dimension received surprisingly little critical analysis—the sudden presence and strength of erotic desire among adolescent white girls. Their responses to male performers—variously described as hysterical, frenzied, wild, and uninhibited—generated great surprise and anxiety. But critics did not question the fact of strong female sexual desire nor the willingness of girls to express it under stimulating conditions. This presents a marked contrast to a decade earlier when, under wartime conditions, female sexuality came under great scrutiny.

As discussed earlier, wartime public discourse had focused primarily on working-class sex delinquents whose sexual desire and expressiveness, associated with social disorder and disease, could be explained as the product of a bad home life, psychopathy, and the absence of restraint generalized to working-class bodies. Toward the end of the war, the sexuality of middle-class girls gradually entered both popular and professional discourse. Experts believed that while sexual feelings formed a part of all adolescent development, active pursuit of sexual experience by middle-class or working-class girls still constituted female delinquency, indicating social or psychological maladjustment. By the mid- to late 1950s, however, as all hell seemed to break loose among female rock 'n' roll fans "all shook up" by the music's sexual beat, journalists and the many experts they consulted did not fundamentally question the openly sexual longings of girls or identify them with "lower-class" origins. Adults in general expressed their disapproval of public displays of "hysteria" and lack of inhibition, but they did not assume that female eroticism, in and of itself, signaled victimization, pathology, or poor and immoral family backgrounds.

A *Life* magazine feature story about rock 'n' roll pictured throngs of enraptured girls above the caption "TEEN ECSTASY." The reporter explained, "It is hard to say what causes the rock 'n' roll rapture . . . [T]he susceptible fans hear something which triggers their emotions and sets off a gale of screams and moans . . . They just *feel* it."[51] Like the bobby-soxer of the 1940s, the starstruck female rock fan of the 1950s represented the "every girl" of postwar youth culture—criticized, but still accepted within the range of normal.

By the late 1950s, even Christian prescriptive literature on teenage sexuality accepted some degree of physical intimacy as part of pre-marital relationships. While advice-givers in the 1940s had said no to kissing under any circumstances, a 1956 advice book for Baptist teen-agers answers the question of kissing on the first date with "No, don't" because "a truly fine fellow" won't pick a girl known for being "easy." Nothing in this answer implies a prohibition against kissing on subsequent dates.[52] Nor does a 1960 article called "Goodnight Prayer or Goodnight Kiss?" In a subsection titled "Kiss or Pray?" the author advises youth on their options: "It is true that we may do either, but it is also true that we may do neither—or both."[53] As couples considered going steady and getting engaged, religious writers condoned some level of sexual intimacy while still warning against the hazards that accompanied such choices. One leaflet cautioned that going steady can rush sexual activity, even though frequent and prolonged kissing, fondling, and caressing "in their proper place and proper time are not evil but good."[54] Similarly, a 1957 Methodist leaflet advised engaged couples on the "common problem" of "excessive fondling and petting," but did not preclude sexual touch that stopped short of "excessive."[55]

What had shifted between the early 1940s and late 1950s to make the existence of adolescent female desire a recognized and relatively uncontroversial fact? The answer lies in the heterosocial high school culture of the postwar years, with its emphasis on dating, dances, and teen romance. By implicitly assuming sexual interest on the part of girls and boys, it had introduced adolescent sexual love into youth culture in a way that had inspired minimal alarm among adult authorities. By the mid-1950s the mutuality of teen love had received recognition in the encouragement of early marriage. Acknowledging that teenagers matured sexually before they became economically self-sufficient or trained for skilled or professional employment, some experts advised that rather than expecting adolescents to adhere to a standard of premarital abstinence, early matrimony provided a way to contain sexuality within marriage. Even without adult approval, many teenagers married while still in high school. A 1959 *Life* magazine article focused on "the marriage bug" that had bit the students of Central High School in Charlotte, North Carolina. Over a period of three years the trend grew so quickly that by 1959, 3 to 4 percent of the student body had married, usually by eloping. Nationally, one of every four eighteen-year-old girls was married, and southern girls and women married, on average, at younger ages than the national rate.[56]

Another reason that the sexuality of adolescent girls engendered little controversy stems from popular conceptualizations of female desire. Press coverage typically depicted the screaming throngs of girls at rock concerts as occasions of mass hysteria, an unplanned and uncontrollable reaction rooted in unconscious desires rather than self-conscious eroticism. Stories about crazed female fans tended to focus on preadolescent eleven- to thirteen-year-olds, thus locating the phenomenon among pubescent girls typically too young to be aware of sexual arousal and their own erotic agency.

These images fit nicely into new psychiatric models of adolescence. In a decade obsessed with juvenile delinquency as a possible indication of the failure of American middle-class family life, theories of male delinquency blamed inattentive parents and comic books, violent movies, hot rods, and other "bad" cultural influences. The problem of female delinquency remained sequestered in medical and psychological discourses, explained not as a direct effect of dangerous cultural influences or family neglect, but as an indirect consequence of dysfunctional family relations that on the surface had little to do with sexuality. Elaborating on theories first proposed in the war and immediate postwar years, child experts argued that strained relations, especially between father and daughter, often found expression in sexual misbehavior.[57] The "hysterical" sexual responses of teenage girls to rock 'n' roll represented "normal" adolescent urges. But when taken beyond norms of teenage "petting," female sexual expression continued to be explained as a product of emotional displacement and generational conflict, not of girls' own erotic agency.

*R*ock 'n' roll helped establish adolescent female sexual desire, expressed through petting, as an accepted "fact." The seemingly smooth entry of girls' sexual desire and activity into standards of ordinary adolescent behavior does suggest a profound change from earlier popular and scholarly beliefs that girls were, by nature, less erotically inclined and more restrained than boys. This new view, however, did not fully recognize teenage girls as self-determining individuals who willingly gave themselves over to rock 'n' roll's stimulating rhythms and lyrics. Yet at least a few teenage girls—young women who gained fame as performers—dared to present their sexuality in these riskier terms.

Ruth Brown, a pioneer of R & B and then rock music, was born in 1928 and grew up in the southern coastal area near Norfolk, Virginia. Brown entered her teens during the war years, finding herself torn between her strict religious upbringing and the social and musical possibilities that surrounded her. Having grown up listening to white country and pop music on the radio, she also heard secular music ("the devil's music," according to her father) broadcast from a local black radio station. She gained more exposure to popular black music by sneaking out at night to hear bands at local clubs, which were packed with customers enriched by the wartime economy.

A self-described rebel who was "desperate to sing," Brown began singing in black USO clubs in her mid-teens, loving "everything about it, especially the soldier boys' response . . . These boys just went wild."[58] When her father, a strict disciplinarian and religious conservative, refused to accept Ruth's sexual and musical choices, she left home at sixteen to pursue her career. A year later she hooked up, onstage in a popular duet act and off the stage as well, with eighteen-year-old Jimmy Brown. Although their musical style was not yet officially labeled "rhythm and blues," by 1946 Ruth Brown and other, mostly male, performers had begun to develop the powerful beat and soulful lyrics that drew "hysterical reactions" from adolescent girls and young women, first under the R & B label and then in the new music called rock 'n' roll. Brown's popularity continued to grow, eventually taking her to Detroit, New York, and Washington, D.C., in a solo act. At age twenty she signed a record contract with Atlantic Records and began recording a string of hits that made her one of the biggest R & B stars of the 1950s.

Ruth Brown did not gain crossover fame, although white mainstream singers regularly covered her songs in hits that made it onto *Billboard*'s pop charts. Nor did her stardom cross into the world of rock 'n' roll despite the fact that in 1952 her hit "5–10–15 Hours (of Your Love)" stayed at number one on the R & B charts for seven weeks and later became the basis, after several transformations, of Bill Haley's breakthrough hit "Rock around the Clock."[59] The hard-driving sexuality of Brown's life and music did not attract the mixed-race audiences that her male contemporaries did, suggesting that the interracial draw of black music in this era operated primarily between black men and audiences of young white women and men. Brown's explicit passion won her fame among black audiences, but seemed to go beyond the unwritten rules of sexual propriety that governed female performance in the 1950s.[60]

Another teenage girl from the South, however, did gain temporary stardom through the hopped-up sound of rockabilly. At age fifteen Janis Martin, already a seasoned performer with her own country radio show in Virginia, signed a record contract with RCA. Born in 1940, Martin grew up with the sounds of country music but also began incorporating into her performances songs by Ruth Brown and LaVern Baker, another African American R & B star. She combined these various sounds into short-lived fame as a rockabilly star often referred to as "the female Elvis." Her powerful, throaty voice merited appearances on *American Bandstand,* the *Tonight Show, Grand Ole Opry,* and other nationally known television and radio shows. She recorded a number of hits, including "My Boy Elvis" and "Will You Willyum."[61]

Like Ruth Brown, Martin openly expressed her sexual longings and appetite in these songs, breaking with the restrictive standards of country music, which expected women to sing about love and romance, whether lost or found, but not about outright sexual desire. In "My Boy Elvis," Martin articulated the effect that Elvis Presley had on girls, changing the passive stance of being overcome by his sex appeal to a more active role as seeker of satisfaction. In the first verse, she takes the role of a "gone" listener who claims Elvis as her own, impatiently stating: "Can't wait for Freddie or for Joe. / Got my blue jeans on and away I go. / I feel like the queen of everything. / Tonight I'll be close to my juke box king." The following verse makes it clear that she is the object of her "juke box king's" love: "All the teeners stomp and shout / When they open the curtains and he walks out. / They know the one he's dreaming of, because I've got his photograph signed 'with love.'" While the lyrics mostly address a fantasy relationship between Elvis and a female fan, making her the "queen of everything," the song puts female adolescents clearly in the role of choicemaker and pleasure seeker.[62]

Martin's hit "Will You Willyum" makes her sexual desire and pleasure much more explicit. The song tells of a girl's boyfriend, William, and his capacity to "thrill me to my finger tips." The chorus describes the thrill of Will's touch and repeats the refrain "Willyum, will you, Willyum." The double entendre of "Will you" as both request for and declaration of satisfaction—"Will, Will, Will you thrill me"—puts the singer in the role of actively requesting and then relishing sexual pleasure, made even more explicit by the repetition of "yum, yum yum" spliced to Will's name. Martin's lyrics made a radical statement in the 1950s, when experts portrayed women's sexuality as passive and responsive, that is, as primarily oriented around male pleasure. In additional verses, Martin rejects other boys because only William can truly "send" her and exclaims dramatically that "when he starts rocking, I yell don't stop." Rejecting the prescribed duty of adolescent girls to stop premarital sexual activity before it went "too far," in her pursuit of sexual pleasure Martin issues a single command to her lover: "Don't stop."[63]

Martin enjoyed some degree of fame from 1956 until 1958, when her career came to a crashing halt. The "female Elvis" had a baby at age eighteen and revealed that she had married secretly when only fifteen. As a teenage wife and mother Martin could no longer sing from the position of the wild and longing teenage girl. Other female rockabilly stars also had brief careers, stifled by the lack of interest shown by record labels and by the disc jockeys who could make or break a singer's career.[64] Martin and her peers made it further than Ruth Brown did in the early world of rock 'n' roll, but a female performer singing about her own sexual desires, satisfactions, frustrations, and fantasies seems to have deviated too far from sexual norms. The men controlling the music industry preferred the dynamic of a sexy male singer eliciting giddy, hysterical reactions from girls.

The constraints on singers like Brown and Martin tell us something about the limits of adolescent sexual self-determination. Girls and women demonstrated their newly won permission to express sexual interest by responding passionately to a music that could turn good girls into wild, screaming, fainting, sexual exhibitionists. But the image of the "hysterical fan" remained crucial to a popular belief that while even "good girls" might feel strong sexual desire, they would stop short of taking control of sexual experience aimed at their own pleasure.

Despite these limits, the image of teenage girls going wild at concerts, dancing with abandon, and singing along to sexually explicit songs continued to trouble adults. They preferred to think of teenage girls, especially middle-class teenage girls, as either innocent of sexual feelings, or at least responsible and concerned enough about pregnancy and loss of reputation to keep their desires well in check, "saving" themselves for marriage. But the 1950s was not an era of saving; it was one of spending. And girls as well as boys consumed their new teen-oriented music as part of a peer culture that openly displayed signs of sexual desire and assertiveness. It was this image of girls, hysterical and "spent" by their uninhibited response to a sexualized music, that proved most disturbing to parents and critics. Public scenes of sexually charged "hysteria" put teenagers' private desires on display, openly expressing needs that moralists believed should, at best, be repressed or at least contained within private settings.

Teenagers spurned this moral standard because they had been quietly cultivating their own peer-based morality for over a decade in the high school culture of heterosexual dating and romance. The seemingly small step from jukebox gatherings at wartime teen canteens to the tumultuous rock 'n' roll concerts of the 1950s caught adults off guard. In their eyes, a music heavily influenced by black and white working-class culture, one that blended racial influences and spoke to youth across class and racial divides, represented a radical break from an earlier cohort of teens jitterbugging at school-sponsored sock hops.

Most threatening of all, rock 'n' roll raised the specter of interracial social interaction and passion, the possibility most feared and hated among southern whites committed to segregation in the name of white superiority.

The perceived danger of "social equality" tells us little about actual racial attitudes among adolescents who in most cases did not extend their musical rebellion into other social or political arenas. The fact that black teens thrilled to Elvis Presley or Bill Haley did not make them more likely to seek out interracial friendships or romances. White adolescents, too, could rave to rhythms and lyrics based in historically African American musical forms without altering their racial beliefs. A girl might sneak away to a blues club on the "wrong" side of the tracks with her boyfriend, dance with abandon, then return to her everyday life of homework and sorority parties. Moreover, because black bands typically performed at exclusively white events like fraternity, high school, or country club dances, teens of different races rarely intermingled; and those occasions when they did interact did not lead rock 'n' roll fans as a group to press for integrated clubs, high schools, or public facilities.[65] Although certainly some teenagers inclined to challenge racial inequality must have used the culture of rock 'n' roll to move in this direction, there is no evidence that this trend was widespread.[66]

To the contrary, the considerable popularity of white pop singer Pat Boone suggests that many teenagers preferred to step over to the wild side, screaming deliriously over Elvis Presley or other rock stars, but then step back into the realm of proper family and community norms. Pat Boone personified a singer who transformed "black" sounds into acceptable "white" pop hits he described as a "vanilla version" of rock 'n' roll.[67] Dressed fastidiously in cardigan sweaters, casual slacks, and his trademark white buck shoes, Boone appealed to teenagers interested in a milder version of rock's lyrics and beat, an experiment in style that left them safely on the side of respectability. Even parents liked Boone, leading publishers to seek him out as a source of advice to teenagers. His book 'Twixt Twelve and Twenty urged youth to pursue a path of spiritual growth, formal education, social responsibility, and financial security. He also discouraged teens from kissing and going steady in the years before maturity (presumably age twenty, from his title).[68] The conclusion that "Pat represented to the middle majority their safe dreams; Elvis, their more dangerous fantasies" seems borne out by a 1957 poll of musical preferences. With Presley at the height of his popularity, the survey revealed that the majority of girls and boys preferred rock to pop. But when asked about their favorite singer, 44 percent of boys and 45 percent of girls named Pat Boone, while only 22 percent of boys and 18 percent of girls chose Elvis Presley.[69]

In retrospect, the rock 'n' roll "rebellion" by itself did not produce radical change. Adolescent interest in rock music simply created an early and powerful entry point for teenagers to pump dollars into an already booming consumer economy, while teen romance typically channeled love into early marriage and motherhood—neither of which was a particularly rebellious outcome. Yet adults perceived a revolutionary challenge to their customary authority. Adolescent girls in particular, whether they held off on sexual intercourse until marriage or not, gave open expression to their sexual feelings and deepest desires without apparent respect for their mothers' wishes, their fathers' authority, or the codes of conduct explicated by parental surrogates like ministers.

In 1960, Muddy Waters, a native Mississippian turned Chicago blues star, played a dance at the all-white University of Mississippi. When university officials witnessed white female students dancing with abandon, skirts flying upward revealing thighs and underwear, they stepped in to halt the dance, turning off the lights and demanding that band members leave the building to wait for their paycheck outside.[70] In this situation and others like it, the sexual and racial threat came less from the black musicians than from young white women refusing to conform to the social and sexual etiquette of their elders. A rejection of etiquette, in turn, intimated a much more profound possibility—a rejection of the very edifice of the South's ruling paradigm. Southern elites justified racial segregation and other discriminatory laws on the grounds that they protected vulnerable white womanhood from black male sexual aggression. But when white high school and college women went wild to the sounds of black R & B or black-influenced rock 'n' roll, segregationists saw the opposite of sexual containment through racial separation: they witnessed white girls responding with apparent sexual abandon to the attractions of black performers—or white performers who enacted "blackness."

Although censorship and protest occurred nationwide, the hostile reaction to rock music was most fervid in southern states, where for both religious and racial reasons adult authorities perceived the burgeoning youth culture as especially threatening. Although the region's institutionalized legal segregation held firm at midcentury, the forces arraigned against segregation moved forcefully ahead in the 1950s. The 1954 *Brown v. Board of Education* ruling against school segregation, followed by the 1955–1956 Montgomery bus boycott, undermined segregation in education and public transportation, launching the civil rights movement's assault on the rule of white supremacy in the South. As regional politicians gathered their forces for legal battles and a strategy of "massive resistance," teenagers appeared on the surface to be moving in the opposite direction. They had created an autonomous popular culture in which the lines of race were becoming more and more blurred as black and white performers shared stages and songs, the airwaves integrated black and white music, and adolescents embraced the music and dance of rock 'n' roll regardless of race. Even more threatening, interracial dancing and socializing went beyond the possibility of legal equality, moving toward "social equality"—a term long used by whites to express their fear of white and black people interacting as equals, no longer bound by hierarchical relations like those between white homemakers and black maids, or white landowners and black tenants.

Within a matter of years, then, longstanding sexual and racial barriers fell vulnerable to a form of popular culture claimed by teenagers as their distinctive birthright. And contained within this commercially powerful music were cultural and political possibilities that ripped against the grain of white southern sensibilities and existing inequalities. Whether first undertaken as purposeful rebellion or thoughtless amusement, the collective embrace of rock 'n' roll posed a genuine threat to the social order. Integrated sounds, bands, and dance floors diminished white control of racialized spaces that were central to the imposition and maintenance of racial hierarchy. White fathers and paternalistic officials had long used their gender authority and an ideology of female sexual vulnerability to keep daughters under strict sexual control, dependent on male protection. But the youth culture of the 1950s challenged the ability of parents to control their children, especially adolescent girls asserting some degree of sexual independence and, thus, disloyalty to "southern" customs.

Given this shift, it makes sense why Ace Carter and his archsegregationist comrades considered rock 'n' roll worthy of political attack and attempted censorship. The bodies, emotions, and relationships of teenagers had long been central to maintaining the existing southern political order. But by the mid- to late 1950s, teenagers' greater social and economic independence, the increasingly overt expressions of female adolescent sexuality, and the shocking popularity of rock 'n' roll signaled potential cracks in the system. Gradual shifts of the 1940s toward a more sexualized adolescent body and a high school culture of love, romance, dating, and marriage became, during the 1950s, critical points of contention in the South. Generational conflict over music merged seamlessly with contemporaneous opposition to the Supreme Court's order to desegregate southern schools with "all deliberate speed."

chapter ten

The Sexual Paradox of High School Desegregation

*I*n September 1957, Americans viewed three powerful images of high school girls, reproduced in newspapers and television news stories across the country. The first, and least etched in historical memory, was a picture of a tall, thin, dignified, but somewhat dazed African American fifteen-year-old walking toward her new high school surrounded by screaming, taunting white teens and adults intent on preventing Dorothy Counts from being the first girl to integrate Harding High School in Charlotte, North Carolina. A very similar photo from a few days later, one reproduced around the world and still recognizable today, featured another tall, poised African American girl, attempting to enter Central High School in Little Rock, Arkansas. Separated from the other eight students trying to integrate the school, Elizabeth Eckford stood alone in a crowd of hateful, jeering faces. Her sunglasses hid any fear her eyes might have betrayed, but in the photo she looks frozen in shock, unsure how to negotiate the danger into which she has unwittingly walked. Yet there remains about her an aura of stately calm that heightens the contrast between Eckford's brave attempt to break down racial barriers and the brutality and rage distorting the faces of white protesters committed to preventing her entry into their prized, all-white school. In another photo from Little Rock, two armed National Guardsmen assigned to Central High point bayonets toward the backs of two white girls walking casually toward school. There is a staged quality to the photo, and the girls look toward the camera conveying a sense of slight discomfort tinged with the thrill of momentary celebrity.[1]

Is it coincidental that the most renowned photographic images from this critical year in the history of school desegregation feature adolescent girls? Black boys are virtually absent and white boys are photographed not in their capacity as students but as unindividuated members of a mob, so hostile to integration that they temporarily forfeit their role as high school students to prevent others from assuming that status. That the most recognized images from the period feature white and black girls at the center of bitter battles over desegregation may be an accident of history, a product of photographic opportunity and editorial selection. But the images arguably signify much more than coincidence. For at the heart of white resistance to school desegregation lay the fear that the children of white parents would somehow end up in intimate relationships with black students, leading to interracial dating, courtship, marriage, and progeny—what segregationists derided as "mixing," "miscegenation," "mongrelization," and "amalgamation." Although in the photo of white Central High girls the soldiers were white, the phallic image of bayonets pointed from behind at a girl's back suggests the possibility of phallic penetration of "innocent" white southern girls lured or forced into sexual relations that would ruin them as representatives of southern white womanhood. The fact that these girls did not seem particularly afraid in this photo suggests a possibility even more unthinkable to southern whites—that adolescent girls might be willing players in the game, rejecting their region's fundamental principle of racial separation.

The striking images of Dorothy Counts and Elizabeth Eckford surrounded by hostile crowds of white protesters symbolize another dimension of the unfolding drama. As lone young black women subject to physical aggression, their images reproduce the historic vulnerability of black women to sexual assaults by white men. But here the image is turned around. For this time, white male aggression and black female vulnerability is made public, shown before the world in a way that could not be hidden, denied, or made to seem like a product of the seductive powers of black women over otherwise respectable white men, especially since screaming white women marched alongside men as equal partners in protest.

One of the most memorable images from the Little Rock school desegregation crisis captures Elizabeth Eckford isolated and walking alone while being taunted and threatened by white segregationists. The dignity of Eckford contrasted with the hatred and aggression of her white peers (behind Eckford), who broke with southern ideals of white female respectability. Library of Congress, NYWTS Photo, LC-USZ62–126826.

Another reversal takes place in these photos. The moral balance of the photo resides on the side of poised, serious African American girls, obstructed by an unruly, hateful crowd. Black adolescent girls stand as individuals—a status rarely granted to them in the dominant culture of the South—demonstrating their own will and mind as they courageously attempt to take their place as "ordinary" high school students. Some of their white female peers stand out in these photographs as taunting, angry, and aggressive. In a visible break with conventions of female respectability, the yelling, spitting, and glaring white girls seem far less like victims than violators, thus reversing conventional representations of white and black womanhood. Al-

In September 1957, the Charlotte, North Carolina, school board selected Dorothy Counts as the single student to desegregate Harding High School. Much like Elizabeth Eckford, she maintains a quiet dignity as she approaches her new school, while white opponents spit, scream, and taunt her from behind. Library of Congress, NYWTS Photo, LC-USZ62–117236.

though Dorothy Counts and Elizabeth Eckford appear starkly isolated in the photos, the context indicates that the girls are attempting to become part of a "student body" in which their bodies and those of white girls would stand together, undifferentiated in physical, moral, or social status.

These reversals hint at two dynamics at the heart of segregationists' fears. On the one hand, they feared that if white students were forced (by law, soldiers, guns) to attend school with black classmates, their white daughters might willingly choose intimate involvements with black boys. The sexuality of average white teenage girls had been powerfully displayed in their enthusiastic response to rock 'n' roll. Having established themselves as sexual actors with their own interests and passions, including their fervor for black singers and musicians, they could no longer be cast purely as female victims of black assailants. Indeed, adolescent white girls had to be considered as potentially willing sexual partners in heretofore unspeakable sexual relationships. Although less a focus of public concern, white sons and black daughters might also choose each other as romantic sexual partners. White men had long enjoyed sexual access to black women's bodies, but in integrated schools, such relationships might occur in the open as part of the legitimate world of high school dating and courtship, adding an element of accountability for male behavior and raising the social standing of black teenage girls to that of "girlfriend" or "date."

As potential coparticipants in the sexualized culture of American high schools, black and white girls helped uncouple notions of sexual virtue from white supremacy. The sexual ideology that painted black and white women as the dirty ground and precious flower, respectively, of southern society had been challenged before by white and black women in the antilynching movement.[2] Now a new generation of young women, whether intentionally or not, was pushing to the limit longstanding sexual dualisms. As the epic struggle over school desegregation heated up, high school girls were central actors in the deconstruction of stable white rule in the South. White men, in particular, responded angrily to their potential loss of power as a racial elite and as patriarchal heads of household.

The 1954 *Brown v. Board of Education* decision mandating desegregation of southern schools generated little immediate political furor. Especially in the upper South, state and local officials assumed that once the Supreme Court had ruled, compliance would soon follow. To go into effect, however, the ruling required states to develop and implement policies for desegregating schools. Even as educators began preparations for the transition, most state governments voiced their opposition to the ruling and waited to see what kind of enforcement guidelines the federal government would issue. The May 1955 Supreme Court directive that schools comply "with all deliberate speed," permitting district courts to work out the legal details, sent a message to southern segregationists that federal pressure would remain minimal. Conflicts would be resolved on southern turf by judges who generally hailed from the South and who supported the existing system of segregation. Moreover, as President Dwight Eisenhower's lukewarm support for *Brown* became widely known, white politicians, business leaders, and citizens groups began to make their opposition to the ruling more vocal.

Nationally known southern politicians increasingly spoke out against compliance to *Brown*. In the spring of 1956, 101 of 128 southern Congressmen signed a "Southern Manifesto" pledging unswerving opposition to any school desegregation. Addressing the *Brown* ruling, Mississippi Senator James Eastland proclaimed that southerners "by and large, will neither recognize, abide by nor comply with this decision. We are expected to remain docile while the pure blood of the South is mongrelized."[3] Eastland's statement presumed that students attending the same schools would create a "mongrelized" race through interracial sexual relationships resulting in pregnancy—a shocking statement given the students' many years of instruction in sexual morality and racial propriety. Other prominent politicians followed Eastland's lead. Senator Strom Thurmond of South Carolina followed the reading of the "Southern Manifesto" into the *Congressional Record* with his own observation that since southern states had improved black schools to the point of equality, the only possible motive for integration was the "mixing of the races."[4]

Beyond such rhetorical flourishes, most politicians quickly shifted public debate away from interracial sex toward principles of law on which they might justify their massive resistance. Political rhetoric centered around issues of states' rights in the face of federal intervention, local control of education, and whether *Brown* actually required integration or merely forbade segregation on the basis of race. Searching for legal justifications, James M. Kilpatrick, the prominent editor of the *Richmond News Leader,* revived the nineteenth-century doctrine of interposition, which claimed that states had a right to reject federal laws to protect their citizens from unconstitutional encroachments by the federal government. Publicly he hoped that the legalism of the concept of interposition would shift the terms of debate from race relations to loftier principles of law. But privately he wrote to an ally that southerners would abandon public schools "for one reason only: To avoid what they regard as the greater catastrophe of a mixed society and an intimate social mingling with the Negro race."[5]

State officials designed policies to block desegregation without appearing openly to defy the new law of the land. State Senator Thomas Pearsall of North Carolina masterminded the Pupil Assignment Act, which put pupil placement in the hands of local school boards, thus avoiding potential state-level lawsuits by the NAACP. Pearsall and other regional leaders argued that *Brown* banned segregation on the basis of race, but did not actually require integration, allowing school boards to assign students to schools according to criteria like residence, intelligence, and even social compatibility with other students. So-called moderates in North Carolina conceded that some token integration would have to take place to indicate minimal compliance with federal law. But they hoped the Pearsall Plan, as it was called, would leave white schools intact by forcing individual black parents to apply for their children's transfer to previously white schools, followed by a time-consuming appeals process after the school boards had denied their requests.

Other states or districts gave parents the option to withdraw their children from any school that black children would attend, providing either for a transfer to an all-white public school or a financial voucher redeemable at private white schools. Some states even permitted school districts to vote to close public schools altogether if faced with integration policies that violated the will of the (white) community. As a result of pupil placement plans and the absolute refusal of some states to make any gesture toward integration, not a single southern state attempted full-scale desegregation in the 1950s, with states like Kentucky, Tennessee, Arkansas, and North Carolina instituting only token integration of a few black students in schools that remained overwhelmingly white.[6]

*W*hen politicians worked through legal channels to overturn *Brown,* they remained focused on the ruling's proper interpretation and on whether federal courts could legally intervene in state-funded, locally administered public education. Generally the more formal, political, or legal the setting, the less was said about issues of interracial sex. But as segregation defenders communicated directly to the public, they were much more likely to make the perceived sexual dangers of integration a prominent part of their rhetoric.

For instance, in 1960 the Georgia General Assembly created the Committee on Schools, composed of nineteen white men and headed by John Sibley, a legislator from Atlanta. The Sibley committee held hearings across the state, inviting local educators, businessmen, pastors, and interested citizens to testify. Of the 1,600 white and two hundred black speakers, almost none raised the specter of interracial sex as a factor in their decision. But Sibley also received numerous letters from citizens who made it clear that their opposition stemmed from fears of interracial intimacy.[7]

In one letter, the president of a private school considered "mixing of the races" from two possible standpoints: "mixing *without social acceptance*" and "mixing *with social acceptance.*" Denied acceptance by white students, black students would inevitably suffer personal trauma, unhappiness, and psychological damage. But if teachers and students did fully accept each race as equal participants in the classroom, in athletics, in sororities and fraternities, in dating, and "in all the intimate contacts of daily living," then "it would be only natural for the races to intermix in the ultimate way and to become only one." Such an outcome, he concluded, would "deny a certain pride of race."[8] Sibley received other personal letters and printed tracts that made the same point, arguing that school desegregation would inevitably lead to interracial marriages contrary to nature, to God's design, and to the best interests of society.

Popular opinion expressed in editorials or in political propaganda raised the issue of interracial sex, marriage, and offspring even more emphatically. In Louisiana, for example, fear of interracial sex entered the annals of law, politics, and protest. In a private communication to State Senator William Rainach, a prominent prosegregationist, Mrs. Harry Crane asked aghast, "What, pray God, is going to happen to the Psyche of genteelly raised white children, particularly little girls . . . when deliberately thrown among those uninhibited, boisterous, undisciplined, unrestrained primitive aborigines?" In response to senti-

ments like this, the Louisiana state legislature outlawed school dancing, parties, entertainment, sports, "and other such activities involving
personal and social contacts."[9]

If the ban on interracial socializing did not explicitly refer to sexual
intimacy, the reference could not have been clearer in the speeches
of ultrasegregationist politicians like Leander Perez. Leading the battle
against Louisiana's 1960 implementation of the *Brown* decision, Perez
exhorted his audience, "Don't let your daughter be raped by those
Congolese. Don't wait until the burr-heads are forced into your
schools."[10] While Perez raised the specter of rape by uncivilized Afri-
cans, other protesters spoke out against interracial "mixing" that might
occur voluntarily. In one prosegregation rally, elementary school children performed a skit featuring four children in black face hugging
and kissing three other children who, without any makeup, remained
"white." The emcee then asked the crowd, "Is this what you want?"
and received a chorus of boos in response. Parents in another protest
carried signs saying, "Keep Our Children White." By substituting
"children" for the more common slogan, "Keep Our Schools White,"
parents revealed their assumption that upon attending "mixed" schools
white children would become involved in racially "mixed" couples,
producing biracial offspring who, as their own grandchildren, would
qualify as "our" children.[11]

Committed segregationists also enlisted religious arguments. A letter to the *Atlanta Constitution* from "A Bible Student" stated that the
Supreme Court decision had forced "our lovely white children" to sit,
socialize, and eat with "the Negro, . . . [which was] a direct violation of the scripture." He then predicted that interracial attractions
between teenagers would result in seeing "white girls the wives of
negroes."[12] A perceptive Tennessee minister wondered if predictions
of interracial marriages did not rely "on the assumption that our
White children are sexually perverted and morally degenerate." He
answered in the negative, however, claiming, "It is normal that when
boys and girls are thrown together in social situations they form ties
that will eventually lead to marriage. School desegregation will lead to
your daughter marrying a Negro boy."[13] Oddly, this minister raises the
possibility that white daughters are "sexually perverted" if attracted to
a Negro boy, but concludes that in integrated settings it is quite normal for interracial intimacies to form and marriages to follow. He was

not the first protester to argue, paradoxically, that "unnatural" relationships would form "naturally" in an integrated society.

White supremacist organizations like citizens councils, the North Carolina Patriots, and the Louisiana Southern Gentlemen deliberately used explicit sexual imagery to persuade followers of the extremely dangerous consequences augured by school desegregation. A common tactic of such groups was to distribute copies of speeches attributed to NAACP leaders. In Mississippi, one mimeographed pamphlet "quoted" an NAACP official addressing his black audience: "It might surprise you to learn that our strongest sympathizers in this particular demand . . . are millions of Southern white women . . . We, the negro man, have long known that the white woman is violently dissatisfied with the white man . . . They, along with us, demand the right to win and love the negro man of their choice and shout to the world, 'This is my man and he is a man in every respect.'"[14] Similar speeches occur in the literature of other white hate groups and in the NAACP's own records of white resistance, making it safe to say that such "recorded" speeches were entirely the creation of white supremacist authors. The author of this tract exhibits tremendous sexual insecurity, recognizing not only white men's mistreatment of white women but also the possibility that the resulting dissatisfaction would lead women right into the arms of a Negro man—in an act of choice. That she might then proudly shout out to the world her preference completed a white man's imagined scenario of abject sexual humiliation.

White hate groups also targeted the world of commercial entertainment and its powerful hold over white teenage girls. In *A Bluebook for Patriots,* a Texas organization complained bitterly about the "veritable parade of Negroidal entertainers" entering American homes via television and exposing white youth to "Negro bobby-sox idols." The handbook warned that if television continued to glamorize black performers, "you may yet see the day when your own daughter will react in similar fashion."[15] A white supremacist newsletter, *The White Sentinel,* expressed special distress over rebellious daughters. The author asserts that if children attend integrated schools, theaters, dances, and pools, "Our mothers, wives, daughters, or sisters" will fall victim to attacks by "negro rapists." Yet the succeeding paragraph abandons the rape narrative and relocates the danger to white solipsism and willful daughters. Urging the Caucasian man (not the white rape victim) to "arise from his slumber to defend himself," the author warns that without action "it will not be long before he will see his daughter run off against his wishes and live with a negro."[16] The literature of white supremacist organizations reveals much more than political opposition to mandated desegregation; it makes manifest that white men of all classes sensed the erosion of patriarchal control in their own families.

The national press concurred that sexuality lay at the core of white resistance to desegregation. Sent to investigate the South's mood in the years after *Brown,* journalists almost always reported that sexual fears were at the forefront of segregationist sentiment. *Look* magazine described the average white parent's fear that a Negro boy would soon be walking the daughter home from school, staying for supper, taking her to the movies, and eventually asking for her hand in marriage. Reporter William Attwood noted that desegregation inevitably brought up one question in southerners' minds: "Would *you* want your daughter to marry a Nigra?"—a question so disturbing that Attwood labeled the fear of integration itself a "sexual neurosis."[17] Across the spectrum, segregationist ministers, politicians, common citizens, and northern journalists all arrived at sexual "mixing" as key to the breadth and depth of southern resistance to school desegregation. The possibility of schoolchildren coming to feel comfortable with and romantically interested in schoolmates of a different race challenged the power of white elites to regulate sexuality and institutionalize black inferiority. More to the point, it also revealed a common fear among southern whites that they might lose control over their own hearts and bodies or those of their children.

As segregationists fixated on the danger of interracial sexual relationships and offspring, they rarely stopped to analyze the reasons such liaisons would occur and why they were by definition harmful. Yet upon scrutiny, both the logic and illogic of their arguments illuminate the sexual and racial assumptions undergirding segregationist views. The most obvious but often unaddressed question in the rhetoric was, If white girls were by nature morally superior and sexually virtuous, what would make such "good girls" turn to black boys for love?

Some segregationists argued from the basis of physical proximity, insinuating that the moral decline of white students would occur simply by being in the same environment as black youth. In a common defense of segregation, opponents referred to high rates of juvenile delinquency, pregnancy, and venereal disease in black communities and in the already desegregated Washington, D.C., schools, where according to Virginia Governor J. Lindsay Almond, Jr., "the livid stench of sadism, immorality and juvenile pregnancy infesting the mixed schools of the District of Columbia and elsewhere" made it abundantly clear why Virginia should remain firm in its opposition to *Brown*.[18] In this environmentally based view, white children associating with black children would, as if by osmosis, take on the moral character of an allegedly inferior race.

Another explanation focused on persistent social interaction. Desegregation would accustom students to socializing at school, then extend beyond the classroom to dating and courtship with the prospect of mixed marriages and biracial children. The danger was exacerbated in secondary education, where large numbers of students shared in both the formal and informal social life of high school culture. To segregationists this situation was especially dire in the context of regional progress in the 1950s, a decade when the number of students graduating from Deep South high schools increased by 70 percent.[19] Yet this is hardly an explanation for why white adolescents, whose parents had instilled notions of racial superiority in them since early childhood, would become sexually involved with black students. Throughout southern history, social proximity had produced interracial liaisons resulting in biracial children. One difference in a newly integrated society would be that relationships between white male and black female students would gain legitimacy and legal standing. Consequently, children of interracial marriages would no longer be treated as illegitimate "black" offspring; they would instead attain standing in both the black and white communities.

To segregationists, prospective marriages between white women and black men proved even more alarming. Despite being raised to fear black men as sexually aggressive potential rapists, white girls were, in this view, still vulnerable to the attractions of black classmates and thus were potentially willing participants in interracial courtship and marriage. Several published letters addressed to President Eisenhower and other politicians quoted a national magazine survey in which an eighteen-year-old white girl attending an integrated school in the North confided, "Almost every white girl I knew had a secret crush on one of the colored boys. The crushes varied from warm friendship to wild infatuation." Exposure created too much temptation, explained one of the girls, given that "we're not all saints."[20]

Southern mothers also feared that their daughters might succumb to temptation. Writing to the governor of Alabama in 1956, a woman describing herself as a "citizen and wife who is concerned about the future of her children" reasoned, "As you know some colored people look even better than some whites and you take a girl who didn't stand in with the white boys so good, right on the start, she might say well, there's a good looking colored boy. I'll just take him."[21] To this concerned mother, it wasn't simply a question of saints and sinners, it was about the complex social world of high school heterosexuality and the choices a girl might make under less-than-ideal conditions.

There lay the primary contradiction in white supremacist arguments. The dreaded event of a black adolescent boy marrying some crestfallen white man's daughter could not be explained away as a product of forced interaction when it lay within the power of white girls to choose associations with black classmates. How then to explain an attraction that most segregationists presented as unnatural and revolting? If indeed girls were not all "saints," did this make them sinners, committing acts that violated both the will of God and the rules of their society? Yet in the many defenses of segregated schools, none claimed that segregation must be preserved because white girls had themselves become immoral and untrustworthy. Only an influence more powerful than adolescent girls' own will or moral upbringing could cause the attractions and resulting relationships between black boys and white girls. That force, to segregationists, was the force of nature.

Yet opponents of *Brown* tended to waffle when assessing the precise role of nature in interracial "mixing." If racial mixing was "unnatural," segregation simply provided a social structure that reflected the laws of nature. Integration, by contrast, would force children into unnatural settings that encouraged unnatural relationships. Racial mixing in the schools, segregationists argued, would produce a domino effect of unnatural acts, from black and white children playing together to dating and eventually intermarriage. Mississippi senator James Eastland contended "the law of nature is on our side," reasoning that "after all, the average American is not a racial pervert."[22] Here Eastland claims that racial separation is a law of nature. Undo this law, and the "average American" might act like a "racial pervert." Since the concept of perversion typically connotes perverse acts of sexuality, by "racial pervert" Eastland suggests that in the wake of unnatural contact between black and white students, sexual perversion would follow in the form of interracial sex. In defying the "law" of nature by complying with the Supreme Court's law of the land, nature would take its revenge in unnatural, or perverse, forms of sexuality.

But others took the opposite tack, asserting that while interracial sex might go against nature, it was only natural that if placed in close proximity, students would experience interracial attractions. Contrary to the first view, here segregation operated as a prophylactic against interracial sex; remove the barriers, and interracial intimacy would develop naturally in an integrated context. In "A Christian View on Segregation," Presbyterian minister G. T. Gillespie warned that if the South believed that intermarriage and a "hybrid" race would improve the welfare and happiness of both races, "then all we need to do is to let down the bars of segregation in the homes, the schools, the churches and in all areas of community life, and let nature take its course." Yet if the course of nature would bring blacks and whites together, on the very next page Gillespie stated, "Segregation Is One of Nature's Universal Laws."[23] Ideologues convinced that segregation was a law of God and nature nevertheless also argued that without intentionally constructed barriers, interracial relationships would naturally occur.

In an article "Mixed Schools and Mixed Blood," Herbert Ravenel Sass wrestled with this very contradiction. He claimed that because same-race preference was a "nearly universal instinct," racial "amalgamation" occurred unnaturally and only at great peril. Given these facts of nature, why worry about placing black and white children in the same educational setting? The problem, according to Sass, was that racial preference was "one of those instincts which develop gradually as the mind develops," and thus required time and cultivation. Shifting from a nature to nurture argument, he believed that children brought up in mixed schools would enter high school lacking the supposedly "natural" instinct toward racial separation. The as yet "unprejudiced" and "defenseless" adolescent mind would be subject to "brain-washing," resulting in "a great increase of racial amalgamation."[24] Believing that children raised in integrated settings and "impregnated" by propaganda would "stop short of interracial mating" was, to Sass, "like going over Niagara Falls in a barrel in the expectation of stopping three fourths of the way down."[25] Combining images of an unstoppable, powerful force of nature, the exciting rush of a waterfall, the specific connection between Niagara Falls and honeymoons, and the process of impregnation, Sass conjured up sexual associations that portrayed school desegregation itself, and not just its dreaded (by him) result, in coded sexual terms.

If some segregationist rhetoric sexualized integration, other language pathologized it with references to social and physical disease. This perspective, too, evaluated interracial "mixing" in terms of the natural world, but this time as a reflection of nature gone awry in a sickened body. Segregationists denounced the "equalitarian virus" that threatened "to undermine all authority in our society from the home through the school."[26] The virus of equalitarianism merged easily with other infectious diseases, especially sexually transmitted ones. An organization called Separate Schools described African Americans as "a vast reservoir of infectious venereal diseases." Since the 1954 *Brown* decision, however, a strategy of containing "this reservoir within that race" had begun to fail. Syphilis rates, which had declined steadily from World War II to 1954, had since exploded in areas where race mixing among young people, especially in sports, entertainment, and social activities, "has been accompanied by a deterioration of sex morality to a level of depravity." Coming close to accusing white adolescents of moral depravity, the author stopped short of charging white youth with having interracial sex by explaining that these diseases spread through unspecified kinds of infectious contact or by germs transferred through drinking fountains and toilets.[27]

Disease metaphors blended easily into notions of pollution. Segregationists saw mixed-race environments as a form of social pollution, then extended this to the "blood" of children born to biracial couples. *New York Times* reporters learned from an ordinary white citizen that white skin "just naturally attracts" black men, leaving him to wonder whether in integrated schools "our white girls won't get so used to being around nigras that after a while they won't pay no attention to color?" White girls dancing "all hugged up" with black boys might end up at the altar together, causing "sex and bad trouble [for] the rest of our days. And once the blood stream is polluted, it won't run clear again in a million years."[28] A letter to an Atlanta newspaper described the normalizing of interracial relationships in terms of crime rather than pollution. "If a person commits a crime long enough it becomes so commonplace that it does not constitute a crime in that person's mind," reasoned Mrs. Dorothy Kaplowitz. "If the youngsters of both races study together, play together, and live in the same neighborhood long enough it becomes such a natural and commonplace thing that marriage between the races wouldn't seem at all out of line to them."[29] Contagious disease, pollution, and crime formed a series of related metaphors that reflected white assumptions about black bodies and black communities as immoral, criminal, and diseased.

Southern writers communicating to a national audience typically tried to describe the "crime" or "virus" of integration in less exaggerated terms, covering up both the vehement hatred and the illogic of more crudely expressed racism. For instance, when distinguished Atlanta columnist John Temple Graves spoke to an audience in Tacoma, Washington, he explained that white southerners loved the Negro but still did not want him in their schools. Asked for a justification, Graves rationalized evasively, "It's a biological thing. Integration in the schools would be a massive thing, throw young people together. There is bound to have a biological effect from all that social contact."[30] Some white southerners concluded that the situation was so complex as to be ultimately insoluble. David Cohn, a well-known southern author, explained in his 1944 article "How the South Feels about the Race Problem" that the average white person felt determined that no white will marry a Negro and especially that no white woman would have relations with a Negro man. In Cohn's view, any "forms of physical propinquity which smack of social equality" might endanger society. "Instinctively the Southerner argues that sex is at the core of life—that it is one of the most profound instincts or desires that animate the human body, and that it is capable of evoking primitive fears and daemonic passions."[31] The erotic fervency historically attributed to black men and women Cohn now acknowledged as part of human, and especially southern, sexuality.

Believing that sex lay at the primal center of life, Cohn suggests that the true threat of integration is not that black students might approach whites, but that white southerners might lose the power to regulate public sexuality and their own primitive passions. Desegregation endangered southern "civilization" because it threatened to release the demonic sexual passions buried under white civility, placing white southerners on the same human and social plane as people of color. In attacking school desegregation, white adults projected a frightening view of their own unrestrained sexual desires onto teenage sons and, even more so, daughters.

Civil rights leaders approached the charges of sexual intent and planned "amalgamation" like one might handle a bomb, walking delicately around the issue while taking cautious steps to defuse it. The NAACP appears to have left the accusations unanswered, taking a "higher" road by dismissing charges of sexual immorality and aggression as not deserving of consideration. These loaded charges were precisely the accusations that had justified a century of lynchings, which primarily involved the murder of black men accused of rape or sexual advances toward white women. To take on the charges at face value granted them credibility and could only harm the burgeoning civil rights movement. Moreover, the NAACP had formerly employed the strategy of insisting that the organization sought legal equality and did not deal with matters of social equality. But in its more aggressive midcentury stance, civil rights leaders were not willing to concede social equality as a meaningful goal. Nor would they deny that in a more just society, white and black persons might more often seek each other out as sexual partners in marriage.

Silence on the topic in this case formed a means of defense, with most black leaders sticking to legal and political civil rights issues. For ordinary black men and women, sexual issues also remained in the distance since even simply to support desegregation publicly put their lives at risk. But one venue in which African Americans could safely challenge the sexual contradictions of segregationist thinking was in letters sent to government officials or to the press. Two letters written by black men to James Folsom during the University of Alabama's 1956 segregation crisis made sure to point out the hypocrisy of white sexual fears. One man reminded the governor that most whites in the south had "color people" (his quotes) working for them as servants and that "if we were the type of people to do any evil against our white race I am sure we could have done it long ago." Using examples of sex-segregated schools converting to coeducation, he reasons that if the boys and girls can mix, "We can mix together also." Taking a more aggressive tone, he continues, "It may come as a shock, but sooner or later things will begin to change . . . If you can mix our money with yours, we can mix also."[32] Another letter to Folsom appears at first to support segregation, stating that integrated education "is wrong in the hearing of God, and Sane man." But the author, an Oklahoma minister originally from Alabama, subtly shifts positions, adding, "If it is wrong for them to be in school together, then it wrong for negroes to enter the white man kitchen or any part of his home." Included in both letters is a reminder, or a veiled threat, that black people have long been in a position to do damage to whites when working in their homes, so that school desegregation is not a "first" instance of white vulnerability in a shared setting.[33]

The national media occasionally provided another opening for African Americans to challenge segregationists. In their *New York Times Magazine* feature story "Inquiry into Southern Tensions," Wilma Dykeman and James Stokely focused on white fears of intermarriage and miscegenation. As the authors sought out black opinion on the subject, one source reminded the journalists that white men had been having children with black women for generations with little public outcry. Not only that, but given that those men's offspring grew up "black" in the black community, black men marrying the daughters of white men already occurred with some frequency. The difference in an integrated school system that resulted in interracial marriages, the commentator noted, would be that black men would not just be having children with the daughters of white men but with the daughters of the wives of white men. With this turn of events, white girls attracted to black boys might, by the South's system of racial definition, someday become mothers of "black" babies.[34]

*O*ne group of southerners had even less to say on the issue of sex and desegregation. Black students involved in token integration of southern high schools ignored the subject or, if asked, disavowed any interest in interracial dating. Ernest Green, one of the "Little Rock Nine," dismissed the whole question as absurd, emphasizing that marriage was not the purpose of education. "Why do I want to go to school?" asked Green rhetorically, replying, "School's not a marriage bureau . . . I'm going there for an education."[35] Yet segregationists did not find Green's opinion persuasive. In their view, integrated schools would lead to a dangerous convergence not only of white and black students, but also of racial status. With students sharing fashions, sitting together in classrooms, and dancing and dating in the open, white teens would experience a relative decline in status as they lost their claim on exclusive, superior social space and standing. Desegregation triggered a generalized fear of falling, as threatened whites imagined their sons and daughters sinking socially, intellectually, and morally to the perceived lower level of African American adolescents. Equally if not more frightening to white parents, white and black teenagers might also converge in each others' arms, entering into loving or playful relationships—that is, possibly falling in love. If their sons and, especially, daughters chose to love black classmates, these relationships would stand as the ultimate affront to the sexual and racial protocol of white southern culture.

In the case of Dorothy Counts and Harding High School, white parents and teenagers did their best to make such a convergence impossible. Although Winston-Salem, Greensboro, and Charlotte prepared to send several children from black schools into previously all-white schools in September 1957, news coverage focused on the one school at which significant opposition formed, Charlotte's Harding High School. When approached by Charlotte's NAACP director, Reverend Herman Counts agreed to have one of his children attend Harding High. His fifteen-year-old daughter Dorothy was a poised, level-headed girl already interested in the civil rights movement. Having spent a week at an interracial Presbyterian youth conference during the summer, she felt prepared to face whatever difficulties she might encounter at Harding. But when the school doors opened on September 4, 1957, neither Dorothy nor her supporters were ready for the level of opposition they encountered. A mob of four hundred white youth and adults pelted her with pebbles and ice while shouting racial epithets and demanding that she "return to Africa." Her calm resolve formed a stark contrast to the white teenage protesters animated by rage, including an eighteen-year-old Harding boy charged with assault and a fifteen-year-old Harding girl accused of spitting on Dorothy.

Later that day police rounded up five white students for hanging an effigy of Dorothy Counts on the school's flagpole, although no arrests followed.[36]

Since North Carolina schools opened earlier than those in Little Rock, Dorothy Counts's brave action received the kind of regional, national, and even international press coverage that soon shifted to Central High School's Little Rock Nine. The contrasting images of unruly, hateful white protesters and the dignified black teenager elicited national and international sympathy for both Dorothy and the cause she represented, putting pressure on North Carolina school officials to make conditions safe. Yet Dorothy Counts's experience at Harding High School lasted only a week. By night her family was receiving threatening phone calls and carloads of hostile nightriders were circling their house, calling out threats. By day hostile teenagers hurled trash at Dorothy, shoved and taunted her, and battered her with racial slurs. Two girls who initially offered friendship suffered so much pressure from white classmates that they quickly joined the rest of Harding's student body in spurning her. On her final day, conditions worsened as Dorothy found her locker ransacked and one of her attackers launched a tin missile that struck Dorothy in the head. On September 12, Dorothy's parents withdrew her from Harding on the grounds that protecting their daughter from harm had to take priority over the cause of integration.[37]

Despite Counts's failed attempt at Harding, Charlotte city leaders heralded their integration plan as a model of success when the three other black students enrolled at previously white city schools managed to stick out the year under less traumatic circumstances.[38] The city received national praise for accomplishing a token display of desegregation that gave the appearance of cooperation with the law, while all but a handful of black students remained in their separate schools and twenty-one whites were permitted to transfer from their assigned schools in order to avoid attendance with black pupils. The Pearsall Plan and pupil placement law worked to evade genuine desegregation while maintaining the state's progressive image of enlightened civility and racial moderation. In fact, by 1961 the rate of desegregation in North Carolina stood at 0.026 percent, lower than rates in Virginia, Arkansas, Tennessee, and Texas.[39]

Several days after Charlotte schools opened in the fall of 1957, school opened in Little Rock, Arkansas, which quickly became the center of national attention as a standoff developed between state and federal authorities. Consequently, Dorothy Counts's week-long trauma at Harding High faded from local and national news as well as from historical memory. But an odd coincidence makes her experience part of a unique and telling story symbolizing some of the broader social tensions around race and the teenage girl in the 1950s.

*Ɛ*xactly one month before Dorothy Counts entered Harding High School, another high-school-aged Dorothy became headline news in Charlotte. Tom McKnight, a Mooresville, North Carolina, newspaper owner and editor, reported that while on an outing to the Duke Power Lake recreational site, he and his cronies had stumbled on a natural wonder, a "statuesque young girl carved from the classical pattern of a Greek goddess" living in primitive conditions unsullied by the dirt and corruption of civilization. Described as tall, lithe, willowy, and very beautiful, Dorothy Brown was a sixteen-year-old white "savage beauty" who had grown up in a "God-forsaken place," living in a cabin with eight siblings and her parents. Over the following days Dorothy Brown, referred to as "Long Sam" after a backwoods barefoot beauty in the syndicated comic strip *Li'l Abner,* was featured as the front page story in the *Charlotte Observer*'s arts and editorial section.[40] Photographs captured her wearing a shirt tied off at the midriff and cut-off shorts that barely reached her thighs. Another shot showed Dorothy floating in a polka dot bathing suit in the nearby Catawba River. This lovely "babe in the woods" stunned her admirers with her womanly beauty and childlike innocence.[41]

Dorothy claimed not to mind her current living conditions except for being forced to leave school after the eighth grade, due to a lack of clothing, to begin a job baby-sitting for a nearby family. Stating a simple desire to attend high school, within a week Dorothy found herself relocated from her "unlettered" parents' "unpainted hovel" to the spacious modern air-conditioned home of her new benefactors. The team of discoverers arranged a vacation at Myrtle Beach for Dorothy to see the ocean while they held off promoters, disc jockeys, "moonstruck college boys," and others who sought a glimpse of this remarkable natural wonder. Modeling agencies, fashion show directors, clothing manufacturers, and publicity agents swarmed around her Charlotte residence while Dorothy's handlers made arrangements for media appearances in New York City. Amid the hoopla an unnamed sponsor promised to fund Dorothy's education at a private high school and college, setting up a fund and financial guardianship to manage whatever fortune came her way. In self-congratulatory tones, the *Observer* gave nearly daily accounts about how "Luscious 'Long Sam' Calmly Starts a New Way of Life."[42]

Dorothy had a flawless figure and face, but what delighted the press even more was how she combined naivete, native intelligence, and wholesome morality. Her sincere religiosity and desire for education came across in homespun sayings like "Knowin' Leads to Living." As for boys, Dorothy impressed her audience with her reticence and level-headed approach to dating, explaining, "I don't look at them. I let them find me." She expressed her disappointment in discovering that "most boys are alike" in that they "start right off bothering me and . . . I always have to end up hitting them."[43] Compared to sexually assertive and knowing teenage girls, Dorothy resurrected a picture of adolescent innocence and girlish charm. Described as "a new kind of star," Dorothy represented "clean and beautiful simplicity," an implicit contrast to the increasingly assertive, sexually informed teenage girls who populated the cities and suburbs of 1950s America.[44] She expressed a preference for Pat Boone over Elvis Presley, having been exposed, despite her "primitive life," to popular culture through magazines, radios, and a television at her workplace. Despite the enormous fanfare, Dorothy remained unintimidated by the media glare and material abundance that surrounded her. She seemed to have a poise and sophistication as natural and genuine as her backwoods charm and innocence.

As national magazines like *Newsweek* and *Life* picked up the story, Dorothy Brown—much like Dorothy Counts—temporarily became a national celebrity, even traveling to New York City and meeting Ed Sullivan, the host of the nation's top-rated variety TV program. Now called "Nature Girl," Dorothy also met cynical New York reporters who grilled her, suspecting a hoax of some sort behind the "Long Sam" phenomenon. According to the *Observer*, Dorothy passed their inspection, winning over disbelievers with her natural beauty and charm. As Dorothy took New York by storm, North Carolinians began

In contrast to Dorothy Counts, Dorothy Brown won the support of white North Carolinians and achieved her goal of a quality high school education. She is shown here returning in August 1957 from New York City, where her transformation from impoverished "Nature Girl" to glamorous teen led to numerous press conferences and a meeting with television star Ed Sullivan. Copyright Don Sturkey, 1957. University of North Carolina at Chapel Hill, North Carolina Collection.

to claim her as their own; one *Observer* article ran under the headline, "Our Dorothy Captures Hearts of New York Press and Sullivan."[45]

Those who met Dorothy commented on two especially pleasing personal qualities. First, she had the grace and poise of a finishing-school valedictorian but in a flash could shift back to a little girl persona—cute, giggly, and attuned to simple pleasures. The caption under one pair of photos read, "One Minute . . . a Girl, the Next . . . a Lovely Woman."[46] She also appealed to the public because her character appeared unchanged, even as she experienced an exterior makeover with a new wardrobe and celebrity status. She turned down a part in a Broadway musical of *Li'l Abner* and an appearance on the $64,000 *Quiz Show*, stating her preference for a solid education back home that would prepare her for a secretarial career. The idea that Dorothy's "pure," "natural" beauty and simple goodness could not be altered by exposure to the big city and the good life gave North Carolinians a sense of nostalgic pride, allowing ordinary white North Carolinians to remain secure in their own cosmopolitanism while claiming a purity of heritage and heart that southerners badly needed in the 1950s. Just as the South became fodder for the national press, which saw the region as horrifyingly backward in its racial bigotry and its willingness to resort to violence, "Nature Girl" Dorothy Brown reversed the image of the benighted South by emphasizing the essential innocence and purity of white southern culture.

Dorothy Brown herself rejected the Long Sam and Nature Girl monikers. Sensing some degree of exploitation, she grumbled, "I hate it. It sounds like I live in a cave and bite the heads off of snakes." She wanted the life that circumstances had prevented, the life of a typical white high school girl. On August 23, 1957, the *Observer* announced that the Long Sam saga was drawing to a close in order to fulfill Dorothy's wish. She returned to North Carolina to enroll in the high school program of the Baptist, coeducational Wingate Junior College, planning to complete high school in two years and continue on to junior college with the financial support of her secret sponsor. On September 12, the *Observer* reported on Dorothy's first days in school accompanied by a photo of Dorothy "swapping girl talk" under the celebratory headline, "Dorothy Goes to School."[47]

One item away on the same page, a different headline announced: "*Life* Covers School Integration: N. C. 'Significantly Different.'"[48] The article reported *Life* magazine's assessment that North Carolina had successfully planned and achieved voluntary integration, avoiding the "school trouble" occurring over desegregation elsewhere in the South.

Yet Thursday, September 12, the day Dorothy Brown began high school, was the very same day that Dorothy Counts's father announced that his daughter would leave Harding High because of the racial harassment and violence she had encountered.

What can we learn from these parallel tales? Both Dorothys were unusually ethical, poised girls unintimidated by a challenge. They also held similar goals—to get a good education and improve their lives by taking advantages of opportunities formerly denied them. Dorothy Brown's achievement substituted for the success narrative that never materialized for Dorothy Counts. Allotted an inferior education due to circumstances beyond her control, Dorothy Brown became a local and state hero, even a national celebrity, when good-hearted liberal citizens discovered the injustice and offered their support, heralding her as "Our Dorothy." Although Dorothy Counts fit a similar profile, making national headlines as she claimed a right to better education, white patrons did not reach out to help her, nor did the state claim her as "ours" or commend her good values, commitment to education, and desire for self-improvement.

Ironically, fifty years earlier white girls like Dorothy Brown had become newsworthy when in large numbers they flocked from the country to the city, bringing with them their low IQs, untutored manners, and sexual assertiveness. There middle-class whites, already threatened by urban crime and commercialism, perceived these young migrants as a degenerate group causing social and sexual havoc. Reformers defined their raw beauty, unsophisticated manners, and sexual appeal as a problem, not a cause for celebration. By the 1950s, however, a poor underprivileged white girl like Dorothy Brown could become a cultural hero because of postwar regional transformations. The percentage of isolated, rural, extremely poor families had declined to the point where their daughters did not present a social threat. Country "bumpkins" like Dorothy Brown might be a regional embarrassment, providing material for acerbic hillbilly jokes, but they might also provide comedic relief by poking fun at sophisticated city life, as they did in *Li'l Abner*, where simple, ignorant country folk appeared at once silly but innocently knowing. Middle-class and elite whites no longer perceived poor whites as the greatest threat confronting them. By midcentury they had turned their full attention to the demands of the most disempowered southerners, African Americans, who were newly insistent on exacting civil rights and legal equality.

Not only was Dorothy Brown nonthreatening; she could even represent an ideal type when compared to typical white and black teenage girls. Unlike black teens clamoring for educational access, Dorothy Brown was a single white individual, notable for uniquely appealing qualities, including the gratitude she exhibited for the patronage of wealthy urban professionals like the McKnight family. Black teens acted on their own initiative and with backing from families and the NAACP, one of the most despised political groups among white southerners. Although she was portrayed by the liberal *Observer* as a victim of racial backwardness, Dorothy Counts was not celebrated by the white press for her beauty, fashion sense, or natural elegance. Black teenagers, no matter how admirable, could not become symbols of purity, beauty, innocence, and wholesome desirability without turning the dominant sexual ideology on its head.

Dorothy Counts was not a heroic figure because her misfortune did not appear as a tragedy in the eyes of most southern whites. Her praiseworthy qualities—grace under fire, educational ambition, and dreams of racial equality—were not attributes that many southern whites sought to cultivate among African Americans in their midst. For most, Dorothy Counts was a villain, not a hero—someone who sought unfair and unwelcome purchase on white public space and social status. To segregationists, she was the girl who made whites look crude, violent, and backward in the eyes of the nation and world, even as they succeeded in scaring her away from Harding High. To liberal whites she was a glitch in the system of token integration, a mistake that betrayed the image of goodwill and progressive attitudes attributed to enlightened white North Carolina. Dorothy Counts revealed the lie to the state's claim of racial moderation, for only Dorothy Brown won the education she desired and deserved. A defeated Dorothy Counts formed a blemish in the self-image of righteous white liberals who preferred the reflection of themselves they saw in the discovery of Dorothy Brown and their own beneficent response to her search for education. In Charlotte, the quaint and bubbly Dorothy Brown stood in for the silently demanding Dorothy Counts, creating an alternative tale of justice and goodwill that overshadowed and outshone the real struggle for access to education and full citizenship being waged in their midst.

*L*ittle Rock, Arkansas, was home to the only desegregation plan of 1957 that actually went into effect in the face of statewide opposition, including the hardline refusal of Governor Orville Faubus to quell violence directed at the nine black students enrolled in the city's Central High School. The story is a familiar one, often told as one of the highlights of the 1950s civil rights movement. Whereas most of the South continued a policy of massive resistance and a few upper South states quietly implemented school desegregation policies, Little Rock, Arkansas, became the site of the first major standoff between a state and the federal government over compliance with the *Brown* decision. Little Rock, like many other school districts, had developed a plan of token integration within a pupil placement procedure that would limit the pace and extent of integration in its schools. In the school district's initial act of compliance, nine African American high school students enrolled in Central High School, the jewel of the city's school system (although it had recently been supplanted by a new high school in an upper-middle-class neighborhood slated to remain all-white that year). Little Rock's White Citizens Council rallied to the cause of parents, many of whom were resentful because their working-class and lower-middle-class children would be attending school with black students while those of wealthier parents would remain in lily-white classrooms. In support of their cause, Governor Faubus ordered the state's National Guard to surround Central High on the first day of school, September 23, 1957, to prevent any of the nine black students from crossing the threshold onto school grounds.

Although Faubus's move was rationalized as a measure to preserve the peace in the face of white hostility and possible violence, it was recognized for what it was: resistance to the federal government's attempt to force desegregation on unwilling state governments. The maneuver resulted in a disastrous first day in which Elizabeth Eckford, who had become separated from the group, found herself a solitary figure trying to face down a mob of angry whites. The image of Eckford isolated in a sea of white hatred triggered an outpouring of northern sympathy and outrage at Faubus's tactics, forcing the hand of President Dwight Eisenhower who, once challenged, federalized the Arkansas troops and sent in additional soldiers to ensure that the nine black students would indeed attend Central High, receiving whatever protection they needed on a day-to-day basis. Eisenhower eventually withdrew the additional troops but maintained the federalized Arkansas National Guard as a presence to ensure that the desegregation of Central High continued throughout the 1957–1958 school year.[49]

This intervention and the efforts of sympathetic school staff offered only minimal protection to the nine students; they endured seemingly endless torture at the hands of white students, who mercilessly taunted, shoved, punched, poked, kicked, and otherwise tormented them in the hallways, staircases, lavatories, classrooms, and lunchroom. Not all white students participated, but those who did not remained aloof, failing on the whole to intervene or offer friendship to their struggling black classmates. The black students were under enormous pressure to remain silent and stoic while enduring white aggression, and the task proved too much for one of the nine, Minniejean Brown, who one day dumped a bowl of chili on the head of a white boy in angry retaliation for the relentless harassment. The principal expelled Brown, inspiring white students to pass out cards that bragged, "One down, eight to go." But the other eight managed to stick out the year, which was long enough to see the lone black senior, Ernest Green, graduate in an auditorium that remained absolutely silent when he advanced to the podium to accept his degree. After surviving a year of hellish trauma, the students found that their victory was a Pyrrhic one at best, since Governor Faubus defied a Supreme Court order and closed the entire public school system the following academic year to prevent the continuation of even token integration. Virginia followed suit, while additional southern states employed other strategies to circumvent the law. From 1958 to 1960, the remainder of Eisenhower's presidency, the number of school districts implementing even token integration fell from 712 during the first three years after the *Brown* ruling to a mere forty-nine.[50]

The failure of meaningful integration in Little Rock and elsewhere in the South shows not only the power of white supremacy, but also the extent to which segregationist fears of sexual mixing and interracial marriages were figments of their own frightened imaginations. Predictions that black and white teenagers lured into communion through a shared love of rock 'n' roll would begin to socialize together and become intimate proved false, as did the expectation that increased social contact in "integrated" schools would spawn close relations and interracial dating. The experience of black students at Central High School was almost exclusively one of painful isolation and loss of peer culture.

Melba Pattillo Beals kept a diary of her year at Central High School that later became the basis of her memoir, *Warriors Don't Cry*. Pattillo survived the everyday terror only by shutting down as many feelings as possible, numbing herself to create a hardened warrior persona. As she toughened her exterior, she mourned the loss of her childhood, a loss she described as "the part of my life that existed before integration," before being jolted into instant adulthood. Sensing a premature transformation, she wrote, "I wasn't ready to be grown up—or to not be Melba." "Being Melba" consisted of living life as a "normal girl," marked by close friendships with other girls who shared her interests in music, fashion, boys, and the still forbidden world of dating. Pressed to become a full-time warrior, she yearned for the black peer group she had lost by leaving Horace Mann High School for Central High. Formerly active in her school's choral groups, honor societies, sports, and popular cliques, Melba, along with her black classmates, was banned by the Central administration from participating in any extracurricular activities. Meanwhile, her Horace Mann friends began to shun her as too controversial or simply not part of their everyday high school world.[51]

Melba's biggest disappointment came when only a single guest showed up at her big "sweet sixteen" birthday party. The contrast between this reality and her expectation that sixteen would be the year of her debut, the year "I had planned to launch my campaign to become a popular girl about school," proved to be one of the most painful experiences of her adolescent life. By the winter of 1958 Pattillo had experienced a devastating loss of self, writing in her diary, "I think only the warrior exists in me now. Melba went away to hide. She was too frightened to stay here."[52] Melba Pattillo understood that her adolescent sense of self depended on shared experiences with an affirming group of peers; only then could the "real" Melba explore dating, love, and its relation to her identity as a middle-class "popular" girl.

Ernest Green did not experience as painful a disruption, since his friends from Horace Mann High School kept in contact and invited him to parties and other school social events. But he also remembered his feelings of exclusion as administrators banned him from the high school prom, the school play, and all graduation activities except the formal ceremony. He remembered what would have been a typical senior year as a completely militarized experience. The students traveled to and from school in an army station wagon with jeeps positioned in front and behind with mounted machine guns and armed soldiers. They entered and exited school circled by troops with drawn bayonets. And they spent the school day with paratroopers posted nearby and helicopters hovering above. According to Thelma Mothershed Wair, another black student, the group found themselves so isolated during the school day that the only time they found for ordinary joking, bonding, and socializing among peers occurred as the group gathered at Mrs. Daisy Bates's house right before and after school.[53]

Given these experiences, the students of the Little Rock Nine commented on how far-fetched they found white fears of interracial dating and marriage. In a roundtable discussion between four white and two black Central High students, set up and televised by NBC in October 1957, the students considered the notion of racial mixing. Sammy Dean Parker, the best known among segregationist girls at Central High, responded to a question about why her white peers did not want to attend schools with Negroes. "Well, I think it is mostly race mixing," she replied. Asked to clarify the point, she explained, "Well, marrying each other." Interestingly, Minniejean Brown responded to Parker by emphasizing that the similarities between white girls and black, not their differences, would prevent interracial marriages. "I'm brown, you are white. What's the difference?" probed Brown. "We are all of the same thoughts. You're thinking about your boy—he's going to the Navy. I'm thinking about mine—he's in the Air Force. We think about the same thing"—to which Sammy Dean Parker replied, "I'll have to agree with you." Despite the fact that their topic was interracial dating, neither of them considered the possibility that "their boy" would not be of their same race. Ernest Green chimed in that school and social life were separable, adding that if he merely wanted new friends, "I don't need to be going to school. I can stand on the corner and socialize."[54]

That fall, the main group of students standing on the corner socializing was composed of white students protesting the integration of their school. Like Sammy Dean Parker, these hard-lined segregationists were the most likely to echo the rhetoric about interracial "mixing" that they heard from adults. Yet ironically, these students were probably more involved in interracial cultural activity than the majority of their peers. Journalists and fellow students described those who boycotted classes and instigated violence in Little Rock and Charlotte as "toughs," especially the renegade boys clad in blue jeans and white T-shirts, sporting slicked-back hair. These working-class teens were also most likely to be avid rock 'n' roll fans, absorbing the influence of black culture through R & B and rock songs playing on the radio, on local jukeboxes, or at popular dance spots. Whether performed by black artists like Ruth Brown or Chuck Berry or white stars like Elvis Presley or Jerry Lee Lewis, the musical and stylistic influences of black culture informed the teenage culture of alienated working-class adolescents, who were rebelling not only against desegregation but also against adult authority in general.[55] White teenagers across the South saw absolutely no contradiction in appreciating black-influenced popular teen culture while hating African American students who entered their social world, even in small numbers via the most token efforts toward school integration.

The recollections of white Central High School students of 1957–1958 reveal less about changing racial consciousness than about the great importance they placed on the ordinary events and special cultural rituals of adolescent social life. School dances, clubs and organizations, special activities, and informal sociability all fed into a romanticized senior year in which teenagers sat on top of their adolescent world, riding the crest of teen culture while looking forward to the approaching transition, which for girls often involved engagement and marriage. As Marcia Webb Lucky recalled, "Most of my memories are the real fun ones—homecoming, cheerleading, research papers, the dances, the people you dated, slumber parties, all the fun things that seventeen-year-olds should be doing."[56] As Webb's memory suggests, the romantic heterosexual culture of high school born in the 1940s had grown even stronger in the 1950s, boosted by increased high school attendance, a teen-oriented commercial market, and greater independence from adult oversight.

Barred from formal events and excluded from informal social circles at Harding and Central High Schools, pioneering black students faced the loss of important rites of adolescence and the everyday teen culture that would have otherwise nurtured their identities as they came of age. Surprisingly, white students describe their experiences as marked by similar losses. Oral historian and psychologist Beth Roy interviewed white adults who had attended Central High during that year. They unanimously described the expectation that their senior year would be some sort of pinnacle, an extended moment of once-in-a-lifetime glory marking both an important ending and a transition into the unknown future. Instead, a majority recalled their sense of invasion by outsiders—not just black students but also the military, governor, president, and press. One former student expressed her strong sense of having suffered an injustice, admitting, "I'm bitter over my senior year, which was ruined because they were forced on us. It was ruined." Another recalled a similar disenchantment, remarking, "I just kept thinking, 'This is my senior year, and this is not what I was looking forward to. This is just unfair.' The main reason . . . I resented it so is because . . . it messed up everything for our senior year."[57]

Roy's informants rarely recalled seeing or even hearing about the physical or verbal abuse directed at their black schoolmates. Instead they saw the past in light of the social losses they suffered, even though dances, proms, and other events went on as planned, with black students excluded. One woman tried to explain her sense of grievance as rooted in the meaning of high school and heterosexuality in the 1950s South, explaining, "Lots of these kids got married right out of high school. You know high school, senior year was really a big thing for us . . . I mean it was really big, so we felt it interfered." A male classmate of hers argued that he continued to believe integration could not have succeeded in that context because the necessary social exclusions, given the racial rules and customs observed by whites of that period, would have destroyed the primary experience of high school, which he saw as fundamentally social and not educational. "I mean, we were going to school to see our friends. This was a social time." He justified his opposition to integration on the grounds that adolescence was about "the fun of every day going to school. They weren't part of it. They couldn't have been."[58] Another classmate recalled that his own worries had little to do with integration, but rather consisted of making the football team and "who I'd take to the dance that weekend, trying to win one of those kewpie dolls out at the state fair for some girl." From his standpoint, he wanted his senior year "to be a big deal, and . . . all this," referring to the politics of integration that marred his senior year, "is taking the focus off of me."[59]

If the life of a high school student was about sports, clubs, dating, and the cultivation of adolescent sociability, it is not hard to see why ardent segregationists feared that impressionable adolescents, spurred on by raucous, sexually charged rock 'n' roll music, might over time fail to uphold longstanding prohibitions against open interracial love. But this did not occur in the late 1950s or anytime soon after. Precisely because participating in "normal" student life held such overwhelming importance for both black and white teenagers, they gave little thought to breaking the social conventions that structured their world. Students wanted to be included, not excluded, from a school-based social life that nurtured romantic and sexual possibilities as some of its many satisfactions. They might happily defy adult authority and claim rock 'n' roll music as their own, but they showed far more reluctance to challenge the authority of peers by attempting anything so bold as interracial dating. This held true in black schools as well as white. Students like Dorothy Counts or Elizabeth Eckford were nearly unique among their peers in forgoing the typical life of segregated southern high schools in order to pioneer school desegregation. For most African American students, integration remained a remote possibility, almost unimaginable given the depth of whites' commitment to their own power and privilege. Consequently, experiences like those of the Little Rock Nine hardly registered on the radar screen of their everyday life. They too poured energy into their own adolescent world, either respecting its social and sexual rules or suffering the consequences of ridicule or ostracism if they carved their own path.

Yet this is only part of the story. That few girls chose to risk their reputation by pursuing a relationship with a boy from a different racial, or even class, background turns out to matter less than that girls had acted independently enough in their social and sexual lives to suggest that they might make such a choice. A majority of white southerners desperately feared the loss of racial power and privilege that a truly successful civil rights movement would achieve. As one response to this fear, young and old alike clung to prohibitions against interracial sexual relations—relations that would erode the carefully constructed barriers between white and black persons assigned unequal status. Women's reputation as southern ladies required that they adhere to this and many other restrictions on their sexuality, while men understood that the existing system ensured their power as white men while still leaving them the prerogative of extramarital interracial sex as long as it remained unacknowledged in public discourse or private family relations.

But this investment had become less secure in the postwar years as a younger generation of adolescents carved out their own social space with values and practices that challenged, usually in small ways but potentially on a grander scale, dominant social and sexual conventions. Girls, in particular, had gravitated toward a kind of sexual forwardness formerly associated in white southern culture with tawdry working-class whites and the majority of blacks. In the process they eroded a core tenet of white supremacy—the belief that white women's pure and passive nature made them especially desirable and inordinately vulnerable to sexual assault by black men, and that they therefore must be constantly protected and regulated. This axiom crumbled in the face of widespread expressions of sexual interest among white and black girls of all classes.

Teenagers, rooted in a changing postwar culture that encouraged adolescent autonomy and consumerism, drifted away from a standard of reserved middle-class propriety closely regulated by parents, toward a more explicitly heterosexual culture oriented around immediate pleasure, dating, courtship, and eventual marriage. Within this new culture, some girls explored sexual relations before marriage that included sexual intercourse or even interracial love. Even the majority that did not take such risks, however, exhibited sexual interest and desire through their embrace of black R & B music and the interracial fusion that was rock 'n' roll. In claiming rock music as their own, adolescent girls in the South also registered the changing sexual parame-

ters of their lives, posing a potential threat to both the sexual and racial status quo.

Despite the reputation of the 1950s for gender rigidity and sexual
containment, the sexual assertiveness of southern adolescent girls
contributed to one of the twentieth century's most lasting musical revolutions as well as one of its most profound and abiding racial battles:
the ferocious struggle over school desegregation. Although the vast
majority did not openly rebel against either the sexual or racial codes
of their time, both black and white adolescent girls asserted their social and sexual interests. In the process, they loosened the foundation
of a southern society that systematically privileged whites over blacks
and men over women. They instigated small changes that allowed
subsequent adolescents, mobilized through the student civil rights
movement, to effect major political changes just a few years after the
end of the reputedly complacent 1950s. The decade may be typically
remembered for its "apolitical" teen culture of sock hops and illicit
back-seat necking and petting to the beat of songs like "Wake Up Little Suzie." But Suzie had awakened already.

Sex, Memory, and the Segregated Past

In 1960 Harper Lee published her first and only novel, *To Kill a Mockingbird,* which became an instant best seller. Lee's book won the 1961 Pulitzer Prize and, like *Gone with the Wind* over thirty years earlier, also became a "classic" movie loved by children and adults alike. The novel tells the story of a young tomboy, Scout, growing up in a small Depression-era Alabama town. The book is not quite a coming-of-age narrative, since Scout is eight and nine years old in the novel. Rather, its two entwined stories lead to the dawning of her social conscience, as she becomes aware of class and racial inequalities as well as the expectations of white "ladyhood." One story is about Scout and her older brother Jem's relationship to a mysterious cloistered neighbor, "Boo" Radley, whose reclusive oddness Scout eventually comes to respect. The second narrative tells how the "sleepy," staid little Alabama town is shaken by the arrest, near lynching, then trial and conviction of an innocent black man accused of raping a white teenage girl. Scout's father, Atticus Finch, an attorney and well-respected town leader, represents the accused man, Tom Robinson. Despite his heroic efforts and brilliance in the courtroom, where he presents certain proof of Robinson's innocence, Atticus fails to win justice for his client, who eventually is shot to death. Yet the novel ends on a hopeful note. Harper Lee takes pains to show subtle changes in racial attitudes among a few of the town's more liberal members, while Scout comes to terms with the unfairness of life under Jim Crow and, to a lesser extent, the restrictive rules of the world of respectable woman-hood, which she will soon enter as she grows into adolescence.

The story is one of a few honorable white people and good-hearted black people whose collective power cannot undo the evil of "com-mon" whites who populate the countryside. The commonness of whites is caricatured in the story's villain, Bob Ewell, a shiftless wid-ower and father to countless children. The family lives adjacent to the town garbage dump and scrapes by on Ewell's county welfare check and the town's picked-over trash. He physically and sexually abuses his oldest daughter, nineteen-year-old Mayella, who is driven to such loneliness that she seeks out the company of Tom Robinson, under the guise of asking for help. She then initiates a deadly kiss that, when witnessed by her father, leads Mayella to cry rape to save her-self from shame and her father's violent wrath. Throughout the trial she sticks by her story with absolute determination, claiming her right to female sexual innocence despite the obvious lies and implausi-bilities revealed in her testimony.[1]

To Kill a Mockingbird contains all the stock characters of southern sexual drama: the innocent black male accused of rape; the town's band of white "ladies" who initiate Scout into ladylike manners and morals in the absence of a mother, but fail to stand up against false claims of virtue; the loyal but asexual older black servant woman; lazy and immoral poor whites; and a dangerous poor white teenage girl who, despite her sympathetic status as victim, commits the unfor-givable act of initiating tabooed sexual intimacy with a black man and then alleges rape to deny her complicity. Her impulsive actions bring the town to the brink of mass violence and irreparable hostilities.

Mayella Ewell fictively represents the poor white girls targeted for "reform" in institutions like Samarcand Manor or declared hopelessly degenerate by state eugenic sterilization programs. By the 1940s she would become the wartime pickup girl; by the 1950s, the trouble-making rock 'n' roller and working-class high school student search-ing for fun, romance, and lasting love in the new interlude between childhood and adulthood afforded by high school. Missing from the story are black teenage girls. Their sexuality once again remains the in-visible but necessary mirror held up to reflect (through contrast) white sexual virtue or (through similarity) poor white sexual degeneracy.

While novelist Harper Lee foreshadowed the possibility of a gradual reduction of racial injustice through the conscientious acts of middle-class white liberals, outside the world of fiction young black women had run out of patience and taken matters into their own hands. They stood up against Jim Crow segregation, poverty, political exclusion, and sexual violence when they joined boys and young men in a powerful grassroots civil rights movement based on Gandhian nonviolence and civil disobedience. Some had participated in NAACP youth groups and experimental interracial forums before 1960, but this year proved the turning point as thousands of young black activists—along with fewer but significant numbers of young white activists—sparked a rejuvenated movement through "sit-ins" at local sites of segregation like drugstores, bus stops, or public parks and swimming pools. Although the movement placed issues of desegregation and voter registration first, activists also took aim at the issue of sexual respect and tried to put an end to sexual terrorism in the forms of rape and lynching.[2]

The coincidental publication of To Kill a Mockingbird and the birth of the student-led sit-in movement in 1960 point to a pivotal moment in southern history. The novel vividly portrays the kind of racially infused sexual politics that characterized the South for most of the twentieth century. In contrast, the bold defiance of southern youth in acts of protest signaled the beginning of a new historical era in which the civil rights movement helped spawn other youth-based protest movements for campus democracy, women's rights, peace, and sexual freedom.

Adolescents formed the front lines of the movement for racial justice, risking assault and arrest more often than cautious elders who had more to protect (including their own children). They also emerged as a significant wing of the movement's leadership through the Student Nonviolent Coordinating Committee, or SNCC. Sexual politics was not made a priority; instead activists generally ignored white opponents' charges that interracial marriage and "social equality" were the ulterior motive of the movement. Yet within a few years, the sexual politics of race could not be ignored as white and black youth of both genders worked and lived side by side in movement "houses" and traveled around the rural South recruiting black residents for voter registration campaigns or general support for the movement.

Soon interracial sexual and romantic relationships became visible within the movement and to observant outsiders. The explosive but seemingly remote possibility of white women choosing black male partners, as well as black women interacting openly with white male partners, had come to be. No longer a dreaded future of racial betrayal, interracial relationships provided immediate evidence of the influence of a movement based on love, mutual respect, and fair and equal treatment for all.

The contrasting figure of Mayella Ewell stood for all the "dirty" little secrets of female adolescent sexuality in the southern past—secrets often hidden behind the romanticized ideal of the southern "belle," who had been modernized as the winsome debutante and popular prom queen. Stories like Mayella's and those of the nonfictional girls who populate the chapters of this book place southern adolescent girls at the center of southern history, making the transition from girlhood to womanhood an important subject of inquiry. Tracing the discourse of adolescent sexuality opens up a new view of how conflicts between, and sometimes within, groups of white and black, rich and poor, men and women were publicly negotiated in political and civil society. From rural migrant girls of the 1920s seeking employment and adventure in the city, to teenage girls of the 1950s fawning and fainting over Elvis Presley, the sexuality of adolescent girls mattered—and it drew the attention of politicians, reformers, moralists, novelists, and social critics. Through ongoing debate and myriad policy decisions, power relations were reconfigured around both the symbol of the endangered or dangerous adolescent girl and actual teenage girls who in their daily lives sought not so much to change the South as to navigate between hard reality and imagined possibility.

Debates about sex delinquency, education, and appropriate adolescent behavior were initially articulated around the divide between the righteous morality of the well-to-do and the presumed immorality of the poor, black or white. The underlying concerns within this class discourse, however, always bespoke racial objectives. Whether aimed at uplift or punishment, programs developed by black and white elites to cultivate morality among the poor of their communities were strategies of racial consolidation or improvement. The attempts of ordinary southerners to survive, enjoy, or better their lives were simultaneously, if not always consciously, imbued with both racial and class meanings. By the 1950s, conflicts originally articulated as a clash of class interests took on an explicitly racial cast. As teens developed a more autonomous and widely shared culture in which girls and boys mixed freely, the "mixing" of races as well as classes threatened the core beliefs and social hierarchies that white southerners clung to as the basis of their "way of life." Conflicts about rock 'n' roll and school desegregation continued to reflect class tensions, but the intense conflagrations over Jim Crow laws and white supremacy made race the most prominent issue in public battles over adolescent lives and lusts.

I tell this story of female adolescence as a southern story not to demonstrate the uniqueness or exceptional place of the South in American history, but rather to emphasize the way that the major tensions of the region played themselves out through issues of gender and generation, sex and sociability. The history of adolescent girlhood and sexuality in the South has a particularly charged quality to it, unlike that of other regions. Yet the trajectories of change in southern adolescent lives and the emerging midcentury youth culture are not unique to the region. This book stands as a contribution to the history of adolescence in the United States, recounting a story that has parallel narratives in other regions. Nevertheless, the particular constellation of racial, class, and regional interests at play in the South shaped the experience of every girl who came of age, making her adolescent experience a regional one as well as part of national trends.

The story ends with a conflict that appears most southern: *Brown v. Board of Education,* massive resistance among whites, and the birth of a civil rights movement led, in significant ways, by African American youth of the South. Yet even as the conflict over desegregation in the South exploded into national and international headlines, exposing the persistent "southernness" of the former Confederate states, the battles fought in the South were over the very issues that would define national politics and culture for the rest of the twentieth century. Bitter conflicts over segregation moved quickly to the North, as did a vibrant civil rights movement sparked by politicized high school and college youth. Adult abhorrence of teenage music, dance, and sexual mores escaped the boundaries of the South as generational conflict became a defining attribute of the 1960s and '70s. The state's regulation of reproductive rights, which by the 1950s turned on the question of the personal right of poor, typically young black women to bear children versus a mandated civic obligation to undergo sterilization, spilled over into public revelations of eugenic sterilization policies affecting women of color in every corner of America. Reproductive issues split into two related conflicts that persist today as major battlegrounds in national politics: the fight over whether women have the right to abortion (and other forms of reproductive control) and an embittered politics about spending public monies on "welfare mothers," who are often portrayed as teenage "children having children" at the public expense.

Yet the regional implications of female sexuality and adolescence remain significant for expanding our understanding of the southern past. Public policy consistently sought to regulate youthful female sexuality in order to preserve existing social relations and hierarchies. The creation of moral reformatories initially only for white girls, racially and economically motivated sterilization programs, the targeting of teenage pickup girls in World War II, attacks on rock 'n' roll, and the furious defense of school segregation indicate a persistent effort to contain, punish, or reform the alleged immorality of girls. But the task proved difficult. Whether based on imagined or accurate observations, the unrestrained teenage girl continued to represent the instability not only of individuals and families, but also of an entire social order— that is, the South's increasingly precarious system of patriarchal white supremacy.

The association of adolescent female sexuality with mutability grows in part from the tendency of adolescents to embrace change. Witness the number of girls who pushed the limits of Victorian respectability toward a new kind of sexual liberalism, from the 1920s flappers to the unassuming midcentury adolescents who imbued high school culture with a pervasively heterosexual orientation. When teenage girls purchased fashionable consumer goods, thrilled to the latest trends in popular music and dance, and used dress to realize a desired romance or cause a dramatic change in life circumstances, they diminished adults' confidence in their ability to preserve the status quo or effect needed reforms. Although adolescent actions do not signal revolutionary intent or outcome, the constant pressure from teenage girls, either as symbols of a disturbed society or as initiators of self-interested change, created small fissures in the region's private and public methods of sexual regulation.

Hairline fractures threatened larger breaks in the system, the shattering of a "southern way of life" rooted in entrenched racism, a severely skewed distribution of wealth, and men's commanding role as heads of household and political power brokers. In some cases adolescents challenged authority directly, by protesting against school policies, refusing to honor the lines separating black from white, or rejecting the sexual double standard in favor of sexual daring or potential equality. In other situations, girls created much quieter challenges to the status quo. The simple act of pursuing—in action or through fantasy—a dream of fancy clothing, a fine job, or a respectful loving provider nourished the possibility of change and conferred value not only on the dream but also on the dreamer, usually a girl demeaned as inferior or lacking in worth by more powerful members of society.

If the push and pull between teenage girls and adult attempts to regulate their sexuality remained a constant between 1920 and 1960, the effects of this continuous tension produced anything but stasis. Sexual regulation met with partial success, as the powers of law and custom continued to constrain young women coming of age, limiting their sexual self-determination, social autonomy, and access to education, financial security, and free expression. Yet the sharp edge of resistance chipped away at the apparently rock "solid South." After decades of adolescent girls' straining at the limits of material circumstance and sexual custom, the myth that linked pure, chaste womanhood to whiteness no longer held up as an axiom of southern society.

As the gulf between sexual behavior and stereotype widened, it joined with other forces of change—increased federal intervention, industrial development, African American migration, grassroots activism, and the actions of a few white liberals who dared to risk their social standing—to weaken southern elites' absolute hold on power. The cumulative threat posed by these forces for change tripped off an explosive reaction among defenders of the system, beginning with the vicious battles over school desegregation in the 1950s and '60s and widening into a virulent defense of the entire system of segregation, black political exclusion, the right of southern states to govern as they pleased, and an economic system that privileged the few to the detriment of the many.

The history of adolescent girls and sexuality touches virtually every aspect of more conventional chronologies that span the rise of the "New South" through the region's "Second Reconstruction" (initiated by the mass movement for civil rights). Any economic, cultural, or political history of this period that leaves out adolescent girlhood is necessarily a partial one. Its inclusion is essential for understanding why the apparently solid South was so vulnerable to challenge during this period. It also helps dispel the notion that the 1960s represent a decade of sudden, almost spontaneous change. The struggle over adolescent female sexuality is part of a much longer history of a gathering storm of resistance and the increased vulnerability of southern elites to attacks from agitators who, far from being from the "outside," had grown up within a system they found increasingly intolerable.[3]

The stories we tell matter. The effects of excluding sexuality and girlhood from the chronicle of southern transformation might, at first glance, appear minimal. To the contrary, segregating histories of sexuality and childhood from more familiar political narratives produces some of the same hazards of segregation in other forms. In her brilliant interrogation of the psychology of southern whites, *Killers of the Dream,* Lillian Smith burrows beneath the covers of southern history to reveal an intriguing web of connections between private, personal experiences of coming of age and the much more studied social hierarchies and political antagonisms of race and class in the South.

Smith identifies one of the midcentury South's central problems as the harm caused by separating what happens inside the body, under the surface, from the body's external layer—skin—that crucial predictor of individual experience and social rank. Using a broad definition of segregation, she draws attention to the psychic separation of sexual desire, labeled "bad," from conscious moral belief, the "good." Likening this split to the public segregation of social spaces through signs indicating "colored" and "white," she recalls, "The lesson on segregation was only a logical extension of the lessons on sex . . . Signs put over doors in the world outside and over our minds seemed natural enough to children like us, for signs had already been put over forbidden areas of our body."[4] From Smith, we can derive a concept of "the body politic" in which the sexual body cannot be separated from social bodies, and interior struggles for power and control are reflections of larger political battles for power and control.

This approach necessitates a retelling of southern history, which Smith proceeds to do. She argues that to truly understand and reckon with the South's past one cannot, must not, separate mind from body, sex from power, bodily surfaces from interiors, and personal memory from political belief. In an extended passage, she explains that it is not easy to select from life

> those strands that have to do only with color, only with Negro-white relationships, only with religion or sex, for they are knit of the same fibers that have gone into the making of the whole fabric, woven into its basic patterns and designs. Religion . . . sex . . . race . . . money . . . avoidance rites . . . malnutrition . . . dreams—no part of these can be looked at and clearly seen without looking at the whole of them. For . . . religion is turned into something different by race, and segregation is colored as much by sex as by skin pigment, and money is no longer a coin but a lost wish wandering through a man's whole life.[5]

To Lillian Smith, psychic segregation—in which people learn to split off sexual desires from their racial beliefs, or split off intimate experience from collective memory—leads to a society based on myth, not history. And myths are killers, she attests, of both people and dreams. Embracing Smith's logic, this history of sexual reckonings blends narratives of growing up, which are often focused on personal and sexual desires, with a larger narrative integrating the history of sexuality into a more familiar history of southern political, economic, and cultural development.

During adolescence, maturing youth begin to see themselves as individuals in their own right, as persons not exclusively defined by family. Teenagers gain a sense of self through a process of identification with friends, family, communities, and other groups that create a sense of belonging or, conversely, through disidentifications and exclusions from other social groupings. The concept of identity, then, implies a narrative of the self that unites personal history to the present, a narrative that makes sense out of a lifetime of identifications, social locations, and personal experiences that come to cohere in a sense of who "I" am.

Individual narrative bleeds over into the collective narratives that constitute shared racial and regional identities, eliminating false distinctions between interior and exterior, private and public, or sex and power. It is at the nexus of personal and social memory that social beliefs form—beliefs that in turn can inspire political action. Notions of "self," coming-of-age stories, communal identities, and the embrace of shared racial or regional experience all depend on a layering of stories. Individual memories merge with stories about who is "us" and who is "them," which then underwrite familiar renditions of the past as unvarnished truth. Historians add another layer of interpretation, similarly influenced by subjective experience and collected data that guide us toward historical conclusions. The individual coming-of-age stories of millions of girls who grew to adulthood during these decades remain largely outside of the available historical record. To the extent that we do come to know them, their histories make up the bits and pieces of historical matter from which we draw broader interpretations. Discoveries about the multiple experiences of growing from southern girlhood to womanhood—from the stirrings of private desire to the public controversies they aroused—make visible a reactive, sensitive underside to the more exposed, accepted public skein of southern history.

The histories we tell also have everything to do with our perceptions of the present. Teenage girls have not stopped being an important locus for signs of societal declension or advancement. For the last several decades, adolescent girls and young women have continued to draw notice as the victims or victors of critical historical developments including the sexual revolution, democratized education, and the rise of second- and now third-wave feminism. They have held greatest prominence in battles over sexual power and control, where they have been cast as the dramatic lead in conflicts over abortion, sex education, the availability and advisability of contraception, and vulnerability to sexual assaults ranging from stranger rape to date rape and incest.

Although adults across the political spectrum have expressed interest in the state of adolescent girlhood, the leading voice comes from a revitalized conservative political movement that has ignited a backlash against the growing autonomy of teenage girls. This view pathologized a rise in female sexual independence as the "epidemic" of teenage pregnancy and/or abortion in the 1980s and '90s. Although rates of teenage pregnancy remained fairly consistent with preceding decades, the much greater number of pregnant adolescents who chose not to marry signaled to conservatives the dissolution of marriage, fiscal responsibility, and "family values." Similarly, defenders of the "traditional" family perceived in adolescent autonomy and rebellion the ghost of "missing children," triggering a moral panic about child kidnappers and a revived sexual slave trade. This is in no way meant to deny the occurrence of tragic incidents of kidnapping and sexual enslavement, or the systemic problems they indicate. But the majority of "missing" girls are teenage runaways who forsake family situations they find abusive or otherwise unbearable. Just as danger lurks not only outside but also within family values and behaviors, concern about endangered girlhood is also not limited to the political right. Liberals and feminists especially have raised public awareness of adolescent eating disorders, the unprecedented pressure on girls and young women to achieve academically and professionally while still committing to marriage and motherhood, or simply the pressure that our fast-paced, highly sexualized society places on girls to grow up "too fast."

Those who view adolescents as harbingers of social ills such as crises in family structure or economic and gender inequalities have responded with abundant policies to redress the perceived problems of girls. Yet some observers see hope where others see harm, touting the growing self-confidence of adolescent girls and marshaling evidence of their increased success in sports, education, and on the pathways to professional and political achievement.

Today, as in the past, adolescent girls serve as both attractive and alarming symbols of social change. Their stories matter. Their coming-of-age experiences, however, never have been divorced from the problems and prospects of adults and the broader society. As in the past, we can look from multiple angles at the desires of teenage girls, their halting steps toward realizing an imagined future, the tragedies that mar their lives, and the ordinary ups and downs of daily life. At the most basic level, we can learn from their stories in order to appreciate and comprehend their lives, to value adolescents for who they are and to better understand and respond to their individual and collective needs. But we can also examine their stories as our own. For both the daily lives and trumped-up myths of female adolescence reveal much about our shared problems and progress, rather than something we can pawn off as a result of either the instability of adolescence or, for that matter, the historical backwardness of the South. The lives of adolescent girls, including their sexual desires and decisions, offer insights into a much more expansive set of societal opportunities and obstacles, shared strengths and vulnerabilities, feelings of pride and shame, and the freedoms and injustices for which we bear collective responsibility.

Notes

Abbreviations

AAA	*Annals of the American Academy of Political and Social Science*
ACE Papers	American Council of Education Papers, Hoover Institution Archives, Stanford University
ADAH	Alabama Department of Archives and History, Montgomery
AHC	Atlanta History Center
AVS Papers	Association of Voluntary Sterilization Papers, Social Welfare History Archives, University of Minnesota
CR-CPL	Carolina Room, Charlotte, North Carolina, Public Library
Johnson Papers	Charles S. Johnson Papers, Fisk University Special Collections
Lewis Papers	Nell Battle Lewis Papers, North Carolina State Archives, Raleigh
McGill Papers	Ralph McGill Papers, Woodruff Library Special Collections, Emory University
NA-RG215	National Archives II, Record Group 215, College Park, Md.
NCC-UNC	North Carolina Collection, University of North Carolina Library, Chapel Hill
NCSA	North Carolina State Archives, Raleigh
ORC-NCSA	Old Records Center, North Carolina State Archives, Raleigh
NU Collection	"Neighborhood Union Collection, 1908–1961," Woodruff Library Archives and Special Collections, Atlanta University Center Consortium
PC-CLCP	Pamphlet Collection, Christian Life Commission Publications, Southern Baptist Historical Library and Archives, Nashville
SBHLA	Southern Baptist Historical Library and Archives, Nashville
SHC-BPL	Southern History Collection, Birmingham, Alabama, Public Library
Sibley Papers	John Sibley Papers, Woodruff Library Special Collections, Emory University
SOHP	Southern Oral History Program, Southern History Collection, University of North Carolina, Chapel Hill

SPBWIC   Records of the State Board of Public Welfare, Institutions, and
                Correction, North Carolina State Archives, Raleigh
SPD   Office of Community War Services, Social Protection Division
Winston Papers Ellen Winston Papers, Jackson Library Special Collections,
                University of North Carolina at Greensboro

Introduction

1. Atlanta Board of Education Minutes, vol. 25 (December 12, 1939), ar-
   chived at the Atlanta Board of Education building; *Atlanta Journal,* December 10, 1939, A14.
2. *Atlanta Constitution,* December 13, 1939, 9.
3. Ibid.; *Atlanta Journal,* December 10, 1939, A14; *Life,* December 25, 1939,
   9–13.
4. "'Gone with the Wind': Atlanta Premiere Stirs South to Tears and Cheers,"
   Life, December 25, 1939, 9; *Atlanta Journal,* December 10, 1939.
5. *Atlanta Journal,* December 10, 1939, A14.
6. Margaret Mitchell, *Gone with the Wind* (New York: Warner Books, 1993),
   65.
7. Ibid., 60, 79, 82.
8. Ibid., 5, 83, 90, 105. On Scarlett O'Hara's modernism, see Elizabeth Fox-
   Genovese, "Scarlett O'Hara: The Southern Lady as New Woman," *American Quarterly* 33 (Fall 1981): 391–411.
9. Zora Neale Hurston, *Their Eyes Were Watching God* (Urbana: University of
   Illinois Press, 1978), 24, 23.
10. Ibid., 29, 44.
11. Ibid., 138–139.
12. Joseph F. Kett, *Rites of Passage: Adolescence in America, 1790 to the Present*
    (New York: Basic Books, 1977); and Harvey J. Graff, *Conflicting Paths:
    Growing Up in America* (Cambridge: Harvard University Press, 1995).
13. See, for example, Kathy Peiss, *Cheap Amusements: Working Women and
    Leisure in Turn-of-the-Century New York* (Philadelphia: Temple University
    Press, 1986); Elizabeth Ewen, *Immigrant Women in the Land of Dollars: Life
    and Culture on the Lower East Side* (New York: Monthly Review Press,
    1985); Susan Glenn, *Daughters of the Shtetl: Life and Labor in the Immi-
    grant Generation* (Ithaca, N.Y.: Cornell University Press, 1990); and Nan
    Enstad, *Ladies of Labor, Girls of Adventure* (New York: Columbia Univer-
    sity Press, 1999). On the South, see Jacquelyn Dowd Hall, "Private Eyes,
    Public Women: Images of Class and Sex in the Urban South, Atlanta,
    Georgia, 1913–1915," *Atlanta History* 36, no. 4 (1993): 24–39; Georgina
    Hickey, *Hope and Danger in the New South: Working-Class Women and Ur-
    ban Development, 1890–1940* (Athens: University of Georgia Press, 2003);
    Tera Hunter, *To 'Joy My Freedom: Southern Black Women's Lives and Labors
    after the Civil War* (Cambridge: Harvard University Press, 1996); and
    Nancy Maclean, "The Leo Frank Case Reconsidered: Gender and Sexual

Politics in the Making of Reactionary Populism," *Journal of American History* 78 (December 1991): 917–948.

14. I am grateful to Rickie Solinger for this insight.

15. On the concept of adolescent girlhood, see Catherine Driscoll, *Girls: Feminine Adolescence in Popular Culture and Cultural Theory* (New York: Columbia University Press, 2002), 2–11, 50–71.

16. Mitchell, *Gone with the Wind,* 333, 557.

17. Hurston, *Their Eyes Were Watching God,* 118–119.

18. I have set the chronological parameters of adolescent girlhood as from thirteen through twenty years old, the teen years to the age of majority.

1. *"Holding Excitement in Their Hands"*

"Holding Excitement in Their Hands" is from Jonathan Daniels, *A Southerner Discovers the South* (New York: Macmillan, 1938), 24.

1. G. Stanley Hall, "Flapper Americana Novissima," *Atlantic Monthly* 129 (June 1922): 776.

2. Lorine Pruett, "The Flapper," in her *The New Generation: The Intimate Problems of Modern Parents and Children* (New York: Macaulay, 1930), 572.

3. Nancy Milford, *Zelda: A Biography* (New York: Harper and Row, 1970); see esp. pp. 27–31 on Fitzgerald's development of female characters.

4. *Atlanta Independent,* October 9, 1915, quoted in Tera Hunter, *To 'Joy My Freedom: Southern Black Women's Lives and Labors after the Civil War* (Cambridge: Harvard University Press, 1996), 173.

5. William J. Robertson, *The Changing South* (New York: Boni and Liveright, 1927), 126.

6. Georgina Hickey, *Hope and Danger in the New South City: Working-Class Women and Urban Development, 1890–1940* (Athens: University of Georgia Press, 2003); and Jacquelyn Dowd Hall, "Private Eyes, Public Women: Images of Class and Sex in the Urban South, Atlanta, Georgia, 1913–1915," *Atlanta History* 36, no. 4 (1993): 24–39.

7. On the South in the 1920s, see George Tindall, *The Emergence of the New South, 1913–1945* (Baton Rouge: Louisiana State University Press, 1967); and William A. Link, *The Paradox of Southern Progressivism, 1880–1930* (Chapel Hill: University of North Carolina Press, 1992).

8. Hunter, *To 'Joy My Freedom;* Shane White and Graham White, *Stylin': African American Expressive Culture from Its Beginnings to the Zoot Suit* (Ithaca, N.Y.: Cornell University Press, 1998); Robin D. G. Kelley, "'We Are Not What We Seem': The Politics and Pleasures of Community," in his *Race Rebels: Culture, Politics and the Black Working Class* (New York: Free Press, 1994), 35–54.

9. Joseph F. Kett, *Rites of Passage: Adolescence in America, 1790 to the Present* (New York: Basic Books, 1977), 11–61.

10. Ibid., 111–143, 173–211.

11. Michel Foucault analyzes the creation of new sexual classifications based

on types of persons, rather than behaviors, in the nineteenth century. This includes the "child" but not the "adolescent." See Foucault, *The History of Sexuality,* vol. 1: *An Introduction,* trans. Robert Hurly (New York: Random House, 1978).

12. Howard P. Chudacoff, *How Old Are You? Age Consciousness in American Culture* (Princeton, N.J.: Princeton University Press, 1989), 65–67; Kett, *Rites of Passage,* 204–210; Emily Cahan et al., "The Elusive Historical Child: Ways of Knowing the Child of History and Psychology," in Glen H. Elder, John Modell, and Russ D. Parke, eds., *Children in Time and Place: Developmental and Historical Insights* (New York: Cambridge University Press, 1993), 215–216.

13. G. Stanley Hall, *Adolescence* (New York: D. Appleton and Co., 1904); Kett, *Rites of Passage,* 205–244; Harvey J. Graff, *Conflicting Paths: Growing Up in America* (Cambridge: Harvard University Press, 1995).

14. G. Stanley Hall, *Youth: Its Education, Regimen, and Hygiene* (New York: D. Appleton, 1907), 135, quoted in Chudacoff, *How Old Are You?,* 677.

15. Kathy Peiss, *Cheap Amusements: Working Women and Leisure in Turn-of-the-Century New York* (Philadelphia: Temple University Press, 1986); Elizabeth Ewen, *Immigrant Women in the Land of Dollars: Life and Culture on the Lower East Side* (New York: Monthly Review Press, 1985); Susan Glenn, *Daughters of the Shtetl: Life and Labor in the Immigrant Generation* (Ithaca, N.Y.: Cornell University Press, 1990); and Nan Enstad, *Ladies of Labor, Girls of Adventure* (New York: Columbia University Press, 1999).

16. Jane Addams, *The Spirit of Youth and the City Streets* (Urbana: University of Illinois Press, 1972).

17. Paula Fass, *The Damned and the Beautiful: American Youth in the 1920s* (New York: Oxford University Press, 1977), 13.

18. Ibid., 260–290; Beth Bailey, *From Front Porch to Back Seat: Courtship in Twentieth-Century America* (Baltimore: Johns Hopkins University Press, 1988), 13–96; Ellen K. Rothman, *Hands and Hearts: A History of Courtship in America* (New York: Basic Books, 1984), 203–244.

19. H. L. Mencken, "Uprising in the Confederacy," *American Mercury* 22 (March 1931): 380.

20. Tindall, *Emergence of the New South,* 184–218.

21. "Digest of Education Statistics," Office of Educational Research and Improvement, Congressional Information Service, Inc., Washington, D.C., March 2000, 17; "120 Years of Education, A Statistical Portrait," U.S. National Center for Education Statistics, 1900–1985, *Digest of Education Statistics,* no. 1425 (1993).

22. Howard W. Odum, *Southern Regions of the United States* (Chapel Hill: University of North Carolina Press, 1936), 502. On Mississippi, see James Anderson, *The Education of Blacks in the South, 1860–1935* (Chapel Hill: University of North Carolina Press, 1988), 235.

23. "Freshmen in Georgia Colleges," *School and Society* 30 (November 23, 1929): 716; and "The Accreditation of the Negro High School," *Journal of Negro Education* 1 (April 1932): 34–43.

24. "Rural Schools in North Carolina," *School and Society* 32 (September 20, 1930): 387; and "Accreditation of the Negro High School," 34–43.

25. By 1930, the average number of school days in U.S. schools, including the South, amounted to 173, while a study of eight southern states showed that the average was 153 days. The term for black students amounted to only 134 days per year—thirty-nine days, or almost eight weeks, less schooling than the average American child received. William G. Carr, "Public Education in the South," *School and Society* 33 (April 11, 1931): 491.

26. National Emergency Council report "Economic Conditions of the South" (1938), cited in a State of Virginia 1939 report on "Expanding Education to Meet the Needs of Rural Community Life," box 5224, folder 5602, "Va. Dept. of Ed.—HS Curriculum Revision, Reports and Pamphlets," General Education Board Papers, Rockefeller Archive Center, Sleepy Hollow, N.Y.

27. O. Latham Hatcher, *Rural Girls in the City for Work* (Richmond: Garrett and Massie, 1930), vii, xv.

28. Ibid., 83–84.

29. Ibid., 41.

30. Ted Ownby, *Subduing Satan: Religion, Recreation, and Manhood in the Rural South, 1865–1920* (Chapel Hill: University of North Carolina Press, 1990), 167–212; Douglas Carl Abrams, *Selling the Old-Time Religion: American Fundamentalists and Mass Culture, 1920–1940* (Athens: University of Georgia Press, 2001), 64–75.

31. Abrams, *Selling the Old-Time Religion*, 66–67, 102; Victor I. Masters, *Making America Christian* (Atlanta: Home Mission Board of the Southern Baptist Convention, 1921), quoted in Ownby, *Subduing Satan*, 203.

32. Robertson, *Changing South*, 126.

33. Hunter, *To 'Joy My Freedom*, 136–140; Jacqueline Anne Rouse, *Lugenia Burns Hope: Black Southern Reformer* (Athens: University of Georgia Press, 1989); Evelyn Brooks Higginbotham, *Righteous Discontent: The Women's Movement in the Black Baptist Church, 1880–1920* (Cambridge: Harvard University Press, 1993), 185–229; Dorothy Salem, *To Better Our World: Black Women in Organized Reform, 1890–1920* (Brooklyn: Carlson Publishing, 1990), 181–197; Christina Simmons, "African Americans and Sexual Victorianism in the Social Hygiene Movement, 1910–40," *Journal of the History of Sexuality* 4 (July 1993): 60.

34. Ted Ownby, *American Dreams in Mississippi: Consumers, Poverty, and Culture, 1830–1998* (Chapel Hill: University of North Carolina Press, 1999), 111–112.

35. Nancy MacLean, *Behind the Mask of Chivalry: The Making of the Second Ku Klux Klan* (New York: Oxford University Press, 1994), 113, 115.

36. "Negro Problems in Cities," *Home Mission College Review* 2 (May 1928): 41.

37. William McGlothlin in the *Gaffney Ledger*, September 8, 1921, quoted in Ownby, *Subduing Satan*, 203.

38. MacLean, *Behind the Mask of Chivalry*, 104.

39. Clifford M. Kuhn, Harlon E. Joye, and E. Bernard West, *Living Atlanta: An*

Oral History of the City, 1914–1948 (Athens: University of Georgia Press, 1990), 37.

40. Ibid., 176, 293–302.
41. Ibid., 173–177, 289–295. On racial interzones, see Kevin J. Mumford, *Interzones: Black/White Sex Districts in Chicago and New York in the Early Twentieth Century* (New York: Columbia University Press, 1997).
42. Edith Farrell, Visiting Teacher Report on Columbus, Georgia; box 2, folder 17, Commonwealth Fund Papers, Rockefeller Archive Center; Mary Lethert Wingerd, "Rethinking Paternalism: Power and Parochialism in a Southern Mill Village," *Journal of American History* 83 (December 1996): 876.
43. A. P. Carter, "Single Girl, Married Girl," A. P. Carter, Peer International Corp. (BMI), 1927.
44. Hatcher, *Rural Girls in the City,* 17, 72.
45. Ibid., 72.
46. Margaret C. Brietz, "Case Studies of Delinquent Girls in North Carolina," master's thesis, University of North Carolina, Chapel Hill, 1927, 84–92; quote, 88.
47. Bruce Bliven, "Away Down South," *New Republic* 10 (1927): 296, quoted in Tindall, *Emergence of the New South,* 98.
48. Tindall, *Emergence of the New South,* 95.
49. William H. Jones, *Recreation and Amusement among Negroes in Washington, D.C.: A Sociological Analysis of the Negro in an Urban Environment* (Washington, D.C.: Howard University Press, 1927), 121.
50. Deborah Gray White, "The Cost of Club Work, the Price of Black Feminism," in Nancy Hewitt and Suzanne Lebsock, eds., *Visible Women: New Essays on American Activism* (Urbana: University of Illinois Press, 1993), 258–260; Higginbotham, *Righteous Discontent,* 185–229; Simmons, "African Americans and Sexual Victorianism," 51–75; Salem, *To Better Our World,* 45–108; Stephanie J. Shaw, *What a Woman Ought to Be and to Do: Black Professional Women Workers during the Jim Crow Era* (Chicago: University of Chicago Press, 1996), 17–30; Hazel V. Carby, "Policing the Black Woman's Body in an Urban Context," *Critical Inquiry* 18 (Summer 1992): 738–755.
51. Mary McLeod Bethune, "Objectives of the National Association of Colored Women, Inc." *Home Mission College Review* 1 (March 1928): 12–13.
52. The quotation is from Simmons, "African Americans and Sexual Victorianism," 61. On the National Training School for Women and Girls, see Higginbotham, *Righteous Discontent,* 210–221; and Victoria W. Woolcott, "'Bible, Bath, and Broom': Nannie Helen Burroughs's National Training School and African-American Racial Uplift," *Journal of Women's History* 9 (Spring 1997): 88–110.
53. *The Campus Mirror,* February 15, 1928, Spelman College Archives.
54. *The Blue Bear,* 1930, College Year Book, Livingstone College Archives.
55. Tindall, *Emergence of the New South,* 273. See also "Enrollment in Negro Universities and Colleges," *School and Society* 28 (September 29, 1928): 401–403. The number rose from 5,231 to 22,609 between 1921 and 1931.

56. Shaw, *What a Woman Ought to Be and to Do*, 21–26, 83–89.

57. Jacquelyn Dowd Hall, *Revolt against Chivalry: Jessie Daniel Ames and the Women's Campaign against Lynching* (New York: Columbia University Press, 1979).

58. Dubose Heyward, *Mamba's Daughters* (New York: Doubleday, 1929). Jack Temple Kirby discusses the novel in *Media-Made Dixie: The South in the American Imagination* (Baton Rouge: Louisiana State University Press, 1978), 64–69.

59. Ibid., 207.

60. Ibid., 249.

61. Ibid., 303.

62. William Faulkner, *Sanctuary* (ca. 1931; New York: Vintage International, 1993). The book sold seven thousand copies in its first two months (compared to *The Sound and the Fury* sales of 1,800 in eighteen months). In 1932 it came out in a new Modern Library edition and continued to sell well, outselling all other Faulkner novels throughout the 1930s. Paramount Pictures bought the film rights and produced the movie as *The Story of Temple Drake* in 1933, followed in 1961 by a Twentieth Century Fox film version called *Sanctuary*. See A. Nicholas Fargnoli and Michael Golay, *William Faulkner A to Z* (New York: Facts on File, 2002), 199; Linda W. Wagner, "William (Cuthbert) Faulkner," *Dictionary of Literary Biography*, vol. 9: *American Novelists, 1910–1945*, ed. James J. Martine (Detroit: Gale Group, 1981), 282–302.

63. Faulkner, *Sanctuary*, 317.

64. Ibid., 51.

65. On the relation of culture to politics, I benefited from Melani McAlister, "A Cultural History of the War without End," *Journal of American History* 89 (September 2000): 441.

2. Spirited Youth or Fiends Incarnate?

1. Faced with possible execution, the young women pleaded guilty even though only two girls admitted they had anything to do with setting the fires. They were advised, erroneously, that even with the guilty plea, the charges would be dropped if their innocence was established. See Lewis Papers, including Samarcand clippings.

2. *Elizabeth City Daily Advance*, April 22, 1931.

3. Documentation on the arson trial and on the institutional history of Samarcand comes from several sources: Lewis Papers; SBPWIC, some of which are located at NCSA and others of which are at ORC-NCSA; "Prisons in North Carolina" clipping file in NCC-UNC; and the published "Biennial Reports of the State Home and Industrial School for Girls" (available at NCC-UNC). See also John Wertheimer and Brian Luskey, "'Escape of the Match-Strikers': Disorderly North Carolina Women, the Legal System, and the Samarcand Arson Case of 1931," *North Carolina Historical Review* 75, no. 4 (1998): 435–460; and Susan Pearson, "Samarcand,

Nell Battle Lewis, and the 1931 Arson Trial," honors essay, April 7, 1989, NCC-UNC.

4. See Ruth Alexander, *The "Girl Problem": Female Sexual Delinquency in New York, 1900–1930* (Ithaca, N.Y.: Cornell University Press, 1995); Joanne J. Meyerowitz, *Women Adrift: Independent Wage Earners in Chicago, 1880–1930* (Chicago: University of Chicago Press, 1988); Mary E. Odem, *Delinquent Daughters: Protecting and Policing Adolescent Female Sexuality in the United States, 1885–1920* (Chapel Hill: University of North Carolina Press, 1995); Regina Kunzel, *Fallen Women, Problem Girls: Unmarried Mothers and the Professionalization of Social Work, 1880–1945* (New Haven: Yale University Press, 1993), 36–64; and Constance A. Nathanson, *Dangerous Passage: The Social Control of Sexuality in Women's Adolescence* (Philadelphia: Temple University Press, 1991).

5. Anne Firor Scott, *The Southern Lady: From Pedestal to Politics, 1830–1930* (Chicago: University of Chicago Press, 1970).

6. Odem, *Delinquent Daughters;* Victoria Getis, "Experts and Juvenile Delinquency, 1900–1935," in Joe Austin and Michael Nevin Willard, eds., *Generations of Youth: Youth Cultures and History in Twentieth-Century America* (New York: New York University Press, 1998), 21–35; and John R. Sutton, *Stubborn Children: Controlling Delinquency in the United States, 1640–1981* (Berkeley: University of California Press, 1988).

7. Odem, *Delinquent Daughters,* 8–37.

8. Twenty-nine of these had been established after 1910, many with federal funds made available during World War I in an effort to eliminate the threat to soldiers' morale and health presented by prostitution and venereal disease. Margaret Reeves, *Training Schools for Delinquent Girls* (New York: Russell Sage, 1929), 18–20, 42–46. See also ibid., 116; Barbara Brenzel, *Daughters of the State: A Social Portrait of the First Reform School for Girls in North America, 1865–1905* (Cambridge: MIT Press, 1983); and Nicole Hahn Rafter, *Partial Justice: Women, Prisons and Social Control* (New Brunswick, N.J.: Transaction, 1990).

9. Of the fifty-seven schools examined by Reeves in 1924, nine were for African American girls; of these only four received primary funding by the state, with the other five depending on private charity. A later study by the Osborne Association found that the only exception to segregationist policies in southern reformatories was Kentucky, although within the institution inmates continued to be segregated by both race and sex. Reeves, *Training Schools,* 42–43; Osborne Association, *Handbook of American Institutions for Delinquent Juveniles,* vol. 2: *Kentucky–Tennessee* (1940), and vol. 4: *Virginia–North Carolina* (1943) (New York: Osborne Association). See also Lee S. Polansky, "I Certainly Hope That You Will Be Able to Train Her: Reformers and the Georgia Training School for Girls," in Elna C. Green, ed., *Before the New Deal: Social Welfare in the South, 1830–1930* (Athens: University of Georgia Press, 1999), 138–159.

10. *Charlotte Observer,* February 19, 1939, in box 163, folder "North Carolina

Industrial Training School for Negro Girls, 1919–1934," SBPWIC, ORC-NCSA.

11. Pearson, "Samarcand," 5.

12. O. Latham Hatcher, *Rural Girls in the City for Work: A Study Made for the Southern Women's Educational Alliance* (Richmond: Garrett and Massie, 1930); Nora Miller, *The Rural Girl in the Rural Family* (Chapel Hill: University of North Carolina Press, 1935), 106–107.

13. *Biennial Reports of the North Carolina Charitable, Penal, and Correctional Institutions* (Raleigh, N.C.: Capital Printing, 1926–1936).

14. "Governor Will Investigate," *American Standard,* October 19, 1928; "An inmate" to Alabama Governor Graves, November 7, 1928, in Alabama Governors (1927–1931): Graves—Admin. files, SG21171, folder 4, "State Training School for Girls," ADAH.

15. "Samarcand Girls Riot in Moore County Jail," *Moore County News,* April 30, 1931. Other reports indicate that this account is highly exaggerated. Nevertheless, it is the description that the residents of Moore County received.

16. *Elizabeth City Daily Advance,* April 22, 1931.

17. On the New South, see Dewey W. Grantham, *The South in Modern America: A Region at Odds* (New York: HarperCollins, 1994); Edward Ayers, *The Promise of the New South: Life after Reconstruction* (New York: Oxford University Press, 1992); Jacqueline Jones, *The Dispossessed: America's Underclass from the Civil War to the Present* (New York: Basic Books, 1992); and Jack Kirby, *Rural Worlds Lost: The American South, 1920–1960* (Baton Rouge: Louisiana State University Press, 1987).

18. Mrs. Herbert Peele, *Elizabeth City Daily Advance,* April 22, 1931; "Rebellious Girls Set Their Bunks Afire to Get Thrill," *Raleigh News and Observer,* May 2, 1931.

19. Arson clippings in box 164, folder "Samarcand Manor, 1918–1924," SBPWIC—Samarcand, ORC-NCSA.

20. "Rebellious Girls," *Raleigh News and Observer,* May 2, 1931; and "Samarcand Girls," *Moore County News,* April 30, 1931.

21. By "modernity" I refer to a regional transformation involving large-scale immigration from rural to urban areas, the growth of a manufacturing sector, the extension of a cash-based consumer economy, and a regional self-consciousness of "becoming modern."

22. According to Lewis's records, nine of the sixteen defendants (including an incest victim) reported having had intercourse between the ages of twelve and fifteen. Several others denied having had intercourse but were strongly suspected by reformatory officials of having committed acts of prostitution and/or having had sexual intercourse.

23. "Rebellious Girls," *Raleigh News and Observer,* May 2, 1931.

24. Biographical information is drawn from the Lewis Papers and from Darden Asbury Pyron, "Nell Battle Lewis (1892–1956) and 'The New Southern Womanhood,'" in James C. Cobb and Charles R. Wilson, eds.,

Perspectives on the American South: An Annual Review of Society, Politics and Culture, vol. 3 (New York: Bordon and Breach Science Publishers, 1985), 63–85 (the *Raleigh News and Observer* quote is on p. 70).

25. Pyron, "Nell Battle Lewis," 73–74.

26. Box 164, folder "Samarcand Manor, 1925–31," SBPWIC—Samarcand, ORC-NCSA.

27. Margaret C. Brietz, "Case Studies of Delinquent Girls in North Carolina," master's thesis, University of North Carolina, Chapel Hill, 1927.

28. Ibid., 65, 51.

29. Clarence C. Church, "The New Psychology Applied to the Adolescent Girl," *South Atlantic Quarterly* 21 (July 1922): 212–213.

30. Brietz, "Case Studies," 122, 134, 177.

31. Ibid., 171–204. On eugenic thought, see Mark H. Haller, *Eugenics: Hereditarian Attitudes in American Thought* (New Brunswick, N.J.: Rutgers University Press, 1984); and Philip R. Reilly, *The Surgical Solution: A History of Involuntary Sterilization in the United States* (Baltimore: Johns Hopkins University Press, 1991).

32. Brietz, "Case Studies," 226.

33. Ibid., 186.

34. Victoria Bynum, *Unruly Women: The Politics of Social and Sexual Control in the Old South* (Chapel Hill: University of North Carolina Press, 1992).

35. Nancy MacLean, "Leo Frank Case Reconsidered: Gender and Sexual Politics in the Making of Reactionary Populism," *Journal of American History* 78 (December 1991): 917–948; Jacquelyn Dowd Hall, "Private Eyes, Public Women: Images of Class and Sex in the Urban South, Atlanta, Georgia, 1913–1915," *Atlanta History* 36, no. 4 (1993): 24–39.

36. Nancy MacLean, *Behind the Mask of Chivalry: The Making of the Second Ku Klux Klan* (New York: Oxford University Press, 1994), 98–124; and Nancy MacLean, "White Women and Klan Violence in the 1920s: Agency, Complicity, and the Politics of Women's History," *Gender and History* 3 (Autumn 1991): 285–303.

37. Rebecca Latimer Felton, "Education of Veterans' Daughters," 1893 speech quoted in LeAnn Whites, "Rebecca Latimer Felton and the Problem of 'Protection' in the New South," in Nancy Hewitt and Suzanne Lebsock, eds., *Visible Women: New Essays on American Activism* (Urbana: University of Illinois Press, 1993), 51.

38. Clippings File, "Reformatories—Ala.—Girls," Southern History Department, Birmingham Public Library.

39. James Goodman, *Stories of Scottsboro* (New York: Vintage, 1994).

40. The only access to working-class opinion I found was in institutional records of parental responses to daughters sentenced to Samarcand. They suggest that although many poor urban and rural parents sought criminal sanctions against their troublesome daughters, they were often dismayed at the harshness of the legal system's response.

41. "The Sisters from Samarcand and Question of Psychiatry," *Raleigh Times*, n.d., Samarcand clippings, Lewis Papers.

42. *Fayetteville Observer,* May 4, 1931.
43. Ibid.
44. "Samarcand Girls Riot," *Moore County News,* April 30, 1931.
45. Arson clippings in box 164, folder "Samarcand Manor, 1918–1924," SBPWIC—Samarcand, ORC-NCSA.
46. Brietz, "Case Studies," 156–160.
47. "Idiots, Imbeciles and Morons at Caswell," *Greensboro Daily News,* December 10, 1922.
48. Elizabeth Lunbeck, "'A New Generation of Women': Progressive Psychiatrists and the Hypersexual Female," *Feminist Studies* 13 (Fall 1987): 513–543.
49. Pamela Haag, "In Search of the 'Real Thing': Ideologies of Love, Modern Romance, and Women's Sexual Subjectivity in the United States, 1920–1940," *Journal of the History of Sexuality* 2, no. 4 (1992): 547–577.
50. Ibid., 547–577. The quote, from p. 557, is from Winifred Richmond, *The Adolescent Girl: A Book for Parents and Teachers* (New York: Macmillan, 1929), 117.
51. *Samarcand Biennial Reports* (Raleigh: Capital Printing, 1920s–1940s).
52. Casebook, Lewis Papers.
53. A particularly helpful conceptualization of identity formation is offered by Lisa Duggan, who defines identity as "a narrative of a subject's location within social structure," or as situating "stories" that "traverse the space between the social world and subjective experience . . . connecting self and world." See Duggan, "The Trials of Alice Mitchell: Sensationalism, Sexology, and the Lesbian Subject in Turn-of-the-Century America," *Signs* 18 (Summer 1993): 793.
54. Brietz, "Case Studies," 187–204.
55. Case book, Lewis Papers.
56. Letter, March 16, 1931, in Governor Graves—Admin. Files, SG19949, folder 1, ADAH.
57. Alexander, *"Girl Problem."*
58. N.d., box 164, SBPWIC—Samarcand, ORC-NCSA.
59. I found additional case-record information on Samarcand residents in the records of former inmates later incarcerated at the State Industrial Farm Colony for Women. To protect the women's privacy, I do not use names from these case records. This quote was from Case 463, Farm Colony Records, "North Carolina Board of Correction and Training—State Industrial Farm Colony for Women, Case Histories," ORC-NCSA.
60. Case 410, Farm Colony Records, ORC-NCSA.
61. Case 17, Farm Colony Records, ORC-NCSA.
62. "Lash Used, Governor Will Investigate," *American Standard,* October 19, 1928; and "An inmate" to Governor Graves, November 7, 1928.
63. Case 600, Farm Colony Records, ORC-NCSA.
64. Case 670, Farm Colony Records, ORC-NCSA.
65. Box 164, folder "Samarcand Manor, 1931," SBPWIC—Samarcand, ORC-NCSA.

66. The 1931 investigation into Samarcand included the finding that "girls giving a great deal of trouble in institution are discharged. Girls have learned that incorrigibility is the quickest method of getting away and some conduct themselves accordingly." Box 164, folder "Samarcand Manor, 1931," SBPWIC—Samarcand, ORC-NCSA.

67. Casebook, Lewis Papers. The incest victim, incarcerated without any charge of criminal wrongdoing, was one of those convicted of arson and committed to state prison.

68. "Prisons in North Carolina," Clippings File, NCC-UNC.

69. Between 1929 and 1947, of North Carolina's 1,901 "eugenic sterilizations" 1,494 were performed on females, with 1,260 of the total performed on "feeble-minded" individuals, a classification that included an overwhelmingly female population. See Eugenics Board of North Carolina, "Biennial Reports," NCC-UNC; Moya Woodside, *Sterilization in North Carolina: A Sociological and Psychological Study* (Chapel Hill: University of North Carolina Press, 1950); Johanna Schoen, *Choice and Coercion: Birth Control, Sterilization, and Abortion in Public Health and Welfare* (Chapel Hill: University of North Carolina Press, 2005); and Edward J. Larson, *Sex, Race, and Science: Eugenics in the Deep South* (Baltimore: Johns Hopkins University Press, 1995).

3. *"Just as Much a Menace"*

1. Loose card in records of the N.C. Training School for Negro Girls, box 163, folder "N.C. Industrial Training School for Negro Girls, n.d., 1919–1934," SBPWIC, ORC-NCSA.

2. North Carolina Federation of Negro Women's Clubs, "An Open Letter to the People of North Carolina," November 22, 1938, box 163, folder "North Carolina Industrial Training School for Negro Girls, 1935–1938," SBPWIC, ORC-NCSA.

3. On African American middle-class reform, see Anne Firor Scott, "Most Invisible of All: Black Women's Voluntary Associations," *Journal of Southern History* 56 (February 1990): 3–22; Stephanie J. Shaw, *What a Woman Ought to Be and to Do: Black Professional Women Workers during the Jim Crow Era* (Chicago: University of Chicago Press, 1996); Dorothy Salem, *To Better Our World: Black Women in Organized Reform, 1890–1920* (Brooklyn: Carlson Publishing, 1990); Deborah Gray White, "The Cost of Club Work, the Price of Black Feminism," in Nancy Hewitt and Suzanne Lebsock, eds., *Visible Women: New Essays on American Activism* (Urbana: University of Illinois Press, 1993), 247–269; Evelyn Brooks Higginbotham, *Righteous Discontent: The Women's Movement in the Black Baptist Church, 1880–1920* (Cambridge: Harvard University Press, 1993); and Paula Giddings, *When and Where I Enter: The Impact of Black Women on Race and Sex in America* (New York: Perennial, 2001).

4. Joan Marie Johnson, "The Colors of Social Welfare in the New South: Black and White Clubwomen in South Carolina, 1900–1930," in Elna

Green, ed., *Before the New Deal: Social Welfare in the South, 1830–1930* (Athens: University of Georgia Press, 1999), 160–180.

5. "Moral Advancement in North Carolina," *Danville Register*, February 20, 1931, in Harriet L. Herring clipping file, NCC-UNC.

6. Deborah Gray White, *Ar'n't I a Woman: Female Slaves in the Plantation South* (New York: W. W. Norton, 1999), 91–118.

7. Giddings, *When and Where I Enter*, 17–32.

8. Higginbotham, *Righteous Discontent*, 185–229; Darlene Clark Hine, "Rape and the Inner Lives of Black Women in the Middle West: Preliminary Thoughts on the Culture of Dissemblance," *Signs* 14 (Summer 1989): 912–920.

9. Martha Hodes, "The Sexualization of Reconstruction Politics: White Women and Black Men in the South after the Civil War," *Journal of the History of Sexuality* 3 (January 1993): 402–417.

10. Giddings, *When and Where I Enter*, 85–118; Hine, "Rape and the Inner Lives of Black Women," 912–920.

11. Higginbotham, *Righteous Discontent*, 88–119.

12. Hazel Carby, "Policing the Black Woman's Body in an Urban Context," *Critical Inquiry* 18 (Summer 1992): 738–739; George Tindall, *The Emergence of the New South, 1913–1945* (Baton Rouge: Louisiana State University Press, 1967), 77–95, 145–148; and Reynolds Farley, "The Urbanization of Negroes in the United States," *Journal of Social History* 1 (1967–1968): 255, 259.

13. Hortense Powdermaker, *After Freedom: A Cultural Study in the Deep South* (ca. 1939; New York: Atheneum, 1968), 70.

14. On urban working-class culture, see Higginbotham, *Righteous Discontent*, 198–200; Carby, "Policing the Black Woman's Body," 737–755; Tara Hunter, *To 'Joy My Freedom: Southern Black Women's Lives and Labors after the Civil War* (Cambridge: Harvard University Press, 1997), 145–186; and Robin D. G. Kelley, "'We Are Not What We Seem': The Politics and Pleasures of Community," in his *Race Rebels: Culture, Politics, and the Black Working Class* (New York: Free Press, 1994), 35–53.

15. "Along the Color Line," *Crisis* 1 (March 1911): 7–8.

16. Sadie Iola Daniel, *Women Builders* (ca. 1931; Washington, D.C.: Associated Publishers, 1970), 53–78; Jacqueline Anne Rouse, *Lugenia Burns Hope: Black Southern Reformer* (Athens: University of Georgia Press, 1989), 57–90.

17. Rouse, *Lugenia Burns Hope*, 65–69; *Chicago Defender* clipping, no title, October 31, 1925, box 7, folder 26, "Neighborhood Union Collection, 1908–1961," NU Collection; and 1925 brochure, box 13, folder 3, NU Collection.

18. Daniel, *Women Builders*, 53–61; and "Virginia Industrial School for Colored Girls," in Osborne Report, *Handbook of American Institutions for Delinquent Juveniles*, vol. 4: *Virginia–North Carolina* (New York: Osborne Association, 1943), 352–354.

19. "Vocational School for Girls—Tullahoma, Tennessee," in Osborne Report,

Handbook, vol. 2: *Kentucky–Tennessee* (New York: Osborne Association, 1940), 205.

20. Box 229, "Dept. of Social Sciences—Studies—Nashville," folder "Juvenile Courts," Johnson Papers; and Osborne Report, "Vocational School for Girls," in *Handbook,* vol. 2, 244–245.

21. Ruby Mitchell Kelley, "An Analysis of the Factors Associated with the Delinquency of Twenty-Five Girls Committed to the Georgia Training School for Negro Girls for 1943–1947," master's thesis, Atlanta University School of Social Work, 1948, 11–14.

22. Glenda Gilmore, *Gender and Jim Crow: Women and the Politics of White Supremacy in North Carolina, 1896–1920* (Chapel Hill: University of North Carolina Press, 1996); and Daniel, *Women Builders,* 137–167.

23. *Sixth Biennial Report of the State Home and Industrial School for Girls and Women (Samarcand Manor), 1928–1930* (Raleigh: Capital Printing, 1930), 7.

24. Deborah Gray White, "The Cost of Club Work, the Price of Black Feminism," in Hewitt and Lebsock, *Visible Women,* 247–269.

25. Kelley, "Analysis," 11–22.

26. Daniel, *Women Builders,* 137–167; and Gilmore, *Gender and Jim Crow,* 177–202.

27. "Virginia State Legislature Commends Race Women," *Chicago Defender,* July 20, 1918, in Janie Porter Barrett Papers, Hampton University Archives.

28. "A Survey of Some Resources for Negroes in North Carolina," n.d. (ca. 1943), in box 225, "Dept. of Public Welfare—Work among Negroes," ORC-NCSA.

29. On rural to urban labor-force migration, see Pete Daniel, *Lost Revolutions: The South of the 1950s* (Chapel Hill: University of North Carolina Press, 2000), 39–47, 91–94; and David R. Goldfield, *Black, White, and Southern: Race Relations and Southern Culture, 1940 to the Present* (Baton Rouge: Louisiana State University Press, 1990).

30. A. W. Cline, Supt. of Welfare of Forsythe County, to Mrs. W. T. Bost, State Commissioner of Public Welfare, in box 163, folder "North Carolina Training School for Negro Girls, 1939–1941," SBPWIC, ORC-NCSA.

31. Maude Barnes Wells, Executive Secretary of the NC Legislative Council, to State Senator Ballentine, February 23, 1943, part 3, box 16, folder 5, "NCLC, Secretary 1940–44," Winston Papers.

32. Daniel, *Women Builders,* 65, 63.

33. Rouse, *Lugenia Burns Hope,* 100.

34. Letter to "North Carolina Awake," April 19, 1921, microfiche reel 2, Charlotte Hawkins Brown Papers, 1900–1961, Schlesinger Library, Radcliffe College.

35. Hope to Eva D. Bowles, March 15, 1922, YWCA folder, NU Collection.

36. Kelley, "Analysis," 47, 33–34.

37. Wilma Loree McCleave, "A Study of the History and Development of the State Training School for Negro Girls, Kinston, North Carolina," master's

thesis, Atlanta University, 1948, 2; Martha Ivory Brown, "Social Types among Delinquent Girls in Atlanta," master's thesis, Atlanta University, 1949, 36.

38. "The Efland Home," *Carolina Times,* February 4, 1939.

39. "An Open Letter," November 22, 1938, box 163, SBPWIC, ORC-NCSA.

40. Evelynn M. Hammonds, "Toward a Genealogy of Black Female Sexuality: The Problematic of Silence," in Jacqui Alexander and Chandra T. Mohanty, eds., *Feminist Genealogies, Colonial Legacies, Democratic Futures* (New York: Routledge, 1997), 175–176.

41. "An Open Letter," November 22, 1938. Charlotte Hawkins Brown made this point explicit when she described black women as wanting "everything—education, power, influence—in fact everything that the white woman wants but her white husband." *Buffalo Progressive Herald,* March 15, 1930, microfiche reel 1, Charlotte Hawkins Brown Papers.

42. Box 163, folder "N.C. Industrial Training School for Negro Girls, 1939–1941," SBPWIC, ORC-NCSA.

43. "A Brief Annual Report of the President of Palmer Memorial Institute to the Board of Trustees for the Academic Year, 1940–41," microfiche reel 4, Charlotte Hawkins Brown Papers.

44. All quotes are from inmates of the TVS, unless otherwise noted and cited. Interview transcripts are in the Johnson Papers, boxes 213–217, "Dept. of Social Science Studies—American Youth Commission Study—Individual Interviews (1937–1942)." The names are the pseudonyms assigned by Johnson or the interviewer, contained in the transcript. The files run alphabetically through the five boxes, integrated with the transcripts of other interviews.

45. Box 216, Johnson Papers.

46. Emma Louise Perry, "A Study of the Background of the First Twenty-Six Girls Admitted to the State Training School for Negro Girls in North Carolina," master's thesis, Atlanta University, 1945. For similar data on Georgia, see Kelley, "Analysis."

47. Perry, "Study," 22–31.

48. Kelley, "Analysis," 3.

49. Perry, "Study," 20–21; ibid., 47.

50. Brown, "Social Types," 25.

51. "Another Home for Delinquent Girls Proposed," *Charlotte Observer,* February 19, 1939.

52. George H. Lawrence to Dr. J. W. Nygard, Director of the Division of Institutions and Corrections, April 12, 1938, box 163, folder "N.C. Industrial School for Negro Girls, 1935–1938," SBPWIC, ORC-NCSA.

53. Report of the Subcommittee of the House Committee on Training Schools (1956); Director's Subject Files, Youth Development Center, Milledgeville Family and Children's Services, box 4, folder "Legislative Committees, 1927–62," Georgia State Department of Archives and History, Morrow.

54. Executive Committee Meeting Minutes, September 11, 1945, North

Carolina Board of Correction and Training, General Correspondence—
Schools, 1943–1947, box 2, folder "Minutes and Reports (Negro Girls'
School)," NCSA.

55. Corrections Commissioner Samuel Leonard to Public Welfare Commissioner Ellen Winston, March 4, 1948, regarding a confidential report of
Richard Clendenen of the Children's Bureau, State Board of Public Welfare Commissioner's Office: Correspondence with State Agencies, Boards,
and Commissions, 1917–1958, box 30B, folder "N.C. Board of Correction
and Training, 1947," NCSA. Earlier reports from the mid-1930s at Efland
indicate that some inmates remained untreated there because of lack
of funds. See "Psycho-Educational Survey of N.C. Industrial School for
Negro Girls," folder "N.C. Industrial Training School for Negro Girls,
1935–1938" and folder "N.C. Industrial Training School for Negro Girls,
Monthly Reports of Admissions and Paroles and Correspondence re: Individual Students, 1926–1952," both in box 163, SBPWIC, ORC-NCSA.

56. McCleave, "Study," 13.

57. Osborne Report, *Handbook,* vol. 2, 229, 259.

58. Ibid., vol. 4, 402, 408, 401.

59. Gilmore, *Gender and Jim Crow,* 119–176.

60. Lula S. Kelsey to Ellen Winston, February 10, 1943, box 16, folder 5,
Winston Papers.

61. Ellen Winston to Lula S. Kelsey, March 2, 1943, box 16, folder 5, Winston
Papers.

62. Elsewhere Winston noted that "in the field of social welfare we often see
harmonious race relations at their best." Speech on "Public Welfare and
Race Relations in North Carolina" given at North Carolina College for Negroes, July 11, 1944, box 20, folder "Speeches 1943–44," Winston Papers.

63. Mrs. A. B. Nelson to Ellen Winston, April 12, 1943, box 16, folder 5,
Winston Papers.

64. September 17, 1949, Report, in N.C. Board of Correction and Training (or
Youth Development) General Correspondence, 1948–1949, box 4, folder
"Negro Advisory Board," NCSA.

65. Advisory Board president Ruth G. Rush to Commissioner of Correction
Samuel E. Leonard, May 24, 1952, in N.C. Board of Correction and
Training, General Correspondence, 1950–1952, box 6, folder "Negro Advi-
sory Board," NCSA.

4. "A Head Full of Diamonds"

1. All quotes in this chapter, unless otherwise noted, are from boxes 213–
217, "Dept. of Social Science—Studies—American Youth Commission
Study—Individual Interviews—1937–1942," Johnson Papers. These interview transcripts, coordinated by Johnson, were conducted for his study
Growing Up in the Black Belt: Negro Youth in the Rural South, prepared for
the American Youth Commission (Washington, D.C.: American Council
on Education, 1941). The names are the pseudonyms assigned by Johnson

or the interviewer, contained in the transcript. The files run alphabetically through the five boxes, integrated with the transcripts from interviews with boys.

2. On slavery see Deborah Gray White, *Ar'n't I a Woman: Female Slaves in the Plantation South* (New York: Norton, 1985). For the postbellum era see Patricia Hill Collins, *Black Feminist Thought: Knowledge, Consciousness, and the Politics of Empowerment* (Boston: Unwin Hyman, 1990); Paula Giddings, *When and Where I Enter: The Impact of Black Women on Race and Sex in America* (New York: Bantam, 1984); and Deborah Gray White, *Too Heavy a Load: Black Women in Defense of Themselves, 1894–1994* (New York: Norton, 1999).

3. John Dollard, *Caste and Class in a Southern Town* (ca. 1937; New York: Doubleday Anchor, 1957), 136–137, 140.

4. Nell Irvin Painter has used the psychological concept of "soul murder" to describe these effects. See Painter, "Soul Murder and Slavery: Toward a Fully Loaded Cost Accounting," *Southern History across the Color Line* (Chapel Hill: University of North Carolina Press, 2002), 15–39. See also Hazel Carby, "Policing and the Black Women's Body in an Urban Context," *Critical Inquiry* 18 (Summer 1992): 738–755; Hortense Spillers, "Interstices: A Small Drama of Words," in Carole S. Vance, ed., *Pleasure and Danger: Exploring Female Sexuality* (Boston: Routledge and Kegan Paul, 1984), 73–100; Hortense Spillers, "Mama's Baby, Papa's Maybe: An American Grammar Book," *Diacritics* 17 (Summer 1987): 65–81; and Evelynn M. Hammonds, "Toward a Genealogy of Black Female Sexuality: The Problematic of Silence," in M. Jacqui Alexander and Chandra Talpade Mohanty, eds., *Feminist Genealogies, Colonial Legacies, Democratic Futures* (New York: Routledge, 1997), 170–183.

5. Daphne Duval Harrison, *Black Pearls: Blues Queens of the 1920s* (New Brunswick, N.J.: Rutgers University Press, 1988); Angela Y. Davis, *Blues Legacies and Black Feminism: Gertrude "Ma" Rainey, Bessie Smith, and Billie Holiday* (New York: Vintage, 1998); Hazel Carby, "It Jus Be's Dat Way Sometime: The Sexual Politics of Women's Blues," *Radical America* 20, no. 4 (1986): 9–22. Harlem Renaissance texts dealing with black girls' sexuality include Zora Neale Hurston, *Their Eyes Were Watching God* (Urbana: University of Illinois Press, 1991); and Jean Toomer, *Cane* (New York: Boni and Liveright, 1923).

6. Records for the American Youth Commission are in ser. 11, ACE Papers.

7. "A Summary of the Prospectus for a Study of the Processes in the Social Conditioning of the Negro Adolescent," box 4, folder 3, "AYC—Negro Youth Study, 1936–37," ACE Papers.

8. The report estimated that of the region's three million rural young people in the fifteen to twenty-five age group maturing between 1900 and 1930, two million—especially those with little education and few job skills— were the most likely to migrate, becoming long-term members of the labor force outside the South. This group had the greatest number of child-bearing years ahead of them; thus they and their children would populate

the country and, experts predicted, reproduce formerly regional problems on a national level. See National Emergency Council, "Report on Economic Conditions in the South" (1938) in David Carlton and Peter Cochlanis, eds., *Confronting Southern Poverty in the Great Depression* (Boston: Bedford/St. Martin's, 1996).

9. Box 4, folder 4, "Proceedings: Conference, AYC, October 12–13, 1936," ACE Papers.

10. By the late 1930s, researchers increasingly framed their work in psychological terms. Studies from this period typically examined family background, education, work, leisure, and sexuality as relevant aspects of overall adolescent personality development in an effort to paint a comprehensive portrait of youth "adjustment" that could serve as the foundation for policy, educational, and social work initiatives.

11. E. Franklin Frazier, *Negro Youth at the Crossways: Their Personality Development in the Middle States* (Washington, D.C.: American Council on Education, 1940); Allison Davis and John Dollard, *The Personality Development of Negro Youth in the Urban South* (Washington, D.C.: American Council on Education, 1940); Ira DeA. Reid, *In a Minor Key: Negro Youth in Story and Fact* (Washington, D.C.: American Council on Education, 1940); W. Lloyd Warner et al., *Color and Human Nature: Negro Personality Development in a Northern City* (Washington, D.C.: American Council on Education, 1941); and Charles S. Johnson, *Growing Up in the Black Belt: Negro Youth in the Rural South* (Washington, D.C.: American Council on Education, 1941).

12. "Revised Prospectus for the Negro Youth Study," box 7, folder 13, "AYC Negro Youth Study—1938," ACE Papers.

13. I judge the interview evidence from this study to be at least as reliable as sexual data gathered by historians from newspaper reports, scientific studies, or social work agencies since, in every instance, reliability depends on both accurate self-reporting and an unbiased telling by the researcher.

14. Unfortunately, I found no comparable body of evidence to make possible a simultaneous consideration of white adolescent sexuality, perhaps because social scientists of the 1930s would have believed it improper to ask white girls—at least those not pregnant or in trouble with the law—such direct and probing questions. Given the incompatibility of sources, I have chosen to plumb the evidence for all it can tell us about the meaning and practice of sexuality among southern black girls.

15. Punctuation, spelling, and abbreviation marks are from the typed transcripts.

16. See for an example, Beth Bailey, *From Front Porch to Back Seat: Courtship in Twentieth-Century America* (Baltimore: Johns Hopkins University Press, 1988). For an exception, see John D'Emilio and Estelle Freedman, *Intimate Matters: A History of Sexuality in America*, 2d ed. (Chicago: University of Chicago Press, 1997), 184–187, 256–265.

17. The sample included the first fifty interviews with boys that included any discussion of sexual thoughts or behavior, a criteria that only excluded a few. Boxes 213–217, Johnson Papers.

18. Group Interview, Shreveport, Louisiana, Johnson Papers.

19. Seven of fifty in my sample mentioned using condoms. Two said they didn't like condoms and chose not to use them; the others saw them as a good option. Because not all interview subjects were asked the same questions, the small percentage who mentioned using condoms (10 percent) cannot be taken as an indication of the actual percentage of condom use.

20. Linda Gordon, *Woman's Body, Woman's Right: A Social History of Birth Control in America* (New York: Grossman, 1976); Leslie Reagan, *When Abortion Was a Crime: Women, Medicine, and the Law in the United States, 1867–1973* (Berkeley: University of California Press, 1997); and Johanna Schoen, *Choice and Coercion: Birth Control, Sterilization, and Abortion in Public Health and Welfare* (Chapel Hill: University of North Carolina Press, 2005).

21. Interviewers speculated that the low rate of pregnancy among their interview subjects occurred because they had sex before they became fertile.

22. North Carolina created some of the earliest birth control clinics in the country, but contraceptives were not available to single women. On southern birth control programs, see Schoen, *Choice and Coercion,* 21–74.

23. D'Emilio and Freedman, *Intimate Matters,* 242–248.

24. Rickie Solinger, *Wake Up Little Susie: Single Pregnancy and Race before Roe v. Wade* (New York: Routledge, 1992); and Regina Kunzel, *Fallen Women, Problem Girls: Unmarried Mothers and the Professionalization of Social Work, 1890–1945* (New Haven: Yale University Press, 1993).

25. "On Being a Negro Youth," p. 25, AYC, box 14, folder 10, "AYC—Negro Youth Study, 1939," ACE Papers.

26. Dollard, *Caste and Class,* 407–409.

27. Davis and Dollard, *Children of Bondage,* 24–25.

28. Ibid., 265–278; quote, 267.

29. Johnson, *Growing Up in the Black Belt,* 224–226.

30. Ibid., 59, 226, 224.

31. Frazier, *Negro Youth at the Crossways,* 230, 234.

32. This ambivalence is even more present in Frazier's better-known monograph on black family life, *The Negro Family in the United States* (Chicago: University of Chicago Press, 1939). On black social scientists, see Daryl Michael Scott, *Contempt and Pity: Social Policy and the Image of the Damaged Black Psyche, 1880–1996* (Chapel Hill: University of North Carolina Press, 1997), 19–55.

33. "On Being a Negro Youth," 25–26, 30–32, box 14, folder 10, "AYC—Negro Youth Study, 1939," ACE Papers.

34. Bailey, *From Front Porch to Back Seat;* Paula Fass, *The Damned and the Beautiful: American Youth in the 1920s* (New York: Oxford University Press, 1977); John Modell, *Into One's Own: From Youth to Adulthood in the United States, 1920–1975* (Berkeley: University of California Press, 1989); Mary C. McComb, "Rate Your Date: Young Women and the Commodification of Depression Era Courtship," in Sherrie A. Innes, ed., *Delinquents and Debutantes: Twentieth-Century American Girls' Cultures* (New York:

New York University Press, 1998), 40–60. The problem with this interpretation is twofold. First, it misses the experience of the "minority" teens who followed a different sexual path, even though evidence of the "majority" view does not establish for certain that indeed most teenagers adopted the normative code put forth by mainstream experts and popular teen movies, magazines, and advice columns. Evidence of the new morality of modern youth is drawn largely from college and high school sources even though a small minority of late adolescents attended college prior to the 1940s and less than half attended high school until the joblessness of the Depression era led a majority of teens to pursue secondary education. Moreover, by failing to explore alternative sexual moralities and behaviors, historians miss an opportunity to see sexual opportunities and dilemmas common to many teenagers across class and culture, aspects of sexual experience excluded from view when focusing primarily on dominant cultural norms.

35. Interviews with Mary Ann Smith and Ethel Ransom, Johnson Papers.

36. Johnson, *Growing Up in the Black Belt,* 223.

37. Here I am using Walter Benjamin's notion of "wish images" as discussed by Nan Enstad in *Ladies of Labor, Girls of Adventure: Working Women, Popular Culture, and Labor Politics at the Turn of the Twentieth Century* (New York: Columbia University Press, 1999), 68–69, 147, 250, n. 7; quote, 69. Enstad analyzes wish images, Benjamin's term for utopian images available in popular culture, as important not because they were "true" but because they "anticipated a potential, emancipatory reality." See also Susan Buck-Morss, *The Dialectics of Seeing: Walter Benjamin and the Arcade Project* (Cambridge: MIT Press, 1989).

38. Lyric from Eurial "Little Brother" Montgomery song, "The Woman I Love Blues" (1935), quoted in Ted Ownby, *American Dreams in Mississippi: Consumers, Poverty, and Culture, 1830–1998* (Chapel Hill: University of North Carolina Press, 1999), 118. "The woman I love / she only sixteen years of age / And she's a full grown woman / but she just got childish ways / She got a head full of diamonds."

5. "Living in Hopes"

1. Margaret Jarman Hagood, *Mothers of the South: Portraiture of the White Tenant Farm Woman* (ca. 1939; New York: W. W. Norton, 1977), 183–192; quote, 192.

2. Edward Ayers, *The Promise of the New South: Life after Reconstruction* (New York: Oxford University Press, 1992), 409–437; George Brown Tindall, *The Emergence of the New South, 1913–1945* (Baton Rouge: Louisiana State University Press, 1967); and Jack Temple Kirby, *Rural Roads Lost: The American South, 1920–1960* (Baton Rouge: Louisiana State University Press, 1987).

3. Donald Davidson et al., *I'll Take My Stand: The South and the Agrarian Tra-*

dition (ca. 1930; Baton Rouge: Louisiana State University Press, 1977), xlii, 206.

4. This argument about consumption is made more generally about rural southerners across age and race by Ted Ownby in *American Dreams in Mississippi: Consumers, Poverty, and Culture, 1830–1998* (Chapel Hill: University of North Carolina Press, 1999).

5. Hagood, *Mothers of the South,* 193–198.

6. Ella Baker, Interview G-8, SOHP.

7. Robert Cecil Cook, *McGowah Place and Other Memoirs* (Hattiesburg, Miss.: Educators' Biographical Press, 1973), 52, quoted by Ownby, *American Dreams,* 96.

8. Grace Elizabeth Hale, *Making Whiteness: The Culture of Segregation in the South, 1890–1940* (New York: Pantheon, 1998).

9. Susan Porter Benson, *Counter Cultures: Saleswomen, Managers, and Customers in American Department Stores, 1890–1940* (Urbana: University of Illinois Press, 1986); and William Leach, *Land of Desire: Merchants, Power, and the Rise of a New American Culture* (New York: Pantheon, 1993).

10. Hagood, *Mothers of the South,* 36, 160–162, and foreword by Anne Firor Scott, vi.

11. Carolyn Kay Steedman, *Landscape for a Good Woman: A Story of Two Lives* (New Brunswick, N.J.: Rutgers University Press, 1987), 38. Steedman's analysis of post–World War II Britain has influenced my interpretation of class-based subjectivities in the very different setting of the American South.

12. Hagood, *Mothers of the South,* 130.

13. Ibid., 143–144.

14. Department of Social Science—Studies—American Youth Commission Study—Individual Interviews, boxes 213–217, Johnson Papers. See also Charles S. Johnson, *Shadow of the Plantation* (Chicago: University of Chicago Press, 1934); Charles S. Johnson, *Growing Up in the Black Belt: Negro Youth in the Rural South* (Washington, D.C.: American Council on Education, 1941); and Hortense Powdermaker, *After Freedom: A Cultural Study in the Deep South* (ca. 1939; New York: Atheneum, 1968).

15. Mozelle Riddle, Interview H-96-2, SOHP.

16. Victoria Byerly, *Hard Times Cotton Mill Girls: Personal Histories of Womanhood and Poverty in the South* (Ithaca, N.Y.: ILR Press, Cornell University, 1986), 20, 23.

17. Douglas Flamming, *Creating the Modern South: Millhands and Managers in Dalton, Georgia, 1884–1984* (Chapel Hill: University of North Carolina Press, 1992), 177. See also Jacquelyn Dowd Hall et al., *Like a Family: The Making of a Southern Cotton Mill World* (Chapel Hill: University of North Carolina Press, 1987).

18. A study of African American teenagers who withdrew from Atlanta's Booker T. Washington High School in the early years of World War II found that a majority of parents did not favor the change, but "did not

feel that they could insist on their staying there when they could not provide for the children in accordance with the standards of their school companions." Sara Carter Campbell, "A Study of the Children Who Withdrew from Booker T. Washington High School and Annex in Atlanta, Georgia, during the First Semester of 1943–44 to Go to Work," master's thesis, Atlanta University, 1944.

19. Wilcox County High School Essays, 1948, ADAH.
20. Byerly, *Hard Times,* 167.
21. Edna Yandell Hargett, Interview H-163, SOHP.
22. Box 214, Johnson Papers.
23. Shirley Abbott, *The Bookmaker's Daughter: A Memory Unbound* (New York: Ticknor and Fields, 1991), 221.
24. Boxes 213–217, Johnson Papers.
25. Margaret Jones Bolsterli, *Born in the Delta: Reflections on the Making of a Southern White Sensibility* (Knoxville: University of Tennessee Press, 1991), 12.
26. Matt Wray and Annalee Newitz, eds., *White Trash: Race and Class in America* (New York: Routledge, 1997); John Shelton Reed, *Southern Folk, Plain and Fancy: Native White Social Types* (Athens: University of Georgia Press, 1986), 34–47.
27. See for example, interviews with Annie Florence Holder, Willie Pearl Horton, and Evangeline Hudson, box 214, Johnson Papers.
28. Margaret C. Brietz, "Case Studies of Delinquent Girls in North Carolina," master's thesis, University of North Carolina, Chapel Hill, 1927, 168.
29. Ann Laura Stoler, *Race and the Education of Desire: Foucault's History of Sexuality and the Colonial Order of Things* (Durham, N.C.: Duke University Press, 1995), 8; Pierre Bourdieu, *Distinction: A Social Critique of the Judgment of Taste,* trans. Richard Nice (Cambridge: Harvard University Press, 1984), 56–57.
30. Icy Norman, Interview H-36, SOHP.
31. Robb Forman Dew, "The Power and the Glory," in Alex Harris, ed., *A World Unsuspected: Portraits of Southern Childhood* (Chapel Hill: University of North Carolina Press, 1987), 108, 110–112, 120.
32. Anne Moody, *Coming of Age in Mississippi* (New York: Dell, 1968), 105–107; quote, 106.
33. Tessie Helms Dyer, Interview H-161, SOHP.
34. Box 214, Johnson Papers.
35. Box 215, Johnson Papers.
36. Evidence on girls' reformatories comes from interviews of inmates at the Tennessee Vocational School for Colored Girls, in Johnson Papers, boxes 213–217, and from records of state reformatories for white girls in North Carolina, Alabama, and Georgia. See records of the "State Board of Public Welfare, Institutions, and Corrections—Samarcand—State Farm Colony for Women," box 165, ORC-NCSA; State Board of Correction and Training, "State Industrial Farm Colony for Women," Correspondence and Misc. Reports, 1929–1947, ORC-NCSA; Clippings File, "Reformatories—

Alabama—Girls," SHC-BPL; and coverage of the Georgia Girls' Training School, *Atlanta Journal* (April–June 1953).

37. "State Industrial Farm Colony for Women, Case Histories," case 644, box 7, ORC-NCSA.

38. Boxes 213 and 215, Johnson Papers.

39. Mabel Kinney Summers, Interview H-146, SOHP.

40. Abbott, *Bookmaker's Daughter* 130. On Abbott's mother, see also Shirley Abbott, *Womenfolks: Growing Up Down South* (New Haven: Ticknor and Fields, 1983).

41. Rosemary Daniell, *Fatal Flowers: On Sin, Sex, and Suicide in the Deep South* (New York: Holt, Rinehart and Winston, 1980), 80, 77.

42. Dew, "Power and the Glory," 121–122.

43. Mary E. Mebane, *Mary: An Autobiography* (Chapel Hill: University of North Carolina Press, 1981), 224–226.

44. Boxes 213–217, Johnson Papers.

45. For this perspective, see Stuart Ewen and Elizabeth Ewen, *Channels of Desire: Mass Images and the Shaping of American Consciousness* (New York: McGraw-Hill, 1982).

46. Original spelling preserved. Wilcox Co. High School Essay, 1948, ADAH.

47. Eva Hopkins, Interview H-167, SOHP.

48. The convergence of material goods, consumer activity, and adolescent desires recasts the Marxist concept of "class-consciousness." As usually understood, class-consciousness—or class identification, in poststructuralist terminology—grows out of comprehending one's social location in relation to people of more and less means. It is a critical awareness rooted in exterior, or social, relations to those around one. But turning this outward gaze inward toward an interior world of feeling, class identification becomes not a political achievement but the experience of oneself as a classed subject. Like current understandings of sexual subjectivity, it resides at the core of a person's sense of being. Sexual subjectivity can, conversely, encompass desires for and relations to a material world grounded in cash, consumption, and economic exchange. It is as much a relation to the empirical world as are class identities.

49. Jacqueline Jones, *The Dispossessed: America's Underclasses from the Civil War to the Present* (New York: Basic Books, 1992).

50. David R. Roediger, *The Wages of Whiteness: Race and the Making of the American Working Class* (New York: Verso, 1991). On the "psychological wage," see W. E. B. DuBois, *Black Reconstruction* (New York: Harcourt Brace, 1935).

51. Paul K. Edwards, *The Southern Urban Negro as a Consumer* (ca. 1932; College Park, Md.: McGrath, 1969).

52. Hortense Powdermaker, *After Freedom: A Cultural Study in the Deep South* (ca. 1939; New York: Atheneum, 1968), 70, 132–133, 282–283.

53. Box 213, Johnson Papers.

54. Hale's *Making Whiteness* proved critical to my understanding of consumption and race.

55. Lillian Smith, *Killers of the Dream* (ca. 1948; New York: Norton, 1978), 96.

56. Wilcox Co. High School Essay, 1948, ADAH.

57. Bolsterli, *Born in the Delta,* 17–19.

58. Box 213, Johnson Papers.

59. Kathy Peiss, *Cheap Amusements: Working Women and Leisure in Turn-of-the-Century New York* (Philadelphia: Temple University Press, 1986); Christine Stansell, *City of Women: Sex and Class in New York, 1789–1860* (New York: Knopf, 1986); Gayle Rubin, "Traffic in Women: Notes on the 'Political Economy' of Sex," in Joan W. Scott, ed., *Feminism and History* (New York: Oxford University Press, 1996), 105–151.

60. Beth Bailey, *From Front Porch to Back Seat: Courtship in Twentieth-Century America* (Baltimore: Johns Hopkins University Press, 1988).

61. Pamela Haag, "In Search of the 'Real Thing': Ideologies of Love, Modern Romance, and Women's Sexual Subjectivity in the United States, 1920–1940," *Journal of the History of Sexuality* 2, no. 4 (1992): 547–577. See also Eva Ilouz, *Consuming the Romantic Utopia: Love and the Cultural Contradictions of Capitalism* (Berkeley: University of California Press, 1977).

62. These dynamics, which arguably encompass middle-class experience as well, perhaps are better captured in an analogy of bumper cars—an arena in which desires crash about, alternately surging ahead and behind, in chaotic fashion with teenage girls at the wheel but in a very tight and difficult-to-manage space.

63. Box 214, Johnson Papers.

64. Quote from inmate testimony given during the "Investigation of State Training School for Girls," SG19949, folder 1, "1931—Ala. State Training School for Girls, no. 1, Alabama Governors (1927–1931): Graves—Admin. Files," ADAH.

6. Sex, Science, and Eugenic Sterilization

1. Eudora Welty, "Lily Daw and the Three Ladies," *A Curtain of Green and Other Stories* (1936; New York: Harcourt, Brace, 1941), 3–20.

2. Edward J. Larson, *Sex, Race and Science: Eugenics in the Deep South* (Baltimore: Johns Hopkins University Press, 1995); Johanna Schoen, *Choice and Coercion: Birth Control, Sterilization, and Abortion in Public Health and Welfare* (Chapel Hill: University of North Carolina Press, 2005); and Phillipa Holloway, "Tending to Deviance: Sexuality and Public Policy in Urban Virginia, Richmond and Norfolk, 1920–1950," Ph.D. diss., Ohio State University, 1999.

3. David Smith and K. Ray Nelson, *The Sterilization of Carrie Buck: Was She Feebleminded or Society's Pawn?* (Far Hills, N.J.: New Horizon, 1989); Daniel J. Kevles, *In the Name of Eugenics: Genetics and the Uses of Human Heredity* (New York: Knopf, 1985), 108–112; Philip J. Reilly, *The Surgical Solution: A History of Involuntary Sterilization in the United States* (Baltimore: Johns Hopkins University Press, 1991), 86–87; Mark H. Haller, *Eugenics:*

Hereditarian Attitudes in American Thought (New Brunswick, N.J.: Rutgers University Press, 1984), 139; Paul Lombardo, "Three Generations of Imbeciles: New Light on *Buck v. Bell*," *New York University Law Review* 60 (April 1985): 30–62; and Stephen J. Gould, "Carrie Buck's Daughter," *Natural History* (July 1984): 14–18.

4. After Virginia's law took effect, other states followed suit: Mississippi passed a sterilization bill in 1928, North Carolina and South Carolina passed such bills in 1929 and 1935, respectively, and Georgia passed the last state law allowing sterilization in 1937. For state-by-state statistics, see Joseph B. Lehane, *The Morality of American Civil Legislation Concerning Eugenical Sterilization* (Washington, D.C.: Catholic University of America Press, 1944), 13–29; Abraham Meyerson et al., *Eugenical Sterilization: A Reorientation of the Problem* (New York: Macmillan, 1936), 7–23; and J. H. Landman, "The Human Sterilization Movement," *Journal of Criminal Law and Criminology* 24 (July–August 1933): 400–408.

5. Elaine Tyler May, *Barren in the Promised Land: Childless Americans and the Pursuit of Happiness* (New York: Basic Books, 1995), 110–111; and Reilly, *Surgical Solution*, 94.

6. Box 7, folder 59, AVS Papers.

7. 1946–1948 Biennial Report of the Eugenics Board of North Carolina, NCSA.

8. Edward J. Larson, "Belated Progress: The Enactment of Eugenic Legislation in Georgia," *Journal of the History of Medicine and Allied Sciences* 46 (January 1991): 44–64. See also Kevles, *In the Name of Eugenics;* and Reilly, *Surgical Solution*.

9. James W. Trent, Jr., *Inventing the Feeble Mind: A History of Mental Retardation in the United States* (Berkeley: University of California Press, 1994), 131–183.

10. May, *Barren*, 106; Haller, *Eugenics*, 70–75; Reilly, *Surgical Solution*, 16–25, 56–70.

11. Reilly, *Surgical Solution*, 138.

12. Larson, *Sex, Race, and Science*, 157.

13. Dorothy Roberts, *Killing the Black Body: Race, Reproduction, and the Meaning of Liberty* (New York: Pantheon, 1997).

14. Quoted in Haller, *Eugenics*, 45.

15. Quoted in Larson, *Sex, Race, and Science*, 68.

16. Smith and Nelson, *Sterilization of Carrie Buck*, 120.

17. Quoted in Larson, *Sex, Race, and Science*, 93.

18. Quoted ibid., 109.

19. Quoted in ibid., 154.

20. Clarence J. Gamble, "Better Human Beings Tomorrow," reprinted from *Better Health* (October 1947), the magazine of the North Carolina Social Hygiene Society. In ephemera collections, AVS Papers.

21. "A Study Relating to Mental Illness, Mental Deficiency, and Epilepsy in a Selected Rural County," issued by the Eugenics Board of North Carolina (May 1948): 9, NCSA.

22. Box 65, folder "North Carolina Industrial Farm Colony for Women," SBPWIC, ORC-NCSA.

23. Smith and Nelson, *Sterilization of Carrie Buck,* 134, quoting testimony of Arthur H. Eastbrook of Cold Spring Harbor Eugenics Record Office in the *Buck v. Bell* case.

24. Moya Woodside, *Sterilization and Social Welfare: A Survey of Current Developments in North Carolina* (New York: Human Betterment Association, 1949), 103.

25. Eleanor Marindin, "How Many Morons Can We Afford?" n.d., box 24, folder "Human Betterment Association Manuscripts—Not Published," AVS Papers.

26. Chester S. Davis, "The Case for Sterilization—Quality versus Quantity," *Winston-Salem Journal and Sentinel,* March 7, 1948.

27. "Idiots, Imbeciles and Morons at Caswell," *Greensboro Daily News,* December 10, 1922.

28. Margaret C. Brietz, "Case Studies of Delinquent Girls in North Carolina," master's thesis, University of North Carolina, Chapel Hill, 1927, 156, 170, 173.

29. The following cases are all drawn from the records of the North Carolina Board of Correction and Training, State Industrial Farm Colony for Women, boxes 1–9, "Case Histories: 1929–1947," ORC-NCSA. I used a sampling method of reading the first twenty-five files of women who were age twenty or younger in every batch of one hundred case files (out of 929 cases). After this sampling method, I also read five additional files from every group of one hundred, pulling the thickest files—assuming they would contain the most detailed records—among those not chosen from the initial sampling technique. Just slightly over 60 percent of inmates in this adult reformatory were under the age of twenty-one at the time of entry. To protect anonymity, I am not using names or initials. Instead I have supplied pseudonyms.

30. Farm Colony Case Histories, record 317.

31. Ibid., record 123.

32. Ibid., record 612.

33. Ibid., record 204.

34. Ibid., record 217.

35. Ibid., record 147.

36. Ibid., record 906.

37. Letter of June 18, 1944, box 2, folder "Public Welfare Superintendents," North Carolina Board of Correction and Training: Correspondence, NCSA. Although it is not clear whether the letter is from her mother, because the majority of correspondence involved mothers I have employed a generic "she."

38. This case is described by Woodside in her *Sterilization and Social Welfare,* 206–208.

39. Randolph County Department of Public Welfare to Samuel E. Leonard,

September 28, 1945, box 2, folder "Public Welfare Superintendents," North Carolina Board of Correction and Training: Correspondence, NCSA.

40. Woodside, *Sterilization and Social Welfare*, 61.

41. Box 247, folder "Negro Feeble Minded Children," Ellen Winston and State Board of Public Welfare Records—Psychological Services, ORC-NCSA.

42. Ibid.

43. Letter from Randolph County Board of Public Welfare, box 2, folder "Public Welfare Superintendents," North Carolina Board of Correction and Training: Correspondence, NCSA.

44. Woodside, *Sterilization and Social Welfare*, 7.

45. Smith and Nelson, *Sterilization of Carrie Buck*, 33–37.

46. Samuel E. Leonard to George H. Lawrence, Superintendent of Public Welfare in Buncombe County, box 4, folder "Public Welfare Superintendents," North Carolina Board of Correction and Training, NCSA.

47. May, *Barren*, 121.

48. Mary Bishop, "Sterilization Survivors Speak Out," *Southern Exposure* 23 (Summer 1995): 15.

49. Woodside, *Sterilization and Social Welfare*, 18.

50. Ibid.

51. Schoen, *Choice and Coercion*.

52. For instance, social workers and child experts developed psychological explanations for white premarital pregnancy that they failed to extend to black adolescent pregnancies, which were still viewed as a product of "natural" African American sexual instincts. This form of racism encouraged sympathetic attention to white adolescent girls while justifying the continued neglect of young black women. See Rickie Solinger, *Wake Up Little Susie: Single Pregnancy and Race before* Roe v. Wade (New York: Routledge, 1992); and Regina Kunzel, *Fallen Women, Problem Girls: Unmarried Mothers and the Professionalization of Social Work, 1890–1945* (New Haven: Yale University Press, 1993).

53. *Asheville Citizen*, September 9, 1954. For other coverage, see North Carolina Clippings File, "Prisons in North Carolina," NCC-UNC.

54. "Shocking Verdict" and "Case Closed?" *Raleigh News and Observer*, September 9, 1954.

55. "The People's Forum: The Death of Eleanor Rush," *Raleigh News and Observer*, September 4, 1954.

56. These statistics were drawn from the published Biennial Reports of the Eugenics Board of North Carolina, NCSA.

57. Larson, *Sex, Race, and Science*, 155.

58. Although teenagers declined as a percentage of North Carolina female sterilizations from 50 percent to 30 percent, their absolute numbers rose due to the increase in the percentage of women relative to men. Statistics drawn from the published Biennial Reports of the Eugenics Board of North Carolina, NCSA. For more on race, age, and marital status, see Schoen, *Choice and Coercion*, 75–138.

59. "Sterilization of Mental Defectives Advised in Light of Record of Rejections in Draft," *Chapel Hill Weekly,* May 10, 1946.
60. Woodside, *Sterilization and Social Welfare,* 6.
61. Undated clippings in Planned Parenthood of Alabama Scrapbooks, Department of Archives and Manuscripts, Birmingham Public Library.
62. David E. Whisnant, *All That Is Native and Fine: The Politics of Culture in an American Region* (Chapel Hill: University of North Carolina Press, 1983).
63. Oliver Wendell Holmes, Supreme Court Opinion, 1927, quoted in Smith and Nelson, *Sterilization of Carrie Buck,* 177–178.

7. The World War II Pickup Girl and Wartime Passions

1. Francis Sill Wickware, "National Defense vs. Venereal Disease," *Life,* October 13, 1941, 128.
2. "Army Cracks Down on Vice That Still Preys on Soldiers," *Newsweek,* August 31, 1942, 27–31; "War on Venereal Ills," *Science News Letter,* November 7, 1942, 300.
3. Marilyn E. Hegarty, "Patriot or Prostitute?: Sexual Discourses, Print Media, and American Women during World War II," *Journal of Women's History* 10 (Summer 1998): 112–136.
4. Wickware, "National Defense vs. Venereal Disease," 128. Wickware cited a military study that identified "ladies of ill fame" as "responsible for practically all venereal disease."
5. Ibid., 130.
6. General Records, 1941–1946, SPD, box 5, folder "Juvenile Delinquency (Case Studies)," entry 37, NA-RG215.
7. Ruth Brown with Andrew Yule, *Miss Rhythm: Autobiography of Ruth Brown, Rhythm and Blues Legend* (New York: Da Capo, 1999), 38–45; quote, 35.
8. "Combating the Victory Girl," *Newsweek,* March 6, 1944, 88.
9. *Life* magazine reported that soldiers from Fort Bragg in North Carolina had "been unable to distinguish between the prostitutes and the nice girls in Fayetteville," in the process stirring up resentment against the military among middle-class residents in the area. Wickware, "National Defense vs. Venereal Disease," 134.
10. Pete Daniel, "Going among Strangers: Southern Reactions to World War II," *Journal of American History* 77 (December 1990): 899.
11. David Goldfield, *Region, Race and Cities: Interpreting the Urban South* (Baton Rouge: Louisiana State University Press, 1997), 249.
12. Subject Classified Files, 1944–1946, SPD, box 1, folder "Research in Social Protection—1944," entry 38, NA-RG215.
13. General Records, 1941–1946, SPD, box 1, folder "Annual Report of Social Protection, 1944," entry 37, NA-RG215.
14. Agnes Meyer, *Journey through Chaos* (New York: Harcourt, Brace, 1943), 184–185.
15. Ibid., 197, 209.
16. Leo Wilson, "Sex Delinquency versus Human Resources," draft of speech

from November 1, 1945, General Records, 1941–1946, SPD, box 1, folder "Articles—Social Protection Division," NA-RG215.

17. Allan Brandt, *No Magic Bullet: A Social History of Venereal Disease in the United States since 1880* (New York: Oxford University Press, 1987), 161–170.

18. Rhetoric for the campaign insisted that cooperation was a form of locally based citizenship, "much like voting," although it failed to note the difference between voting as an option to participate in a democratic elective process and the complete absence of choice or democratic procedure in mandatory blood testing and quarantine. "Fight against Syphilis," *Science News Letter,* June 23, 1945, 394–397.

19. "War on Venereal Ills," *Science News Letter,* November 7, 1942, 300.

20. The *Fayetteville Observer* in North Carolina charged the FBI with contemptible and dangerous violations of civil rights, arresting girls for FBI "interviews" and then browbeating them into a confession of misconduct that then served as evidence for conviction. See "Contemptible and Dangerous," *Fayetteville Observer* (n.d., ca. Fall 1943), in General Records, 1941–1946, SPD, box 9, folder "Prostitution and Promiscuity," entry 37, NA-RG215.

21. "War on Venereal Ills," *Science News Letter,* November 7, 1942, 300. Emphasis added. For SPD's rationale, see Subject Classified Files, 1944–1946, SPD, box 1, folder "Region 7, 1945," entry 38, NA-RG215. Under the charge of promiscuity, minors could be packed off to a state reformatory for an indefinite term of rehabilitation, followed by an extended probationary period. Although public health and social work leaders claimed to feel great concern over the fate of the diseased "girl," public health facilities often withheld treatment from syphilis carriers who had passed into a noninfectious stage of the disease and could not pass along the infection to soldiers, sailors, or defense plant workers, although they themselves could suffer and possibly die.

22. Grace Palladino, *Teenagers: An American History* (New York: Basic Books, 1996), 80–81.

23. Josephine D. Abbott, "Report on Study of Youth Problems in Wartime," American Social Hygiene Association to the SPD (October 16, 1944), box 1, folder "American Social Hygiene Association," entry 37, NA-RG215.

24. *Statistical Abstract of the United States, 1947,* Bureau of the Census Publication (Washington, D.C.: U.S. Government Printing Office, 1947), 34.

25. Elisabeth S. Magee, "Impact of the War on Child Labor," *AAA* 236 (November 1944): 101.

26. Ibid., 103.

27. Alice Scott Nutt, "Juvenile Delinquency and the War," *Christian Century,* October 20, 1943, 1195.

28. James Plant, "Social Significance of War Impact on Adolescents," *AAA* 236 (November 1944): 1–7.

29. Evelyn Emig Mellon, "Living and Letting Live with Adolescents," *Parents Magazine* 21 (October 1946): 106.

30. James H. S. Bossard, "Family Backgrounds of Wartime Adolescents," *AAA* 236 (November 1944): 42.

31. Gladys Denny Shultz, "Romance in Teen Time," *Ladies' Home Journal* 64 (March 1947): 270.
32. George E. Gardner, "Sex Behavior of Adolescents in Wartime," *AAA* 236 (November 1944): 66.
33. Poor whites, blacks, and other racial/ethnic minorities suffered from high rates of syphilis and other infectious diseases because the conditions of poverty—medical neglect, malnutrition, poor sanitation, and residence in dense urban neighborhoods—caused diseases to spread quickly.
34. "Draft Aids Syphilis Study," *Science News Letter,* June 26, 1943, 409.
35. Walter Reckless, "The Impact of War on Crime, Delinquency, and Prostitution," *American Journal of Sociology* 48 (November 1942): 385–386.
36. "Office of War Information Report on Juvenile Delinquency," p. 5, General Records, SPD, box 5, folder "Juvenile Delinquency," NA-RG215.
37. Walter Clarke, M.D., "About VD," *New York Times Magazine,* February 2, 1947, 15, 44.
38. Helen Buckler, "What They Want Is FUN!" *Parents Magazine* 19 (March 1944): 20.
39. Ellen Herman, *The Romance of Psychology: Political Culture in the Age of Experts* (Berkeley: University of California Press, 1995), 77–84.
40. Ibid., 83–121.
41. Caroline B. Zachry, "Customary Stresses and Strains of Adolescence," *AAA* 236 (November 1944): 137.
42. Gladys Schultz, "Does Your Daughter Think She's in Love?" *Reader's Digest* 44 (May 1944): 64.
43. General Records, SPD, box 2, folder "Evolution of a Government Pamphlet ('Challenge to Community Action')," 2, NA-RG215.
44. Ibid., 3.
45. Pamela S. Haag, "In Search of 'The Real Thing': Ideologies of Love, Modern Romance, and Women's Sexual Subjectivity in the United States, 1920–40," *Journal of the History of Sexuality* 2, no. 4 (1992): 550. Haag argues that modernist sexual discourses that defined men as conscious, self-possessed sexual actors never granted women a similar self-sovereignty. Instead they saw sexual desire as inhabiting an unruly subconscious domain of the psyche, driving women toward sexual acts they did not choose as "a rational female self capable of claiming and acting upon desires."
46. Rickie Solinger, *Wake Up Little Susie: Single Pregnancy and Race before Roe v. Wade* (New York: Routledge, 1992); and Regina Kunzel, *Fallen Women, Problem Girls: Unmarried Mothers and the Professionalization of Social Work, 1890–1945* (New Haven: Yale University Press, 1993).
47. Speech, "The Role of Women in the Fight for Freedom," June 1943, reel 1 of Charlotte Hawkins Brown (1883–1961) Papers, (1900–1961), Schlesinger Library, Radcliffe College.
48. Report to Whitcomb H. Allen, Regional SPD Representative, on New Orleans (January 2, 1945). In the same series see also Dorothy C. Lawson re-

port on Lexington, Kentucky (May 30, 1945), SPD, box 15, entry 38, NA-RG215.

49. "Report of the Negro Coordinating Council of the Committee on Social Protection," n.d, SPD., box 10, folder "Georgia," entry 38, NA-RG215.

50. I tracked wartime attitudes toward delinquency in the black press, choosing the southern newspapers *Norfolk Journal and Guide* and *Baltimore Afro American.*

51. See these articles, all from *Ebony:* "Sex in High School" (December 1950): 25–32; "Teen-Age Love Clubs," (April 1952): 83–86; quote, 83; and "Child Brides," (March 1953): 25–30.

52. "How Moral Are Our Co-Eds?" *Ebony* (July 1952): 100–104.

53. "Sex in High School," 28.

54. SPD, box 9, folder "Prostitution and Promiscuity," entry 37, NA-RG215.

55. Palladino, *Teenagers,* 117.

56. Thomas Hine, *The Rise and Fall of the American Teenager* (New York: Bard, 1999), 230–231.

57. Palladino, *Teenagers,* 49–79.

58. Eleanor Lake, "The Younger Set," and SPD, box 1, folder "American Social Hygiene Association," entry 37, NA-RG215.

59. On a Danville, Virginia, teenage club for African Americans see Ellen E. Wood, "Investment, $1,000: Dividends in Citizenship, Unlimited," *Recreation* 39 (May 1945): 81, 105.

60. The club eventually closed because it could no longer manage its large membership or prevent itself from becoming the hangout for students from a single high school.

61. W. C. Yancy, "Now Youth Has a Chance!" *Recreation* 38 (July 1944): 191–192; Eleanor Lake, "The Younger Set," *Survey Graphic* 33 (August 1944): 348; and "Centers All Their Own," *Recreation* 37 (August 1943): 275–277.

62. Yancy, "Now Youth Has a Chance!" 191–192; Lake, "The Younger Set," 348; and Roy Sorenson, "Wartime Recreation for Adolescents," *AAA* 236 (November 1944): 145–151.

63. Palladino, *Teenagers,* 84–93.

64. Catherine Mackenzie, "Teen-Age Centers," *New York Times Magazine,* May 20, 1945, 29.

65. "Boys, Girls—and Dates," *New York Times Magazine,* December 5, 1943, 32.

66. Charles Ansell, "They 'Just Jump'," *Recreation* 37 (October 1943): 374.

67. Ibid., 376.

68. Paul Whiteman, "God Bless the Jitterbug," *American Magazine* 128 (September 1939): 160.

69. Henry Bowman, Ph.D., "Are Girls Becoming Pursuers?" *American Magazine* 139 (April 1945): 33.

70. Ibid., 104.

71. Mona Gardner, "Chastity and Syphilis," *Ladies' Home Journal* 62 (January 1945): 23, 78.

72. Ernest Groves, "Too Much Kissing?" *American Magazine* 128 (December 1939): 22–23, 124–125; quote, 124.
73. *Norfolk Journal and Guide*, September 15, 1941, 6.
74. Ibid., December 13, 1941, 6.
75. For a view of expert advise to teenagers, see Paul Popenoe, "So You're in Love: A Talk to Youth on Sex," *Reader's Digest* 38 (January 1941): 32–34. Popenoe was recognized as a foremost expert in the field of sex education and marriage.
76. Schultz, "Does Your Daughter Think She's in Love?" 63–64.
77. Schultz, "Romance in Teen Time," 272, 270.

8. School Days

1. *Co-Ed Leader*, March 3, 1942, "Commercial High School" subject file, AHC.
2. *Girls' High Times*, February 21, 1941, Girls' High School Collections, box 12, ms. 365, AHC.
3. John D'Emilio, *Sexual Politics, Sexual Communities: The Making of a Homosexual Minority in the United States, 1940–1970* (Chicago: University of Chicago Press, 1983); Elaine Tyler May, *Homeward Bound: American Families in the Cold War Era* (New York: Basic Books, 1988).
4. I used a variety of sources to get a general picture of high school life, usually through school newspapers, yearbooks, or newspaper clippings. See Subject File—Public Schools—Georgia, AHC; CR-CPL; Subject Files, Special Collections, Woodruff Library, Atlanta University Center; subject files, SHC-BPL; and Wilcox High School Essay, 1948, ADAH. Also helpful were published oral histories, including William H. Chafe et al., ed., *Remembering Jim Crow: African Americans Tell about Life in the Segregated South* (New York: New Press, 2001), 152–204; and Clifford M. Kuhn et al., ed., *Living Atlanta: An Oral History of the City, 1914–1948* (Athens: University of Georgia Press, 1990), 130–171.
5. Jeffrey P. Moran, *Teaching Sex: The Shaping of Adolescence in the Twentieth Century* (Cambridge: Harvard University Press, 2000); and Susan K. Freeman, *Up for Discussion: Adolescent Girls and Sex Education in the Mid-Twentieth Century* (Urbana: University of Illinois Press, 2007).
6. On segregated schools and *Brown v. Board of Education*, see James T. Patterson, Brown v. Board of Education: *Civil Rights Milestone and Its Troubled Legacy* (New York: Oxford University Press, 2001); and Richard Kluger, *Simple Justice: The History of* Brown v. Board of Education *and Black America's Struggle for Equality* (New York: Knopf, 2004). See also Philip N. Racine, "Atlanta's Schools: A History of the Public School System, 1869–1955," Ph.D. diss., Emory University, 1969; and William Bagwell, *School Desegregation in the Carolinas: Two Case Studies* (Columbia: University of South Carolina Press, 1972).
7. For Harding High School student photographs and descriptions of student activities, see the *Acorn* yearbooks from the 1940s, CR-CPL.

8. This estimated percentage is based on the difference between the number of students shown in photographs of ninth-grade home rooms and the number of senior photographs in the *Acorn*, CR-CPL. This estimate is consistent with statistical data. In 1940, slightly more than half of urban whites graduated from high school. Working-class urban whites and poor small-town and rural whites shared many of the disadvantages of black students. By 1950 white youth completed a median of twelve years of school, African American girls completed approximately nine years, and African American boys, eight years. Among rural farming youth of the South, white girls completed nine to ten years of schooling, white boys just under nine years, African American girls seven to eight years, and African American boys less than six years on average. See Daniel O. Price, U.S. Bureau of the Census, *Changing Characteristics of the Negro Population* (Washington D.C.: U.S. Government Printing Office, 1969); and Lani Guinier, "From Racial Liberalism to Racial Literacy: *Brown v. Board of Education* and the Interest-Divergence Dilemma," *Journal of American History* 91 (June 2004): 103.

9. Elisabeth S. Magee, "Impact of the War on Child Labor," *AAA* 236 (November 1933): 103.

10. J. M. Gaskin, *The Modern Dance on Trial* (Norman: Oklahoma University Press, 1945); Christian Life Commission Publications, Pamphlet Collection, Southern Baptist Historical Library and Archives, Nashville, Tenn.

11. *The Cornellian*, Booker T. Washington High School Yearbook, Special Collections, Woodruff Library, Atlanta University Center Archives.

12. *Herald* (September 1946), Second Ward High School newspaper, vertical files—North Carolina High Schools, CR-CPL.

13. Mary E. Mebane, *Mary: An Autobiography* (Chapel Hill: University of North Carolina Press, 1981), 137–138.

14. Wilcox County High School Essay (1948), ADAH.

15. "Parent Teacher Activities," *Birmingham Age Herald* (September 17, 1943), folder "Education and School—Public—Birmingham—High School," SHC-BPL.

16. Clippings from *Birmingham News*, January 13, 1949, and January 12, 1958, SHC-BPL.

17. Charlotte Central High School *Rambler* (April 25, 1952), CR-CPL.

18. Evidence of high school beauty and homecoming queens comes from the yearbooks of multiple schools available at the CPL, the AHS, and Special Collections, Woodruff Library, Atlanta University Center Archives. On black beauty queens, see Maxine Leeds Craig, *Ain't I a Beauty Queen: Black Women, Beauty, and the Politics of Race* (New York: Oxford University Press, 2002).

19. *Snips and Cuts*, Charlotte Central High School (1926), CR-CPL.

20. Ibid. (1942), CR-CPL.

21. *Harding Hi-Lites*, April 25, 1947, CR-CPL.

22. Ibid., October 10, 1946, CR-CPL.

23. "Psychology Proves Practical," *Harding Hi-Lites,* October 24, 1946, CR-CPL.

24. May, *Homeward Bound,* 92–134; John D'Emilio and Estelle B. Freedman, *Intimate Matters: A History of Sexuality in America,* 2d ed. (Chicago: University of Chicago Press, 1997), 260–262, 291–295.

25. Vanessa Siddle Walker, *Their Highest Potential: An African American School Community in the Segregated South* (Chapel Hill: University of North Carolina Press, 1996), 2.

26. "Biggest Negro High School," *Ebony* (June 1950): 15–20; Melvel Arvina Bradford, "The Syphilitic Patient as Person," master's thesis, Fisk University, 1943, in box 237, Department of Social Science, folder "Student Papers," Johnson Papers.

27. Ruby Alma Clowers, "A Study of the Recreational Interests and Needs of 100 Negro Students of Macon, Georgia," master's thesis, Atlanta University, 1947.

28. *Charlotte Observer,* September 2, 1979, and *Charlotte News,* December 9, 1976, in folder "Charlotte Public High Schools, Ward Two," CR-CPL. The quote is from *Charlotte News.*

29. Walker, *Their Highest Potential.*

30. Mebane, *Mary,* 140–142, 192–193.

31. All quotes in the following sections come from the *Acorn* yearbooks of Bob Weddington (1943), Alice Nivens (1946–1950), and June Platt (1952) of Harding High School, CR-CPL. I will not cite page numbers, since some yearbooks and end pages were not paginated. With one yearbook for each, the year will be clear in the case of Weddington and Platt. For Alice Nivens, rather than provide repetitive citations I will state either the year or her grade in the text.

32. Grace Palladino, *Teenagers: An American History* (New York: Basic Books, 1996), 97–115.

33. Beth L. Bailey, *From Front Porch to Back Seat: Courtship in Twentieth-Century America* (Baltimore: Johns Hopkins University Press, 1988); and John Modell, *Into One's Own: From Youth to Adulthood in the United States, 1920–1975* (Berkeley: University of California Press, 1989).

34. Sarah Pardee, "Fifteen," *Lace and Pig Iron* (1940), 24–26, CR-CPL.

35. Suzanne Walker, "Trudy at the Sea Shore," *Lace and Pig Iron* (1940), 62–66, CR-CPL.

36. Moran, *Teaching Sex;* and Freeman, *Making Sense of Sex.*

37. D'Emilio and Freedman, *Intimate Matters,* 280–295.

38. See for example, "Sex in the Classroom," *Time,* March 22, 1948, 71–72; "Youth and Shall Our Schools Teach Sex," *Newsweek,* May 19, 1947, 100; and Elizabeth Force, "High School Education for Family Living," *AAA* 272 (November 1950): 156–162.

39. John Newton Baker, *Sex Education in High Schools* (New York: Emerson Books, 1942).

40. May, *Homeward Bound,* 16–36, 114–134. On the juvenile delinquency scare of the 1950s, see James Gilbert, *A Cycle of Outrage: America's Reac-*

tion to the Juvenile Delinquent in the 1950s (New York: Oxford University Press, 1986).

9. Would Jesus Dance?

1. Earlier that April, Carter had organized a group of white thugs to storm the stage during a Nat King Cole concert played for a white Birmingham audience. See Michael T. Bertrand, *Race, Rock, and Elvis* (Urbana: University of Illinois Press, 2000), 112–114.
2. *Newsweek,* April 23, 1956, 32.
3. Phillip Ennis, *The Seventh Stream: The Emergence of Rock 'n' Roll in American Popular Music* (Hanover, N.H.: Wesleyan University Press, 1992), 121.
4. Pete Daniel, *Lost Revolutions: The South in the 1950s* (Chapel Hill: University of North Carolina Press/Smithsonian Institution, 2000), 121–147.
5. Peter Guralnick, *Sweet Soul Music: Rhythm and Blues and the Southern Dream of Freedom* (New York: Harper and Row, 1986), 24.
6. Daniel, *Lost Revolutions,* 121–147; Ennis, *Seventh Stream,* 161–192; and Bertrand, *Race, Rock, and Elvis,* 59–79.
7. Ennis, *Seventh Stream,* 132–136.
8. Daniel, *Lost Revolutions,* 131–147; and ibid., 176–180.
9. Budding performers like Elvis Presley, Johnny Cash, Jerry Lee Lewis, and Buddy Holly listened as well to the many local country music "barn dance" shows that featured regular acts and bands on tour. Although these shows did not as a rule attract crossover audiences of black youth, performers like Little Richard and Chuck Berry absorbed the sounds of country music into their own artistry, which they later introduced to black audiences.
10. Covers represented a mixed achievement, because often a white singer's success meant simply a loss of sales for the original black artist. Especially when the white version used the exact same musical arrangements as the original hit, black performers viewed white copycat singers as stealing not only their music but also their profits.
11. Guralnick, *Sweet Soul Music,* 11; Daniel, *Lost Revolutions,* 166–172.
12. Peter Guralnick, *Last Train to Memphis: The Rise of Elvis Presley* (Boston: Little, Brown, 1994), 96.
13. "Rock 'n' Roll Rolls On 'n' On," *Life,* December 22, 1958, 37.
14. Les Brown, "In the Whirl," *Down Beat,* September 19, 1956, 45.
15. Gertrude Samuels, "Why They Rock 'n' Roll—And Should They?" *New York Times Magazine,* January 12, 1956, 16; "The Great Rock 'n' Roll Controversy," *Look,* June 26, 1956, 40–42.
16. *Newsweek,* June 18, 1956, 42.
17. "Yeh-Heh-Heh-Hes, Baby," *Time,* June 18, 1956, 54.
18. Gael Sweeney, "The King of White Trash Culture: Elvis Presley and the Aesthetics of Excess," in Matt Wray and Analee Newitz, eds., *White Trash: Race and Class in America* (New York: Routledge, 1997), 249–266.

19. Ralph J. Gleason, "Fats Domino: Not Responsible," *Down Beat*, September 19, 1956, 40.
20. Richard Welch, "Rock 'n' Roll and Social Change: The Making of the American Dream," *History Today* 40 (February 1990): 36.
21. Journalist Jack O'Brien after Presley's appearance on the *Ed Sullivan Show*, quoted in David P. Szatmary, *Rockin' Time: A Social History of Rock-and-Roll*, 4th ed. (Upper Saddle River, N.J.: Prentice Hall, 2000), 47.
22. "Rock 'n' Roll Rolls on 'n' On," 42.
23. Richard Schickel, "The Big Revolution in Records," *Look*, April 15, 1958, 28.
24. Ibid., 49.
25. "Hillbilly on a Pedestal," *Newsweek*, May 11, 1956, 82.
26. "A Psychologist's Viewpoint," *Down Beat*, September 19, 1956, 42.
27. Quoted in Guralnick, *Last Train*, 189, 285. On the Jacksonville incident, see Guralnick, *Last Train*, 189–190, 321–322; and Albert Goldman, *Elvis* (New York: McGraw Hill, 1981), 159.
28. Quoted in Guralnick, *Last Train*, 370.
29. Ennis, *Seventh Stream*, 238.
30. Guralnick, *Sweet Soul Music*, 25.
31. Gleason, "Fats Domino," 40.
32. Bertrand, *Race, Rock, and Elvis*, 182.
33. Marybeth Hamilton, "Sexual Politics and African-American Music," *History Workshop Journal* 46 (Autumn 1998): 161–176; quote, 162.
34. Chuck Berry, *Chuck Berry: The Autobiography* (New Youk: Harmony, 1987), 183.
35. Samuels, "Why They Rock 'n' Roll," 16.
36. Schickel, "Big Revolution," 28.
37. J. M. Gaskin, "The Modern Dance on Trial," pamphlet, 1945, 17, PC-CLCP, SBHLA.
38. Ibid., 15, 10.
39. Ennis, *Seventh Stream*, 214.
40. Pamphlets, PC-CLCP, SBHLA.
41. Woodson Arms, "Shall We Dance?" PC-CLCP, SBHLA; and Mrs. Claude Rhea, Jr., "Music and Morality," *Baptist Young People*, August 23, 1959, 27.
42. "Teen Talk about Rock 'n' Roll," pamphlet, 1959, PC-CLCP, SBHLA.
43. "Teen Talk about Dancing," pamphlet, 1960, PC-CLCP, SBHLA.
44. Ibid.
45. "Teen Talk about Rock 'n' Roll."
46. "Teen Talk about Dancing."
47. Daniel, *Lost Revolutions*, 173.
48. Szatmary, *Rockin' Time*, 21.
49. Steve Alves, from the film script for *A History of American Teenagers* (Greenfield, Mass.: Hometown Productions), 51, in author's possession.
50. Szatmary, *Rockin' Time*, 48–49.
51. "Rock 'n' Roll Rolls On 'n' On," 42. Emphasis in original.
52. Fayly H. Cothern, *I've Been Wondering* (Nashville: Broadman Press, 1956), 17.

53. H. Y. Mullikin, "Goodnight Prayer or Goodnight Kiss?" *Baptist Young People,* May 1, 1960, 19.
54. C. Newman Hogle, "Going Steady—Pros and Cons," Christian Education Service Leaflet, Department of the Christian Family in Co-operation with the Youth Department Board of Education, The Methodist Church, Nashville, 1957, 6, SBHLA.
55. Oliver M Butterfield, "Now You Are Engaged," Christian Education Service Leaflet, Department of the Christian Family in Co-operation with the Youth Department Board of Education, The Methodist Church, Nashville, 1957, 6, SBHLA.
56. "The Costly Hazard of Young Marriage," *Life,* April 13, 1959, 119–130; U.S. Bureau of the Census, *Statistical Abstract of the United States: 1959* (Washington D.C.: U.S. Government Printing Office, 1959), 71–72.
57. I am indebted to Rachel Devlin's analysis in her "Female Juvenile Delinquency and the Problem of Sexual Authority in America, 1945–1965," in Sherrie A. Inness, ed., *Delinquents and Debutantes: Twentieth-Century American Girls' Cultures* (New York: New York University Press, 1988), 83–106. See also Devlin, *Relative Intimacy: Fathers, Adolescent Daughters, and Postwar American Culture* (Chapel Hill: University of North Carolina Press, 2005).
58. Ruth Brown with Andrew Yule, *Miss Rhythm: The Autobiography of Ruth Brown, Rhythm and Blues Legend* (New York: Da Capo, 1999), 38.
59. Ennis, *Seventh Stream,* 212–213.
60. Brown with Yule, *Miss Rhythm,* 46–81.
61. Gillian G. Gaar, *She's a Rebel: The History of Women in Rock and Roll* (Emeryville, Calif.: Seal Press, 1992), 20–21; and Mary A. Bufwack and Robert K. Oermann, *Finding Her Voice: The Saga of Women in Country Music* (New York: Crown, 1993), 222–223.
62. "My Boy Elvis," copyright Janis Martin Lyrics, www.rockabilly.nl/lyrics3/m0020.htm (accessed March 31, 2006).
63. "Will You, Willyum," copyright, Janis Martin Lyrics, www.lyricsdownload.com/janis-martin-william-lyrics.html (accessed March 31, 2006).
64. Bufwack and Oermann, *Finding Her Voice,* 222–223.
65. For example, white girls like Sammie Dean Parker, from Little Rock, Arkansas, danced on the local afternoon teen music show, *Steve's Show.* But that she enjoyed a music largely created through African American influences did not make a dent in her segregationist beliefs: she became one of the most prominent white student leaders of the resistance to desegregating Little Rock's Central High School. Daniel, *Lost Revolutions,* 164–165.
66. See ibid., 174–175, for the argument that rock music held great possibility for such a racial transformation.
67. Szatmary, *Rockin' Time,* 24–25.
68. "Pat Boone Boom: He Sets a New Style in U.S. Teen-Age Idols," *Life,* February 2, 1959, 75–58. See also Ennis, *Seventh Stream,* 244–253.
69. This survey was conducted among Illinois teenagers and although not

stated explicitly, seems to have questioned white teens only. James S. Coleman, *The Adolescent Society: The Social Life of the Teenager and Its Impact on Education* (New York: Free Press, 1961), 23.

70. Daniel, *Lost Revolutions*, 167–169.

10. The Sexual Paradox of High School Desegregation

1. "Crowds Heckle Fifteen-Year-Old Dorothy Counts," *Charlotte Observer*, September 5, 1957, A1; "Rejected with Jeers," *Arkansas Gazette*, September 5, 1957, 1; "Bayonets in the Backs of Schoolgirls," *U.S. News and World Report*, October 4, 1957, 69 [UPI photograph].

2. Paula Giddings, *When and Where I Enter: The Impact of Black Women on Race and Sex in America* (New York: Perennial, 2001), 81–118; Jacquelyn Dowd Hall, *Revolt against Chivalry: Jessie Daniel Ames and the Women's Campaign against Lynching* (New York: Columbia University Press, 1979).

3. Quoted in Liva Baker, *The Second Battle of New Orleans: The Hundred-Year Struggle to Integrate the Schools* (New York: HarperCollins, 1996), 223.

4. Ibid., 276.

5. Quoted from James J. Thorndike, "'The Sometimes Sordid Level of Race and Segregation': James M. Kilpatrick and the Virginia Campaign against *Brown*," in Matthew D. Lassiter and Andrew B. Lewis, eds., *The Moderates' Dilemma: Massive Resistance to School Desegregation in Virginia* (Charlottesville: University Press of Virginia, 1998), 66.

6. William Chafe, *Civilities and Civil Rights: Greensboro, North Carolina, and the Black Struggle for Freedom* (New York: Oxford University Press, 1981), 42–70; William Chafe, *The Unfinished Journey: America since World War II*, 3d ed. (New York: Oxford University Press, 1995), 153–171; and Adam Fairclough, *Better Day Coming: Blacks and Equality, 1890–2000* (New York: Viking, 2001), 218–225.

7. Sibley Papers.

8. Dr. E. L. Wright to John Sibley, January 22, 1958, box 151, folder "Segregation: Correspondence, 1956–1966," Sibley Papers. Emphasis in original.

9. Adam Fairclough, *Race and Democracy: The Civil Rights Struggle in Louisiana, 1915–1972* (Athens: University of Georgia Press, 1995), 169, 205.

10. Ibid., 244.

11. Baker, *Second Battle*, 339–416; quote, 414.

12. Box 24, folder "Readership Correspondence—Integration, 1957," McGill Papers.

13. *Augusta Courier*, June 17, 1957, 3; in William Hartsfield Papers, box 37, folder "Printed Material—Newsclippings, 1957," Special Collections, Woodruff Library, Emory University.

14. Box 58, folder "Subject Files: Integration, 1954," McGill Papers.

15. *A Bluebook for Patriots* (San Antonio, Tex.: American Heritage Protective Committee, 1956), 77–78; part 20, reel 13, "General Office Files, Reprisals—WCC and KKK, 1956," Papers of the NAACP (microform), ed. Au-

gust Meier, Mark Fox, and Randolph Boehm (Bethesda, Md.: University Publications of America, 1981).

16. *The White Sentinel,* National Citizens Protective Association, Inc. of St. Louis, Missouri; hand dated in file as 5/20/57; part 20, reel 13, NAACP Papers.

17. William Attwood, "Fear Underlies the Conflict," *Look,* April 3, 1956, 27. Emphasis in original.

18. Helen Hill Miller, "Private Business and Public Education in the South," *Harvard Business Review* (July–August, 1960): 87–88; quoting the *Richmond Times Dispatch,* January 29, 1959.

19. "The 'Deep South'—Land with a Future: A New Survey," *U.S. News and World Report,* November 6, 1961, 66.

20. Box 152, folder "School Study Commission—Personal Correspondence, 1961," Sibley Papers.

21. Letter to Governor Folsom, February 9, 1956, in Alabama Governor (1955–1959: Folsom) Administrative Files, SG 1395, folder 3, "Univ. of Ala.—'Miss Lucy,' Feb. 7, 1956–Feb. 13, 1956," ADAH.

22. *Arkansas Faith* (December 1955): 10; part 20, reel 13, NAACP Papers.

23. Rev. G. T. Gillespie, "A Christian View of Segregation," address from November 4, 1954, to the Synod of Mississippi of the Presbyterian Church, in part 20, reel 13, NAACP Papers.

24. Herbert Ravenel Sass, "Mixed Schools and Mixed Blood," reprinted from the November 1956 *Atlantic Monthly,* distributed by States' Rights Council of Georgia, Inc., box 151, folder "Segregation: Correspondence, 1956–1966," Sibley Papers.

25. Ibid.

26. Carleton Putnam, letter of April 29, 1960, box 152, folder "School Study Commission—Personal Correspondence, 1961," Sibley Papers.

27. Boyd Taylor, "VD Explosion," *Separate Schools* (May 1961): 2.

28. Wilma Dykeman and James Stokely, "Inquiry into the Southern Tensions," *New York Times Magazine,* October 13, 1957, 20.

29. Letter from Dorothy Kaplowitz, November 3, 1957, in box 24, folder "Readership Correspondence—Integration, Nov. 3 1957–Oct. 1, 1962," McGill Papers.

30. "No Surrender on Integration, Says Speaker," *Tacoma Washington News Tribune,* October 31, 1957.

31. David Cohn, "How the South Feels about the Race Problem," *Atlantic Monthly* (January 1944): 48–49.

32. Letter from February 9, 1956, Alabama Governor (1955–1959: Folsom) Administrative Files, SG 1395, folder 3, "Univ. of Alabama—'Miss Lucy,' Feb. 7, 1956–Feb. 13, 1956," ADAH.

33. Rev. E. D. Lewis to Folsom, February 25, 1956, in ibid.

34. Dykeman and Stokely, "Inquiry," 20.

35. "A Roundtable Discussion," in Clayborne Carson et al., *The Eyes on the Prize Civil Rights Reader* (New York: Penguin, 1991), 105.

36. For daily coverage of Dorothy Counts's attempted integration of Harding High School, see *Charlotte Observer* (September 5–September 13, 1957).

37. Dorothy Counts was not alone in suffering defeat at the hands of racist white teenagers and adults. In Birmingham, Alabama, in August 1957, longtime civil rights activist Reverend Fred Shuttlesworth petitioned the school board to admit black children to three of Birmingham's all-white schools. Rebuffed by the school board, in September Shuttlesworth tried again by bringing four children, two of them his daughters, directly to school to enroll on the first day of classes. They walked into a mob of angry protesters who beat the group back toward their car. By the time they left the area, Shuttlesworth had been badly beaten, his wife had been stabbed in the leg, and his daughter's ankle had been nearly broken by someone who slammed the car door as she attempted to get in. The following day white students boycotted school, with some boys forming a rock-throwing brigade. The Ku Klux Klan took matters into their own hands, randomly selecting two black men for torture and castration as a message to the black community that school desegregation would not come without a severe price. These actions ended integration efforts in Alabama for the 1957 school year. See Andrew M. Manis, *A Fire You Can't Put Out: The Civil Rights Life of Birmingham's Reverend Fred Shuttlesworth* (Tuscaloosa: University of Alabama Press, 1999), 145–163; and Glenn T. Eskew, *But for Birmingham: The Local and National Movement in the Civil Rights Struggle* (Chapel Hill: University of North Carolina Press, 1997), 121–151. See also David Garrow, ed., *Birmingham, Alabama, 1956–1963: The Black Struggle for Civil Rights* (Brooklyn: Carlson Publishers, 1989).

38. Frye Gaillard, *The Dream Long Deferred* (Chapel Hill: University of North Carolina Press, 1988), 3–17.

39. Chafe, *Unfinished Journey,* 161.

40. As "Long Sam," Dorothy Brown was a familiar figure to southerners of the 1950s. The sexually magnetic but "innocent" poor white girl was portrayed by Erskine Caldwell in his *Tobacco Road* (1932) characters Ellie May and her sister Pearl; as the "over-sexed" mill girl in Caldwell's next sensational novel, *God's Little Acre* (1933); by William Faulkner's character Dewey Dell in *As I Lay Dying* (1930); as Daisy Mae in Al Capp's comic strip *Li'l Abner* (1934); and as Elly May Clampett on the 1960s hit television series *Beverly Hillbillies.*

41. Coverage ran in the *Charlotte Observer* from August 4 to September 12, 1957.

42. *Charlotte Observer,* August 11, 1957, A3.

43. Ibid.

44. Ibid., August 16, 1957, B1.

45. Ibid., August 17, 1957, A1.

46. Ibid., A5. Ellipses in original.

47. Ibid., August 23, 1957, A1; and September 12, 1957, A3.

48. Ibid., September 12, 1957, A3.

49. Among the many works on the Little Rock desegregation story, see Elizabeth Jacoway and C. Fred Williams, eds., *Understanding the Little Rock Crisis: An Exercise in Remembrance and Reconciliation* (Fayetteville: University of Arkansas Press, 1999); Jane Cassels Record and Wilson Record, eds., *Little Rock, U.S.A.: Materials for Analysis* (San Francisco: Chandler, 1960); Will Counts, *A Life Is More than a Moment: The Desegregation of Little Rock's Central High* (Bloomington: Indiana University Press, 1999); Elizabeth Huckaby, *Crisis at Central High, Little Rock: 1957–58* (Baton Rouge: Louisiana State University Press, 1980); Mary L. Dudziak, *Cold War and Civil Rights: Race and the Image of American Democracy* (Princeton, N.J.: Princeton University Press, 2000), 115–151; and Pete Daniel, *Lost Revolutions: The South in the 1950s* (Chapel Hill: University of North Carolina Press, 2000), 251–283.

50. Chafe, *Unfinished Journey,* 158–159. On Virginia, see Robert A. Pratt, *The Color of Their Skin: Education and Race in Richmond, Virginia, 1954–1989* (Charlottesville: University of Virginia Press, 1992); and Lassiter and Lewis, *Moderates' Dilemma.*

51. Melba Patillo Beals, *Warriors Don't Cry: A Searing Memoir of the Battle to Integrate Little Rock's Central High* (New York: Pocket Books, 1994), 156.

52. Ibid., 246.

53. Henry Hampton and Steve Fayer, *Voices of Freedom: An Oral History of the Civil Rights Movement from the 1950s through the 1980s* (New York: Bantam, 1991), 48–51.

54. "A Roundtable Discussion," in Carson et al., *Eyes on the Prize Civil Rights Reader,* 105.

55. Daniel, *Lost Revolutions,* 263–274.

56. Hampton and Fayer, *Voices of Freedom,* 50.

57. Beth Roy, *Bitters in the Honey: Tales of Hope and Disappointment across Divides of Race and Time* (Fayetteville: University of Arkansas Press, 1999), 159, 206.

58. Ibid., 255.

59. Ibid., 280.

Conclusion

1. Harper Lee, *To Kill a Mockingbird* (Philadelphia: J. B. Lippincott, 1960).

2. Danielle L. McGuire, "'It Was like All of Us Had Been Raped': Sexual Violence, Community Mobilization, and the African American Freedom Struggle," *Journal of American History* 91 (December 2004): 906–931.

3. Although rarely part of a concerted effort for racial justice, the history of adolescent girls and the sexual reckonings they prompted fits into a concept, broadened beyond organized protest, of "the long civil rights movement" written about by Jacquelyn Dowd Hall, "The Long Civil Rights

Movement and the Political Uses of the Past," *Journal of American History* 91 (March 2005): 1233–1263.

4. Lillian Smith, *Killers of the Dream* (New York: W. W. Norton, 1949), 84–85.

5. Ibid., 17.

Acknowledgments

$\mathcal{M}$any organizations and individuals provided invaluable assistance as I researched and wrote this book. Several small grants from the Baldy Center for Research on Law and Social Policy (of the University at Buffalo Law School in Buffalo, New York) funded research trips to southern archives and libraries. A travel grant from the Rockefeller Archive Center allowed me to do a week of research at the Rockefeller Archive in New York State. A Stanford Humanities Center Fellowship provided a year away from teaching, and a challenging, supportive intellectual community as I drafted early chapters of the book. Finally, a grant from the University at Buffalo's College of Arts and Science Subvention Fund covered the costs of photo duplication and obtaining copyright permissions for the songs and photos used in this book.

Good friends assisted in the research process by opening their homes and contributing their ideas during many summers of research. I thank Anne Enke, Nan Enstad, Mary Jo Festle, Maureen Fitzgerald, Scott Harris, Pauline Klein, Leisa Meyer, and Nick Radel for their generous hospitality and friendship. Other friends and colleagues offered invaluable support by reading all or parts of the manuscript at various points along the way. Tim Dean, Paula Ebron, Gabrielle Hecht, Karen Sawislak, and members of the Stanford Humanities Center (1997–1998) read early chapters and provided valuable critiques. I also received excellent commentary on later chapters and conference papers from Karen Anderson, Margot Canaday, John D'Emilio, Marge Frantz, Estelle Freedman, Nancy Hewitt, Pippa Holloway, Leila Rupp, and Lynn Sacco. Nan Enstad and Liz Kennedy remain my unfailingly reliable and staunchest supporters as well as my toughest critics.

Colleagues at the University at Buffalo read all or parts of the manuscript in its first full draft. Special thanks to Mike Frisch, Michael Lansing, Patrick

McDevitt, Ramya Sreenivasan, Hershini Bhana Young, and Jason Young for their close readings. Colleagues from around the university who attended the Baldy Center Manuscript Workshop contributed valuable advice on revising the manuscript. Lynn Mather showed great acumen and generosity in organizing the workshop and arranging for outside commentators Annalise Orleck and Rickie Solinger. Each provided a thorough critique of the manuscript that helped me refine and extend my argument as well as trust my own instincts and judgments. Pete Daniel and Jacquelyn Hall, who read the manuscript for Harvard University Press, offered incisive criticism and clarifying questions as well as saved me from some factual errors. This book is a much better work of history as a result of the keen insights of these four historians.

Thanks as well to the editorial staff at the *Journal of Women's History* for their early interest in and publication of "Spirited Youth or Fiends Incarnate" (Winter 1998), an article that in altered form became the basis of Chapter 2. On a more practical level, I have been blessed with three research assistants— Shannon O'Connor, Lisa Krieger, and Katrina Sinclair—whose bibliographic research made my work easier at the beginning, middle, and end stages (respectively) of the project. Students in graduate and undergraduate seminars on southern history and the history of adolescence asked hard questions that forced me to think through "the obvious" and fueled my energy for writing about southern adolescent girls. They also contributed their own research and ideas about rock 'n' roll music and the *Brown v. Board of Education* decision and its aftermath.

Various professionals provided critical assistance in locating sources and pointing me to rich collections. Historian and independent scholar Pamela Grundy not only opened up her home to me but also made every conversation an informal workshop on ideas and sources; in particular, she informed me about extremely useful materials at the University of North Carolina– North Carolina Collection (UNC-NCC, at Chapel Hill) and the Charlotte Public Library. Archivists and librarians at these and many other state archives, public libraries, college and university libraries, and special collections across the South shared their knowledge of manuscript collections and published documents. Especially helpful were the committed and creative archivists at the North Carolina State Archives, the Southern History Collection of the Birmingham Public Library, the Charlotte Public Library, the Atlanta History Center, and at special collections at Fisk University, Spelman and Livingstone colleges, the Atlanta University Center, Emory University, and the University of North Carolina at Chapel Hill and at Greensboro. All of these helpful professionals guided me through manuscript collections, clippings files, and institutional records. Kim Cumber at the North Carolina State Archives, Stephen Fletcher at UNC-NCC, and various staff members of the Library of Congress went out of their way to find photos and speed up the ordering and duplication process.

Joyce Seltzer, my editor at Harvard University Press, stood behind this project from its very inception, when I could provide only the barest sketch of its content and significance and had yet to write a single word. Her unwavering encouragement, knowledge of how to craft a book, and acute sense of when to push and when to back off made this book distinctly better than it would have been without her editorial skill and personal support. I am grateful as well to her assistant, Jennifer Banks, for guiding me through the process of gaining copyright permissions for songs and photographs, and to Julie Carlson, who did an extraordinary job copyediting the manuscript.

This book would never have been completed without the support of some medical professionals who taught me that being "under a doctor's care" was not the same as being underneath a doctor's thumb. To Elizabeth Biggart, John Barry, Judith Feld, Mediha Mirza, Emily Ets-Hokin, and Nancy Somit, thank you for your kindness and expertise. Emily Ets-Hokin, in particular, contributed insight on adolescence and reminders that all writing is creative. She along with Elizabeth Biggart dared me to enjoy—rather than suffer—the writing process, a challenge I sometimes met.

As always, my mother, Gretchen Cahn, and siblings—Ellen (who proofread the manuscript with generosity and eagle eyes), Peter, Lisa, and Steve—supplied me with love and laughter in just the right doses, as did my beloved friends Liz Martin-Garcia, Kathleen Duffy, Gretchen Pullen, Diane Kowalczyk, Dan Morneau, and Hershini Bhana Young—all writers or talented creative spirits. Tandy Hamilton has, without reading a single completed chapter, contributed to this book in countless ways, from the mundane—computer expertise and organizational skills—to the sublime, sustaining my mind and spirit.

Index

Abbott, Shirley, 138, 145
Abortion, 116–117, 309, 313
Abstinence, sexual, 112, 113, 211
Acker, Peggy, 217
Addams, Jane, 22
Adolescence: changing conception of, 20–23; definitions of, 164; delinquency and, 52–53; history of, 308; meaning of, 10–12; psychiatric models of, 260; "teenager" as term, 200; wartime conceptions of, 190, 194–197
Adolescence (Hall), 21–22
Adolescents, female: in category of "women workers," 13–14; instability of, 7; in literary stereotype, 4; men as danger and desire, 29–30; rock 'n' roll music and, 251; sexual self-determination and, 59, 66, 264; urban workers, *19;* women's history and, 9. *See also* High school students; Teenagers
Adoption programs, 118
Adults: generational divide and, 16; girls' clothing and, 139; middle class white courtship and, 38; postwar youth guidance and, 235–237; rock 'n' roll music and, 240, 258–259; school desegregation fears of, 285; in World War II, 188
Agrarians, 132
Agriculture: black women's fertility as

cheap labor for, 179–180; children in farm labor, 24; crisis in, 18, 25, 46–47; decline of, 143; New Deal programs and, 100; transition to wage labor, 54, 129, 131
Aid to Dependent Children, 176–177
Alabama, 13, 17, 69, 101, 186, 281; desegregation in, 285; Girls' Training School, 55; high school students in, 104, 217; Montgomery bus boycott, 177, 199, 267; Scottsboro case, 56; wartime defense industries in, 183; White Citizens Council of, 241
Alcohol consumption, 16, 17, 29, 110; delinquency and, 63, 81; domestic violence and, 88; "mixing" of races and, 28
Almond, Lindsay J., Jr., 280
"Amateur girls," 182, 184, 208
American Bandstand (TV show), 250–251, 262
American Council on Education, 100
American Dream, 26
American Eugenics Association, 162
American Youth Commission (AYC), 100, 101, 120, 121, 122, 123
Ames, Jessie Daniel, 77
Amusement parks, 22
Antebellum period, 54, 72
Antilynching movement, 34, 72, 273

9 780674 063938